Lecture Notes in Computer Science   11092

Commenced Publication in 1973
Founding and Former Series Editors:
Gerhard Goos, Juris Hartmanis, and Jan van Leeuwen

More information about this series at http://www.springer.com/series/7408

Christoph Benzmüller · Francesco Ricca
Xavier Parent · Dumitru Roman (Eds.)

Rules and Reasoning

Second International Joint Conference, RuleML+RR 2018
Luxembourg, Luxembourg, September 18–21, 2018
Proceedings

 Springer

Editors
Christoph Benzmüller
Computer Science
Freie Universität Berlin
Berlin
Germany

Francesco Ricca
University of Calabria
Rende
Italy

Xavier Parent
Université du Luxembourg
Esch-sur-Alzette
Luxembourg

Dumitru Roman
SINTEF/University of Oslo
Oslo
Norway

ISSN 0302-9743   ISSN 1611-3349   (electronic)
Lecture Notes in Computer Science
ISBN 978-3-319-99905-0   ISBN 978-3-319-99906-7   (eBook)
https://doi.org/10.1007/978-3-319-99906-7

Library of Congress Control Number: 2018952566

LNCS Sublibrary: SL2 – Programming and Software Engineering

This Springer imprint is published by the registered company Springer Nature Switzerland AG
The registered company address is: Gewerbestrasse 11, 6330 Cham, Switzerland

Preface

These are the proceedings of the Second International Joint Conference on Rules and Reasoning (RuleML+RR). RuleML+RR joined the efforts of two well-established conference series: the International Web Rule symposia (RuleML) and the Web Reasoning and Rule Systems (RR) conferences.

The RuleML symposia and RR conferences have been held since 2002 and 2007, respectively. The RR conferences have been a forum for discussion and dissemination of new results on Web reasoning and rule systems, with an emphasis on rule-based approaches and languages. The RuleML symposia were devoted to disseminating research, applications, languages, and standards for rule technologies, with attention to both theoretical and practical developments, to challenging new ideas, and to industrial applications. Building on the tradition of both, RuleML and RR, the joint conference series RuleML+RR aims at bridging academia and industry in the field of rules, and at fostering the cross-fertilization between the different communities focused on the research, development, and applications of rule-based systems. RuleML+RR aims at being the leading conference series for all subjects concerning theoretical advances, novel technologies, and innovative applications about knowledge representation and reasoning with rules.

To leverage these ambitions, RuleML+RR 2018 was organized as part of the Luxembourg Logic for AI Summit (LuxLogAI 2018). This summit was hosted by the University of Luxembourg on the Campus Belval in Esch-sur-Alzette, Luxembourg. With its special focus theme on "Methods and Tools for Responsible AI," a core objective of LuxLogAI 2018 was to present and discuss the latest developments and progress made concerning the crucial question of how to make AI more transparent, responsible, and accountable. To this end, LuxLogAI 2018 brought together a range of events with related interests. In addition to RuleML+RR, this included the 4th Global Conference on Artificial Intelligence (GCAI 2018), the DecisionCAMP 2018, the Reasoning Web Summer School (RW 2018), the workshop on Mining and Reasoning with Legal Texts (MIREL 2018), and the Annual Meeting of the German National Interest Group in Deduction Systems (Deduktionstreffen 2018).

The RuleML+RR conference, moreover, included several subevents:

1. Doctoral Consortium, organized by Kia Teymourian (Boston University, US) and Paul Fodor (Stony Brook University, USA). The doctoral consortium is an initiative to attract and promote student research in rules and reasoning, with the opportunity for students to present and discuss their ideas and benefit from close contact with leading experts in the field.
2. Industry Track, organized by Silvie Spreeuwenberg (LibRT, The Netherlands) and Sven Mühlenbrock (KPMG, Luxembourg): The industry track provides a forum for all sectors of industry and business (as well as public sectors) to present, discuss, and propose existing or potential rule-based applications.

3. International Rule Challenge, organized by Giovanni De Gasperis (University of L'Aquila, Italy), Wolfgang Faber (Alpen-Adria-Universität Klagenfurt, Austria), and Adrian Giurca (BTU Cottbus-Senftenberg, Germany): The aim of this initiative is to provide competition among work in progress and new visionary ideas concerning innovative rule-oriented applications, aimed at both research and industry.

The technical program of the main track of RuleML+RR 2018 included the presentation of ten full research papers, five long technical communications, and seven short papers including technical communications and system demonstrations. These contributions were carefully selected by the Program Committee among 33 high-quality submissions to the event. Each paper was reviewed by at least three reviewers; most papers additionally received meta-reviews. The technical program also included papers from the Doctoral Consortium and the Rule Challenge.

At RuleML+RR 2018 the following invited keynotes and tutorials were presented by experts in the field:

- Keynote by Hanna Bast (Universität Freiburg, Germany): "Efficient and Convenient Search on Very Large Knowledge Bases"
- Keynote by Georg Gottlob (University of Oxford, UK, and TU Wien, Austria): "Vadalog: A Language and System for Knowledge Graphs"
- Keynote by Guido Governatori (CSIRO/Data61, Australia): "Modal Rules: Extending Defeasible Logic with Modal Operators"
- Tutorial by Bob Kowalski, Migual Calejo, and Fariba Sadri (all Imperial College, London, UK): "Logic and Smart Contracts"
- Tutorial by Monica Palmirani (University of Bologna, Italy) and Guido Governatori (CSIRO/Data61, Australia): "LegalRuleML"

The chairs sincerely thank the keynote and tutorial speakers for their contribution to the success of the event. The chairs also thank the Program Committee members and the additional reviewers for their hard work in the careful assessment of the submitted papers. Further thanks go to all authors of contributed papers, in particular, for their efforts in the preparation of their submissions and the camera-ready versions within the established schedule. Sincere thanks are due to the chairs of the additional tracks and subevents, namely, the Doctoral Consortium, the Rule Challenge and the Industry Track, and to the chairs of all co-located LuxLogAI events. The chairs finally thank the entire organization team including the publicity, sponsorship, financial, and proceedings chairs, who actively contributed to the organization and the success of the event.

A special thanks goes to all the sponsors of RuleML+RR 2018 and LuxLogAI 2018: Binarypark; the Computer Science and Communications (CSC) Research Unit at the University of Luxembourg; the Department of Mathematics and Computer Science at the University of Calabria; the Interdisciplinary Centre for Security, Reliability and Trust (SnT) and the Interdisciplinary Lab for Intelligent and Adaptive Systems (ILIAS) at the University of Luxembourg; LogicalContracts; the Luxembourg National

Research Fund (FNR); oXygen; and Springer. A special thanks also goes to the publisher, Springer, for their cooperation in editing this volume and publishing the proceedings.

July 2018

Christoph Benzmüller
Francesco Ricca
Xavier Parent
Dumitru Roman

Organization

Summit Chair (LuxLogAI)

Leon van der Torre   University of Luxembourg, Luxembourg

General Chair (RuleML+RR)

Xavier Parent   University of Luxembourg, Luxembourg

Program Chairs

Christoph Benzmüller   University of Luxembourg and Freie Universität
     Berlin, Germany
Francesco Ricca   University of Calabria, Italy

Proceedings Chair

Dumitru Roman   SINTEF/University of Oslo, Norway

Industry Track Chair

Silvie Spreeuwenberg   LibRT, The Netherlands

Doctoral Consortium Chairs

Kia Teymourian   Boston University, USA
Paul Fodor   Stony Brook University, USA

International Rule Challenge Chairs

Giovanni De Gasperis   University of L'Aquila, Italy
Wolgang Faber   Alpen-Adria-Universität Klagenfurt, Austria
Adrian Giurca   BTU Cottbus-Senftenberg, Germany

Reasoning Web (RW) Summer School

Claudia d'Amato   University of Bari, Italy
Martin Theobald   University of Luxembourg, Luxembourg

Publicity Chairs

Amal Tawakuli	University of Luxembourg, Luxembourg
Frank Olken	Frank Olken Consulting, USA

Financial Chair

Martin Theobald	University of Luxembourg, Luxembourg

Poster Chair

Alexander Steen	University of Luxembourg, Luxembourg

Program Committee

Sudhir Agarwal	Stanford University, USA
Nick Bassiliades	Aristotle University of Thessaloniki, Greece
Christoph Benzmüller (Chair)	Freie Universität Berlin, Germany
Leopoldo Bertossi	Carleton University, Canada
Mehul Bhatt	University of Bremen, Germany, and Örebro University, Sweden
Pedro Cabalar	University of Corunna, Italy
Diego Calvanese	Free University of Bozen-Bolzano, Italy
Iliano Cervesato	Carnegie Mellon University, USA
Horatiu Cirstea	Loria Nancy, France
Stefania Costantini	Università dell'Aquila, Italy
Juergen Dix	Clausthal University of Technology, Germany
Thomas Eiter	Vienna University of Technology, Austria
Esra Erdem	Sabanci University, Turkey
Wolfgang Faber	Alpen-Adria-Universität Klagenfurt, Austria
Fred Freitas	Universidade Federal de Pernambuco, Brazil
Daniel Gall	Ulm University, Germany
Giancarlo Guizzardi	Federal University of Espirito Santo, Brazil
Michael Kifer	Stony Brook University, USA
Matthias Klusch	DFKI Saarbrücken, Germany
Michael Kohlhase	FAU Erlangen-Nürnberg, Germany
Roman Kontchakov	Birkbeck University of London, UK
Manolis Koubarakis	National and Kapodistrian University of Athens, Greece
Domenico Lembo	Sapienza University of Rome, Italy
Francesca Lisi	Università di Bari, Italy
Thomas Lukasiewicz	University of Oxford, UK
Marco Maratea	University of Genoa, Italy
Alessandra Mileo	Dublin City University, Ireland
Marco Montali	Free University of Bozen-Bolzano, Italy

Angelo Montanari	University of Udine, Italy
Marie-Laure Mugnier	University of Montpellier, France
Sven Mühlenbrock	KPMG Luxembourg, Luxembourg
Raghava Mutharaju	GE Global Research Center Niskayuna, USA
Magdalena Ortiz	Vienna University of Technology, Austria
Adrian Paschke	Freie Universität Berlin, Germany
Andreas Pieris	The University of Edinburgh, UK
Luca Pulina	POLCOMING-University of Sassari, Italy
Jan Rauch	Prague University of Economics, Czech Republic
Francesco Ricca (Chair)	University of Calabria, Italy
Fabrizio Riguzzi	University of Ferrara, Italy
Livio Robaldo	University of Luxembourg, Luxembourg
Konstantin Schekotihin	Alpen-Adria Universität Klagenfurt, Austria
Stefan Schlobach	Vrije Universiteit Amsterdam, The Netherlands
Rolf Schwitter	Macquarie University, Australia
Giorgos Stoilos	Athens University of Economics and Business, Greece
Umberto Straccia	ISTI-CNR Pisa, Italy
Mirek Truszczynski	University of Kentucky, USA
Anni-Yasmin Turha	TU Dresden, Germany
Neng-Fa Zhou	CUNY Brooklyn College and Graduate Center, USA

Additional Reviewers

Jean-Paul Calbimonte	Cleyton Rodrigues
Giuseppe Cota	Silvie Spreeuwenberg
Robson Fidalgo	Alexandru Todor
Valeria Fionda	Despoina Trivela
Eugene Pinsky	Riccardo Zese

RuleML+RR 2018 Sponsors

Fonds National de la
Recherche Luxembourg

UNIVERSITÉ DU
LUXEMBOURG

DIPARTIMENTO DI
MATEMATICA E INFORMATICA

Keynote Talks

Efficient and Convenient Search on Very Large Knowledge Bases

Hannah Bast

Department of Computer Science, University of Freiburg, 79110 Freiburg,
Germany
bast@cs.uni-freiburg.de

Abstract. Knowledge bases like Freebase or Wikidata have hundreds of millions of entities and billions of triples. Searching such knowledge bases is challenging in many ways. First, already importing the data dumps from such knowledge bases into standard triples stores is hard: it can take forever or does not work at all without preprocessing. Second, even relatively simple queries can take a very long time to process, in particular queries with large result sets. Third, formulating queries in SPARQL is hard even for experts, since it requires knowledge of the exact names or ids of the involved predicates and entities. Fourth, it is often desirable to combine knowledge base search with keyword search, but basic SPARQL provides little support for this. We will present ideas and solutions for all four of these challenges, as well as various demos based on these ideas and solutions.

Logic and Smart Contracts

Robert Kowalski[1], Miguel Calejo[2], and Fariba Sadri[3]

[1] Imperial College, London, UK
{r.kowalski,f.sadri}@imperial.ac.uk
[2] logicalcontracts.com
mc@logicalcontracts.com
[3] Imperial College, London, UK

Abstract. The idea of using logic to improve the analysis and drafting of legal documents was advocated most notably already in the 1950s by the legal theorist Layman Allen [1]. It was given a boost in the 1980s with the use of logic programming (LP) to implement a large portion of the British Nationality Act [7]. Arguably, since then, LP in one form or another has been the dominant approach in the field of AI and Law.

In the meanwhile, a new, related field has emerged with the development of blockchains and smart contracts. However, the main programming languages being used in this new field, such as Solidity and Serpent, have been developed without attention to AI approaches. As a result, there is a large gap between smart contracts in these programming languages and their specifications in the natural language of the law. The resulting systems are hard to verify and difficult for non-programmers to understand.

The gap between conventional programming languages for smart contracts and logic-based languages for AI and Law has inspired several recent applications of AI approaches to the implementation of smart contracts and other legal documents. In this tutorial, we will survey these recent developments, focusing on three main examples: the simplified loan agreement developed by Flood and Goodenough [3], the rock, paper scissors example used in a blockchain lecture course at the University of Maryland [2], and the delayed delivery example of the Accord Project [6], https://www.accordproject.org/.

We will discuss alternative implementations of these examples, and show how they can be implemented in the logic and computer language LPS [4, 5], with an open source implementation over SWISH [8], the online version of SWI Prolog. Attendees can experiment with the examples, using their own laptops or tablets during the tutorial. A brief introduction to LPS and a link to the online implementation can be found at http://lps.doc.ic.ac.uk/.

References

1. Allen, L.E.: Symbolic logic: a razor-edged tool for drafting and interpreting legal documents. Yale LJ, **66**, 833 (1956)
2. Delmolino, K., Arnett, M., Kosba, A., Miller, A., Shi, E.: Step by step towards creating a safe smart contract: lessons and insights from a cryptocurrency lab. In: Clark, J., Meiklejohn, S., Ryan, P., Wallach, D., Brenner, M., Rohloff, K. (eds.) FC 2016. LNCS, vol. 9604, 79–94. Springer, Heidelberg (2016)
3. Flood, M., Goodenough, O.: Contract as automaton: the computational representation of financial agreements. Technical report, Office of Financial Research, U.S. Department of the Treasury (2017)
4. Kowalski, R., Sadri, F.: Reactive computing as model generation. New Gener. Comput. **33**(1), 33–67 (2015)
5. Kowalski, R., Sadri, F.: Programming in logic without logic programming. TPLP **16**, 269–295 (2016)
6. Selman, D.: Template specification. Logic and smart contracts Kowalski, Calejo and Sadri (2018)
7. Sergot, M.J., Sadri, F., Kowalski, R.A., Kriwaczek, F., Hammond, P., Cory, H.T.: The british nationality act as a logic program. CACM **29**(5), 370–386 (1986)
8. Wielemaker, J., Riguzzi, F., Kowalski, R., Lager, T., Sadri, F., Calejo, M.: Using swish to realise interactive web based tutorials for logic based languages. (2018, submitted for publication)

Contents

Invited Papers

Vadalog: A Language and System for Knowledge Graphs

Luigi Bellomarini[1,2], Georg Gottlob[1,3], Andreas Pieris[4], and Emanuel Sallinger[1(✉)]

[1] University of Oxford, Oxford, UK
emanuel.sallinger@cs.ox.ac.uk
[2] Banca d'Italia, Rome, Italy
[3] TU Wien, Vienna, Austria
[4] University of Edinburgh, Edinburgh, UK

1 Introduction

With the introduction of its Knowledge Graph [20], Google has coined the name for a new generation of knowledge-based systems that go beyond what was previously expected of areas that include graph databases, knowledge bases, machine-learning systems and rule-based logical reasoners. Beyond Google, companies are recognizing the need for making use of their vast amounts of data and knowledge in the form of enterprise knowledge graphs [20]. In the same way that databases created the need for Database Management Systems (DBMS) and knowledge bases fostered the creation of Knowledge Base Management Systems (KBMS), the interest in Knowledge Graphs creates a need for academia and industry to understand and develop *knowledge graph management systems* (KGMS).

There are a variety of requirements for a KGMS. For a detailed discussion of such requirements, we refer to [4,13]. Yet at its core, a KGMS must be expressive enough to represent knowledge beyond mere facts, but at the same time provide scalability in the presence of very large amounts of data and complex reasoning tasks. The most wide-spread form of knowledge that has been adopted over the last decades has been in the form of rules, be it in rule-based systems, ontology-based systems or other forms. The nature of graphs makes the presence of recursion in these rules a particularly important aspect. The need to refer to unknown or missing information makes the presence of existential quantification essential. At the same time, a KGMS has to provide methods and tools for data analytics and machine learning. Moreover, a KGMS needs interfaces to many heterogeneous data sources, including: corporate RDBMS, NoSQL stores, the web, machine-learning and analytics packages. We represent a short summary of a KGMS reference architecture in Fig. 1.

The search for *knowledge representation and reasoning* formalisms that satisfy some or all of these criteria has led the community to develop a wide range of languages. In this paper, we give a short introduction to the Vadalog language and system, a KGMS that satisfies the requirements summarized above. The logical core of Vadalog is Warded Datalog$^\pm$ [2,15]. The prominent feature

© Springer Nature Switzerland AG 2018
C. Benzmüller et al. (Eds.): RuleML+RR 2018, LNCS 11092, pp. 3–8, 2018.
https://doi.org/10.1007/978-3-319-99906-7_1

of Warded Datalog$^\pm$ is that it (1) includes all of Datalog, (2) is able to express SPARQL under set semantics and the OWL 2 QL entailment regime and (3) still has polynomial time data complexity. The VADALOG system [5–7] follows the reference architecture shown in Fig. 1 and exploits the theoretical underpinnings of relevant Datalog$^\pm$ languages, combining them with existing and novel techniques from database engineering and AI practice. A more detailed introduction to the Vadalog language and system is given in [4]. Yet, PTIME data complexity, while sufficient for many conventional applications, can be prohibitive for "Big Data" scenarios. One such example is towards building knowledge graphs that consider huge elections in the area of computational social choice [12]. Many more could be named. Therefore, we describe sub-languages, in particular *strongly warded* Datalog$^\pm$, which are suited for such scenarios.

This survey includes, in abbreviated form, material from a number of previous papers on the topic [4–7]. The VADALOG system is Oxford's contribution to VADA [17], a joint project of the universities of Edinburgh, Manchester, and Oxford. We reported first work on the overall VADA approach to data wrangling in [13]. In this paper, we focus on the VADALOG system at its core. Our system currently fully implements the core language and is already in use for a number of industrial applications.

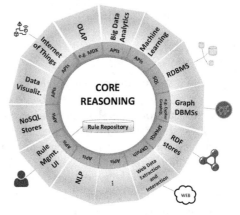

Fig. 1. KGMS reference architecture [4].

2   The VADALOG Core Language

VADALOG is a Datalog-based language. It belongs to the Datalog$^\pm$ family of languages that extend Datalog by existential quantifiers in rule heads, as well as by other features, and restricts at the same time its syntax in order to achieve decidability and data tractability; see, e.g., [8–11]. The logical core of the VADALOG language corresponds to *Warded Datalog$^\pm$* [2,15], which captures plain Datalog as well as SPARQL queries under the entailment regime for OWL 2 QL [14], and is able to perform ontological reasoning tasks. Reasoning with the logical core of VADALOG is computationally efficient. VADALOG is obtained by extending Warded Datalog$^\pm$ with additional features of practical utility. We now illustrate the logical core of VADALOG, more details about extensions can be found in [4].

The logical core of VADALOG relies on the notion of wardedness, which applies a restriction on how the "dangerous" variables of a set of existential rules are used. Note that existential rules are also known as tuple-generating dependencies (tgds), i.e., Datalog rules were existential quantification is allowed in the head.

Intuitively, a "dangerous" variable is a body-variable that can be unified with a labeled null value when the chase algorithm is applied, and it is also propagated to the head of the rule. For example, given the set Σ consisting of the rules

$$P(x) \rightarrow \exists z\, R(x, z) \quad \text{and} \quad R(x, y) \rightarrow P(y),$$

the variable y in the body of the second rule is "dangerous" (w.r.t. Σ) since starting, e.g., from the database $D = \{P(a)\}$, the chase will apply the first rule and generate $R(a, \nu)$, where ν is a null that acts as a witness for the existentially quantified variable z, and then the second rule will be applied with the variable y being unified with ν that is propagated to the obtained atom $P(\nu)$.

The goal of wardedness is to tame the way null values are propagated during the construction of the chase instance by posing the following conditions: (i) all the "dangerous" variables should coexist in a single body-atom α, called the *ward*; (ii) the ward can share only "harmless" variables with the rest of the body, i.e., variables that are unified only with database constants during the construction of the chase.

Warded Datalog$^\pm$ consists of all the (finite) sets of warded existential rules. As an example of a warded set of rules, the following rules encode part of the OWL 2 direct semantics entailment regime for OWL 2 QL (see [2,15]):

$$\underline{\text{Type}(x, y)}, \text{Restriction}(y, z) \rightarrow \exists w\, \text{Triple}(x, z, w)$$
$$\underline{\text{Type}(x, y)}, \text{SubClass}(y, z) \rightarrow \text{Type}(x, z)$$
$$\underline{\text{Triple}(x, y, z)}, \text{Inverse}(y, w) \rightarrow \text{Triple}(z, w, x)$$
$$\underline{\text{Triple}(x, y, z)}, \text{Restriction}(w, y) \rightarrow \text{Type}(x, w).$$

It is easy to verify that the above set is warded, where the underlined atoms are the wards. Indeed, a variable that occurs in an atom of the form Restriction$(\cdot, \cdot)$, or SubClass$(\cdot, \cdot)$, or Inverse$(\cdot, \cdot)$, is trivially harmless. However, variables that appear in the first position of Type, or in the first/third position of Triple can be dangerous. Thus, the underlined atoms are indeed acting as the wards.

3   Efficient Sub-languages in VADALOG

Reasoning in Warded Datalog$^\pm$ is PTIME-complete in data complexity [2,15]. Although polynomial time data complexity is desirable for conventional applications, PTIME-hardness can be prohibitive for "Big Data" applications; in fact, this is true even for linear time data complexity. This raises the question whether there are fragments of Warded Datalog$^\pm$ that guarantee lower data complexity, but at the same time maintain the favourable properties discussed above. Of course, such a fragment should be weaker than full Datalog since Datalog itself is already PTIME-complete in data complexity. On the other hand, such a fragment should be powerful enough to compute the transitive closure of a binary relation, which is a crucial feature for reasoning over graphs, and, in particular, for capturing SPARQL queries under the entailment regime for OWL 2 QL. Therefore, the complexity of such a refined fragment is expected to be NLOGSPACE-complete.

Such a fragment of Warded Datalog$^\pm$, dubbed *Strongly-Warded*, can be defined by carefully restricting the way recursion is employed. Before giving the definition, let us recall the standard notion of the predicate graph of a set Σ of existential rules, which essentially encodes how the predicates in Σ interact. The *predicate graph* of Σ, denoted $PG(\Sigma)$, is a directed graph (V, E), where the node set V consists of all the predicates occurring in Σ, and we have an edge from a predicate P to a predicate R iff there exists $\sigma \in \Sigma$ such that P occurs in the body of σ and R occurs in the head of σ. Consider a set of nodes $S \subseteq V$ and a node $R \in V$. We say that R is Σ-*reachable* from S if there exists at least one node $P \in S$ that can reach R via a path in $PG(\Sigma)$. We are now ready to introduce strong-wardedness.

A set of existential rules Σ is called *strongly-warded* if Σ is warded, and, for each $\sigma \in \Sigma$ of the form

$$\varphi(\bar{x}, \bar{y}) \;\rightarrow\; \exists \bar{z}\, (P_1(\bar{x}, \bar{z}) \wedge \ldots \wedge P_n(\bar{x}, \bar{z})),$$

there exists at most one atom in $\varphi(\bar{x}, \bar{y})$ whose predicate is Σ-reachable from $\{P_1, \ldots, P_n\}$. *Strongly-Warded Datalog$^\pm$* consists of all the (finite) sets of existential rules that are strongly-warded. Intuitively, in a strongly-warded set of existential rules, each rule σ is either non-recursive, or it employs a mild form of recursion in the sense that an atom generated by σ during the construction of the chase instance can affect exactly one body-atom of σ. Let us clarify that the additional syntactic condition posed on warded existential rules in order to obtain strongly-warded existential rules, is the same as the condition underlying *Piecewise Linear Datalog*; see, e.g., [1].

It can be shown that our main reasoning task of tuple inference under Strongly-Warded Datalog$^\pm$ is NLOGSPACE-complete in the data complexity. Moreover, this refined language remains powerful enough for capturing OWL 2 QL, and, extended by a mild form of negation, can express every SPARQL query under the entailment regime for OWL 2 QL. As already explained above, the NLOGSPACE data complexity immediately excludes full Datalog. However, Strongly-Warded Datalog$^\pm$ includes some important and well-studied fragments of Datalog: (i) *Non-Recursive Datalog*, where the underlying predicate graph is acyclic, and (ii) *IDB-Linear Datalog*, where each rule can have at most one intensional predicate (i.e., it appears in the head of at least one rule) in its body, while all the other predicates are extensional.

A lightweight fragment of Strongly-Warded Datalog$^\pm$ that is *FO-Rewritable* is *Linear Datalog$^\pm$*, where each existential rule can have exactly one body-atom [9]. FO-Rewritability means that, given a pair $Q = (\Sigma, \text{Ans})$, we can construct a (finite) first-order query Q_{FO} such that, for *every* database D, $Q(D)$ coincides with the evaluation of Q_{FO} over D. This immediately implies that tuple inference under Linear Datalog$^\pm$ is in AC$_0$ in data complexity. Despite its simplicity, Linear Datalog$^\pm$ is expressive enough for expressing every OWL 2 QL axiom. However, it cannot compute the transitive closure of a binary relation, which is unavoidable to ensure FO-Rewritability. This makes it unsuitable for querying RDF graphs under the entailment regime for OWL 2 QL.

4 The VADALOG System

The functional architecture of the VADALOG system, our KGMS, is depicted in Fig. 1. The knowledge graph is organized as a repository, a collection of VADALOG rules. The external sources are supported by means of *transducers*, intelligent adapters that integrate the sources into the reasoning process.

The Big Data characteristics of the sources and the complex functional requirements of reasoning are tackled by leveraging the underpinnings of the core language, which are turned into practical execution strategies. In particular, in the reasoning algorithms devised for Warded Datalog$^{\pm}$, after a certain number of chase steps (which, in general, depends on the input database), the chase graph [9] (a directed acyclic graph where facts are represented as nodes and the applied rules as edges) exhibits specific periodicities and no new information, relevant to query answering, is generated. The VADALOG system adopts an *aggressive recursion and termination control* strategy, which detects such redundancy as early as possible by combining compile-time and runtime techniques. In combination with a highly engineered architecture, the VADALOG system achieves high performance and an efficient memory footprint.

At compile time, as wardedness limits the interaction between the labeled nulls, the engine rewrites the program in such a way that joins on specific values of labeled nulls will never occur. This exploits work on schema mapping composition and optimization [16,19]. More details on the Vadalog system can be found in [7]. The system includes many other features, such as data extraction with OXPath, which is in use with our collaborators at dblp [18].

5 Conclusion

The VADALOG system is already in use for a number of industrial applications. We believe that the VADALOG system is a well-suited platform for knowledge graph applications that integrate machine learning (ML) and data analytics with logical reasoning. We are currently implementing applications of this type and will report about them soon. Other extensions that we envision in the scope of efficient sub-languages are in the area of inconsistency, in particular towards efficient fragments of consistent query answering [3].

Acknowledgments. This work has been supported by the EPSRC Programme Grant EP/M025268/1. The VADALOG system is IP of the University of Oxford.

References

1. Afrati, F.N., Gergatsoulis, M., Toni, F.: Linearisability on datalog programs. Theor. Comput. Sci. **308**(1–3), 199–226 (2003)
2. Arenas, M., Gottlob, G., Pieris, A.: Expressive languages for querying the semantic web. In: PODS, pp. 14–26 (2014)
3. Arming, S., Pichler, R., Sallinger, E.: Complexity of repair checking and consistent query answering. In: ICDT, vol. 48, LIPIcs. SD-LZI (2016)

4. Bellomarini, L., Gottlob, G., Pieris, A., Sallinger, E.: Swift logic for big data and knowledge graphs. In: IJCAI, pp. 2–10 (2017)
5. Bellomarini, L., Gottlob, G., Pieris, A., Sallinger, E.: Swift logic for big data and knowledge graphs. In: Tjoa, A.M., Bellatreche, L., Biffl, S., van Leeuwen, J., Wiedermann, J. (eds.) SOFSEM 2018. LNCS, vol. 10706, pp. 3–16. Springer, Cham (2018). https://doi.org/10.1007/978-3-319-73117-9_1
6. Bellomarini, L., Gottlob, G., Pieris, A., Sallinger, E.: The Vadalog system: swift logic for big data and enterprise knowledge graphs. In: AMW (2018)
7. Bellomarini, L., Sallinger, E., Gottlob, G.: The vadalog system: Datalog-based reasoning for knowledge graphs. PVLDB **11**(9), 975–987 (2018)
8. Calì, A., Gottlob, G., Kifer, M.: Taming the infinite chase: query answering under expressive relational constraints. J. Artif. Intell. Res. **48**, 115–174 (2013)
9. Calì, A., Gottlob, G., Lukasiewicz, T.: A general datalog-based framework for tractable query answering over ontologies. J. Web Sem. **14**, 57–83 (2012)
10. Calì, A., Gottlob, G., Lukasiewicz, T., Marnette, B., Pieris, A.: Datalog+/-: a family of logical knowledge representation and query languages for new applications. In: LICS, pp. 228–242 (2010)
11. Calì, A., Gottlob, G., Pieris, A.: Towards more expressive ontology languages: the query answering problem. Artif. Intell. **193**, 87–128 (2012)
12. Csar, T., Lackner, M., Pichler, R., Sallinger, E.: Winner determination in huge elections with mapreduce. In: AAAI, pp. 451–458. AAAI Press (2017)
13. Furche, T., Gottlob, G., Neumayr, B., Sallinger, E.: Data wrangling for big data: towards a lingua franca for data wrangling. In: AMW (2016)
14. Glimm, B., Ogbuji, C., Hawke, S., Herman, I., Parsia, B., Polleres, A., Seaborne, A.: SPARQL 1.1 entailment regimes. W3C Recommendation, 21 March 2013
15. Gottlob, G., Pieris, A.: Beyond SPARQL under OWL 2 QL entailment regime: rules to the rescue. In: IJCAI, pp. 2999–3007 (2015)
16. Kolaitis, P.G., Pichler, R., Sallinger, E., Savenkov, V.: Limits of schema mappings. Theory Comput. Syst. **62**(4), 899–940 (2018)
17. Konstantinou, N., et al.: The VADA architecture for cost-effective data wrangling. In: SIGMOD, ACM (2017)
18. Michels, C., Fayzrakhmanov, R.R., Ley, M., Sallinger, E., Schenkel, R.: Oxpath-based data acquisition for dblp. In: JCDL, pp. 319–320. IEEE CS (2017)
19. Sallinger, E.: Reasoning about schema mappings. In: Data Exchange, Information, and Streams, volume 5 of Dagstuhl Follow-Ups, pp. 97–127. SD-LZI (2013)
20. Wikipedia: Knowledge graph. https://en.wikipedia.org/wiki/Knowledge_Graph (2017). Accessed 3 Mar 2018

Modal Rules: Extending Defeasible Logic with Modal Operators

Guido Governatori[(✉)]

Data61, CSIRO, Dutton Park 4102, Australia
guido.governatori@data61.csiro.au

Abstract. In this paper we present a general methodology to extend Defeasible Logic with modal operators. We motivate the reasons for this type of extension and we argue that the extension will allow for a robust knowledge framework in different application areas.

1 Introduction

Since the revival of modal logic at the beginning of the 20th century the debate whether there is a genuine need for modal logic has gone on and on with alternate fortune. Originally modern modal logic [37,38] has been proposed as an alternative knowledge representation formalism to obviate the problems of classical logic with material implication. The main drawback at that time was the lack on an intuitive (set theoretic or Tarskian) semantics. The situation changed in the second part of the 50s with the introduction of the so called possible worlds semantics [33], that offers a very intuitive reading and explanation of the modal operators. This made it possible for modal logic to flourish again.

In the same years the seminal work by Hintikka [28] established the foundations of the analysis of epistemic and doxastic notions (i.e., knowledge and belief) in terms of modal operators, paving thus the way to the field of agents and multi-agent systems. In this field modal operators proved to be very powerful conceptual tools to describe the internal (mental) states of agents as well as interactions among agents.

von Wright [47] started the study of deontic logic, where modal operators are associated to normative notions such as obligation, permission and so on. Deontic logic is nowadays one of the most promising instruments for the formalisation of institutionalised organisation and the mutual relationships (normative position) among the actors in such models. Deontic Logic plays an important role in the formalisation of contracts [11,35].

What we want to stress out here is that modal logic is appropriate to provide a conceptual model for describing agents as well as many other intensional notions, in particular normative notions such as obligations, permissions, rights and so on which are important for policies, e-commerce and e-contracts. While modal logic offers a very elegant and powerful tool to describe conceptual models in the above area, as well as many others, it suffers from two main drawbacks: (i) Its computational complexity is to high for any real practical application;

© Springer Nature Switzerland AG 2018
C. Benzmüller et al. (Eds.): RuleML+RR 2018, LNCS 11092, pp. 9–30, 2018.
https://doi.org/10.1007/978-3-319-99906-7_2

(ii) in real life situations one has to reason with somehow incomplete and sometimes conflicting information, and modal logics being usually based on classical logic are, in general, not able to deal with such situations appropriately.

To mitigate the above drawbacks several extensions of defeasible logic, a rule based non-monotonic logic designed to deal with these issues, have been proposed to provide a feasible computationally oriented non-monotonic rule based account of modal logic. Different extensions of defeasible logic with modal operators have already been presented, thus the objective of the paper is not just to introduce some new modal defeasible logic. The aim of the paper is twofold. We want to advocate and motivate the design choices behind modal defeasible logic and to show that the approach is conceptually sound and grounded in well understood logical principles; in addition, we want to show a basic framework for defining modal defeasible logics.

To achieve our goal, we first answer the questions whether it is better to have modal operators or modalities (i.e., predicates) for the modal notions. Our answer will be that modal operators (and consequently modal logic) offer a better alternative. At that point we can present our general methodology to combine modalities and Defeasible Logic.

2   Modalities and Modal Logics

Let us now discuss a main objection to modal logic. Since the introduction of the possible world semantics there has been a proliferation of modal logics. In part this is a consequence of the many interpretations one can give to the modal operators. Given the multiplicity of interpretations it is clear that it is not possible to have a one size fits all (or most) situation, given the many facets of modalities. It is recognised [36] that, apart some special cases[1], there is no one modal logic even for a particular interpretation, and thus the designer of a particular application has to choose case by case which proprieties/principles are satisfied by the modal operators. The designer has to identify which notions are better modelled by modal operators and which are suitable to be captured by predicates.

Given the issues above a supporter of modalities (particular *ad hoc* predicates whose interpretation is that of modal operators) might argue that modalities offer a more convenient approach since there is no need to create a new logic every time we have a new notion. Everything can be represented in first-order logic. After all, it is hard to distinguish between notions to be modelled by ordinary predicates and notions to be modelled by modal operators. In addition, from a computational point of view first-order logic is semi-decidable while often modal logics are decidable, and there are examples where properties can be encoded easily in modal logic but they require high-order logic representations.

A first answer to this objection, following Scott's advice [46], is that rather than adding ad hoc predicates to the language, improvements must be made

---

[1] For example the modal logic of provability where the interpretation of □ as the provability predicate of Peano Arithmetics forces a one to one mapping.

by adding modal operators so as to achieve a richer language that can represent the behaviour of modal notions in a more natural and applicable manner. The advantage of this approach is to incorporate general and flexible reasoning mechanisms within the inferential engine.

A formal representation language should offer concepts close to the notions the language is designed to capture. For example, contracts typically contain provisions about deontic concepts such as obligations, permissions, entitlements, violations and other (mutual) normative positions that the signatories of a contract agree to comply with. Accordingly, a contract language should cater for those notions. In addition, the language should be supplemented by either a formal semantics or facilities to reason with and about the symbols of the language to give meaning to them. As usual, the symbols of the language can be partitioned in two classes: logical symbols and extra logical symbols. The logical symbols are meant to represent general concepts and structures common to every contract while extra logical symbols encode the specific subject matter of given contracts. In this perspective the notions of obligation and permission will be represented by deontic modalities while concepts such as price, service and so on are better captured by predicates since their meaning varies from contract to contract.

In general, we believe that the approach with modal operators is superior to the use of ad hoc predicates at least for the following aspects[2]:

- *Ease of expression and comprehension.* In the modal approach the relationships among modal notions are encoded in the logic and reasoning mechanism while for ad hoc predicates knowledge bases are cluttered with rules describing the logical relationships among different modes/representations of one and the same concept. For example, in a set of rules meant to describe a contract, given the predicate $pay(X)$, we have to create predicates such as $obligatory\_pay(X)$, $permitted\_pay(X)$, ... and rules such as

$$obligatory\_pay(X) \rightarrow permitted\_pay(X)$$

  and so on. Thus ad hoc predicates do not allow users to focus only and exclusively on aspects related to the content of a contract, without having to deal with any aspects related to its implementation.
- *Clear and intuitive semantics.* It is possible to give a precise, unambiguous, intuitive and general semantics to the notions involved while each ad hoc predicate requires its own individual interpretation, and in some cases complex constructions (for example reification) are needed to interpret some ad hoc predicates.

---

[2] In addition to the aspects we discuss here, we would like to point out that it has been argued [27,29] that deontic logic is better than a predicate based representation of obligations and permissions when the possibility of norm violation is kept open. As we have argued elsewhere [20] a logic of violation is essential for the representation of contracts where rules about violations are frequent. Obviously this argument only proves that modal operators are superior to deontic modalities, but we are confident that the argument can be extended to other modal notions.

- *Modularity.* A current line of research proposes that the combination of deontic operators with operators for speech acts and actions faithfully represent complex normative positions such as delegation, empowerment as well as many others that may appear in contracts [10,30]. In the modal approach those aspects can be added or decomposed modularly without forcing the user to rewrite the predicates and rules to accommodate the new facilities, or to reason at different granularity.

3   What Is a Rule?

A *rule* describes the relationship between a set of formulas (premises) and a formula (conclusion), or in the parlance of Input/Output logic [41] a rule provides a mechanism to process an input (premises) to obtain its output (conclusion). In this prospective a rule can be seen as an element of a relation with the following signature

$$2^{Input} \times Output$$

where, given a fixed logical language $\mathcal{L}$, *Input* is the set of formulas of $\mathcal{L}$ that can be used as input/premises, and *Output* the set of formulas of $\mathcal{L}$ that can be used as the conclusions/output of the rules.

Given a domain, multiple relations with the same signature are possible, and so are reading of the nature and properties of the relationship between premises and conclusion. Thus, we can ask how strong is such a relation. We can then investigate the nature of such a relationship. Given two sets, we have the following seven possible relationships describing the "strength" of the connections between the premises and the conclusion of a rule:

premises always conclusion
premises sometimes conclusion
premises not complement conclusion
premises no relationship conclusion
premises always complement conclusion
premises sometimes complement conclusion
premises not conclusion

Accordingly, as far as the strength of rules is concerned we distinguish between *strict rules* for the "always" cases, *defeasible rules* for the "sometimes" cases and *defeaters* for the "not" cases; the seventh case is when there is no relationship between the premises and the conclusion. In addition to the strength of the relationship we can study the mode the rule connects the antecedent and the conclusion. As usual, rules allow us to derive new conclusions given a set of premises. Since rules have a mode, the conclusions will be modal formulas (formulas within the scope of a modal operator). For the modes one can have one set of rules (base rules) describing the inference principles of the basic logic plus one mode for each modal operator of the language (modal rules). As we will see, the idea of modal rules is to introduce modalised conclusions. Accordingly, if we have a modal rule for p for a modal operator $\Box_i$, this means that the rule allows for the derivation of $\Box_i p$. In the next sections we are going to examine how to implement such idea in a computationally oriented logic, Defeasible Logic, and the focus is on the properties of rules and not on the logical structure of formulas. In Defeasible Logic formulas are limited to literals, and then modal literals when extended with modal rules; in addition we will discuss how to incorporate the "violation/compensation" operator introduced in [20] and that can be used a degree of acceptability for the conclusions.

4   Defeasible Logic

Defeasible Logic (DL) [3, 42] is a simple, efficient but flexible non-monotonic formalism that can deal with many different intuitions of non-monotonic reasoning [4], and efficient and powerful implementations have been proposed [6, 40]. DL and its variants have been applied in many fields.

The language of DL is restricted to literals (atomic propositions and their negation). Knowledge in DL can be represented in two ways: facts and rules.

Facts are indisputable statements, represented in form of states of affairs (literal and modal literal). Facts are represented by predicates. For example, "the price of the spam filter is $50" is represented by

$$Price(SpamFilter, 50).$$

In Defeasible Logic strict rules, defeasible rules and defeaters are represented, respectively, by expressions of the form

- $A_1, \ldots, A_n \rightarrow B$,
- $A_1, \ldots, A_n \Rightarrow B$,
- $A_1, \ldots, A_n \leadsto B$,

where $A_1, \ldots, A_n$ is a possibly empty set of prerequisites and B is the conclusion of the rule. We only consider rules that are essentially propositional. Rules containing free variables are interpreted as the set of their ground instances.

Strict rules are rules in the classical sense: whenever the premises are indisputable then so is the conclusion. Thus, they can be used for definitional clauses. An example of a strict rule is "A 'Premium Customer' is a customer who has spent $10000 on goods":

$$TotalExpense(X, 10000) \rightarrow PremiumCustomer(X).$$

Defeasible rules are rules that can be defeated by contrary evidence. An example of such a rule is "Premium Customer are entitled to a 5% discount":

$$PremiumCustomer(X) \Rightarrow Discount(X).$$

The idea is that if we know that someone is a Premium Customer then we may conclude that she is entitled to a discount *unless there is other evidence suggesting that she may not be* (for example if she buys a good in promotion).

Defeaters are a special kind of rules. They are used to prevent conclusions not to support them. For example:

$$SpecialOrder(X), PremiumCustomer(X) \rightsquigarrow \neg Surcharge(X).$$

This rule states that premium customers placing special orders might be exempt from the special order surcharge. This rule can prevent the derivation of a "surcharge" conclusion. However, it cannot be used to support a "not surcharge" conclusion.

DL is a "skeptical" non-monotonic logic, meaning that it does not support contradictory conclusions.[3] Instead, DL seeks to resolve conflicts. In cases where there is some support for concluding A but also support for concluding $\neg A$, DL does not conclude neither of them (thus the name "skeptical"). If the support for A has priority over the support for $\neg A$ then A is concluded.

As we have alluded to above, no conclusion can be drawn from conflicting rules in DL unless these rules are prioritised. The *superiority relation* is used to define priorities among rules, that is, where one rule may override the conclusion of another rule. For example, given the defeasible rules

$$r : PremiumCustomer(X) \Rightarrow Discount(X)$$
$$r' : SpecialOrder(X) \Rightarrow \neg Discount(X)$$

which contradict one another, no conclusive decision can be made about whether a Premium Customer, who has placed a special order, is entitled to the 5% discount. But if we introduce a superiority relation $>$ with $r' > r$, we can indeed conclude that special orders are not subject to discount.

We now give a short informal presentation of how conclusions are drawn in DL. Let D be a theory in DL (i.e., a collection of facts, rules and a superiority relation). A *conclusion* of D is a tagged literal and can have one of the following four forms:

$+\Delta q$ meaning that q is definitely provable in D (i.e., using only facts and strict rules).

$-\Delta q$ meaning that we have proved that q is not definitely provable in D.

$+\partial q$ meaning that q is defeasibly provable in D.

$-\partial q$ meaning that we have proved that q is not defeasibly provable in D.

Strict derivations are obtained by forward chaining of strict rules, while a defeasible conclusion p can be derived if there is a rule whose conclusion is p, whose prerequisites (antecedent) have either already been proved or given in the case at hand (i.e. facts), and any stronger rule whose conclusion is $\neg p$ has prerequisites that fail to be derived.

---

[3] To be precise contradictions can be obtained from the monotonic part of a defeasible theory, i.e., from facts and strict rules.

In other words, a conclusion p is derivable when:

- p is a fact; or
- there is an applicable strict or defeasible rule for p, and either
  - all the rules for $\neg p$ are discarded (i.e., are proved to be not applicable) or
  - every applicable rule for $\neg p$ is weaker than an applicable strict[4] or defeasible rule for p.

The formal definitions of derivations in DL are in the next section.

Maher [39] has shown that the extension of a theory in DL can be computed in time linear in the number of rules and literals in the theory.

5   Modal Defeasible Logic

As we have seen in Sect. 1, modal logics have been put forward to capture many different notions somehow related to the intensional nature of agency as well as many other notions. Usually modal logics are extensions of classical propositional logic with some intensional operators. Thus, any modal logic should account for two components: (1) the underlying logical structure of the propositional base and (2) the logic behaviour of the modal operators. Alas, as is well-known, classical propositional logic is not well suited to deal with real life scenarios. The main reason is that the descriptions of real-life cases are, very often, partial and somewhat unreliable. In such circumstances, classical propositional logic might produce counterintuitive results insofar as it requires complete, consistent and reliable information. Hence any modal logic based on classical propositional logic is doomed to suffer from the same problems.

On the other hand, the logic should specify how modalities can be introduced and manipulated. Some common rules for modalities are, e.g.,

$$\frac{\vdash \varphi}{\vdash \Box\varphi}\text{Necessitation} \qquad \frac{\vdash \varphi \to \psi}{\vdash \Box\varphi \to \Box\psi}\text{RM}$$

Both dictates conditions to introduce modalities based purely on the derivability and structure of the antecedent. These rules are related to the well-known problem of logical omniscience and put unrealistic assumptions on the capability of an agent. However, if we take a constructive interpretation, we have that if an agent can build a derivation of φ then she can build a derivation of $\Box\varphi$. We want to maintain this intuition here, but we want to replace derivability in classical logic with a practical and feasible notion like derivability in DL. Thus, the intuition behind this work is that we are allowed to derive $\Box_i p$ if we can prove p with the mode $\Box_i$ in DL.

To extend DL with modal operators we have two options: (1) to use the same inferential mechanism as basic DL and to represent explicitly the modal

---

[4] Notice that a strict rule can be defeated only when its antecedent is defeasibly provable.

operators in the conclusion of rules [43]; (2) introduce new types of rules for the modal operators to differentiate between modal and factual rules.

For example, the "deontic" statement "The Purchaser shall follow the Supplier price lists" can be represented as

$$AdvertisedPrice(X) \Rightarrow O_{purchaser} Pay(X)$$

if we follow the first option and

$$AdvertisedPrice(X) \Rightarrow_{O_{purchaser}} Pay(X)$$

according to the second option, where $\Rightarrow_{O_{purchaser}}$ denotes a new type of defeasible rule relative to the modal operator $O_{purchaser}$. Here, $O_{purchaser}$ is the deontic "obligation" operator parametrised to an actor/role/agent, in this case the purchaser.

The differences between the two approaches, besides the fact that in the first approach there is only one type of rules while the second accounts for factual and modal rules, is that the first approach has to introduce the definition of p-incompatible literals (i.e., a set of literals that cannot hold when p holds) for every literal p. For example, we can have a modal logic where $\Box p$ and $\neg p$ cannot be both true at the same time. Moreover, the first approach is less flexible than the second: in particular in some cases it must account for rules to derive $\Diamond p$ from $\Box p$; similarly, conversions (see Sect. 6.3) require additional operational rules in a theory, thus the second approach seems to offer a more conceptual tool than the first one. The second approach can use different proof conditions based on the modal rules to offer a more fine grained control over the modal operators and it allows for interaction between modal operators.

As usual with non-monotonic reasoning, we have to specify (1) how to represent a knowledge base and (2) the inference mechanism used to reason with the knowledge base. The language of Modal Defeasible Logic consists of a finite set of modal operators $Mod = \{\Box_1, \ldots, \Box_n\}$ and a (numerable) set of atomic propositions $Prop = \{p, q, \ldots\}$.[5]

In the same way Modal Logic is an extension of classical propositional logic, Modal Defeasible Logic is an extension of Defeasible Logic. This means that in Modal Defeasible Logic we will have a mechanism to handle non-modal conclusions (the standard mechanism of basic Defeasible Logic) plus mechanisms for the modal operators. Given the rule based nature of Defeasible Logic what we have is a set of rule (called base-rule) to manipulate non-modal conclusions (and we use the standard rules of Defeasible Logic), plus for each modal operator we have a set of rules to determine the conditions under which we can conclude a literal in the scope of the modal operator. The inference mechanism for these set

---

[5] The language can be extended to deal with other notions. For example to model agents, we have to include a (finite) set of agents, and then the modal operators can be parameterised with the agents. For a logic of action or planning, it might be appropriate to add a set of atomic actions/plans, and so on depending on the intended applications.

of rules is again the mechanism of Defeasible Logic. In other terms what we have is that, for a modal logic with n modal operators, we combine $n + 1$ defeasible logics: one for each modal operator, and one for the basic inference mechanism.

We supplement the usual definition of literal (an atomic proposition or the negation of it), with the following clauses

- if l is a literal then $\Box_i l$, and $\neg\Box_i l$, are literals if l is different from $\Box_i m$, and $\neg\Box_i m$, for some literal m.

The above condition prevents us from having sequences of modalities where we have successive occurrences of one and the same modality; however, iterations like $\Box_i\Box_j$ and $\Box_i\Box_j\Box_i$ are legal in the language.

Given a literal l with $\sim l$ we denote the complement of l, that is, if l is a positive literal p then $\sim l = \neg p$, and if $l = \neg p$ then $\sim l = p$.

According to the previous discussion a Modal Defeasible Theory D is a structure

$$(F, R, \succ)$$

where

- F is a set of facts (literals or modal literals),
- $R = R^B \cup \bigcup_{1 \leq i \leq n} R^{\Box_i}$, where R^B is the set of base (un-modalised) rules, and each $R^{\Box_i}$ is the set of rules for $\Box_i$ and
- $\succ \subseteq R \times R$ is the superiority relation.

A rule r is an expression $A(r) \hookrightarrow_X C(r)$ such that $(\hookrightarrow \in \{\rightarrow, \Rightarrow, \rightsquigarrow\}$, X is B, for a base rule, and a modal operator otherwise), $A(r)$ the antecedent or body of r is a (possible empty) set of literals and modal literals, and $C(r)$, the consequent or head of r is a literal if r is a base rule and either a literal or a modal literal Yl where Y is a modal operator different from X. Given a set of rules R we use R_{sd} to denote the set of strict and defeasible rules in R, and $R[q]$ for the set of rules in R whose head is q.

The derivation tags are now indexed with modal operators. Let X range over Mod. A conclusion can now have the following forms:

$+\Delta_X q$: q is definitely provable with mode X in D (i.e., using only facts and strict rules of mode X).

$-\Delta_X q$: we have proved that q is not definitely provable with mode X in D.

$+\partial_X q$: q is defeasibly provable with mode X in D.

$-\partial_X q$: we have proved that q is not defeasibly provable with mode X in D.

Thus $+\partial_{\Box_i} q$ means that we have a defeasible proof for $\Box_i q$.

Formally provability is based on the concept of a *derivation* (or proof) in D. A derivation is a finite sequence $P = (P(1), \ldots, P(n))$ of tagged literals satisfying the proof conditions (which correspond to inference rules for each of the kinds of conclusion). $P(1..n)$ denotes the initial part of the sequence P of length n.

Before introducing the proof conditions for the proof tags relevant to this paper we provide some auxiliary notions.

Let $\#$ be either Δ or ∂. Let $P = (P(1), \ldots, P(n))$ be a proof in D and q be a literal; we will say that q is $\#$-*provable* in P, or simply $\#$-provable, if there is a line $P(m)$ of the derivation such that either:

1. if $q = l$ then
   - $P(m) = +\#l$ or
   - $\Box_i l$ is $\#$-provable in $P(1..m-1)$ and $\Box_i$ is reflexive[6]
2. if $q = \Box_i l$ then
   - $P(m) = +\#_i l$ or
   - $\Box_j \Box_i l$ is $\#$-provable in $P(1..m-1)$, for some $j \neq i$ such that $\Box_j$ is reflexive.
3. if $q = \neg\Box_i l$ then
   - $P(m) = -\#_{\Box_i} l$ or
   - $\Box_j \neg \Box_i l$ is $\#$-provable in $P(1..m-1)$, for some $j \neq i$ such that $\Box_j$ is reflexive.

A literal q is $\#$-rejected in P, or simply $\#$-provable, if there is a line $P(m)$ of the derivation such that either:

1. if $q = l$ then
   - $P(m) = -\#l$ and
   - $\Box_i \sim l$ is $\#$-provable in $P(1..m-1)$ and $\Box_i$ is reflexive.
2. if $q = \Box_i l$ then
   - $P(m) = -\#_{\Box_i} l$ and
   - $\Box_j \Box_i \sim l$ is $\#$-provable in $P(1..m-1)$, for some $j \neq i$ such that $\Box_j$ is reflexive.
3. if $q = \neg\Box_i l$ then
   - $P(m) = +\#_{\Box_i} l$ or
   - $\Box_j \neg \Box_i \sim l$ is $\#$-provable in $P(1..m-1)$, for some $j \neq i$ such that $\Box_j$ is reflexive.

For example, we can say that a literal $\Box_i l$ is ∂-rejected if, in a derivation, we have a line $-\partial_{\Box_i} l$, and the literal $\neg\Box_i \neg l$ is ∂-rejected if we have $+\partial_{\Box_i} \neg l$ and so on.

Let X be a modal operator and $\#$ is either Δ or ∂. A literal l is $\#_X$-*provable* if the modal literal Xl is $\#$-provable; l is $\#_X$-rejected if the literal Xl is $\#$-rejected.

Let X be a modal operator or B and $\# \in \{\Delta, \partial\}$. Given a rule r we will say that the rule is $\#_X$-*applicable* iff

1. $r \in R^X$ and $\forall a_k \in A(r)$, a_k is $\#$-provable; or
2. if $X \neq B$ and $r \in R^B$, i.e., r is a base rule, then $\forall a_k \in A(r)$, a_k is $\#_X$-provable.

Given a rule r we will say that the rule is $\#_X$-*discarded* iff

1. $r \in R^X$ and $\exists a_k \in A(r)$, a_k is $\#$-rejected; or
2. if $X \neq B$ and $r \in R^B$, i.e., r is a base rule, then $\exists a_k \in A(r)$, a_k is $\#$-rejected.

---

[6] A modal operator $\Box_i$ is reflexive iff the truth of $\Box_i \phi$ implies the truth of ϕ. In other words $\Box_i$ is reflexive when we have the modal axiom $\Box_i \phi \rightarrow \phi$.

Based on the above definition of provable and rejected literals we can give the conditions to determine whether a rule is applicable or the rule cannot be used to derive a conclusion (i.e., the rule is discarded).

The proof conditions for $+\Delta$ correspond to monotonic forward chaining of derivations.

$+\Delta_X$: If $P(n+1) = +\Delta_X q$ then
      (1) $q \in F$ if $X = B$ or $\Box_i q \in F$ and $X = \Box_i$ or
      (2) $\exists r \in R_s[q]$: r is Δ_X-applicable.

For $-\Delta$ we have

$-\Delta_X$: If $P(n+1) = +\Delta_X q$ then
      (1) $q \notin F$ if $X = B$ and $\Box_i q \notin F$ and $X = \Box_i$ and
      (2) $\forall r \in R_s[q]$: r is Δ_X-discarded.

We give now the proof condition for defeasible conclusions (i.e., conclusions whose tag is $+\partial$). Defeasible derivations have an argumentation like structure divided in three phases. In the first phase, we put forward a supported reason (rule) for the conclusion we want to prove. Then, in the second phase, we consider all possible (actual and not) reasons against the desired conclusion. Finally, in the last phase, we have to rebut all the counterarguments. This can be done in two ways: we can show that some of the premises of a counterargument do not obtain, or we can show that the argument is weaker than an argument in favour of the conclusion. This is formalised by the following (constructive) proof conditions.

$+\partial_X$: If $P(n+1) = +\partial_X q$ then
      (1) $+\Delta_X q \in P(1..n)$, or
      (2) $-\Delta_X \sim q \in P(1..n)$ and
          (2.1) $\exists r \in R_{sd}[q]$: r is ∂_X-applicable and
          (2.2) $\forall s \in R[\sim q]$ either s is ∂_X-discarded or
               $\exists w \in R[q]$: w is ∂_X-applicable and $w \succ s$.

For $-\partial$ we have

$-\partial_X$: If $P(n+1) = -\partial_X q$ then
      (1) $-\Delta_X q \in P(1..n)$, and either
      (2) $+\Delta_X \sim q \in P(1..n)$ or
          (2.1) $\forall r \in R_{sd}[q]$: r is ∂_X-discarded or
          (2.2) $\exists s \in R[\sim q]$: s is ∂_X-applicable and
               $\forall w \in R[q]$: either w is ∂_X-discarded or $w \not\succ s$.

The above conditions are, essentially, the usual conditions for defeasible derivations in DL, we refer the reader to [3,21,42] for more thorough treatments. The only point we want to highlight here is that base rules can play the role of modal rules when all the literals in the body are $\partial_{\Box_i}$-derivable. Thus, from a base rule $a, b \Rightarrow_B c$ we can derive $+\partial_{\Box_i} c$ if both $+\partial_{\Box_i} a$ and $+\partial_{\Box_i} b$ are derivable while this is not possible using the rule $a, \Box_i b \Rightarrow_B c$ (see the next section about *conversions* for the intuition behind this feature). Notice that this feature correspond to the □-introduction rule

$$\frac{\phi \vdash \psi}{\Box\phi \vdash \Box\psi}$$

in sequent calculi for material implication for modal logic. This condition applies only for base rules, and in our framework base rule play the same role as material implication in standard modal logic.

Let HB_T be the Herbrand base of a given defeasible theory T (i.e., the set of all literals, and their negations, occurring in the facts and rules of a theory). The extension of a theory is the 4-tuple

$$(\Delta^+, \Delta^-, \partial^+, \partial^-)$$

where, for $\# \in \{\Delta, \partial\}$

$$\#^\pm = \{l \in HB_T : \exists\Box \in Mod \cup \{B\},\ T \vdash \pm\#_\Box p\}.$$

where, as usual $T \vdash \pm\#_\Box p$ means that there is a derivation from T of $\pm\#_\Box p$. Similarly, we can define the extension for each modal operator. [3] proved (for basic DL) that (i) $\partial^+ \cap \partial^- = \emptyset$, and (ii) $l, \sim l \in \partial^+$ only if $l, \sim l \in \Delta^+$. We will say that a DL is *coherent* if the properties (i) and (ii) just introduced hold for the logic. The coherence result shows that DL is resilient to contradiction unless the contradiction appears in the monotonic part of a theory.[7]

Proposition 1. *1. Modal DL is coherent.*
2. The extension of a theory in Modal DL can be computed in time linear to the size of the theory.

These results are straightforward since Modal DL is essentially a combination of n-disjoint basic defeasible logics. Thus the complexity results is a corollary of the result by [39].

6   Modal Defeasible Logic with Interactions

Notice that the proof condition for $+\partial$ given in Sect. 4 and then those for the other proof tags are the same as those of basic DL as given in [3]. What we have done is essentially to consider $n + 1$ non-monotonic consequence relation defined in DL and compute them in parallel. In the previous sections, we have argued that one of the advantages of modal logic is the ability to deal with

---

[7] All the coherency results stated in this paper are a consequence of using the principle of strong negation to define the proof conditions. The principle mandates that the conditions for proof tags $+\#$ and $-\#$ are the strong negation of each other, where the strong negation transforms conjunctions in disjunctions, disjunctions in conjunctions, existential in universal, universal in existential, conditions for a tag $-@$ in $+@$ and conditions for $+@$ in $-@$. [17] proves that if the proof conditions are defined using such a principle then the corresponding logic is coherent.

complex notions composed by several modalities, or by interactions of modal operators. Thus, we have to provide facilities to represent such interactions. In the rest of this section we examine the most basic relationships between two modal operators.

As we have seen in the previous section DL is able to handle gracefully conflicts arising in the defeasible part of a theory, and contradictions can be obtained only form the strict part. In designing the interaction in Modal DL we have taken the same approach. Contradictions can be obtained from interaction with strict rules and facts. To illustrate the interactions and their properties we concentrate only on the defeasible part of theories. Thus in stating the results we assume to have theory where there are no strict rules and facts are consistent (i.e., $l, \sim l \notin F$).

In Modal DL it is possible to distinguish three types of interactions: inclusion, conflicts and conversions. In the next two sections, we will motivate them and we show how to capture them in our framework.

6.1   Inclusion

Let us take a simple inclusion axiom of multi-modal logic relating two modal operators $\Box_1$ and $\Box_2$.

$$\Box_1 \phi \rightarrow \Box_2 \phi \tag{1}$$

The meaning of this axiom is that every time we are able to prove $\Box_1 \phi$, then we are able to prove $\Box_2 \phi$. Thus, given the intended reading of the modal operators in our approach –a modal operator characterises a derivation using a particular mode, it enables us to transform a derivation of $\Box_1 \phi$ into a derivation of $\Box_2 \phi$. Therefore, to model (1) in Modal DL what we have to do is just to add the following clause to the proof conditions for $+\partial_{\Box_2}$ (and the other proof tags accordingly) with the condition

$$+ \partial_{\Box_1} q \in P(1..n) \tag{2}$$

Proposition 2. *For a Modal DL extended with 2,*[8]

1. *The logic is coherent.*
2. $\partial_{\Box_1}^{+} \subseteq \partial_{\Box_2}^{+}$.
3. *The extension of a theory can be computed in time linear to the size of the theory (i.e., rules and literals).*

Notice that Proposition (2.2) gives us the property determined by $\Box_1 \phi \rightarrow \Box_2 \phi$.

---

[8] The proofs of these results as well as that of Propositions 3 and 4 are modifications and generalisation of the proofs given in [21].

6.2   Conflicts

If a theory/logic is consistent (and serial for classical modal logic[9]), we also have that $\Box_1\phi \rightarrow \Box_2\phi$ implies that it is not possible to prove $\Box_2\neg\phi$ given $\Box_1\phi$, i.e.,

$$\Box_1\phi \rightarrow \neg\Box_2\neg\phi.$$

However, this idea is better illustrated by the classically equivalent formula

$$\Box_1\phi \wedge \Box_2\neg\phi \rightarrow \bot. \tag{3}$$

When the latter is expressed in form of inference rule

$$\frac{\Box_1\phi, \Box_2\neg\phi}{\bot} \tag{4}$$

it suggests that it is not possible to obtain $\Box_1\phi$ and $\Box_2\neg\phi$ together. This does not mean that $\Box_1\phi$ implies $\Box_2\phi$, but that the modal operators $\Box_1$ and $\Box_2$ are in conflict with each other. Modal DL is able to differentiate between the two formulations: For the inclusion version (i.e., $\Box_1\phi \rightarrow \Box_2\phi$) what we have to do is just to add the following clause to the proof conditions for $+\partial_{\Box_2}$ (and the other proof tags accordingly) with the condition

$$+\partial_{\Box_1}q \in P(1..n)$$

For the second case (i.e., $\Box_1\phi \wedge \neg\Box_2\phi \rightarrow \bot$), we have to give a preliminary definition.

   To capture this conflict we have to give a preliminary definition. Given a modal operator $\Box_i$, $\mathcal{F}(\Box_i)$ is the set of modal operators in conflict with $\Box_i$. If the only conflict axiom we have is $\Box_1\phi \wedge \Box_2\phi \rightarrow \bot$ then $\mathcal{F}(\Box_1) = \{\Box_2\}$. With $R^{\mathcal{F}(\Box_i)}$ we denote the union of rules in all $R^{\Box_j}$ where $\Box_j \in \mathcal{F}(\Box_i)$.

   At this point to implement the proof condition for the conflict all we have to do is to replace clause 2.2 of the definition of $+\partial_{\Box_i}q$ with the clause

(2.2)$\forall s \in R^{\mathcal{F}(\Box_i)}[\sim q]$ either s is ∂_X-discarded or
$\exists w \in R[q]$: w is ∂_X-applicable and $w \succ s$.

The notion of conflict has been proved useful in the area of cognitive agents, i.e., agent whose rational behaviour is described in terms of mental and motivational attitudes including beliefs, intentions, desires and obligations. Classically, agent types are characterised by stating conflict resolution methods in terms of orders of overruling between rules [7,21]. For example, an agent is *realistic* when rules for beliefs override all other components (i.e., intentions, desires); she is *social* when obligations are stronger than the other components with the exception of beliefs. Agent types can be characterised by stating that, for any types of rules X and Y, for every r and r', $r \in R^X[q]$ and $r' \in R^Y[\sim q]$, we have that $r > r'$.

---

[9] Notice that the 'seriality' axiom $\Box\phi \rightarrow \Diamond\phi$ more generally corresponds to the 'consistency' of the modal operator. Given the interpretation of the modal operators given in modal logic as derivability in DL and the consistency of DL, this reading is appropriate for the present context.

Proposition 3. *For a Modal DL with modified clause 2.2:*

1. *The logic is coherent.*
2. $\partial_{\square_1}^+ \cap \partial_{\square_2}^+ = \emptyset.$
3. *The extension of a theory can be computed in time linear to the size of the theory (i.e., rules and literals).*

Notice that Proposition (3.2) gives us the property determined by 4.

6.3   Conversions

Another interesting feature that could be explained using our formalism is that of *rule conversion*. Indeed, this feature allows us to model the interactions between different modal operators. In general, notice that in many formalisms it is possible to convert from one type of conclusion into a different one. For example, the right weakening rule of non-monotonic consequence relations (see [32])

$$\frac{B \vdash C \quad A \mathrel{|\!\sim} B}{A \mathrel{|\!\sim} C}$$

allows the combination of non-monotonic and classical consequences.

Suppose that a rule of a specific type is given and all the literals in the antecedent of the rule are provable in one and the same modality. If so, is it possible to argue that the conclusion of the rule inherits the modality of the antecedent? To give an example, suppose we have that $p, q \Rightarrow_{\square_i} r$ and that we obtain $+\partial_{\square_j} p$ and $+\partial_{\square_j} q$. Can we conclude $\square_j r$? In many cases this is a reasonable conclusion to obtain. For example suppose that an agent has to obey the norm that p and q make r obligatory, and then the agent intends both p and q, thus if the agent usually complies with the norm, then the agent should form the intention of r. For more discussion about this issue see, [19,21].

For this feature we have to declare which modal operators can be converted and the target of the conversion. Given a modal operator $\square_i$, with $\mathcal{V}(\square_i)$ we denote the set of modal operators $\square_j$ that can be converted to $\square_i$. In addition, we assume that base rules can be converted to all other types of rules. The condition to have a successful conversion of a rule for $\square_j$ into a rule for $\square_i$ is that all literals in the antecedent of the rules are provable modalised with $\square_i$. Formally we have thus to add (disjunctively) in the support phase (clause 2.1) of the proof condition for $\partial_{\square_i}$ the following clause

(2.1b) $\exists r \in R^{\mathcal{V}(\square_i)}[q]$ such that r is $\partial_{\square_i}$-applicable

The notion of conversion enables us to define new interesting agent types [21].

We conclude this section with a formalisation of the Yale Shooting Problem that illustrates the notion of conversion. Let INT be the modal operator for intention. The Yale Shooting Problem can be described as follows[10]

$$liveAmmo, load, shoot \Rightarrow_B kill$$

---

[10] Here we will ignore all temporal aspects and we will assume that the sequence of actions is done in the correct order.

This rule encodes the knowledge of an agent that knows that loading the gun with live ammunitions, and then shooting will kill her friend. This example clearly shows that the qualification of the conclusions depends on the modalities relative to the individual acts "load" and "shoot". In particular, if the agent intends to load and shoot the gun (INT(*load*), INT(*shoot*)), then, since she knows that the consequence of these actions is the death of her friend, she intends to kill him ($+\partial_{\text{INT}}kill$). However, in the case she has the intention to load the gun ($+\partial_{\text{INT}}load$) and for some reason shoot it (*shoot*), then the friend is still alive ($-\partial kill$).

Proposition 4. *For a Modal DL with conversion:*

1. *The logic is coherent.*
2. *The extension of a theory can be computed in time linear to the size of the theory (i.e., rules and literals).*

7   From Single Conclusion to Alternative Conclusions

In this section we introduce the non-classical operator devised in [20] to model the combination of violation and compensatory obligations and then extended to model degree of acceptability or preferences for conclusions [8,16]. The main intuition is that now a rule is an expression

$$A_1, \ldots, A_n \hookrightarrow_\square C_1 \otimes C_2 \otimes \cdots \otimes C_m \tag{5}$$

where the reading of the conclusion is that $\square C_1$ is the best/ideal conclusion that follows from the set of premises $A_1, \ldots, A_n$, but if C_1 does not hold (with some mode) then, $\square C_2$ is the second best (acceptable) alternative, or we can say it is "plan B", and so on, until we reach C_m, concluding $\square C_m$ which is the least we can do.

To accommodate such construction the first step is to amend the language and give the restriction on what types of formulas can appear in the parts (body and head) of rules.

The formation rules for $\otimes$-expressions are:

1. every literal is an $\otimes$-expression;
2. if A is an $\otimes$-expression and b is a literal then $A \otimes b$ is an $\otimes$-expression.

Notice, the modalised literal cannot occur in an $\otimes$-expression. In addition, we stipulate that $\otimes$ obeys the following properties:

1. $a \otimes (b \otimes c) = (a \otimes b) \otimes c$ (associativity);
2. $\bigotimes_{i=1}^{n} a_i = (\bigotimes_{i=1}^{k-1} a_i) \otimes (\bigotimes_{i=k+1}^{n} a_i)$ where there exists j such that $a_j = a_k$ and $j < k$ (duplication and contraction on the right).

For rules we stipulate the body of a rule r, $A(r)$ is a set of literals and modal literals, while the conclusion or head $C(r)$ is an $\otimes$-expression. In case of a logic with multiple modes, one can group modes in classes of modes, and for each class of mode, there is an $\otimes_i$ operator for that class of modes. The restriction is the defined that the mode of the rule an the $\otimes$-expression are for the same class of modes.

For the proof conditions we have to consider that now if we want to conclude c_k for some $\otimes$-expression $c_1 \otimes_i \cdots \otimes_i c_n$, we have to determine the proof state for all the elements c_j in the expression preceding it. We illustrate how to define such conditions for a basic notion of obligation. Thus, the reading of 5 is that, if the conditions in the antecedent holds, then C_1 is obligatory, but if we have a violation, i.e., $\neg C_1$ holds, then C_2 is the obligation whose fulfilment compensates the violation of the obligation of C_1 (and so on).

Accordingly, condition (2.1) and (2.2) of $+\partial_\square$ look like

(2.1) $\exists r \in R_{sd}^{\square}[q, i]$ such that $\forall c_k, 1 \leq k < i \in C(r)$: $+\partial_\square c_k, -\partial c_k \in P(1..n)$.

(2.2) $\forall s \in R^{\square}[\sim q, j]$: either $\exists c_k, 1 \leq k < i \in C(s)$: $-\partial_\square c_k \in P(1..n)$ or $+\partial c_k \in P(1..n)$,...

Furthermore, it is possible to modify the conditions for c_k to account for different types of burden describing what counts as evidence (or lack of it) for a violation/or compliance. $-\partial c_k$ means that we are not able to prove c_k, but it does not necessarily mean that $\neg c_k$ holds. We refer to [11,15,16] for the full details of how to define the prof conditions for a proper deontic logics with interactions between obligations and permissions and for for logic for richer interactions among modalities (and mode of different types). For the issue of how to distinguish different types of burden for compliance and violation we refer to [12].

Proposition 5. *For a Modal DL with $\otimes$-expression.*

1. *The logic is coherent.*
2. *The extension of a theory can be computed in time linear to the size of the theory (i.e., rules and literals).*

8 Implementation

The reasoning process of Modal Defeasible Logic has three phases. In the preprocessing phase, the theory is loaded into the mechanism and is transformed into an equivalent theory without superiority relation and defeaters. In the next phase, the rule loader, which parses the theory obtained in the first phase, generates the data structure for the inferential phase. Finally, the inference engine applies modifications to the data structure, where at every step it reduces the complexity of the data structure.

Theory Transformation: The transformation operates in three steps. The first two steps remove the defeaters rules and the superiority relation among rules by applying the transformations similar to those of [21]. Essentially, the hierarchy of the modal operators is generated from the conflicting relationship among these operators. The modal operator on the top of the hierarchy plays the role of the BEL operator as in [21]. This amounts to take the rules for the modal operator at the top of the hierarchy as the set of base rules. The third step performs conversions of every modal rule into a rule with a new modal operator as specified by the theory.

Rule Loader: The rule loader creates a data structure as follows: for every (modal) literal in the theory, we create an entry whose structure includes:

- a list of (pointers to) rules having the literal in the head. In order to simplify the data structure, a modal literal from the head of a rule is built from the head atom and the modal operator of the corresponding rule.
- a list of (pointers to) rules having the literal in the body
- a list of (pointers to) entries of complements of the literal. Notice that the complements of a literal should take into account of the occurrence the modal operator. For example, the complements of the literal $\Box_i l$ are $\neg\Box_i l$ and $\Box_i \sim l$; if the operator is reflexive we have to include also l as a complement of $\Box_i l$.
- a list of entries of literals which conflict with the literal. The conflict relationship is derived from the conflicting modal operators dictated by the theory. In addition, a modal literal $\Box_i l$ always conflicts with $\sim l$ when $\Box_i$ is reflexive.

In order to improve the computational performance, every list in the data structure is implemented as a hash table.

Inferential Engine: The Engine is based on an extension of the Delores algorithm proposed in [40] as a computational model of Basic Defeasible Logic. In turn, the engine

- Assert each fact (as a literal) as a conclusion and removes the literal from the rules, where the literal positively occurs in the body, and "deactivate" the rules where either its complements or its conflicting literals occur in the body.
- Scan the list of active rules for rules with the empty body. Take the (modal) literal from the head, remove the rule, and put the literal into the pending facts. The literal is removed from the pending facts and adds to the list of facts if either there is no such rule (of the appropriate type) whose head contains the complements of the literal or literals with conflicting modes, or it is impossible to prove these literals.
- It repeats the first step.
- The algorithm terminates when one of the two steps fails.[11] On termination, the algorithm outputs the set of conclusions from the list of facts.

For the full details of for an efficient and optimised implementation based on Delores [40] called SPINdle, see [34]. An alternative implementation based on the meta-program [4,19] and DR-Prolog [1] is described in [5], and an implementation based on DR-device [6] and a series of transformations to map modalities to predicates is presented in [31].

---

[11] This algorithm outputs $+\partial$; $-\partial$ can be computed by an algorithm similar to this with the "dual actions". For $+\Delta$ we have just to consider similar constructions where we examine only the first parts of step 1 and 2. $-\Delta$ follows from $+\Delta$ by taking the dual actions.

9   Conclusion and Discussion

In this paper we have shown how to integrate (non-monotonic) rules and modal operators. In particular we discussed on how to add modal operators on top of the Defeasible Logic framework advanced in [3,4], where one of the advantage of such a framework is that it defines variants of the logic to accommodate different (and sometimes incompatible) intuitions of non-monotonic reasoning without the need to modify a knowledge base. Here, we have illustrated the extension taking one the (so called ambiguity blocking, team defeat) variant presented in [3], but the underlying idea can be applied without modifications to other variants. Recently [14] proved that the use of modal literals allows for the integration of different variants in a transparent way for the semantics of the variants. Thus, given a single rule $a \Rightarrow_\Box c$ one can derive both $\Box_{ab}c$ and $\Box_{ap}c$ where the first adopts the proofs conditions for the ambiguity blocking variant, while $\Box_2$ corresponds to provability under ambiguity propagation. The modalities derived in this way can be used under the semantics for other variants without affecting the semantics.

The closest work to our is the Defeasible Deontic Logic propose by Nute [43]. However, the major difference is that this version of Defeasible Deontic Logic takes the alternative approach where there is only one type of rules and the modality is a property of the conclusion and not of the rules. In addition to what we discussed in Sect. 5, the resulting logic is not able to differentiate between the conditions to derive conclusion with different mode from the same set of rules.

Input/Output logic [41,44] is another logical framework where modal outcomes (output) are generated from rules. The major difference is that the formulas in the input (antecedent) do not admit modal formulas. However, Governatori [13] provides an example (from the legal domain) where the antecedents of rules essentially contain modal (deontic) formulas. Such examples are not uncommon in the legal domain. While it has been proposed that the input of rules are modal formulas [45], we believe that such proposals are a bit premature, since, the reasoning mechanisms of the logic require an underlying consequence relation (typically the consequence relation of classical logic), but if modal formulas are in the input, then the consequence relation should be defined by the Input/Output logic itself (and all such logics must admit reusable output. However, we believe that this topic needs further research.

A typical objection to Defeasible Logic is that the logic is only defined proof-theoretically and that there is not semantics. While, in general the objection is not valid –sequent and natural deduction systems have been used to give semantics for logics, and semantics have been given for Defeasible Logic, the issue of devising a possible world semantics for modal Defeasible Logic remained. [25] defines a possible world semantics (neighbourhood based) and proves characterisation for the different options apart conversion (the issues of how to characterise it is an open question), and the topic how to adapt the sequence semantics of [8] for $\otimes$ is left for further work.

The framework we have outlined in the previous sections present the basic interaction mechanism for interactions between modal operators (i.e., inclusion, conflicts, conversion). The framework has proven robust enough to represent and reason with different scenarios and applications, from business contracts [11,18] to normative reasoning [2,15,22,26], policy/rule based cognitive agents [9,16,17,21], and workflow systems and regulatory process compliance [23,24]. The main reason of the success, we believe, is due to the fact that Modal DL conceptually strengthen the expressive power of DL with modal operators, but at the same time it maintains the constructive and computational flavour of DL. Indeed, we have proved that the complexity of Modal DL as outlined here is linear. This makes the logic very attractive for knowledge intensive applications requiring different types or mode to assert the conclusions determined by the underlying knowledge bases.

References

1. Antoniou, G., Bikakis, A.: DR-Prolog: a system for defeasible reasoning with rules and ontologies on the semantic web. IEEE Trans. Knowl. Data Eng. **19**(2), 233–245 (2007)
2. Antoniou, G., Billington, D., Governatori, G., Maher, M.J.: On the modeling and analysis of regulations. In: Proceedings of the Australian Conference Information Systems, pp. 20–29 (1999)
3. Antoniou, G., Billington, D., Governatori, G., Maher, M.J.: Representation results for defeasible logic. ACM Trans. Comput. Logic **2**(2), 255–287 (2001)
4. Antoniou, G., Billington, D., Governatori, G., Maher, M.J., Rock, A.: A family of defeasible reasoning logics and its implementation. In: Horn, W. (ed.) ECAI 2000, Proceedings of the 14th European Conference on Artificial Intelligence, pp. 459–463. IOS Press, Amsterdam (2000)
5. Antoniou, G., Dimaresis, N., Governatori, G.: A modal and deontic defeasible reasoning system for modelling policies and multi-agent systems. Expert Syst. Appl. **36**(2), 4125–4134 (2009)
6. Bassiliades, N., Antoniou, G., Vlahavas, I.: A defeasible logic reasoner for the semantic web. Int. J. Semant. Web Inf. Syst. (IJSWIS) **2**(1), 1–41 (2006)
7. Broersen, J., Dastani, M., Hulstijn, J., van der Torre, L.: Goal generation in the BOID architecture. Cogn. Sci. Q. **2**(3–4), 428–447 (2002)
8. Calardo, E., Governatori, G., Rotolo, A.: Sequence semantics for modelling reason-based preferences. Fundamenta Informaticae **158**, 217–238 (2018)
9. Dastani, M., Governatori, G., Rotolo, A., van der Torre, L.: Programming cognitive agents in defeasible logic. In: Sutcliffe, G., Voronkov, A. (eds.) LPAR 2005. LNCS (LNAI), vol. 3835, pp. 621–636. Springer, Heidelberg (2005). https://doi.org/10.1007/11591191_43
10. Gelati, J., Governatori, G., Rotolo, A., Sartor, G.: Normative autonomy and normative co-ordination: declarative power, representation, and mandate. Artif. Intell. Law **12**(1–2), 53–81 (2004)
11. Governatori, G.: Representing business contracts in RuleML. Int. J. Cooper. Inf. Syst. **14**(2–3), 181–216 (2005)
12. Governatori, G.: Burden of compliance and burden of violations. In: Rotolo, A. (ed.) 28th Annual Conference on Legal Knowledge and Information Systems, Frontieres in Artificial Intelligence and Applications, pp. 31–40. IOS Press, Amsterdam (2015)

13. Governatori, G.: Thou Shalt is not you will. In: Atkinson, K. (ed.) Proceedings of the Fifteenth International Conference on Artificial Intelligence and Law, pp. 63–68. ACM, New York (2015)

14. Governatori, G., Maher, M.J.: Annotated defeasible logic. Theor. Pract. Logic Programm. **17**(5–6), 819–836 (2017)

15. Governatori, G., Olivieri, F., Rotolo, A., Scannapieco, S.: Computing strong and weak permissions in defeasible logic. J. Philos. Logic **42**(6), 799–829 (2013)

16. Governatori, G., Olivieri, F., Scannapieco, S., Rotolo, A., Cristani, M.: The rational behind the concept of goal. Theor. Pract. Logic Programm. **16**(3), 296–324 (2016)

17. Governatori, G., Padmanabhan, V., Rotolo, A., Sattar, A.: A defeasible logic for modelling policy-based intentions and motivational attitudes. Logic J. IGPL **17**(3), 227–265 (2009)

18. Governatori, G., Pham, D.H.: DR-CONTRACT: an architecture for e-contracts in defeasible logic. Int. J. Bus. Process Integr. Manag. **4**(3), 187–199 (2009)

19. Governatori, G., Rotolo, A.: Defeasible logic: agency, intention and obligation. In: Lomuscio, A., Nute, D. (eds.) DEON 2004. LNCS (LNAI), vol. 3065, pp. 114–128. Springer, Heidelberg (2004). https://doi.org/10.1007/978-3-540-25927-5_8

20. Governatori, G., Rotolo, A.: Logic of violations: a Gentzen systems for dealing with contrary-to-duty obligations. Australas. J. Logic **3**, 193–215 (2005)

21. Governatori, G., Rotolo, A.: BIO logical agents: norms, beliefs, intentions in defeasible logic. J. Autonom. Agents Multi Agent Syst. **17**(1), 36–69 (2008)

22. Governatori, G., Rotolo, A.: A computational framework for institutional agency. Artif. Intell. Law **16**(1), 25–52 (2008)

23. Governatori, G., Rotolo, A.: A conceptually rich model of business process compliance. In: Link, S., Ghose, A. (eds.) 7th Asia-Pacific Conference on Conceptual Modelling, CRPIT, vol. 110, pp. 3–12. ACS (2010)

24. Governatori, G., Rotolo, A.: Norm compliance in business process modeling. In: Dean, M., Hall, J., Rotolo, A., Tabet, S. (eds.) RuleML 2010. LNCS, vol. 6403, pp. 194–209. Springer, Heidelberg (2010). https://doi.org/10.1007/978-3-642-16289-3_17

25. Governatori, G., Rotolo, A., Calardo, E.: Possible world semantics for defeasible deontic logic. In: Ågotnes, T., Broersen, J., Elgesem, D. (eds.) DEON 2012. LNCS (LNAI), vol. 7393, pp. 46–60. Springer, Heidelberg (2012). https://doi.org/10.1007/978-3-642-31570-1_4

26. Governatori, G., Rotolo, A., Sartor, G.: Temporalised normative positions in defeasible logic. In: 10th International Conference on Artificial Intelligence and Law (ICAIL05), pp. 25–34. ACM Press (2005)

27. Herrestad, H.: Norms and formalization. In: Proceedings of the 3rd International Conference on Artificial Intelligence and Law, ICAIL 1991, pp. 175–184. ACM Press (1991)

28. Hintikka, J.: Knowledge and Belief. Cornell University Press, Ithaca (1962)

29. Jones, A.J.I., Sergot, M.: On the characterization of law and computer systems: the normative systems perspective. In: Meyer, J.-J.C., Wieringa, R.J. (eds.) Deontic Logic in Computer Science: Normative System Specification, pp. 275–307. Wiley (1993)

30. Jones, A.J.I., Sergot, M.: A formal characterisation of institutionalised power. J. IGPL **4**(3), 429–445 (1996)

31. Kontopoulos, E., Bassiliades, N., Governatori, G., Antoniou, G.: A modal defeasible reasoner of deontic logic for the semantic web. Int. J. Semant. Web Inf. Syst. **7**(1), 18–43 (2011)

32. Kraus, S., Lehmann, D., Magidor, M.: Nonmonotonic reasoning, preferential models and cumulative logics. Artif. Intell. **44**, 167–207 (1990)
33. Kripke, S.A.: A completness theorem in modal logic. J. Symbolic Logic **24**, 1–14 (1959)
34. Lam, H.-P., Governatori, G.: The making of SPINdle. In: Governatori, G., Hall, J., Paschke, A. (eds.) RuleML 2009. LNCS, vol. 5858, pp. 315–322. Springer, Heidelberg (2009). https://doi.org/10.1007/978-3-642-04985-9_29
35. Lee, R.M.: A logic model for electronic contracting. Decis. Support Syst. **4**, 27–44 (1988)
36. Lemmon, E.J.: Is there only one correct system of modal logic? In: Proceedings of the Aristotelian Society. Supplementary Volume, vol. XXXIII, pp. 23–40. Harrison & Sons, London (1959)
37. Lewis, C.I.: A Survey of Symbolic Logic. University of California, Berkley (1918)
38. Lewis, C.I., Langford, C.H.L: Symbolic Logic. Dover, New York (1932). 2nd edn. (1959)
39. Maher, M.: Propositional defeasible logic has linear complexity. Theor. Pract. Logic Programm. **1**(6), 691–711 (2001)
40. Maher, M.J., Rock, A., Antoniou, G., Billington, D., Miller, T.: Efficient defeasible reasoning systems. Int. J. Artif. Intell. Tools **10**(4), 483–501 (2001)
41. Makinson, D., van der Torre, L.: Input/output logics. J. Philos. Logic **29**(4), 383–408 (2000)
42. Nute, D.: Defeasible logic. In: Handbook of Logic in Artificial Intelligence and Logic Programming, vol. 3, pp. 353–395. Oxford University Press, Oxford (1994)
43. Nute, D.: Norms, priorities and defeasibility. In: McNamara, P., Prakken, H. (eds.) Norms, Logics and Information Systems. New Studies in Deontic Logic, pp. 83–100. IOS Press, Amsterdam (1998)
44. Parent, X., van der Torre, L.: Detachment in normative systems: examples, inference patterns, properties. IFCoLog J. Logic Appl. **4**(9), 2295–3038 (2017)
45. Parent, X., van der Torre, L.: The pragmatic oddity in norm-based deontic logics. In: Proceedings of the 16th edition of the International Conference on Artificial Intelligence and Law, ICAIL 2017, London, United Kingdom, 12–16 June 2017, pp. 169–178 (2017)
46. Scott, D.: Advice in modal logic. In: Lambert, K. (ed.) Philos. Probl. Logic, pp. 143–173. Reidel, Dordrecht (1970)
47. von Wright, G.H.: Deontic logic. Mind **60**, 1–15 (1951)

Full Papers

Mixing Logic Programming and Neural Networks to Support Neurological Disorders Analysis

Francesco Calimeri[1], Francesco Cauteruccio[1], Aldo Marzullo[1(✉)],
Claudio Stamile[2], and Giorgio Terracina[1]

[1] DEMACS, University of Calabria, Rende, Italy
{calimeri,cauteruccio,marzullo,terracina}@mat.unical.it
[2] CREATIS; CNRS UMR5220; INSERM U1044, Université de Lyon,
Université Lyon 1, INSA-Lyon, Villeurbanne, Lyon, France
stamile@creatis.insa-lyon.fr

Abstract. The incidence of neurological disorders is constantly growing, and the use of Artificial Intelligence techniques in supporting neurologists is steadily increasing. Deductive reasoning and neural networks are two prominent areas in AI that can support discovery processes; unfortunately, they have been considered as separate research areas for long time. In this paper we start from a specific neurological disorder, namely Multiple Sclerosis, to define a generic framework showing the potentially significant impact of mixing rule-based systems and neural networks. The ambitious goal is to boost the interest of the research community in developing a more tight integration of these two approaches.

Keywords: Deductive reasoning · Neural networks
Neurological disorders · Rule-based systems

1 Introduction

Artificial Intelligence covers a large number of fields, and a huge amount of work has been spent by the research community for addressing different goals with diverse approaches to achieve them [18,32]. Two prominent research areas, that lately fostered a significant interest, consist of deductive reasoning [3–5,11,17,33] and Artificial Neural Networks (ANN) [19]. In the former, typical approaches rely on rules that are used to accurately and concisely model the problem at hand, its "structure"; input data is then mapped onto the model, and proper answers

---

G. Terracina—This work was partially supported by the Italian Ministry for Economic Development (MISE) under the project "Smarter Solutions in the Big Data World", funded within the call "HORIZON2020" PON I&C 2014–2020, and by the Italian Ministry of University and Research under project "Dottorato innovativo a caratterizzazione industriale" PON R&I FSE-FESR 2014–2020.

C. Benzmüller et al. (Eds.): RuleML+RR 2018, LNCS 11092, pp. 33–47, 2018.
https://doi.org/10.1007/978-3-319-99906-7_3

are found by means of proper algorithms that compute well-defined, model-theoretic semantics. On the contrary, with ANNs the problem is not actually modeled, and its structure is almost unknown; rather, approaches progressively "learn", usually by examples, the best answers to provide for given inputs.

Intuitively, the main advantages of deductive approaches consist of the high level of certainty in obtained answers and the capability of easily expressing, by rules, very complex problems. However, rule-based formalisms are not the ultimate, comprehensive solution, as some kind of problems can be hardly encoded by rules; furthermore, highly complex problems may imply severe performance issues, even for the best performing rule-based systems [8]. On the other hand, ANNs can learn and model non-linear complex relationships, and even generalize acquired knowledge in order to infer new properties over unseen data; moreover, once trained, a neural network can be extremely fast in providing answers to complex problems. Unfortunately, obtained results have only statistical significance, and can not be considered as "certain"; precision may also strongly depend on the training phase and on the quality of the training data. Finally, as for deductive reasoning, not all problems can be properly solved by ANNs.

For a long time, these two areas of AI have been considered as separate both in academia and in practice, and there is almost none, or very limited, integration between the two; furthermore, most of existing proposals consider one of the two approaches just as an aid to improve the other. In particular, in the latest years, some work have been carried out for "coupling" inductive approaches with declarative ones. Many are geared towards increasing performance of declarative systems, such in the case of Answer Set Programming (ASP), for instance by inductively choosing configurations, algorithms selection, and proper coupling of subsystems [13,15,28]; other approaches are related to the use of inductive solutions in order to "guide" the reasoning, the generation of logic programs or optimizations [10,24,25]; most are still at a preliminary stage.

Integration is available, to some extent. In particular, there are different works with approaches mixing statistical analysis and ASP [2,16,29], where the aim is the extension of logic programs with probabilistic reasoning, either by a direct integration or embedding external predicates. Furthermore, thanks to external built-in constructs available in language extensions supported by some ASP-based systems [1,6,7,14,30], it is possible to invoke external functions and define custom constraints; via such invocations, one might in principle place a call to a neural network. Unfortunately, to the best of our knowledge, a fully integrated environment or framework is not available; this is unsurprising, as it is not straightforward to find a way for effectively combining a reasoning model strictly based on logic rules with an inductive model based on neural networks. In particular, a major drawback is due to the intrinsic nature of the latter, namely the impossibility of defining precise reasons that make constraints violated; and these are needed in a rule-based system in order to explore the search space of the problem. Hence, this ends up in an exhaustive search. Nonetheless, we strongly believe that a tight integration between deductive reasoning and neural network capabilities might have a significant impact on applications in complex contexts, where parts of the problem can be easily and precisely modeled by rules while others are easier to be solved as "black-boxes" by neural networks.

The present work stems from the ambitious idea of mixing rule-based reasoning systems and neural networks. Given the amount of work required for moving towards the goal, we decided to start from defining a strategy for the aforementioned integration in a specific context, in order to prove the effectiveness of the idea first, and define its boundaries. In particular, we focus here on the healthcare context, and introduce an extensible framework to support doctors at understanding the complex mechanisms underlying the evolution of neurological disorders; more specifically, we address Multiple Sclerosis (MS) [35].

The approach herein proposed is not meant to be a definitive solution to the problem; rather, it should be intended as a proof-of-concept showing how the integration of rule-based systems and neural networks can provide a remarkable impact in simplifying the study of complex mechanisms. The current implementation of the framework relies on the well known rule-based Answer Set Programming (ASP) system DLV [1,4,27] and extends our previous work for an early detection of the disease based on neural networks [9]. Although it still lacks of the tight integration we wish to oversee, the framework already provides sufficient building blocks for achieving an accurate analysis of the problem. Furthermore, we carry out a preliminary experimental activity in order to point out the effectiveness of the proposal and its potentialities.

The remainder of the paper is structured as follows. In Sect. 2 we describe the medical problem we address and point out limitations of existing technologies, whereas in Sect. 3 we introduce the general framework and the role deductive and inductive approaches play therein; Sect. 4 describes the experimental campaign demonstrating the potentialities of the approach. Eventually, in Sect. 5 we draw our conclusions.

2 Background and Problem Description

The incidence of neurological disorders is constantly growing, also because population is aging in most countries; hence, the efforts to design approaches capable of determining the onset of these disorders and monitoring their course in patients are intensifying [12,20,36]. Furthermore, the tools supporting neurologists in their activities are becoming more complex and sophisticated (think, for instance, of magnetic resonance imaging (MRI) or of new electroencephalograms (EEG) with 256 electrodes, instead of the classical ones with 19 electrodes). These important advances foster the need for handling new data formats, like images and temporal series, that are hard to be analyzed by human experts. In these scenarios, automatic tools for the analysis are becoming mandatory.

In many neurological investigations a key role is played by the connections between brain areas, that can be studied either by means of MRI or EEG, for example; graph theory, and specifically network analysis tools, may hence provide insights to evaluate the health state of the brain. A challenging issue is to find suitable representations of brain areas as a network, and then proper tools for interpreting them. Multiple Sclerosis (MS) is a chronic disease of the central nervous system that disrupts the flow of information within the brain, and between brain and body. In 2015, about 2.3 million people resulted as affected, globally, with rates varying widely among different regions and different populations [35]. The disease onset starts with a first acute episode, called Clinically Isolated Syndrome (CIS), that evolves either into the Relapsing-Remitting (RR) course with a probability of 85%, or into the Primary Progressive (PP) course with a probability of 15%; RR patients will then evolve into the Secondary Progressive (SP) course after about 10–20 years [23,34].

Determining the current clinical profile of a patient has a major impact on the treatment one gets; unfortunately, it is not an easy task. Recent approaches make use of graph-based features (graph density, assortativity, transitivity, global efficiency, modularity and characteristic path length) obtained from DTI data and support vector machines [23] to classify clinical profiles of multiple sclerosis. Other approaches [21] exploit state-of-the-art classifiers (such as Support Vector Machines, Linear Discriminant Analysis and Convolutional Neural Networks) to classify Multiple Sclerosis courses using features extracted from Magnetic Resonance Spectroscopic Imaging (MRSI) combined with brain tissue segmentations of gray matter, white matter, and lesions.

Beyond the identification of the current clinical profile, predicting a patient's evolution and response to a therapy based on clinical, biological and imaging markers still represents a challenge for neurologists. In particular, it would be highly interesting to simulate the course of the disease by simulating brain connections degradation, in order to understand which kind of modifications might mostly determine an evolution of the disease into a worst state, or which recovery processes might induce a remission state. Unfortunately, this process represents a not trivial challenge due to various reasons, including the fact that the mechanisms guiding the evolution of the pathology are still unknown. One possible solution would be to simulate the progress of the pathology by means of a set of custom-defined logic rules for modeling the disruption of the brain structure, which may involve a certain background knowledge. However, this is still not enough as, since the mechanism is unknown, it is not possible to validate a hypothetical reasoning model. Hence, an approach able to explore and discover this underlying mechanism is needed. From this point of view, the spectrum of machine learning techniques offers useful approaches; nevertheless, it's not straightforward to exploit ANNs to selectively alter data structures.

In this context, quite an effective "weapon" could consist of the use of an integrated environment which allows the application of a set of rules, based on constraints, that identify minimal alterations of brain connections inducing a change of state in the disease; the possible change of state can be in turn detected exploring latent relations learnt from samples by neural networks. Unfortunately, as pointed out in the Introduction, current available solutions directly coupling deductive rule systems and ANN would require an exhaustive search of all possible alterations; in the ideal solution, the ANN should guide the deductive engine in finding minimal modifications. Addressing the aforementioned issues and the broader clinical problem is part of our future objectives. In this work we focus on a more specific scenario based on fixed sets of alterations, and we define a modular framework which, once advances in related technologies will be available, can be easily enhanced and hence pave the way to a fully integrated environment combining logic-based reasoning with machine learning approaches.

3   Framework and Methodology

In this section we present a framework to support the analysis of neurological disorders. The framework is general, and can be adapted to several kind of disorders; we focus here on Multiple Sclerosis. We first introduce the general workflow of the framework, and then we illustrate its components.

The general workflow is presented in Fig. 1. Intuitively, it takes a brain representation as input, classifies the current stage of the disease, and then simulates the disease course by "damaging the brain". The newly obtained brain representation is then classified, and used for the next steps. These steps are iterated until some condition holds. More in detail, the framework takes as input a representation of the brain of a patient, which can be, for example, obtained by an MRI. This is transformed into a weighted graph $G^0 = (V, E_0, \omega_0)$ representing the brain connectoma of the patient, that is processed by an ANN which outputs a set of probability values (the probability of the patient to belong to each class). In our application context, the ANN classifies the brain connectoma and outputs four probability values related to MS classes, namely $(P_{CIS}, P_{PP}, P_{RR}, P_{SP})$. Obviously, the framework can be applied to other kind of pathologies, by changing the ANN module. The connectoma is then processed by the LP module, which takes as input a graph G^i and determines a set of edges $E' \in E$ that should be altered in the next step. Here, logic programs and rules are used to define the particular kind of structures of the connectoma that one wishes to study; rules allow to easily specify and identify even complex structures in graphs. Then, an altering function $f : (G^i, E') \rightarrow G^{i+1}$ is applied to the selected edges. Any modification useful for the analysis can be applied; intuitively, depending on the application context, an edge weight set to 0 may indicate the virtual deletion of the edge itself. The newly obtained graph G^{i+1} is then given as input to the ANN, and possibly used as input of the next iteration. The process is reiterated until a certain condition α is satisfied. Eventually, when the process stops, the

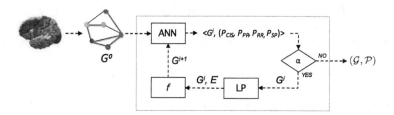

Fig. 1. Architecture of the proposed framework

result of the framework is represented by a pair $(\mathcal{G}, \mathcal{P})$ where $\mathcal{G}$ is the set of the computed graphs and $\mathcal{P}$ is the set of the corresponding probability values computed by the ANN for each $G \in \mathcal{G}$. More details about the modules are reported next.

3.1 From MRI to Graphs

Translation of MRI images to graphs is carried out by means of the approach presented in [23], and illustrated in Fig. 2: *(i)* each voxel of the T1-weighted MR image is labeled in five classes, depending on the corresponding tissue type [white matter (WM), cortical GM, sub-cortical GM, cerebro-spinal fluid (CSF)]; *(ii)* the diffusion image is pre-processed by applying correction of Eddy-current distortions and skull stripping; *(iii)* GM segmentation and WM tractography are then exploited to obtain a connectivity matrix A; *(iv)* A represents the adjacency matrix of the weighted undirected graph $G = (V, E, \omega)$ where V is the set containing the segmented GM brain regions and weights in ω are related to the number of fibers connecting two nodes.

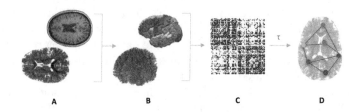

Fig. 2. Illustration of the graph creation steps

3.2 Brain Damage Simulation Module

In the study of MS, metrics over graphs related to brain structures have been considered in literature [31]; however, it is still unclear how they influence the progress of the disease. In the proposed framework, logic programs are used as a fast and effective tool for the definition and identification of specific graph substructures that could be involved in MS course. LP module contains a logic program that, given a certain graph $G = (V, E, \omega)$, defines a connectoma modification criterion and singles out a set of edges related to a subgraph satisfying a specific property. Examples of interesting criteria and returned edges are described next. *(i)* *Maximum Clique* (simply *Clique*), that contains the greatest subset of vertices in G such that every two distinct vertices in the clique are adjacent; in this case, LP returns the edges E' linking the vertices in the clique. *(ii)* *Independent Set*, i.e., the greatest subset of vertices in G such that no two vertices in the set are adjacent; in this case LP returns the edges E' having exactly one vertex in the independent set. *(iii)* *Max-degree node*, i.e., the node showing the maximum degree in G; in this case LP returns the edges connected to it. *(iv) k-hub*, i.e., the set of k nodes having the highest degree; in this case LP returns the edges connected to the *k-hub*. *(v) Minimum Vertex Cover*, i.e., the smallest set of vertices MVC such that each edge of the graph is incident onto at least one vertex of the set; in this case LP returns the edges E' such that both vertices of the edge are in MVC.

For an undirected graph G^i, the logic program of choice is coupled to an extensional knowledge base consisting of a set of facts of the form node(X) and edge(X,Y,W), which identify nodes and edges of G^i, respectively, and outputs a set of atoms of the form e(X,Y,W) which represent the set of edges E' to be modified. Given that, in our context, edge weights are related to the number of fibers linking two points in the brain, an edge edge(X,Y,W) with W = 0 is considered inactive and not contributing to the network, i.e., the corresponding nodes are considered not connected.

As an example, Fig. 3 reports an ASP encoding for the *Clique* problem. For space reasons, we refrain from discussing in detail the encoding, and point out that it complies with the ASP-Core-2 standard; the interested reader can refer to the vast literature on Answer Set Programming for more insights. Intuitively, the program "guesses" the nodes that belong to a clique in the graph G^i by means of the choice rule {clique(X)} :- node(X), and then "checks", by means of the "strong" constraint :- clique(X), clique(Y), X < Y, not activeEdge(X,Y), that the inclusion of two unconnected nodes in the candidate clique set is forbidden. Cardinality of the clique is maximized using the "weak" constraint :~ node(X), not clique(X). [1@1,X], that penalizes the exclusion of a node in the candidate clique set. Finally, intended output, i.e., the set of the edges connecting the nodes within the resulting clique, is represented by the extension of predicate e(X,Y,W), which is built according to the first rule appearing in the encoding. All ASP encodings for considered criteria can be found at https:// www.mat.unical.it/calimeri/exp/rr2018/.

```
e(X,Y,W)  :- edge(X,Y,W), clique(X), clique(Y).
{ clique(X) } :- node(X).
activeEdge(X,Y) :- edge(X,Y,W), W!=0.
:- clique(X), clique(Y), X < Y, not activeEdge(X,Y).
:~ node(X), not clique(X). [1@1,X]
```

Fig. 3. An ASP encoding for the *Clique* problem.

3.3 Classification of Multiple Sclerosis Clinical Courses

The classification step is carried out by an extension of the approach we introduced in [9], which uses a Convolutional Neural Network [26] (CNN) to characterize patients in the corresponding MS profiles. The CNN takes as input a graph G^i representing a connectoma and outputs a probability value for each MS class. The model architecture contains two Convolutional layers which filter G^i

with 3 kernels of size $3 \times 3 \times 1$ with a stride of 1 using *tanh* activation function. The resulting output is processed by two Fully Connected layers of size 128 with ReLU activation function. Eventually, a Fully Connected layer consisting of 4 units (one per class) with *softmax* activation is used to perform the classification task. It is worth noting that the softmax function calculates the probability distribution of the event over n different events; in particular, by means of it, we are able to determine the probability of each target class over all possible target classes and the target clinical course is the one with the highest probability.

In Sect. 4.2 we show that this new version of the classifier considerably increases reliability with respect to the proposal in [9]. This is an important result, as the precision of the classification over unseen samples is fundamental in studying brain connectoma alterations.

4 Experiments

We test the proposed framework via a preliminary, yet extensive, experimental campaign. The aim is to determine whether there is a latent relation between the presence/absence of particular graph structures in the connectoma and the stage of the MS disease. In particular, we are interested in verifying if and how modifications on the connectoma of a patient, simulated by modifications on the graph representing it, can modify the classification returned by the neural network. Observe that, as a side effect, understanding these relations could provide at least partial motivations for ANN classifications; this is still an open issue in ANN. In the following, we first introduce the dataset and the setup of the experiments; then, we discuss the results.

4.1 Dataset Description and Preprocessing

T1 and diffusion tensor imaging (DTI) have been used to obtain structural connectivity matrices for each subject. On the overall, 578 samples (distributed into the four aforementioned categories as 63 CIS, 199 RR, 190 SP, 126 PP, respectively) were considered for the experiments, and for each sample the corresponding graph G has been induced as explained in Sect. 3.1. Each graph consists of 84 vertices with an average of 2036.31 ± 139.19 edges for samples in CIS, 1951.25 ± 235.43 in RR, 1634.56 ± 315.27 in SP and 1760.96 ± 293.58 in PP. It is important to point out that, in order to keep experiments coherent, we filtered out some samples; in particular, given that the correct classification of each sample is known a priori and we are not evaluating accuracy of the classification step, after the training of the neural network all misclassified samples have been filtered out; hence, we avoid to propagate initial classification errors in the framework. As a consequence, after the training phase carried out over all initial 578 samples, a total of 55 CIS, 189 RR, 187 SP and 109 PP samples have been fed as input to the framework.

As already introduced, and as it will be better outlined next, we considered different test cases, each using a different way of altering the connectoma by means of different logic programs. According to the evolution of the pathology, it is not possible for a patient classified in a particular stage to be classified in an healthier stage after a disruption of the connectoma; then, during the experiments, and even if this occurred in a very limited set of cases, we disregarded those samples apparently showing remission after a distruption, because these cases are certainly misclassifications of the neural network. In particular, among all the test cases, we removed on average 8.6, 11.2, 3.8 and 19.4 samples for initial stages CIS, RR, SP and PP, respectively.

4.2   Training and Evaluation of the ANN

In the following, we provide some further details on the performance obtained by the ANN after the training phase. Indeed, although it does not constitute a core contribution of the present work, it is worth illustrating the improvements on the neural-network based classification algorithm introduced in [9].

As for training and classification settings, 80% of the dataset is used to perform the training of the ANN; performance was computed on the remaining 20%. The neural network model was trained using Adamax [22] with learning rate 0.001 for 50 epochs. Cross validation with 10 folds was used to provide a more robust evaluation of the model. The quality of the classification was compared by means of the average Precision, Recall and F-Measure[1] achieved during the cross validation. Table 1 reports the evaluation results: it can be observed how the ANN is particularly effective in determining the right stage of the pathology under consideration. We consider this a crucial factor in the framework, as studying the impact of the variations in the connectoma on the course of the disease requires a very high precision in the classification step.

Notably, the new classification model adopted in this paper allows to reach an average F-Measure of 94%, which represents a significant improvement with respect to the 80% reached in [9] for the same quality measure. The interested reader can find in [9] a more complete reference to obtained improvements.

Table 1. Average Precision, Recall and F-Measure (± standard deviation) achieved during cross validation (10 folds). Results are computed per class (CIS, PP, RR, SP) and with respect to all classes (Tot).

	Precision (±$stdev$)	Recall (±$stdev$)	F-Measure (±$stdev$)
CIS	0.88 (±0.09)	1.00 (±0.00)	0.93 (±0.05)
PP	0.93 (±0.08)	0.96 (±0.06)	0.94 (±0.04)
RR	0.96 (±0.04)	0.91 (±0.08)	0.93 (±0.05)
SP	0.97 (±0.06)	0.94 (±0.05)	0.95 (±0.04)
Tot	0.96 (±0.03)	0.93 (±0.05)	0.94 (±0.04)

---

[1] Classification report has been generated by using the `scikit-learn` framework available at http://scikit-learn.org.

4.3   Experimental Setting

As previously pointed out, we are interested in studying the possible variations of each *stage* of the MS clinical course according to different *criteria* for modifying the connectoma. We describe next experimental settings and actual instantiations of the general framework introduced in Sect. 3; each presented experiment collects runs for a pair ⟨ *stage, criterion* ⟩ (e.g., ⟨ *CIS, Clique* ⟩), where input to the framework consist of samples classified as *stage* and the LP module is instantiated with *criterion* (we tested all criteria introduced in Sect. 3.2). Each experiment collects probability values for each stage, for each criterion. The f function is intended to simulate the disrupting process of the MS disease on the portion of brain connectoma identified by LP; hence, we designed f to act as a degradation function on the weights of selected edges, thus simulating a degradation in the strength of the connection. In particular, given the initial graph G^0 a *degradation coefficient* is computed for each edge (x, y, w_{xy}) in G^0 as $d_{xy} = w_{xy} \times p$, where p is a percentage of degradation set as a parameter for the experimentation. Once the logic program LP singles out the set of edges E' in G^i to modify, each edge (x, y, w_{xy}) in E' is changed to $(x, y, max\{w_{xy} - d_{xy}, 0\})$. Here, a weight set to 0 means a deletion of the edge from the resulting graph, and consequently a complete distruption of the corresponding connection; in this case, the subsequent iteration and the corresponding logic program will no longer consider this edge as belonging to the graph. In the experiments we considered both $p = 25\%$ and $p = 50\%$. As for the exit condition α, we simply set it as a counter on the total number of iterations, requiring to stop each test case after 4 iterations. The value has been set empirically, given that, as a matter of facts, we observed that after four iterations a severe disruption occurs, making it hard for the ANN to properly classify the sample. Finally, in order to evaluate the significance of obtained results, for each test case we considered also a *random test*, designed as follows: at each iteration, given the number n of edges to modify as identified by LP, we select n *random* edges and apply f to them. In other words, we are interested in evaluating whether the variations in classification results depend on the structure of the modified portion of connectoma, or simply on the number of varied edges.

Due to space constraints, we discuss in detail only the results of a subset of the experiments we carried out. In particular, we show results for modification criteria defined by *Clique, Vertex Cover* and *k-hub*, and using $p = 50\%$. Results are shown in Figs. 4 and 5. The complete set of results is available at https://www.mat.unical.it/calimeri/exp/rr2018/.

4.4   Discussion of the Results

Figures 4 and 5 report the overall results. For each stage of the pathology, we report the probability values (indicated by a group of four vertical bars, for each iteration) computed by the ANN, both for framework results and random test. In particular, from left to right, one can observe the variation of the average probability values for each class. As an example, the first bar in the leftmost

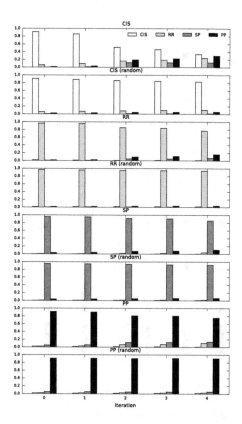

Fig. 4. Average probability values for iterations $i = 0..4$ with LP = *Clique*. For each stage, framework results (upper) and random test (lower) are reported.

group of the first bar chart in Fig. 4 represents the probability associated with the CIS stage for a CIS classified patient. The same bar in subsequent groups shows variations of this probability through iterations 1–4 with LP = *Clique*; the same bar in the second bar chart shows variations of the same probability with random alterations of the connectoma.

Results show interesting variations, when testing the framework with the *Clique* criterion. Figure 4 shows probability values computed by our approach for each stage, for each iteration: it is worth noting that *Clique* seems to affect mostly the CIS stage, as CIS probability values significantly decrease. Interestingly, this behaviour seems not to be simply related to the amount of disrupted edges: random tests show a constant probability value across iterations. More interestingly, the aforementioned behaviour is not observable for the other stages RR, SP and PP, where the disruption of cliques does not actually induce significant changes. This absence of variations is not related to the absence of cliques to change, or to their different cardinalities; indeed, the number of edges modified in all stages are comparable being on average 258.37 ± 34.30 from iteration 1 to

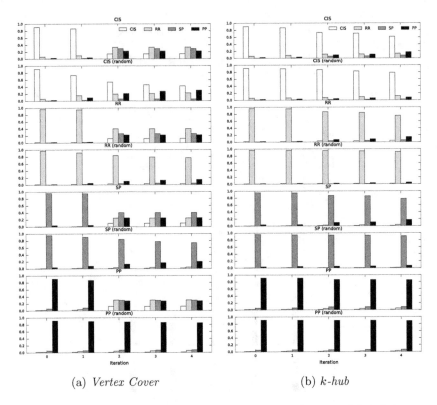

(a) *Vertex Cover*   (b) *k-hub*

Fig. 5. Average probabilities for logic programs *Vertex Cover* and *k-hub* (iterations $i = 0..4$). For each stage, framework results and random test are reported.

iteration 2, and 130.38 ± 5.34 from iteration 3 to iteration 4. The results for the CIS starting stage also show that probabilities of PP actually increase through iterations, even if not sufficiently enough to allow a guess over a change of state.

Figure 5(a) shows the probability obtained by the ANN using the *Vertex Cover* within the LP module. Here, significant variations can be observed in all stages. This indicates a potentially strong correlation between vertex cover disruption criteria and pathology evolution, apart from the CIS case: even if it shows a significant probability decrease across iterations, this happens also for the random case; as a consequence nothing can be said about CIS in this experiment. If we consider RR from iteration 2, we can observe a dramatic decrease of the probability value associated to this stage: all probability values become similar and, consequently, it is not possible anymore to conclude that the modified sample can be classified as RR. The same applies to SP and PP. As far as this behaviour is concerned, starting from iteration 2, no minimum vertex cover could be identified in the modified graph through steps 3 and 4. This explains the substantially constant behaviour of the classification through the subsequent iterations. Furthermore, as already observed for Clique, the number of modified

Table 2. Difference of average probability values between normal and random tests across all stages and problems *Clique, Vertex Cover* and *k-hub* for each iteration $i = 1..4$.

	Clique				Vertex Cover				k-hub			
Iteration	1	2	3	4	1	2	3	4	1	2	3	4
CIS	.04	.31	.34	.44	.12	.35	.28	.25	.02	.12	.11	.16
RR	.01	.09	.09	.16	.04	.39	.36	.34	.00	.08	.09	.16
SP	.00	.02	.02	.06	.05	.42	.36	.32	.01	.06	.07	.13
PP	.02	.11	.11	.14	.02	.50	.50	.49	.00	.03	.02	.01

edges across stages and iterations is stable, being on average 1490.45 ± 147.12 from iteration 1 to iteration 2. It is also interesting to correlate the high number of modified edges with the substantially constant probability values of the random tests. This strengthen the intuition about the correlation between vertex covers and the RR, SP and PP stages.

Figure 5(*b*) reports results of experiments with the *k-hub* criterion, and can be considered a counter-example of previous results. In fact, even if the number of modified edges is significant and comparable with *Clique*, i.e., $301.47 \pm 22, 82$ from iteration 1 to iteration 2, and $202, 99 \pm 26, 47$ from iteration 3 to iteration 4, probability values across iterations are almost constant and very similar to the random tests. This leads us to conclude that k-hub structures are not characterizing any stage of the disease. Eventually, Table 2 numerically enriches data shown in Figs. 4 and 5 by reporting numerical values about the average difference of probabilities computed by the ANN between the normal and random tests across iterations. The results confirm the considerations outlined above.

5   Conclusion

This paper introduced a general and extensible framework supporting neurologists in studying the evolution of neurological disorders. We have shown that the combination of a rule-based approach and of a neural-network based one can be very effective, in such a framework. Indeed, logic-based modules greatly simplify the exploration of different, possibly complex, variations in the structure of the connectoma, and ANNs allow to immediately check the potential impact of such variations in the course of the disease. Preliminary tests prove the potential impact of the framework on the discovery process. It is worth noting that, once technological limitations related with the integration of deductive engines with neural networks will be overcome, effectiveness in supporting these kind of studies will boost. As an example, the problem of finding minimal changes to the connectoma that determine a change of state could be explored. Based on the results of our work and on these observations, it is part of our future interest to work on getting a tight coupling of deductive engines and neural networks.

References

1. Alviano, M., et al.: The ASP system DLV2. In: Balduccini, M., Janhunen, T. (eds.) LPNMR 2017. LNCS (LNAI), vol. 10377, pp. 215–221. Springer, Cham (2017). https://doi.org/10.1007/978-3-319-61660-5_19
2. Beck, H., Dao-Tran, M., Eiter, T., Fink, M.: LARS: A logic-based framework for analyzing reasoning over streams. In: AAAI, pp. 1431–1438. AAAI Press (2015)
3. Bratko, I.: Prolog Programming for Artificial Intelligence, 4th edn. Addison-Wesley (2012)
4. Brewka, G., Eiter, T., Truszczynski, M.: Answer set programming at a glance. Commun. ACM **54**(12), 92–103 (2011)
5. The CADE ATP System Competition (2011). http://www.cs.miami.edu/~tptp/CASC
6. Calimeri, F., Cozza, S., Ianni, G., Leone, N.: An ASP system with functions, lists, and sets. In: Erdem, E., Lin, F., Schaub, T. (eds.) LPNMR 2009. LNCS (LNAI), vol. 5753, pp. 483–489. Springer, Heidelberg (2009). https://doi.org/10.1007/978-3-642-04238-6_46
7. Calimeri, F., Fuscà, D., Perri, S., Zangari, J.: I-DLV: the new intelligent grounder of DLV. Intelligenza Artificiale **11**(1), 5–20 (2017)
8. Calimeri, F., Gebser, M., Maratea, M., Ricca, F.: Design and results of the fifth answer set programming competition. Artif. Intell. **231**, 151–181 (2016)
9. Calimeri, F., Marzullo, A., Stamile, C., Terracina, G.: Graph based neural networks for automatic classification of multiple sclerosis clinical courses. In: Proceedings of the European Symposium on Artificial Neural Networks, Computational Intelligence and Machine Learning (ESANN 18) (2018, forthcoming)
10. Chabierski, P., Russo, A., Law, M., Broda, K.: Machine comprehension of text using combinatory categorial grammar and answer set programs. In: COMMONSENSE. CEUR Workshop Proceedings, vol. 2052. CEUR-WS.org (2017)
11. Constraint Handling Rules (2011). http://dtai.cs.kuleuven.be/CHR/
12. Duun-Henriksen, J., Madsen, R., Remvig, L., Thomsen, C., Sorensen, H., Kjaer, T.: Automatic detection of childhood absence epilepsy seizures: toward a monitoring device. Pediatric Neurol. **46**(5), 287–292 (2012)
13. Fuscà, D., Calimeri, F., Zangari, J., Perri, S.: I-DLV+MS: preliminary report on an automatic ASP solver selector. In: RCRA@AI*IA. CEUR Workshop Proceedings, vol. 2011, pp. 26–32. CEUR-WS.org (2017)
14. Gebser, M., Kaminski, R., Kaufmann, B., Ostrowski, M., Schaub, T., Wanko, P.: Theory solving made easy with clingo 5. In: ICLP (Technical Communications). OASICS, vol. 52, pp. 2:1–2:15. Schloss Dagstuhl - Leibniz-Zentrum fuer Informatik (2016)
15. Gebser, M., Kaminski, R., Kaufmann, B., Schaub, T., Schneider, M.T., Ziller, S.: A portfolio solver for answer set programming: preliminary report. In: Delgrande, J.P., Faber, W. (eds.) LPNMR 2011. LNCS (LNAI), vol. 6645, pp. 352–357. Springer, Heidelberg (2011). https://doi.org/10.1007/978-3-642-20895-9_40
16. Gelfond, M.: Knowledge representation language P-Log – A short introduction. In: de Moor, O., Gottlob, G., Furche, T., Sellers, A. (eds.) Datalog 2.0 2010. LNCS, vol. 6702, pp. 369–383. Springer, Heidelberg (2011). https://doi.org/10.1007/978-3-642-24206-9_21
17. Gerevini, A., Long, D.: Plan constraints and preferences in PDDL3 - the language of the fifth international planning competition. Technical report (2005). http://cs-www.cs.yale.edu/homes/dvm/papers/pddl-ipc5.pdf

18. Ginsberg, M.L.: Essentials of Artificial Intelligence. Morgan Kaufmann (1993)
19. Goodfellow, I.J., Bengio, Y., Courville, A.C.: Deep Learning. Adaptive Computation and Machine Learning. MIT Press, Cambridge (2016)
20. Hornero, R., Abásolo, D., Escudero, J., Gómez, C.: Nonlinear analysis of electroencephalogram and magnetoencephalogram recordings in patients with Alzheimer's disease. Philos. Trans. Roy. Soc. London A Mathe. Phys. Eng. Sci. **367**(1887), 317–336 (2009)
21. Ion-Mărgineanu, A., et al.: A comparison of machine learning approaches for classifying multiple sclerosis courses using MRSI and brain segmentations. In: Lintas, A., Rovetta, S., Verschure, P.F.M.J., Villa, A.E.P. (eds.) ICANN 2017. LNCS, vol. 10614, pp. 643–651. Springer, Cham (2017). https://doi.org/10.1007/978-3-319-68612-7_73
22. Kingma, D.P., Ba, J.: Adam: A method for stochastic optimization. CoRR abs/1412.6980 (2014)
23. Kocevar, G., et al.: Graph theory-based brain connectivity for automatic classification of multiple sclerosis clinical courses. Frontiers Neurosci. **10**, 478 (2016)
24. Law, M., Russo, A., Broda, K.: Learning weak constraints in answer set programming. TPLP **15**(4–5), 511–525 (2015)
25. Law, M., Russo, A., Broda, K.: Iterative learning of answer set programs from context dependent examples. TPLP **16**(5–6), 834–848 (2016)
26. LeCun, Y., Bottou, L., Bengio, Y., Haffner, P.: Gradient-based learning applied to document recognition. Proce. IEEE **86**(11), 2278–2324 (1998)
27. Leone, N., et al.: The DLV system for knowledge representation and reasoning. ACM Trans. Comput. Log. **7**(3), 499–562 (2006)
28. Maratea, M., Pulina, L., Ricca, F.: A multi-engine approach to answer-set programming. Theor. Pract. Logic Program. **14**(6), 841–868 (2014)
29. Nickles, M., Mileo, A.: Web stream reasoning using probabilistic answer set programming. In: Kontchakov, R., Mugnier, M.-L. (eds.) RR 2014. LNCS, vol. 8741, pp. 197–205. Springer, Cham (2014). https://doi.org/10.1007/978-3-319-11113-1_16
30. Redl, C.: The dlvhex system for knowledge representation: recent advances (system description). TPLP **16**(5–6), 866–883 (2016)
31. Rubinov, M., Sporns, O.: Complex network measures of brain connectivity: Uses and interpretations. NeuroImage **52**(3), 1059–1069 (2010)
32. Russell, S.J., Norvig, P.: Artificial Intelligence - A Modern Approach (3. internat. edn.). Pearson Education (2010). http://vig.pearsoned.com/store/product/1,1207, store-12521_isbn-0136042597,00.html
33. smt-lib-web: The Satisfiability Modulo Theories Library (2011). http://www.smtlib.org/
34. Stamile, C., et al.: A longitudinal model for variations detection in white matter fiber-bundles. In: 2015 International Conference on Systems, Signals and Image Processing (IWSSIP), pp. 57–60 (2015)
35. Vos, T., Allen, C., Arora, M., Barber, R., Bhutta, Z., Brown, A.: Gbd 2015 disease and injury incidence and prevalence collaborators. global, regional, and national incidence, prevalence, and years lived with disability for 310 diseases and injuries, 1990–2015: a systematic analysis for the global burden of disease study 2015. Lancet **388**(10053), 1545–1602 (2016)
36. Wieser, H., Schindler, K., Zumsteg, D.: EEG in Creutzfeldt-Jakob disease. Clinical Neurophysiol. **117**(5), 935–951 (2006)

On the k-Boundedness
for Existential Rules

Stathis Delivorias[✉], Michel Leclère, Marie-Laure Mugnier,
and Federico Ulliana

University of Montpellier, LIRMM, CNRS, Inria, Montpellier, France
jazzcrazysta@yahoo.com

Abstract. The chase is a fundamental tool for existential rules. Several chase variants are known, which differ on how they handle redundancies possibly caused by the introduction of nulls. Given a chase variant, the halting problem takes as input a set of existential rules and asks if this set of rules ensures the termination of the chase for any factbase. It is well-known that this problem is undecidable for all known chase variants. The related problem of boundedness asks if a given set of existential rules is bounded, i.e., whether there is an upper bound on the depth of the chase, independently from any factbase. This problem is already undecidable in the specific case of datalog rules. However, knowing that a set of rules is bounded for some chase variant does not help much in practice if the bound is unknown. Hence, in this paper, we investigate the decidability of the k-boundedness problem, which asks whether a given set of rules is bounded by an integer k. After introducing a general framework which motivates a breadth-first approach to problems related to chase termination for any chase variant, we prove that k-boundedness is decidable for three chase variants.

1 Introduction

Existential rules (see [CGK08,BLMS09,CGL09] for the first papers and [GOPS12,MT14] for introductory courses) are a positive fragment of first-order logic that generalizes the deductive database query language Datalog and knowledge representation formalisms such as Horn description logics (see e.g. [CGL+05,KRH07,LTW09]). These rules offer the possibility to model the existence of unknown individuals by means of existentially quantified variables in rule heads, which enables reasoning on incomplete data with the open-domain assumption. Existential rules have the same logical form as database constraints known as tuple-generating dependencies, which have long been investigated [AHV95]. Reborn under the names of existential rules, Datalog$^\exists$ or Datalog$^+$, they have raised significant interest in the last years as ontological languages, especially for the ontology-mediated query-answering and data-integration issues.

© Springer Nature Switzerland AG 2018
C. Benzmüller et al. (Eds.): RuleML+RR 2018, LNCS 11092, pp. 48–64, 2018.
https://doi.org/10.1007/978-3-319-99906-7_4

A knowledge base (KB) is composed of a set of existential rules, which typically encodes ontological knowledge, and a factbase, which contains factual data. The forward chaining, also known as the *chase* in databases, is a fundamental tool for reasoning on rule-based knowledge bases and a considerable literature has been devoted to its analysis. Its ubiquity in different domains comes from the fact it allows one to compute a *universal model* of the knowledge base, i.e., a model that maps by homomorphism to any other model of the knowledge base. This has a major implication in problems like answering queries with ontologies since it follows that a (Boolean) conjunctive query is entailed by a KB if and only if it maps by homomorphism to a universal model.

Several variants of the chase have been defined: *oblivious* or naive chase (e.g. [CGK08]), *skolem* chase [Mar09], *semi-oblivious* chase [Mar09], *restricted* or standard chase [FKMP05], *core* chase [DNR08] (and its variant, the equivalent chase [Roc16]). All these chase variants compute logically equivalent results.[1] Nevertheless, they differ on their ability to detect the redundancies that are possibly caused by the introduction of unknown individuals (often called *nulls*). Note that, since redundancies can only be due to nulls, all chase variants coincide on rules without existential variables (i.e., Datalog rules, also called range-restricted rules [AHV95]). Then, for rules with existential variables the chase produces iteratively new information until no new rule application is possible. The (re-)applicability of rules is depending on the ability of each chase variant to detect redundancies. Evidently this has a direct impact on the termination. Of course, if a KB has no finite universal model then none of the chase variants will terminate. This is illustrated by Example 1.

Example 1. Take the KB $\mathcal{K} = (F, \mathcal{R})$, where $\mathcal{R}$ contains the rule $R = \forall x (Human(x) \rightarrow \exists y \, (parentOf(y, x) \wedge Human(y)))$ and $F = \{Human(Alice)\}$. The application of the rule R on the initial factbase F, entails the existence of a new (unknown) individual y_0 (a *null*) generated by the existential variable y in the rule. This yields the factbase $\{Human(Alice), parentOf(y_0, Alice), Human(y_0)\}$, which is logically translated into an existentially closed formula: $\exists y_0 (Human(Alice) \wedge parentOf(y_0, Alice) \wedge Human(y_0))$. Then, R can be applied again by mapping x to y_0 thereby creating a new individual y_1. It is easy to see that in this case the forward chaining does not halt, as the generation of each new individual enables a novel rule application. This follows from the fact that the universal model of the knowledge base is infinite.   △

However, for the case of KBs which have a *finite* universal model, all chase variants can be totally ordered with respect to the inclusion of the sets of factbases on which they halt: oblivious < semi-oblivious = skolem < restricted < core. Here, $X_1 < X_2$ means that when X_1 halts on a KB, so does X_2, and there are KBs for which the reciprocal is false. The oblivious chase is the most redundant kind of the chase as it performs all possible rule applications, without checking

---

[1] In addition, the *parsimonious chase* was introduced in [LMTV12]. However, this chase variant, aimed towards responding at atomic queries, does not compute a universal model of the KB, hence it is not studied here.

for redundancies. The core chase is the less redundant chase as it computes a minimal universal model by reducing every intermediate factbase to its core. In between, we find the semi-oblivious chase (equivalent to the skolem-chase) and the restricted chase. The first one does not consider isomorphic facts that would be generated by consecutive applications of a rule according to the same mapping of its frontier variables (i.e, variables shared by the rule body and head). The second one discards all rule applications that produce "locally redundant" facts. The chase variants are illustrated by Example 2 (for better presentation, universal quantifiers of rules will be omitted in the examples):

Example 2. Consider the knowledge bases $\mathcal{K}_1 = (F, \{R_1\}), \mathcal{K}_2 = (F, \{R_2\})$, and $\mathcal{K}_3 = (F', \{R_3\})$ built from the facts $F = \{p(a, a)\}$ and $F' = \{\exists w\ p(a, w)\}$ and the rules $R_1 = p(x, y) \rightarrow \exists z\ p(x, z)$, $R_2 = p(x, y) \rightarrow \exists z\ p(y, z)$ and $R_3 = p(x, y) \rightarrow \exists z\ (p(x, x) \wedge p(y, z))$. Then, the oblivious chase does not halt on $\mathcal{K}_1$ while the semi-oblivious chase does. Indeed, there are infinitely many different rule applications on the atoms $p(a, z_0)$, $p(a, z_1)$, ... that can be generated with R_1; yet, all rule applications map the frontier variable x to the same constant a, and are therefore filtered by the semi-oblivious chase. In turn, the semi-oblivious chase does not halt on $\mathcal{K}_2$ while the restricted chase does. Here again, there are infinitely many rule applications on the atoms $p(a, z_0), p(z_0, z_1), \dots$ that can be generated with R_2; since each of them maps the frontier variables to new existentials, they are all performed by the semi-oblivious chase. However, all generated atoms are redundant with the initial atom $p(a, a)$ and the restricted chase deems the first (and then all successive) rule applications as redundant. On the other hand, the restricted chase does not halt on $\mathcal{K}_3$ while the core chase does. In this case, the first rule application yields $\exists w \exists z_0 (p(a, w) \wedge p(a, a) \wedge p(w, z_0))$. This is logically equivalent to $p(a, a)$ i.e., its core, which leads to the core-chase termination at the next step. However, the restricted chase checks only for redundancy of the newly added atoms with respect to the previous factbase, and does not take into account that the addition of new atoms can cause redundancies elsewhere in the factbase (in this example, the previous atom $p(a, w)$ together with the new atom $p(w, z_0)$ are redundant with respect to the new atom $p(a, a)$). So with the restricted chase, R_3 will be always applicable. Finally, note that $p(a, a)$ is a (finite) universal model for all knowledge bases $\mathcal{K}_1, \mathcal{K}_2$, and $\mathcal{K}_3$.   △

The termination problem, which asks whether for a given set of rules the chase will terminate on any factbase, is undecidable for all chase variants [DNR08, BLM10, GM14]. The related problem of *boundedness* asks whether termination is ensured for a given set of rules within a predefined number of steps, that is, within a bound which is independent from *any* factbase. In this, the boundedness problem assumes a breadth-first definition of the chase where, at each step, all possible rule applications are first computed and then applied in parallel while complying to the specific redundancy criterion of the chase variant. Given a breadth-first chase variant X, a set of rules is said to be X-*bounded* if there is k (called the bound) such that, for any factbase, the X-chase stops after at most k breadth-first steps. Of course, since chase variants differ with respect to termination, they also differ with respect to boundedness.

Boundedness ensures several semantic properties. Indeed, if a set of rules is X-bounded with k the bound, then, for any factbase F, the saturation of F at rank k (i.e., the factbase obtained from F after k X-chase breadth-first steps) is a universal model of the KB; the reciprocal also holds true for the core chase. Moreover, boundedness also ensures the UCQ-rewritability property (also called the finite unification set property [BLMS11]): any (Boolean) conjunctive query q can be rewritten using the set of rules $\mathcal{R}$ into a (Boolean) union of conjunctive queries Q such that for any factbase F, q is entailed by $(F, \mathcal{R})$ if and only if Q is entailed by F. It follows that many interesting static analysis problems such as query containment under existential rules become decidable when a ruleset is bounded. Note that the conjunctive query rewriting procedure can be designed in a such a way that it terminates within k breadth-first steps with k the bound for the core chase [LMU16]. Finally, from a practical viewpoint, the degree of boundedness can be seen as a measure of the recursivity of a ruleset, and most likely, this is reflected in the actual number of breadth-first steps required by the chase for a given factbase or the query rewriting process for a given query, which is expected to be much smaller than the theoretical bound.

As illustrated by Example 1, the presence of existential variables in the rules can make the universal model of a knowledge base infinite and so the ruleset unbounded, even for the core chase. However, the importance of the boundedness problem has been recognized already for rules without existential variables. Indeed, the problem has been first posed and studied for Datalog, where it has been shown to be undecidable [HKMV95, Mar99]. Example 3 illustrates some cases of bounded and unbounded rulesets in this setting.

Example 3. Consider the rulesets $\mathcal{R}_1 = \{R\}$ and $\mathcal{R}_2 = \{R, R'\}$ where $R = p(x, y) \land p(y, z) \rightarrow p(x, z)$ and $R' = p(x, y) \land p(u, z) \rightarrow p(x, z)$. The set $\mathcal{R}_1$ contains a single transitivity rule for the predicate p. This set is clearly unbounded as for any integer k there exists a factbase $F = \{p(a_i, a_{i+1}) \mid 0 \le i < 2^k\}$ that requires k chase steps. On the other hand, $\mathcal{R}_2$ also contains a rule that joins individuals on disconnected atoms. In this case, we have that (i) if R generates some facts then R' generates these same facts as well and (ii) R' needs to be applied only at the first step, for any F, as it does not produce any new atom at a later step. Therefore, $\mathcal{R}_2$ is bounded with the bound $k = 1$. Note that since these examples are in Datalog, the specificities of the chase variants do not play any role. △

Finally, the next example illustrates boundedness for non-Datalog rules.

Example 4. Consider the ruleset $\mathcal{R} = \{p(x, y) \rightarrow \exists z (p(y, z) \land p(z, y))\}$ and the fact $F = \{p(a, b)\}$. With all variants, the first chase step yields $F_1 = \{p(a, b), p(b, z_0), p(z_0, b)\}$. Then, two new rule applications are possible, which map $p(x, y)$ to $p(b, z_0)$ and $p(z_0, b)$, respectively. The oblivious and semi-oblivious chases will perform these rule applications and go on forever. Hence, the chase on $\mathcal{R}$ is not bounded for these two variants. On the other hand, the restricted chase does terminate. It will not perform any of these rule applications on F_1. Indeed, the first application would add the facts $\{p(z_0, z_1), p(z_1, z_0)\}$, which can "folded" into F_1 by a homomorphism that maps z_1 to b (while leaving z_0 fixed), and this is similar for the second rule application. We can check that actually the restricted chase will stop on any factbase, and is bounded with $k = 1$. The same holds here for the core chase. $\triangle$

Despite the relatively negative results on boundedness, knowing that a set of rules is bounded for some chase variant does not help much in practice anyway, if the bound is unknown or even very large. Hence, the goal of this paper is to investigate the k-boundedness problem, which asks, for a given chase variant, whether for any factbase, the chase stops after at most k breadth-first steps.

Our main contribution is to show that k-boundedness is indeed decidable for the oblivious, semi-oblivious and restricted chases. Actually, we obtain a stronger result by exhibiting a property that a chase variant may fulfill, namely consistent heredity, and prove that k-boundedness is decidable as soon as this property is satisfied. We show that it is the case for all the known chase variants except for the core chase. Hence, the decidability of k-boundedness for the core chase remains an open question.

The paper is organized as follows. Section 2 presents the formal setting, while Sect. 3 outlines the importance of breadth-first derivations for k-boundedness. Section 4 is devoted to the decidability results.

2   Preliminaries

We consider a first-order setting with constants but no other function symbols. A term is either a constant or a variable. An atom is of the form $r(t_1, \ldots, t_n)$ where r is a predicate of arity n and the t_i are terms. Given a set of atoms A, we denote by $vars(A)$ and $terms(A)$ the set of its variables and terms. A *factbase* is a set of atoms, logically interpreted as the existentially closed conjunction of these atoms. A *homomorphism* from a set of atoms A to a set of atoms B (notation: $\pi : A \rightarrow B$), is a substitution $\pi : vars(A) \rightarrow terms(B)$ such that $\pi(A) \subseteq B$. In this case, we also say that A maps to B (by π). We denote by $\models$ the classical logical consequence and by $\equiv$ the logical equivalence. It is well-known that, given sets of atoms A and B seen as existentially closed conjunctions, there is a homomorphism from A to B if and only if $B \models A$.

An *existential rule* (or simply rule), denoted by R, is a formula $\forall \bar{x} \forall \bar{y} (B(\bar{x}, \bar{y}) \rightarrow \exists \bar{z} \, H(\bar{x}, \bar{z}))$ where B and H, called the body and the head of the rule, are conjunctions of atoms, $\bar{x}$ and $\bar{y}$ are sets of universally quantified variables, and $\bar{z}$ is a set of existentially quantified variables. We call *frontier* the variables shared by the body and head of the rule, that is $frontier(R) = \bar{x}$. In the following we will refer to a rule as a pair of sets of atoms (B, H) by interpreting their common variables as the frontier. A *knowledge base* (KB) $\mathcal{K} = (F, \mathcal{R})$ is a pair where F is a factbase and $\mathcal{R}$ is a set of existential rules. We implicitly assume that all the rules as well as the factbase employ disjoint sets of variables, even if, for convenience, we reuse variable names in examples.

Let F be a factbase and $R = (B, H)$ be an existential rule. We say that R is *applicable* on F via π if there exists a homomorphism π from its body B to F. We call the pair (R, π) a *trigger*. We denote by π^s a *safe* extension of π which maps all existentially quantified variables in H to fresh variables as follows: for each existential variable z we have that $\pi^s(z) = z_{(R,\pi)}{}^2$. The factbase $F \cup \pi^s(H)$ is called an *immediate derivation* from F through (R, π). Given a factbase F and a ruleset $\mathcal{R}$ we define a *derivation* from F and $\mathcal{R}$, denoted by $\mathcal{D}$, as a (possibly infinite) sequence of triples $D_0 = (\emptyset, \emptyset, F_0), D_1 = (R_1, \pi_1, F_1), D_2 = (R_2, \pi_2, F_2), \ldots$ where $F_0 = F$ and every F_i $(i > 0)$ is an *immediate derivation* from F_{i-1} through a new trigger (R_i, π_i), that is, $(R_i, \pi_i) \neq (R_j, \pi_j)$ for all $i \neq j$. The *sequence of rule applications associated* with a derivation is simply the sequence of its triggers $(R_1, \pi_1), (R_2, \pi_2), \ldots$ A *subderivation* of a derivation $\mathcal{D}$ is any derivation $\mathcal{D}'$ whose sequence of rule applications is a subsequence of the sequence of rule applications associated with $\mathcal{D}$.

We will introduce four chase variants, namely oblivious (**O**), semi-oblivous (**SO**), restricted (**R**), equivalent chase (**E**). As explained later, some pairs of chase variants introduced in the literature have similar behavior, in which case we chose to focus on one of the two. All the chase variants are derivations that comply with some condition of applicability of the triggers.

Definition 1. Let $\mathcal{D}$ be a derivation of length n from a factbase F and a ruleset $\mathcal{R}$, and F_n the factbase obtained after the n rule applications of $\mathcal{D}$. A trigger (R, π) is called:

1. **O**-*applicable* on $\mathcal{D}$ if R is applicable on F_n via π.
2. **SO**-*applicable* on $\mathcal{D}$ if R is applicable on F_n via π and for every trigger (R, π') in the sequence of triggers associated with $\mathcal{D}$, the restrictions of π and π' to the frontier of R are not equal.
3. **R**-*applicable* on $\mathcal{D}$ if $R = (B, H)$ is applicable on F_n via π and π cannot be extended to a homomorphism $\pi' : B \cup H \rightarrow F_n$.
4. **E**-*applicable* on $\mathcal{D}$ if $R = (B, H)$ is applicable on F_n via π and it does not hold that $F_n \equiv F_n \cup \pi^s(H)$.

Note that for $X \in \{\mathbf{O}, \mathbf{R}, \mathbf{E}\}$, the applicability of the trigger only depends on F_n (hence we can also say the trigger is X-*applicable* on F_n), while for the **SO**-chase we have to take into account the previous triggers. Note also that the definitions of **O**- and **SO**- trigger applicability allow one to extend a derivation with a rule application that does not add any atom, i.e., $F_{n+1} = F_n$; however, this is not troublesome since no derivation can contain twice the same triggers.

Given a derivation $\mathcal{D}$, we define the *rank* of an atom as follows: $rank(A) = 0$ if $A \in F_0$, otherwise let $R = (B, H)$ and (R, π) be the first trigger in the

---

^{2} This fixed way to choose a new fresh variable allows us to always produce the same atoms for a given trigger and that is without loss of generality since each trigger appears at most once on a derivation.

sequence $\mathcal{D}$ such that $A \in \pi^s(H)$, then $rank(A) = 1 + \max_{A' \in \pi(B)}\{rank(A')\}$. Intuitively, the rank of an atom corresponds to the chase step at which it has been generated, when considering a breadth-first chase. This notion is naturally extended to triggers: $rank((R, \pi)) = 1 + \max_{A' \in \pi(B)}\{rank(A')\}$.

The *depth* of a finite derivation is the maximal rank of one of its atoms. Finally, a derivation $\mathcal{D}$ is X-*breadth-first* (where $X \in \{\mathbf{O}, \mathbf{SO}, \mathbf{R}, \mathbf{E}\}$) if it satisfies the following two properties:

- (1) *rank compatibility:* for all elements D_i and D_j in $\mathcal{D}$ with $i < j$, the rank of the trigger of D_i is smaller or equal to the rank of the trigger of D_j, and
- (2) *rank exhaustiveness:* for every rank k of a trigger in $\mathcal{D}$, let $D_i = (R_i, \pi_i, F_i)$ be the last element in $\mathcal{D}$ such that $rank((R_i, \pi_i)) = k$. Then, every trigger which is X-applicable on the subderivation $D_1, ..., D_i$ is of rank $k + 1$.

Definition 2 (Chase variants) . Let F be a factbase and $\mathcal{R}$ be a ruleset. We define four *variants* of the chase:

1. An **oblivious chase** is any derivation $\mathcal{D}$ from F and $\mathcal{R}$.
2. A **semi-oblivious chase** is any derivation $\mathcal{D}$ from F and $\mathcal{R}$ such that for every element $D_i = (R_i, \pi_i, F_i)$ of $\mathcal{D}$, the trigger (R_i, π_i) is **SO**-applicable to the subderivation $D_0, D_1, ..., D_{i-1}$ of $\mathcal{D}$.
3. A **restricted chase** is any derivation $\mathcal{D}$ from F and $\mathcal{R}$ such that for every element $D_i = (R_i, \pi_i, F_i)$ of $\mathcal{D}$, the trigger (R_i, π_i) is **R**-applicable to the subderivation $D_0, D_1, ..., D_{i-1}$ of $\mathcal{D}$.
4. An **equivalent chase** is any **E**-breadth-first derivation $\mathcal{D}$ from F and $\mathcal{R}$ such that for every element $D_i = (R_i, \pi_i, F_i)$ of $\mathcal{D}$, the trigger (R_i, π_i) is **E**-applicable to the subderivation $D_0, D_1, ..., D_{i-1}$ of $\mathcal{D}$.

We will abbreviate the above chase variants with **O**-chase, **SO**-chase, **R**-chase, and **E**-chase, respectively. Unless otherwise specified, when we use the term X-chase derivation, we will be referring to any of the four chase variants. Furthermore, with *breadth-first* X-chase derivation we will always imply X-breadth-first X-chase derivation.

Let us point out that the semi-oblivious and skolem chases, both defined in [Mar09], lead to similar derivations. Briefly, the skolem chase consists of first skolemizing the rules (by replacing existentially quantified variables with skolem functions whose arguments are the frontier variables) then running the oblivious chase. Both chase variants yield isomorphic results, in the sense that they generate exactly the same sets of atoms, up to a bijective renaming of nulls by skolem terms. Therefore, we chose to focus on one of the two, namely the semi-oblivious chase. The core chase [DNR08] and the equivalent chase [Roc16] have similar behaviors as well. The core chase proceeds in a breadth-first manner and, at each step, performs in parallel all rule applications according to the restricted chase criterion, then computes a core of the resulting factbase. We remind that a core of a set of atoms is one of its minimal equivalent subsets. Hence, the core chase may remove at some step atoms that were introduced at a former step. If the equivalent chase is run in a breadth-first manner, it performs the same steps as the core chase. This follows from the fact that $F_i \equiv F_{i+1}$ if and only if $core(F_i)$ is equal to $core(F_{i+1})$ (up to bijective variable renaming). However, the equivalent chase is more convenient to handle from a formal point of view because of its monotonicity, in the sense that within a derivation $F_i \subseteq F_{i+1}$.

An X-chase derivation $\mathcal{D}$ from F and $\mathcal{R}$ is *exhaustive* if for all $i \geq 0$, if a trigger (R, π) is X-applicable on the subderivation $D_1, ..., D_i$, then there is a $k \geq i$ such that one of the two following holds:

1. $D_k = (R, \pi, F_k)$ or
2. (R, π) is not X-applicable on $D_1, ..., D_k$.

An X-chase derivation is *terminating* if it is both exhaustive and finite. And we say that the X-chase is *terminating* or *halts* on $(F, \mathcal{R})$ if there exists an X-chase derivation from F and $\mathcal{R}$ that terminates. It is well-known that for $X \in \{\mathbf{O}, \mathbf{SO}, \mathbf{E}\}$, if there exists a terminating derivation for a given KB, then all exhaustive derivations on this KB are terminating. This does not hold for the restricted chase, because the order in which rules are applied matters, as illustrated by the next example:

Example 5. We assume two rules $R_1 = p(x, y) \to \exists z\, p(y, z)$ and $R_2 = p(x, y) \to p(y, y)$ and $F = \{p(a, b)\}$. Let $\pi = \{x \mapsto a, y \mapsto b\}$. Then (R_1, π) and (R_2, π) are both **R**-applicable. If (R_2, π) is applied first, then the derivation is terminating. However if we apply (R_1, π) first, and (R_2, π) second we produce the factbase $F_2 = \{p(a, b), p(b, z_{(R_1, \pi)}), p(b, b)\}$ and with $\pi' = \{x \mapsto b, y \mapsto z_{(R_1, \pi)}\}$ we have that (R_1, π') as well as (R_2, π') are again both **R**-applicable. Consequently, if we always choose to apply R_1 before R_2 then the corresponding derivation will be infinite. $\triangle$

We now introduce some notions that will be central for establishing our results on k-boundedness for the different chase variants.

Definition 3 (Restriction of a derivation). Let $\mathcal{D}$ be a derivation from F and $\mathcal{R}$. For any $G \subseteq F$, the *restriction of $\mathcal{D}$ induced by G* denoted by $\mathcal{D}_{|G}$, is the maximal derivation from G and $\mathcal{R}$ obtained by a subsequence of the trigger sequence of $\mathcal{D}$.

The following example serves to demonstrate how a subset of the initial factbase induces the restriction of a derivation:

Example 6. Take $F = \{p(a, a), p(b, b)\}$, $R = p(x, y) \to \exists z\, p(y, z)$ and

$$\mathcal{D} = (\emptyset, \emptyset, F), (R, \pi_1, F_1), (R, \pi_2, F_2), (R, \pi_3, F_3), (R, \pi_4, F_4)$$

with $\pi_1 = \{x/y \mapsto a\}$, $\pi_2 = \{x/y \mapsto b\}$, $\pi_3 = \{x \mapsto a, y \mapsto z_{(R, \pi_1)}\}$, and $\pi_4 = \{x \mapsto z_{(R, \pi_1)}, y \mapsto z_{(R, \pi_3)}\}$.
The derivation $\mathcal{D}$ produces the factbase

$$F_4 = F \cup \{p(a, z_{(R, \pi_1)}), p(b, z_{(R, \pi_2)}), p(z_{(R, \pi_1)}, z_{(R, \pi_3)}), p(z_{(R, \pi_3)}, z_{(R, \pi_4)})\}$$

Then, if $G = \{p(a,a)\}$, we have $\mathcal{D}_{|G} = (\emptyset, \emptyset, G), (R, \pi_1, G_1), (R, \pi_3, G_2),$ (R, π_4, G_3) is the restriction of $\mathcal{D}$ induced by G where

$$G_3 = G \cup \{p(a, z_{(R,\pi_1)}), p(z_{(R,\pi_1)}, z_{(R,\pi_3)}), p(z_{(R,\pi_3)}, z_{(R,\pi_4)})\}$$

$\triangle$

Definition 4 (Ancestors). Let $D_i = (R_i, \pi_i, F_i)$ be an element of a derivation $\mathcal{D}$. Then every atom in $\pi_i(B_i)$ is called a *direct ancestor* of every atom in $(F_i \setminus F_{i-1})$. The (indirect) *ancestor* relation between atoms is defined as the transitive closure of the direct ancestor relation. The direct and indirect ancestor relations between atoms are extended to triggers: let $D_j = (R_j, \pi_j, F_j)$ where $j < i$. Then (R_j, π_j) is a *direct ancestor* of (R_i, π_i) if there is an atom in $(F_j \setminus F_{j-1})$ which is a direct ancestor of the atoms in $(F_i \setminus F_{i-1})$. We will denote the ancestors of sets of atoms and triggers as $Anc(F, \mathcal{D})$ and $Anc((R, \pi), \mathcal{D})$, respectively. The inverse of the ancestor relation is called the *descendant* relation.

There is an evident correspondance between the notion of ancestors and the notions of rank and depth. Suppose a ruleset with at most b atoms in the rules' bodies. The following lemma results from the fact that each atom has at most b direct ancestors and a chain of ancestors cannot exceed the depth of a derivation.

Lemma 1 (The ancestor clue). Let $\mathcal{D}$ be an X-derivation from F and $\mathcal{R}$. Then for any atom A of rank k in $\mathcal{D}$, $|F \cap Anc(A, \mathcal{D})| \leq b^k$; also for any trigger (R, π) of rank k in $\mathcal{D}$, $|F \cap Anc((R, \pi), \mathcal{D})| \leq b^k$.

This lemma will be instrumental for proving our results on k-boundedness as it allows one to characterize the number of atoms that are needed to produce a new atom at a given chase step.

In the next section, we turn our attention to the properties of the derivations that are key to study k-boundedness.

3   Breadth-First Chase

To derive our results on k-boundedness we will focus on derivations that are *breadth-first*. Informally speaking, a derivation which is *not* breadth-first, can be seen as a derivation where the rules are applied with priority on a subset of the factbase. This can have a significant effect, particularly on the (non-)termination of the restricted chase. That is because as demonstrated in Example 5 of the previous section, in the restricted chase the order of application of the rules can have a decisive impact on whether a derivation will terminate or not.

The oblivious and the semi-oblivious chase have the property that if one derivation terminates on a particular knowledge base, then all derivations will terminate and have the same length and depth. Hence, it suffices to consider breadth-first derivations when investigating problems related to the termination and depth of derivations for **O**-chase and **SO**-chase. In addition, the equivalent chase is by definition breadth-first (as is the core chase). This leaves the restricted chase as the last chase variant where we have to question the effectiveness of the breadth-first approach.

Indeed, the restricted chase was not initially conceived to be necessarily working in a breadth-first manner. However, as we show below, breadth-first derivations suffice for studying its termination, just as is the case for the other chase variants as well. Moreover, breadth-first derivations have the smallest depth.

Proposition 1. For each terminating **R**-derivation from F and $\mathcal{R}$ there exists a breadth-first terminating **R**-derivation from F and $\mathcal{R}$ of smaller or equal depth.

Proof. Let $\mathcal{D}$ be a terminating **R**-chase derivation from F and $\mathcal{R}$. Let $\mathcal{T_D}$ its sequence of associated triggers and let $\mathcal{T'_D}$ be a sorting of $\mathcal{T_D}$ such that the rank of each element is greater or equal to the rank of its predecessors. Let $\mathcal{D'}$ be the derivation by applying, when **R**-applicable, the triggers using the order of $\mathcal{T'_D}$. Because of the sorting, some of the triggers in $\mathcal{T'_D}$ may no longer be **R**-applicable. However, $\mathcal{D'}$ respects the rank compatibility property. Suppose now that there is a new trigger $(R, \pi) \notin \mathcal{T_{D'}}$ which is **O**-applicable on $\mathcal{D'}$. Then (R, π) is **O**-applicable on $\mathcal{D}$, because $(R, \pi) \in \mathcal{T_D}$ if and only if $(R, \pi) \in \mathcal{T_{D'}}$. However, as $\mathcal{D}$ is **R**-terminating, the trigger (R, π) is not **R**-applicable on $\mathcal{D}$. This means that π can be extended to an homomorphism π' that maps $B \cup H$ in a set of atoms which belong to the factbase resulting from $\mathcal{D}$. We know that $\pi'(B)$ also belongs to the factbase resulting from $\mathcal{D'}$. Then, if this is the case also for $\pi'(H)$ we conclude that (R, π) is also not **R**-applicable on $\mathcal{D'}$. Otherwise, let $G \subseteq \pi'(H)$ the maximal set of atoms that do not belong to the factbase resulting from $\mathcal{D'}$. The atoms in G have been generated by a sub-sequence of triggers of $\mathcal{T_D}$ that are not **R**-applicable while building $\mathcal{D'}$. By composing all the homomorphisms that contribute to the non-**R**-applicability of these triggers on $\mathcal{D'}$ we can build a homomorphism π'' that maps G to a subset of the factbase resulting from $\mathcal{D'}$. By composing π' and π'' we conclude that (R, π) is also not **R**-applicable on $\mathcal{D'}$. $\square$

We now consider the question of whether there is a way to predetermine the depth of derivations, especially when a particular ruleset is considered and the initial factbase can vary. This gives birth to the notion of boundedness, which we now define.

Definition 5. Let $X \in \{\mathbf{O}, \mathbf{SO}, \mathbf{R}, \mathbf{E}\}$. A ruleset $\mathcal{R}$ is X-bounded if there is k such that for every factbase F, all breadth-first X-chase derivations are of depth at most k.

Note that we could have defined boundedness by considering all X-chase derivations instead of all breadth-first X-chase derivations, but the notion would have been weaker for the restricted chase, as suggested by Proposition 1.

As already mentioned, boundedness is shown to be undecidable for classes of existential rules like Datalog. However, the practical interest of this notion lies more on whether we can find the particular bound k, rather than knowing that there exists one and thus the ruleset is bounded. Because even if we cannot know whether a ruleset is bounded or not, it can be useful to be able to check a particular bound k. To this aim, we define the notion of k-boundedness where the bound is known, and we prove its decidabity for three of the four chase variants.

4   Decidability of k-boundedness for Some Chase Variants

Definition 6 (k-**boundedness**). Given a chase variant X, a ruleset $\mathcal{R}$ is X-k-*bounded* if for every factbase F, any breadth-first X-chase derivation is terminating with depth at most k.

Note that a ruleset which is k-bounded is also bounded, but the converse is not true. Our approach for testing k-boundedness is to construct a finite set of factbases whose size depends solely on k and $\mathcal{R}$, that acts as representative of *all* factbases for the boundedness problem. From this one could obtain the decidability of k-boundedness. Indeed, for each representative factbase one can compute all breadth-first derivations of depth k and check if they are terminating.

For analogy, it is well-known that the oblivious chase terminates on all factbases if and only if it terminates on the so-called critical instance (i.e., the instance that contains all possible atoms on the constants occurring in rule bodies, with a special constant being chosen if the rule bodies have only variables) [Mar09]. However, it can be easily checked that the critical instance does not provide oblivious chase derivations of maximal depth, hence is not suitable for our purpose of testing k-boundedness. Also, to the best of our knowledge, no representative sets of all factbases are known for the termination of the other chase variants.

In this section, we prove that k-boundedness is decidable for the oblivious, semi-oblivious (skolem) and restricted chase variants by exhibiting such representative factbases. A common property of these three chase variants is that redundancies can be checked "locally" within the scope of a rank, while in the equivalent chase, redundancies may be "global", in the sense by adding an atom we can suddenly make redundant atoms added by previous ranks.

Following this intuition, we define the notion of hereditary chase.

Definition 7. The X-chase is said to be *hereditary* if, for any X-chase derivation $\mathcal{D}$ from F and $\mathcal{R}$, the restriction of $\mathcal{D}$ induced by $F' \subseteq F$ is an X-chase derivation.

A chase is hereditary if by restricting a derivation on a subset of a factbase we still get a derivation with no redundancies. This captures the fact that redundancies can be tested "locally". This property is fulfilled by the oblivious, semi-oblivious and restricted chase variants; a counter-example for the equivalent chase is given as the end of this section.

Proposition 2. The X-chase is hereditary for $X \in \{\mathbf{O}, \mathbf{SO}, \mathbf{R}\}$.

Proof. We assume that $\mathcal{D}$ is an X-chase derivation from F and $\mathcal{R}$, and $\mathcal{D}_{|F'}$ is the restriction of $\mathcal{D}$ induced by $F' \subseteq F$.

Case O By definition, an **O**-chase derivation is any sequence of immediate derivations with distinct triggers, so the restriction of a derivation from a subfact of F is an **O**-chase derivation.

Case SO The condition for **SO**-applicability is that we do not have two triggers which map frontier variables in the same way. As $\mathcal{D}$ fulfills this condition its subseqence $\mathcal{D}_{|F'}$ also fulfills it.

Case R The condition for **R**-applicability imposes that for a trigger (R, π) there is no extension of π that maps the head of R to F. Since $\mathcal{D}_{|F'}$ generates a factbase included in the factbase generated by $\mathcal{D}$ we conclude that **R**-applicability is preserved. □

Note however that the fact that $\mathcal{D}$ is breadth-first does not ensure that its restriction induced by F' is still breadth-first (because the rank exhaustivness might not be satisfied). It is actually the case for the oblivious chase (since all triggers are always applied), but not for the other variants since some rule applications that would be possible from F' have not been performed in $\mathcal{D}$ because they were redundant in $\mathcal{D}$ given the whole F. The next examples illustrate these cases.

Example 7 (Semi-oblivious chase).
Let $F = \{p(a,b), r(a,c)\}$ and $\mathcal{R} = \{R_1 = p(x,y) \rightarrow r(x,y); R_2 = r(x,y) \rightarrow \exists z\, q(x,z); R_3 = r(x,y) \rightarrow t(y)\}$. Let $\mathcal{D}$ be the (non terminating) breadth-first derivation of depth 2 from F whose sequence of associated triggers is (R_1, π_1), (R_3, π_2), (R_2, π_2), (R_3, π_1) with $\pi_1 = \{x \mapsto a, y \mapsto b\}$ and $\pi_2 = \{x \mapsto a, y \mapsto c\}$ which produce $r(a,b), q(a, z_{(R_2,\pi_2)}), t(c), t(b)$; the trigger (R_2, π_1) is then **O**-applicable but not **SO**-applicable, as it maps equally the frontier variables as (R_2, π_2). Let $F' = \{p(a,b)\}$. The restriction of $\mathcal{D}$ induced by F' includes only $(R_1, \pi_1), (R_3, \pi_1)$ and is a **SO**-chase derivation of depth 2, however it is not breadth-first since now (R_2, π_1) is **SO**-applicable at rank 2 (thus the rank exhaustiveness is not satisfied).   △

Example 8 (Restricted chase).
Let $F = \{p(a,b), q(a,c)\}$ and $\mathcal{R} = \{R_1 = p(x,y) \rightarrow r(x,y); R_2 = r(x,y) \rightarrow \exists z\, q(x,z); R_3 = r(x,y) \rightarrow t(x)\}$. Let $\mathcal{D}$ be the (terminating) breadth-first derivation of depth 2 from F whose sequence of associated triggers is $(R_1, \pi), (R_3, \pi)$ with $\pi = \{x \mapsto a, y \mapsto b\}$ which produces $\{p(a,b), q(a,c), r(a,b), t(a)\}$; this application permits the trigger (R_2, π) to be **SO**-applicable, which is however not **R**-applicable because of the presence of $q(a,c)$ in F. Let $F' = \{p(a,b)\}$. The restriction of $\mathcal{D}$ induced by F' is a restricted chase derivation of depth 2, however it is not breadth-first since now (R_2, π) is **R**-applicable at rank 2 and thus has to be applied (to ensure the rank exhaustiveness of a breadth-first derivation).   △

Heredity is not sufficient for our decidability proof. Hence, we define a stronger property, namely consistent heredity, which ensures that the restriction of a breadth-first derivation $\mathcal{D}$ induced by F' *can be extended* to a breadth-first derivation (still from F').

Definition 8. The X-chase is said to be *consistently hereditary* if for any fact-base F and any breadth-first X-derivation $\mathcal{D}$ from F and $\mathcal{R}$, the restriction of $\mathcal{D}$ induced by $F' \subseteq F$ is a subderivation of a breadth-first X-derivation $\mathcal{D}'$ from F' and $\mathcal{R}$.

Proposition 3. The X-chase is consistently hereditary for $X \in \{\mathbf{O}, \mathbf{SO}, \mathbf{R}\}$.

Proof. Let $\mathcal{D}$ be a breadth-first X-chase derivation from F and $\mathcal{R}$ and $\mathcal{D}_{|F'}$ the restriction of $\mathcal{D}$ induced by $F' \subseteq F$.

Case O Since $\mathcal{D}$ is breadth-first, it is rank compatible, and since the ordering of triggers is preserved in $\mathcal{D}_{|F'}$ we get that $\mathcal{D}_{|F'}$ is rank compatible. Similarly by the rank exhaustiveness of $\mathcal{D}$, all triggers which are descendants of F' appear in $\mathcal{D}$, so $\mathcal{D}_{|F'}$ is also rank exhaustive. Hence $\mathcal{D}$ is breadth-first.

Case SO As before, we can easily see that triggers in $\mathcal{D}_{|F'}$ are ordered by rank. Now, suppose that $\mathcal{D}_{|F'}$ is not rank exhaustive, i.e. there are rule applications (descendants of F') that were *skipped* in $\mathcal{D}$ because they mapped the frontier variables of a rule R in the same way that earlier rule applications issued from $F \setminus F'$ did. Then new triggers will be applicable in $\mathcal{D}_{|F'}$ raising to a breadth-first derivation $\mathcal{D}'$. We want to show that $\mathcal{D}'$ is rank exhaustive and that $\mathcal{D}_{|F'}$ is a subsequence of $\mathcal{D}'$. For every new trigger (R, π) that appears in $\mathcal{D}'$ but not in $\mathcal{D}_{|F'}$ there is a trigger (R, π') that appears in $\mathcal{D}$ but not in $\mathcal{D}_{|F'}$, such that π and π' map the frontier variables of R to the same terms. Therefore, as every rank of $\mathcal{D}$ is exhaustive the same holds for $\mathcal{D}'$. Then, all triggers of $\mathcal{D}_{|F'}$ remain **SO**-applicable in $\mathcal{D}'$ so $\mathcal{D}_{|F'}$ can be considered a subsequence of $\mathcal{D}'$.

Case R Let $\mathcal{D}'$ be the *breadth first completion* of $\mathcal{D}_{|F'}$ constructed as follows: for every breadth-first level κ, after applying all triggers of $\mathcal{D}_{|F'}$ of rank κ, we apply all other possible **R**-applicable triggers of rank κ (in any order). By definition, $\mathcal{D}'$ is rank exhaustive. We want to show also that $\mathcal{D}_{|F'}$ is a subsequence of $\mathcal{D}'$, that is, that all triggers of $\mathcal{D}_{|F'}$ are still **R**-applicable in $\mathcal{D}'$. We do so by induction on the size of $\mathcal{D}'$.

For the first element of $\mathcal{D}'$, this is trivial because we start $\mathcal{D}'$ by adding all triggers of $\mathcal{D}_{|F'}$ of rank 1. By induction hypothesis, assume now that all the $n-1$ first triggers of $\mathcal{D}_{|F'}$ are **R**-applicable (hence retained) in $\mathcal{D}'$. Let (R, π) be the n-th trigger of $\mathcal{D}_{|F'}$. We denote with F'_{n-1} the resulting factbase after applying the first $n-1$ triggers of $\mathcal{D}_{|F'}$ and with G the resulting factbase after applying all triggers of $\mathcal{D}'$ up to (R, π). Let $(R_1, \pi_1), ..., (R_m, \pi_m)$ be the triggers that were not **R**-applicable in $\mathcal{D}$ but were **R**-applicable and were added in $\mathcal{D}'$. It holds that $G = F'_{n-1} \cup \pi_1^s(H_1) \cup \cdots \cup \pi_m^s(H_m)$.

Now, we assume that (R, π) is not **R**-applicable on $\mathcal{D}'$. Hence, by the condition of **R**-applicability, there exists a homomorphism $\sigma : \pi^s(H) \to G$ (so also $\sigma(\pi^s(H)) \subseteq G$), which behaves as the identity on $\pi(B)$. We denote with F_i the factbase produced until applying (R, π) on $\mathcal{D}$. We have that $F'_{n-1} \subseteq F_i$, hence we get that $G \subseteq F_i \cup \pi_1^s(H_1) \cup \cdots \cup \pi_m^s(H_m)$ and so $\sigma : \pi^s(H) \rightarrow$ $F_i \cup \pi_1^s(H_1) \cup \cdots \cup \pi_m^s(H_m)$. Now, because $(R_1, \pi_1), \ldots, (R_m, \pi_m)$ were not $\mathbf{R}$-applicable in $\mathcal{D}$ we know that there exist respective homomorphisms $\sigma_j :$ $\pi_j^s(H_j) \rightarrow F_i$ (so also $\sigma_j(\pi_j^s(H_j)) \subseteq F_i$), that behave as the identity on $\pi_j(B_j)$, for all $j \in \{1, \ldots, m\}$. As all σ_j differ have disjoint domains, and each one of them essentially applies only to the existential variables of its respective $\pi_j^s(H_j)$, we can define $\dot{\sigma} := \bigcup_{i \leq m} \sigma_i$ from which we get $\dot{\sigma} \circ \sigma(\pi^s(H)) \subseteq$ $\dot{\sigma}(F_i \cup \pi_1^s(H_1) \cup \cdots \cup \pi_m^s(H_m))$ which yields $\dot{\sigma} \circ \sigma(\pi^s(H)) \subseteq F_i$. As the substitution $\dot{\sigma} \circ \sigma$ has as domain only the set of newly created variables in $\pi^s(H)$, hence qualifies as an extension of π, and from (3) we conclude that (R, π) is not $\mathbf{R}$-applicable in $\mathcal{D}$. That is a contradiction, hence it must be the case that (R, π) is indeed $\mathbf{R}$-applicable in $\mathcal{D}'$. Therefore we have shown that all triggers of $\mathcal{D}_{|F'}$ appear in $\mathcal{D}'$, so indeed $\mathcal{D}_{|F'}$ is a subderivation of an exhaustive breadth-first sequence from F'. □

The next property exploits the notion of consistent heredity to bound the size of the factbases that have to be considered.

Proposition 4. Let b be the maximum number of atoms in the bodies of the rules of a ruleset $\mathcal{R}$. Let X be any consistently hereditary chase. If there exist an F and a breadth-first X-chase $\mathcal{R}$-derivation from F that is of depth at least k, then there exist an F' of size $|F'| \leq b^k$ and a breadth-first X-chase $\mathcal{R}$-derivation from F' with depth at least k.

Proof. Let $\mathcal{D}$ be a breadth-first $\mathcal{R}$-derivation from F of depth k. Let (R, π) be a trigger of $\mathcal{D}$ of depth k. Let F' be the set of ancestors of (R, π) in F, and by Lemma 1 we know that $|F'| \leq b^k$. Since we consider consistently hereditary chases, the restriction $\mathcal{D}_{|F'}$ (which trivially includes (R, π)) is still a derivation sequence of the considered chase and moreover it is a subderivation of an exhaustive breadth-first X-chase $\mathcal{R}$-derivation $\mathcal{D}'$ from F'. Since $\mathcal{D}'$ was constructed as breadth-first completion of $\mathcal{D}$, the ranks of common triggers are preserved from $\mathcal{D}$ to $\mathcal{D}_{|F'}$ and $\mathcal{D}'$. And since $\mathcal{D}'$ includes (R, π) in its sequence of associated rule applications, we have that (R, π) has also rank k in $\mathcal{D}'$, hence $\mathcal{D}'$ is of depth at least k. □

We are now ready to prove the main result.

Theorem 1. Determining if a set of rules is X-k-bounded is decidable for any consistently hereditary X-chase. This is in particular the case for the oblivious, semi-oblivious and restricted chase variants.

Proof. By Proposition 4, to check if all breadth-first $\mathcal{R}$-derivations are of depth at most k, it suffices to verify this property on all factbases of size less or equal to b^k. For a given factbase F, there is a finite number of (breadth-first) $\mathcal{R}$-derivations from F of depth at most k, hence we can effectively compute these derivations, and check if one of them can be extended to a derivation of depth $k + 1$. □

Finally, the following example shows that the **E**-chase (hence the core chase as well) is not hereditary, therefore not consistently hereditary.

Example 9 (Equivalent (Core) chase). Let $F = \{p(a, a), p(a, b), p(b, c), s(b)\}$ and $\mathcal{R}$ the following set of rules:

$$R_1 = p(x, x) \wedge p(x, y) \wedge p(y, z) \rightarrow \exists w \big(p(w, z) \wedge r(w) \big)$$
$$R_2 = p(x, y) \rightarrow \exists u \; p(u, x)$$
$$R_3 = s(y) \wedge p(y, z) \wedge p(w, z) \wedge r(w) \rightarrow q(w)$$
$$R_4 = p(x, y) \wedge p(y, z) \rightarrow t(y)$$
$$R_5 = t(y) \rightarrow r(y)$$

Here we can verify that any exhaustive E-chase $\mathcal{R}$-derivation from F is of depth 3. Consider such a derivation $\mathcal{D}$ that adds atoms in the following specific order at each breadth-first level (for clarity, we do not use standardized names for the nulls):

$$1 : t(a), t(b), p(w_1, c), r(w_1), p(w_2, b), r(w_2), p(w_3, a), r(w_3)$$
$$2 : r(a), r(b), q(w_1), p(u_1, w_1)$$
$$3 : q(b)$$

Let $F' = F \setminus \{s(b)\}$. Let $\mathcal{D}'$ be the restriction of $\mathcal{D}$ induced by F'. It includes the application of R_2 that produces $p(u_1, w_1)$. More precisely, at level 2, $\mathcal{D}'$ still produces $r(a)$, $r(b)$ and $p(u_1, w_1)$ but not $q(w1)$. However, $\mathcal{D}'$ is not an **E**-chase derivation because the rule application that produces $p(u_1, w_1)$ is now redundant (this is due to the absence of $q(w1)$). We conclude that the equivalent chase is not hereditary. Note also that any exhaustive **E**-chase derivation from F' is of depth 2 and not 3 as from F.   △

5   Conclusion

In this paper, we investigated the problem of determining whether a ruleset is k-bounded, that is when the chase always halts within a predefined number of steps independetly of the factbase. We have shown that k-boundedness is decidable for some relevant chase variants by first outlining the importance of breadth-first derivations, and then by establishing a common property that ensures decidability, namely "consistent heredity". The complexity of the problem is independent from any data since the size of the factbases to be checked depends only on k and the size of the rule bodies. Our results indicate an EXPTIME upper bound for checking k-boundedness for both the **O**-chase and the **SO**-chase. For the **R**-chase, as the order of the rule applications matters, one needs to check all possible derivations. This leads to a 2-EXPTIME upper bound for the **R**-chase. We leave for further work the study of the precise lower complexity bound according to each kind of chase. Finally, we leave open the question of the decidability of the k-boundedness for the core (or equivalent) chase.

References

[AHV95] Abiteboul, S., Hull, R., Vianu, V. (eds.): Foundations of Databases: The Logical Level, 1st edn. Addison-Wesley Longman Publishing Co., Inc, Boston (1995)

[BLM10] Baget, J.-F., Leclère, M., Mugnier, M.-L.: Walking the decidability line for rules with existential variables. In: KR 2010 (2010)

[BLMS09] Baget, J.-F., Leclère, M., Mugnier, M.-L., Salvat, E.: Extending decidable cases for rules with existential variables. IJCAI **2009**, 677–682 (2009)

[BLMS11] Baget, J.-F., Leclère, M., Mugnier, M.-L., Salvat, E.: On rules with existential variables: walking the decidability line. Artif. Intell. **175**(9–10), 1620–1654 (2011)

[CGK08] Calì, A., Gottlob, G., Kifer, M.: Taming the infinite chase: query answering under expressive relational constraints. In: KR 2008, pp. 70–80 (2008)

[CGL+05] Calvanese, D., De Giacomo, G., Lembo, D., Lenzerini, M., Rosati, R.: DL-lite: tractable description logics for ontologies. In: AAAI, pp. 602–607 (2005)

[CGL09] Calì, A., Gottlob, G., Lukasiewicz, T.: A general datalog-based framework for tractable query answering over ontologies. PODS **2009**, 77–86 (2009)

[DNR08] Deutsch, A., Nash, A., Remmel, J.B.: The chase revisited. In: PODS, pp. 149–158 (2008)

[FKMP05] Fagin, R., Kolaitis, P.G., Miller, R.J., Popa, L.: Data exchange: semantics and query answering. Theor. Comput. Sci. **336**(1), 89–124 (2005)

[GM14] Gogacz, T., Marcinkowski, J.: All-instances termination of chase is undecidable. In: Esparza, J., Fraigniaud, P., Husfeldt, T., Koutsoupias, E. (eds.) ICALP 2014. LNCS, vol. 8573, pp. 293–304. Springer, Heidelberg (2014)

[GOPS12] Gottlob, Georg, Orsi, Giorgio, Pieris, Andreas, Šimkus, Mantas: Datalog and its extensions for semantic web databases. In: Eiter, Thomas, Krennwallner, Thomas (eds.) Reasoning Web 2012. LNCS, vol. 7487, pp. 54–77. Springer, Heidelberg (2012). doi: 10.1007/978-3-642-33158-9_2

[HKMV95] Hillebrand, G.G., Kanellakis, P.C., Mairson, H.G., Vardi, M.Y.: Undecidable boundedness problems for datalog programs. J. Log. Program. **25**(2), 163–190 (1995)

[KRH07] Krötzsch, M., Rudolph, S., Hitzler, P.: Complexity boundaries for Horn description logics. In: Proceedings of AAAI, pp. 452–457. AAAI Press (2007)

[LMTV12] Leone, N., Manna, M., Terracina, G., Veltri, P.: Efficiently computable datalog$^\exists$ programs. In: Proceedings of the Thirteenth International Conference on Principles of Knowledge Representation and Reasoning, KR 2012, pp. 13–23. AAAI Press (2012)

[LMU16] Leclère, M., Mugnier, M.-L., Ulliana, F.: On bounded positive existential rules. In: Proceedings of the 29th International Workshop on Description Logics (2016)

[LTW09] Lutz, C., Toman, D., Wolter, F.: Conjunctive query answering in the description logic $\mathcal{EL}$ using a relational database system. In: Proceedings of IJCAI, pp. 2070–2075 (2009)

[Mar99] Marcinkowski, J.: Achilles, turtle, and undecidable boundedness problems for small datalog programs. SIAM J. Comput. **29**(1), 231–257 (1999)

[Mar09] Marnette, B.: Generalized schema-mappings: from termination to tractability. In: PODS, pp. 13–22 (2009)

[MT14]   Mugnier, M.-L., Thomazo, M.: An introduction to ontology-based query answering with existential rules. Reasoning Web **2014**, 245–278 (2014)

[Roc16]   Rocher, S.: Querying Existential Rule Knowledge Bases: Decidability and Complexity. (Interrogation de Bases de Connaissances avec Règles Existentielles: Décidabilité et Complexité). Ph.D. thesis, University of Montpellier, France (2016)

Cardinality Restrictions Within Description Logic Connection Calculi

Fred Freitas[1]([⊠]) and Ivan Varzinczak[2]

[1] Informatics Center, Federal University of Pernambuco (CIn - UFPE),
Recife, Brazil
fred@cin.ufpe.br
[2] CRIL, University of Artois & CNRS, Arras, France
varzinczak@cril.fr

Abstract. Recently, we have proposed the θ-connection method for the description logic (DL) $\mathcal{ALC}$, the $\mathcal{ALC}$ θ-CM. It replaces the usage of Skolem terms and unification by additional annotation and introduces blocking through a new rule in the connection calculus, to ensure termination in the case of cyclic ontologies. In this work, we enhance this calculus and its representation to take on $\mathcal{ALCHQ}^=$, an extended fragment that includes role hierarchies, qualified number restrictions and (in)equalities. The main novelty of the calculus lies in the introduction of equality, as well as in the redefinition of connection to accommodate number restrictions, either explicitly or expressed through equality. The new calculus uses the Eq system, thus introducing substitutivity axioms for each concept or role name. The application of Bibel's equality connections appears here as a first solution to deal with equality.

Keywords: Description logic · Connection method · Inference system
Cardinality restrictions · Role hierarchies · Reasoning

1 Introduction

Particularly after the appearance of the Semantic Web, Description Logic (DL) [1] has attracted growing attention in the Informatics' mainstream, with applications in many areas. The possibility of supplying Web users with query answers obtained by complex, albeit decidable reasoning may constitute the main reason for such interest.

At least in the last two decades, the field of DL reasoning has been taken over by tableaux calculi and reasoners. The DL family of languages has spread to include very expressive fragments such as $\mathcal{SROIQ}$ [15]; cutting-edge reasoning performance was accordingly achieved, with the development of DL-specific optimization techniques.

On the one hand, a clear advantage for tableaux calculi against the growing array of DL constructs - which demand particular treatment during reasoning - may lie in its easy adaptability. Dealing with a new construct may only require conceiving a new tableaux rule, maybe along with some optimization companion.

On the other hand, promising methods may have been neglected in such a scenario, in which the tough competition is often focused on gains through optimizations.

C. Benzmüller et al. (Eds.): RuleML+RR 2018, LNCS 11092, pp. 65–80, 2018.
https://doi.org/10.1007/978-3-319-99906-7_5

Therefore, perhaps there is still room available for "basic research" on DL reasoning, in the sense that other efficient calculi need to be adapted to DL, tuned and tested.

Recently, we have embarked in such an endeavor. Departing from the successful first-order logic (FOL) Connection Method (CM) - whose matrix representation provides a parsimonious usage of memory compared to other methods -, we designed, a first connection calculus for DL, the $\mathcal{ALC}\,\theta$-CM [6]. It incorporates several features of most DL calculi: blocking (implemented by a new rule in connection calculi), lack of variables, unification and Skolem functions.

Moreover, RACCOON [7], the reasoner which embodied this calculus, displayed surprisingly promising performance for an engine which has no DL optimizations. In most of our benchmarking for $\mathcal{AL}, \mathcal{ALE}$ and $\mathcal{ALC}$, it was only clearly surpassed by Konclude [15] (even against FacT ++ [16] and Hermit [8] – see Sect. 5), even considering that these reasoners were designed to face more complex DL fragments than $\mathcal{ALC}$, a disadvantage for them. Nonetheless, this fact corroborates connection calculi as fair, competitive choices for DL ontology querying and reasoning.

In an attempt to extend the expressivity of the ontologies it can cope with, in this work we enhance this calculus and its representation to take on $\mathcal{ALCHQ}^=$, an extended fragment that includes role $\mathcal{H}$ierarchies, $\mathcal{Q}$ualified number restrictions and (in)equalities. The main novelty lies in the introduction of (in)equalities, as well as the redefinition of connection to accommodate number restrictions, either explicitly or expressed through equalities. The application of Bibel's eq-connections (equality connections) [4] appears here as a first solution to deal with (in)equalities, although cardinality restrictions do not need equality connections, once, in this case, an equality connects only to an inequality, given a proper θ-substitution for the pair is available. Surely, there are other more efficient solutions to dealing with equality, such as paramodulation [13] and RUE (Resolution and Unifications with Equality) [5], not to speak on the many advanced techniques already applied in the DL setting. The aim of the new $\mathcal{ALCHQ}^=\theta$-connection calculus is providing a first solution and roadmap on how to deal with equality and number restrictions, based on its semantics.

The text is organized as follows. Section 2 provides an explanation of the FOL CM. Section 3 introduces $\mathcal{ALCHQ}^=$; its normalization is shown in Sect. 4. Section 5 explains our formal connection calculus for $\mathcal{ALCHQ}^=$. Section 6 discusses related work on equality handling in FOL and DL. Section 7 concludes the article. The calculus' termination, soundness and completeness are proven in www.cin.ufpe.br/ ∼ fred/RR.pdf.

2   The Connection Method

The connection method has a long tradition in automated deduction. Conceived by W. Bibel in the early 80's, it is a *validity procedure* (opposed to *refutation procedures* like tableaux and resolution), i.e., it tries to prove whether a formula, theorem or query is valid. It consists of a matrix-based deduction procedure designed to be economical in the use of memory, as it is not *generative* as tableaux and resolution, in the sense that it does not create intermediary clauses or sentences during proof search. We explain how it works below, preceded by necessary definitions.

A (first-order) *literal*, denoted by L, is either an atomic formula or its negation. The complement $\neg L$ of a literal L is P if L is of the form $\neg P$, and $\neg L$ otherwise. A formula in *disjunctive normal form (DNF)* is a disjunction of conjunctions (like $C_1 \vee \ldots \vee C_n$), where each *clause* C_i has the form $L_1 \wedge \ldots \wedge L_m$ and each L_i is a literal. The *matrix* of a formula in DNF is its representation as a set $\{C_1, \ldots, C_n\}$, where each C_i has the form $\{L_1, \ldots, L_m\}$ with literals L_i. In the *graphical matrix* representation, clauses are represented as columns.

2.1 Method Representation

Suppose we wish to entail whether $KB \models \alpha$ is valid using a direct method, like the Connection Method (CM). By the Deduction Theorem [3], we must then prove directly $KB \rightarrow \alpha$, or, in other words, if $\neg KB \vee \{\alpha\}$ is valid. This opposes to classical refutation methods, like tableaux and resolution, which builds a proof by testing whether $KB \cup \{\neg\alpha\} \models \bot$. Hence, in the CM, the whole knowledge base KB should be negated, including instantiated predicates, like $A(a)$, where a is a constant or individual. Given $KB = \{\alpha_1, \alpha_2, \ldots, \alpha_n\}$, α_i being FOL formulae, in this work we define *query* as a matrix $\neg KB \vee \{\alpha\}$ (i.e., $\neg\alpha_1 \vee \neg\alpha_2 \vee \ldots \vee \neg\alpha_n \vee \alpha$) to be proven valid, where α is the query *consequent*. A query represented in this way is said to be in *positive DNF*.

Besides, the effects for a negated KB in a DNF representation are: (i) axioms of the form $E \rightarrow D$ (in DL, $E \sqsubseteq D$) translate into $E \wedge \neg D$; (ii) in a matrix, variables are existentially quantified; (iii) FOL Skolemization works over universally quantified variables, instead of existential ones; and (iv) the consequent α is not negated.

Example 1 (Query, positive DNF, clause, matrix). The query

$$\{\forall w\, Animal(w) \wedge \exists z(hasPart(w,z) \wedge Bone(z)) \rightarrow Vertebrate(w), \forall x\, Bird(x) \rightarrow$$
$$Animal(x) \wedge \exists y(hasPart(x,y) \wedge Bone(y)) \wedge \exists v(hasPart(x,v) \wedge Feather(v))\}$$
$$\models \forall t\, Bird(t) \rightarrow Vertebrate(t)$$

is represented by the following positive DNF matrix and graphical matrix, where variables y, v and t were skolemized by functions $f(x), g(x)$ and constant c (Fig. 1):

$\{\{Animal(w), hasPart(w,z), Bone(z), \neg Vertebrate(w)\}, \{Bird(x), \neg Animal(x)\}, \{Bird(x), \neg hasPart(x, f(x))\}, \{Bird(x), \neg Bone(f(x))\}, \{Bird(x), \neg hasPart(x, g(x))\}, \{Bird(x), \neg Feather(g(x))\}, \{\neg Bird(c)\}, \{Vertebrate(c)\}\}$.

$$\begin{bmatrix} A(w) & B(x) & B(x) & B(x) & B(x) & B(x) & \neg B(c) & V(c) \\ h(w,z) & \neg A(x) & \neg h(x,f(x)) & \neg Bo(f(x)) & \neg h(x,g(x)) & \neg F(g(x)) & & \\ Bo(z) & & & & & & & \\ \neg V(w) & & & & & & & \end{bmatrix}$$

Fig. 1. A FOL query in disjunctive clausal form represented as a matrix and graphical matrix (with literals abridged, e.g. $A(w)$ stands for *Animal(w)*, etc.)

2.2   Method Intuition and Functioning

We have represented a FOL query in DNF with clauses as columns, i.e., we are dealing with the matrix vertically. If we change our perspective, traversing the matrix horizontally in all possible ways (or *paths*), with each column supplying only one literal in a path, and group these paths conjunctively, we are indeed converting the query to the conjunctive normal formal (in the most inefficient way). For instance, in the matrix above, two of the paths are (randomly) listed below:

$$\{A(w), B(x), B(x), \neg Bo(f(x)), \neg h(x, g(x)), B(x), \neg B(c), V(c)\}$$
$$\{h(w, z), \neg A(x), B(x), \neg Bo(f(x)), \neg h(x, g(x)), \neg F(g(x)), \neg B(c), V(c)\}.$$

The conjunctive formula would look like (with all variables quantified):

$$\ldots \wedge (A(w) \vee B(x) \vee B(x) \vee \neg Bo(f(x)) \vee \neg h(x, g(x)) \vee B(x) \vee \neg B(c) \vee V(c)) \wedge \ldots$$
$$\wedge (h(w, z) \vee \neg A(x) \vee B(x) \vee \neg Bo(f(x)) \vee \neg h(x, g(x)) \vee \neg F(g(x)) \vee \neg B(c) \vee V(c)) \wedge \ldots$$

It is now easy to see that such a formula (or matrix) is valid iff every path has a connection, i.e., a σ-complimentary pair of literals, where σ is the (most general) unifier between them. For instance, the first path above is true, once it contains the valid subformula $B(x) \vee \neg B(c)$, with $\sigma = \{x/c\}$; the second is true because it has the subformula $h(w, z) \vee \neg h(x, g(x))$, with $\sigma = \{x/c, w/c, z/g(c)\}$, and so on.

The method then must check all paths for connections in a systematic way. Note that a connection prunes many paths in a single pass, due to the matricial arrangement of clauses, a relevant source of reasoning efficiency.

Example 2 (Connection Method). Figure 2 shows the step-by-step query solution. The reader may note, e.g., that the first connection (step 1) solves 16 paths.

Each connection can create up to two sets of literals still to be solved, one in each clause (column) involved in the connection. The first of these literals in each clause is marked in each step of the Figure with an arrow.

Otten [11] proposed a "sequent-style" calculus formalization, alternatively to the graphical matricial one. Our calculus is based on his; it is explained in Sect. 5.

3   The Description Logic $\mathcal{ALCHQ}^=$

An ontology in $\mathcal{ALCHQ}^=$ is a set of axioms over a signature $\Sigma = (N_C, N_R, N_O)$, where N_C is the *set of concept names* (unary predicate symbols), N_R is the *set of role or property names* (binary predicate symbols), and N_O is the set of *individual names* (constants) [1]. The sets are mutually disjoint. The set of $\mathcal{ALCHQ}^=$ *concept expressions* (**C**) is recursively defined as follows (with $n \in \mathbb{N}^*$, and C a concept expression, i.e., $C \in \mathbf{C}$):

$$C ::= N_C \,|\, C \sqcap C \,|\, C \sqcup C \,|\, \neg C \,|\, \exists r.C \,|\, \forall r.C \,|\, \geq nr \,|\, \geq nr.C \,|\, \leq nr \,|\, \leq nr.C$$

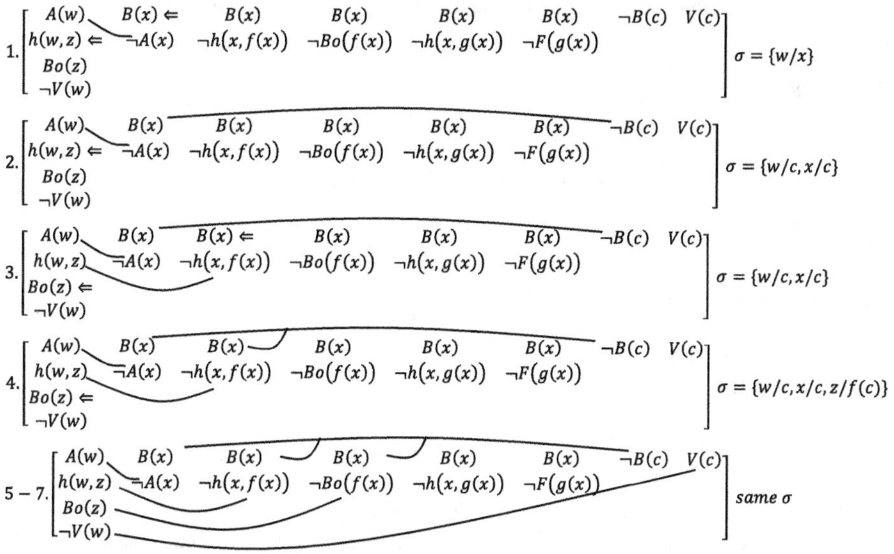

Fig. 2. The query solution, with literals abridged. Arrows stand for pending sets of literals.

$\mathcal{ALCHQ}^=$ allows for a set of basic axioms (TBox, RBox), and a set of axioms of a particular situation (ABox). In the definitions below $a, b \in N_O, r, s \in N_R, D, E \in \mathbf{C}$ and $i, n \geq 1$. A TBox axiom is a subsumption like $D \sqsubseteq E$; an RBox one is like $r \subseteq s$; and an ABox $\mathcal{A}$ w.r.t. a TBox $\mathcal{T}$, an RBox $\mathcal{R}$ is a finite set of assertions (or *instances*) of three types: (i) *concept assertions* like $C(a)$; (ii) *role assertions* $r(a, b)$; (iii) *(in)equality assertions* $a = b$ (or $a \neq b$). An ontology O is an ordered tuple $(\mathcal{T}, \mathcal{R}, \mathcal{A})$

An interpretation I has a domain Δ^I and an interpretation function $.^I$ that maps to every $A \in N_C$ a set $A^I \subseteq \Delta^I$; to every $r \in N_R$ a relation $r^I \subseteq \Delta^I \times \Delta^I$; and to every $a \in N_O$ an element $a^I \in \Delta^I$. The function $.^I$ extends to concepts as depicted in Table 1.

An interpretation I satisfies an axiom $\alpha(I \models \alpha)$ iff all I axioms and α are satisfied, i.e., I satisfies $C \sqsubseteq D$ iff $C^I \subseteq D^I$, $C(a)$ iff $a^I \in C^I$, $r(a, b)$ iff $\langle a, b \rangle \in r^I$, $r \subseteq s$ iff $r^I \subseteq s^I$. O entails $\alpha(O \models \alpha)$ iff every model of O is also a model of α. In this paper, variables are denoted by x, y, z, possibly with subscripts. Terms are variables or individuals.

4 Normal Form and Matrix Representation for $\mathcal{ALCHQ}^=$

Matrices with (qualified) number restrictions can be represented in two ways: the *abridged form*, i.e., with the number restrictions explicit, and the *expanded form*, with number restrictions substituted by axioms containing concepts, roles and (in)equalities that correspond to the semantic definitions. Besides, to take on (in)equalities, *substitutivity axioms* (e.g., $\forall x \forall y (x = y) \rightarrow (E(x) \rightarrow E(y))$ for concept names, and $\forall x \forall y \forall z \forall k (x = z) \wedge (y = k) \rightarrow (r(x, y) \rightarrow r(z, k))$ for role names) are represented as clauses for every concept and role name in the query.

Table 1. Syntax and semantics of $\mathcal{ALCHQ}^=$ constructors

Construct	Syntax	Semantics
Atomic negation	$\neg C$	Δ^I / C^I
Conjunction	$C \sqcap D$	$C^I \cap D^I$
Disjunction	$C \sqcup D$	$C^I \cup D^I$
Exist. restriction	$\exists r.C$	$\{x \in \Delta^I \mid \langle x,y \rangle \in r^I \wedge y \in C^I\}$
Value restriction	$\forall r.C$	$\{x \in \Delta^I \mid \langle x,y \rangle \in r^I \rightarrow y \in C^I\}$
(In)equality	$a = b \backslash \neq$	$a^I = b^I \backslash a^I \neq b^I$
Qualified number restriction[a] (for simple number restrictions, drop $\wedge y_i \in C^I$ from the semantics)	$\leq nr.C$	$\{x \in \Delta^I \mid \bigwedge\limits_{i=1}^{n+1} \langle x,y_i \rangle \in r^I \wedge y_i \in C^I \bigwedge\limits_{i,j=1, i \neq j}^{n} y_i \neq y_j$ $\bigwedge\limits_{i=1}^{n-1} y_i \neq y_{n+1} \rightarrow y_n = y_{n+1}\}$
	$\geq nr.C$	$\{x \in \Delta^I \mid \bigwedge\limits_{i=1}^{n+1} \langle x,y_i \rangle \in r^I \wedge y_i \in C^I \bigwedge\limits_{i,j=1, i \neq j}^{n+1} y_i \neq y_j\}$

[a]Note that we have relied on an unusual semantics for number restrictions, instead of $\{x \in \Delta^I \mid \# \langle x,y_i \rangle \in r^I \wedge y_i \in C^I \leq | \geq n\}$. The semantics presented here indeed consists of the basis for the number restrictions rules ($\leq | \geq$-rules [1]) in tableaux calculi.

Next, the matrix is converted to a specific DNF, introduced here. This DNF, with definitions concerning representation as matrices for the calculus, is presented below.

Definition 1 ($\mathcal{ALCHQ}^=$ literal, formula, clause, matrix). $\mathcal{ALCHQ}^=$ *literals* are atomic concepts or roles, possibly negated and/or instantiated, or *(in)equalities*. Literals involved in universal or existential restrictions are underlined. In case a restriction involves more than one clause, literals are indexed (in the top of the literal) with a same new column index number. An $\mathcal{ALCHQ}^=$ formula in DNF is a disjunction of conjunctions (like $C_1 \vee \ldots \vee C_n$), where each C_i has the form $L_1 \wedge \ldots \wedge L_m$, with each L_i being a literal. The *matrix* of an $\mathcal{ALCHQ}^=$ formula in DNF is a set $\{C_1, \ldots, C_n\}$, where each *clause* C_i has the form $\{L_1, \ldots, L_m\}$ with literals L_i.

Definition 2 (Substitutivity clauses, graphical matrix). $\mathcal{ALCHQ}^=$ matrices representing number restrictions also contain *substitutivity clauses* for every concept and role name, in the forms $\{x \neq y, E(x), \neg E(y)\}$ and $\{x \neq z, y \neq k, r(x,y), \neg r(z,k)\}$ with $E \in N_C, r \in N_R$.

In the *graphical matrix* representation, clauses are represented as columns, and restrictions as lines; restrictions with indexes are horizontal; without are vertical (see Example 3 – substitutivity axioms are not presented). Literals participating in a universal restriction in an axiom's left-hand side (LHS) or in an existential restriction in the right-hand side (RHS) are underlined; otherwise, they are sidelined.

Example 3 (Query, clause, $\mathcal{ALCHQ}^=$ matrix, abridged/expanded forms). Figure 3 shows query $O = \{ > 1 \text{ hasPart.Wheel} \sqsubseteq \text{Vehicle}, \text{Car} \sqsubseteq \geq 3 \text{ hasPart.Wheel}\}$, $\alpha = \text{Car} \sqsubseteq \text{Vehicle}$ in abridged form. The index marks clauses involved in a same restriction).

$\{\{\geq \underline{1\text{hasPart, Wheel}}, \neg\text{Vehicle}\}, \{\text{Car}, \underline{\leq 3 \neg\text{hasPart}^1}\}, \{\text{Car}, \underline{\neg\text{Wheel}^1}\}, \{\text{Vehicle(a)}\},$
$\{\neg\text{Car(a)}\}\}$

$$\begin{bmatrix} \geq 1 \text{ hasPart} & \text{Car} & \text{Car} & \neg\text{Car(a)} & \text{Vehicle(a)} \\ \text{Wheel} & \underline{\leq 3 \neg\text{hasPart}} & \neg\text{Wheel} & & \\ \neg\text{Vehicle} & & & & \end{bmatrix}$$

Fig. 3. The query from Example 1 represented as an $\mathcal{ALCHQ}^=$ matrix in abridged form

The negations in literals $\underline{\leq 3\neg\text{hasPart}^1}$ and $\neg\text{Wheel}^1$ constitute merely a notational convention that facilitates the connections. They reflect the transformation to the expanded form, where these literals are converted into negated literals and equalities.

The number restriction expanded form, according to the semantics defined in Table 1, replaces $\geq \underline{1\text{hasPart, Wheel}}$ by $\text{hasPart}(x, y_1) \sqcap \text{Wheel}(y_1) \sqcap \text{hasPart}(x, y_2)$ $\sqcap \text{Wheel}(y_2) \wedge y_1 \neq y_2$ and $\underline{\leq 3 \neg\text{hasPart}^1}$ by $\bigwedge_{i=1}^{3} \text{hasPart}(x, v_i) \sqcap \text{Wheel}(v_i) \sqcap v_1 \neq$ $v_2 \sqcap v_1 \neq v_3 \to v_2 = v_3$ before creating the matrix. The resulting matrix is depicted in Fig. 4. For the sake of space, substitutivity axioms are not shown.

$\{\{\underline{\text{hasPart, Wheel}(y_1)}, \underline{\text{hasPart, Wheel}(y_2)}, y_1 \neq y_2, \neg\text{Vehicle}\}, \{\text{Car}, \underline{\neg\text{hasPart}^1}\}, \{\text{Car}, \underline{\neg\text{Wheel}(v_1)^1}\}, \{\text{Car}, \underline{\neg\text{hasPart}^2}\}, \{\text{Car}, \neg\text{Wheel}(v_2)^2\}, \{\text{Car}, \underline{\neg\text{hasPart}^3}\}, \{\text{Car}, \underline{\neg\text{Wheel}(v_3)^3}\}, \{\text{Car}, v_1 = v_2\}, \{\text{Car}, v_1 = v_3\}, \{\text{Car}, v_2 = v_3\}, \{\text{Vehicle(a)}\}, \{\neg\text{Car(a)}\}\}$

$$\begin{bmatrix} h & C & C & C & C & C & C & C & C & C & \neg C(a) & V(a) \\ W(y_1) & \neg h & \neg W(v_1) & \neg h & \neg W(v_2) & \neg h & \neg W(v_3) & v_1=v_2 & v_1=v_3 & v_2=v_3 & & \\ h & & & & & & & & & & & \\ W(y_2) & & & & & & & & & & & \\ y_1 \neq y_2 & & & & & & & & & & & \\ \neg V & & & & & & & & & & & \end{bmatrix}$$

Fig. 4. Same example in expanded form, showing the (in)equalities (again, literals are abridged, i.e., C means Car, h means hasPart, etc.)

$$i)\ 1NF: \begin{bmatrix} E_1 \\ \vdots \\ E_n \\ \neg D_1 \\ \vdots \\ \neg D_m \end{bmatrix} \quad ii)\ 2NF: \begin{bmatrix} E & \cdots & \cdots & E \\ \neg r & \neg D_1 & \cdots & \neg D_n \end{bmatrix} \quad iii)\ 3NF: \begin{bmatrix} \neg r & D_1 & \cdots & D_m \\ \neg E & \cdots & \cdots & \neg E \end{bmatrix}$$

Fig. 5. Examples of the three two-lined normal forms' representations in $\mathcal{ALCHQ}^=$

Definition 3 (Impurity, pure conjunction/disjunction). *Impurity* in an $\mathcal{ALCHQ}^=$ formula is a disjunction in a conjunction, or a conjunction in a disjunction. A *pure conjunction* (PC) or *disjunction* (PD) does not contain impurities (see Definition in [6]).

Example 4 (Impurity, pure conjunction/disjunction). (a) $\exists r.A$ and $\bigwedge_{i=1}^{n} A_i$ are PCs if A and each A_i are also PCs; (b) $(\forall r.(D_0 \sqcup \ldots \sqcup D_n \sqcup (E_0 \sqcap \ldots \sqcap E_m) \sqcup (A_0 \sqcap \ldots \sqcap A_p))$ is not a PD, as it contains two impurities: $(E_0 \sqcap \ldots \sqcap E_m)$ and $(A_0 \sqcap \ldots \sqcap A_p)$.

Definition 4 (Two-lined disjunctive normal form). An $\mathcal{ALCHQ}^=$ axiom is in *two-lined DNF* iff it is in DNF and in one of the following normal forms (NFs): (i) $\widehat{E} \sqsubseteq \widecheck{D}$; (ii) $E \sqsubseteq \widehat{E}$; (iii) $\widecheck{D} \sqsubseteq E$, where E is a concept name[1] $\widehat{E}$ is a PC, and $\widecheck{D}$ is a PD.

Example 5 (Two-lined disjunctive normal form). The axioms (i) $\widehat{E} \sqsubseteq \widecheck{D}$; (ii) $E \sqsubseteq \exists r.\widehat{E}$ and (iii) $\forall r.\widecheck{D} \sqsubseteq E$, where $\widehat{E} = \bigwedge_{i=1}^{n} E_i$ and $\widecheck{D} = \bigvee_{j=1}^{m} D_j$ (Fig. 5).

Definition 5 (Cycle, cyclic/acyclic ontologies and matrices). If A and B are atomic concepts in an ontology O, A *directly uses* B, if B appears in the right-hand side of a subsumption axiom whose left-hand side is A. Let the relation *uses* be the transitive closure of *directly uses*. A *cyclic ontology* or *matrix* has a cycle when an atomic concept *uses* itself; otherwise it is *acyclic* [1]; e.g., $O = \{A \sqsubseteq \exists r.B, B \sqsubseteq \exists s.A\}$ is cyclic.

5   The $\mathcal{ALCHQ}^=$ θ-Connection Calculus ($\mathcal{ALCHQ}^=$ θ-CM)

The $\mathcal{ALCHQ}^=$ θ-Connection Method (henceforth $\mathcal{ALCHQ}^=$ θ-CM) differs from the FOL Connection Method (CM) by replacing Skolem functions and unification by θ-substitutions, and, just as typical DL systems, employs blocking to assure termination.

Besides, equality connections, proposed by Bibel [4], are needed here as a first attempt to address (in)equalities, and thus (qualified) cardinality restrictions. The idea is to include substitutivity axioms for each concept and role name, e.g., for concept P: $x = y \rightarrow (P(x), \rightarrow P(y))$, represented as a single column $\{x = y, P(x), \neg P(y)\}$

Moreover, w.r.t. $\mathcal{ALC}$ θ-CM, $\mathcal{ALCHQ}^=$ θ-CM expands the notion of connection to include equality, which is used to express number restrictions. An ontology represented as a matrix with the equalities is said to be in the *expanded form* and is explained in the next section. The *abridged form*, with number restrictions without equalities, is tackled in Subsect. 4.2.

5.1   Expanded Form - Representation and Reasoning

Definition 6 (Path, connection, θ-substitution, θ-complementary connection). A *path through a matrix M* contains exactly one literal from each clause/column in M. A *connection* is a pair of literals in three forms: (i) $\{E, \neg E\}$ with the same concept/role name, instantiated with the same instance(s) or not; (ii) $\{x = y, x \neq y\}$, with x and y instantiated with the same instance or not. A θ-*substitution* assigns each (possibly omitted) variable an individual or another variable, in an $\mathcal{ALCHQ}^=$ literal. A θ-*complementary* connection is a

---

[1] The symbols E and $\widehat{E}$ were chosen here to designate a concept name and a pure conjunction rather than the usual C and $\widehat{C}$, to avoid confusion with clauses, that are also denoted by C.

pair of $\mathcal{ALCHQ}^=$ literals $\{E(x), \neg E(y)\}$ or $\{p(x,v), \neg p(y,u)\}$, with $\theta(x) = \theta(y)$, $\theta(v) = \theta(u)$. The complement $\overline{L}$ of a literal L is E if $= \neg E$, and it is $\neg E$ if $L = E$.

Remark 1 (θ-substitution). Simple term unification without Skolem functions is used to calculate θ-substitutions. The application of a θ-substitution to a literal is an application to its variables, i.e. $\theta(E) = E(\theta(x)), x$ fresh, and $\theta(r) = r(\theta(x), \theta(y))$, where E is an atomic concept and r is a role. For notation, $x^\theta = \theta(x)$.

Definition 7 (Set of concepts). The *set of concepts* $\tau(x)$ of a term x contains all concept names instantiated by x so far, defined as $\tau(x) \underset{def}{=} \{E \in N_C | E(x) \in Path\}$.

Definition 8 (Skolem condition). The *Skolem condition* ensures that at most one concept name is underlined for each term in the graphical matrix form. If i is an index, this condition is defined as $\forall a \mid \{\underline{E^i} \in N_C \big| E^i(a) \in Path\} \mid \leq 1$.

Definition 9 ($\mathcal{ALCHQ}^=$ connection calculus). Figure 6 brings the formal $\mathcal{ALCHQ}^=$ connection calculus ($\mathcal{ALCHQ}^=$ θ-CM), adapted from the FOL CM [11]. The rules of the calculus are applied in an analytic, bottom-up way. The basic structure is the tuple $<C, M, Path>$, where clause C is the open sub-goal, M the matrix corresponding to the query $O \models \alpha$ (O is an $\mathcal{ALCHQ}^=$ ontology) and $Path$ is the *active path*, i.e. the (sub-)path being currently checked. The index $\mu \in \mathbb{N}$ of a clause C^μ denotes that C^μ is the μ-th copy of clause C, increased when Cop is applied for that clause (the variable x in C^μ is denoted x_μ) – see example of copied clauses in Fig. 13a. When Cop is applied, it is followed by the application of Ext or Red, to avoid non-determinism in the rules' application. The *Blocking Condition* states that, when a cycle finishes, the last new individual x_μ^θ (if it is new, then $x_\mu^\theta \notin N_O$, as in the condition) has a set of concepts $\tau(x_\mu^\theta)$ which is not a subset of the set of concepts of the previous copied individual, i.e., $\tau(x_\mu^\theta) \not\subseteq \tau\left(x_{\mu-1}^\theta\right)$ [14]. If this condition is not satisfied, blocking occurs.

$$Axiom\ (Ax) \quad \frac{}{\{\}, M, Path}$$

$$Start\ Rule\ (St) \quad \frac{C_1, M, \{\}}{\varepsilon, M, \varepsilon} \quad with\ C_1 \in \alpha$$

$$Reduction\ Rule\ (Red) \quad \frac{C, M, Path \cup \{L_2\}}{C \cup \{L_1\}, M, Path \cup \{L_2\}}$$
$$with\ \theta(L_1) = \theta(\overline{L_2})\ and\ the\ Skolem\ condition\ holds$$

$$Extension\ Rule\ (Ext) \quad \frac{C_1 \setminus \{L_2\}, M, Path \cup \{L_1\} \quad C, M, Path}{C \cup \{L_1\}, M, Path}$$
$$with\ C_1 \in M,\ L_2 \in C_1, \theta(L_1) = \theta(\overline{L_2})\ and\ the\ Skolem\ condition\ holds$$

$$Copy\ Rule\ (Cop) \quad \frac{C \cup \{L_1\}, M \cup \{C_2^\mu\}, Path}{C \cup \{L_1\}, M, Path}$$
$$with\ C_2^\mu\ is\ a\ copy\ of\ C_1, L_2 \in C_2^\mu, \theta(L_1) = \theta(\overline{L_2})\ and\ the\ blocking\ condition\ holds$$

Fig. 6. The connection calculus $\mathcal{ALCHQ}^=$ θ-CM

Lemma 1 (Matrix characterization). A matrix M is valid iff there exist an index μ, a set of θ-substitutions $\langle \theta_i \rangle$ and a set of connections S, s.t. every path through M^μ, the matrix with copied clauses, contains a θ-complementary connection $\{L_1^\theta, L_2^\theta\} \in S$, i.e. a connection with $\theta(L_1) = \theta(\overline{L_2})$. The tuple $\langle \mu, \langle \theta_i \rangle, S \rangle$ is called a *matrix proof*.

Clause copying and its multiplicity μ already existed in the original CM, but neither a copy rule nor blocking were necessary, as FOL is semi-decidable. To regain termination, the new *Copy* rule implements blocking [1], when no alternative connection is available and cyclic ontologies are being processed. The rule regulates the creation of new individuals, blocking when infinite cycles are detected. The *Skolem condition* solves the FOL cases where the combination of Skolemization and unification correctly prevents connections (see Soundness Theorem in WWW.cin.ufpe.br/∼fred/RR.pdf).

In the *Ext* and *Red* rules, θ-substitutions replace implicit variables by terms in the current path. A restriction avoids the situation in FOL matrices, where unification is tried with distinct Skolem functions: any individual x can have in its set of concepts $\tau(x)$ at most a single concept name with a column index in the matrix, stated by the condition $\forall a \left| \left\{ E^i \in N_C \middle| E^i(a) \in Path \right\} \right| \leq 1$.

Example 6 ($\mathcal{ALCHQ}^=$ connection calculus). Figures 7 and 8 show the proof of the query from Example 1 using the matrix representation and the calculus, respectively.

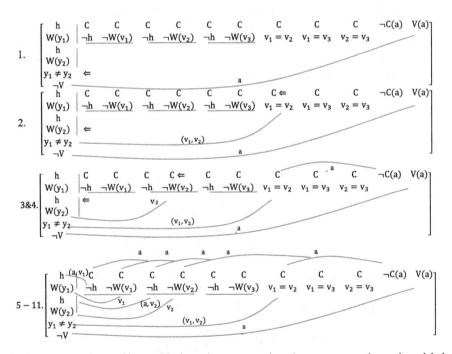

Fig. 7. The query's proof in graphical matrix representation. Arcs are connections whose labels are the names of the involved individual(s)/variable(s). Arrows indicate pending literals' lists.

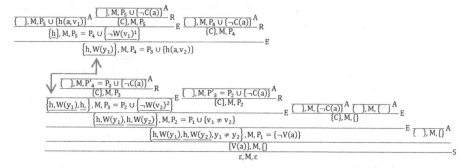

Fig. 8. The proof of the query using the calculus, where M is an abbreviation for $\{\{h, W(y_1), h, W(y_2), y_1 \neq y_2, \neg V\}, \{C, \underline{\neg h}^1\}\}$, $\{C, \neg W(v_1)^1\}, \{C, \underline{\neg h}^2\}\}, \{C, \neg W(v_2)^2\}, \{C, \underline{\neg h}^3\}\}$, $\{C, \neg W(v_3)^3\}, \{C, v_1 = v_2\}, \{C, v_1 = v_3\}, \{C, v_2 = v_3\}, \{V(a)\}, \{\neg C(a)\}\}$. The double-ended arrow just copies the proof part to save text space.

Furthermore, when equality between pairs of individuals are being dealt, equality connections [4] with substitutivity axioms, in explicit or implicit form, can be relied upon. One can solve, e.g., $\{P(a), a = b\} \vDash P(b)$, as portrayed in Fig. 9. Figure 9(i) displays the equality connections performed in the usual way, with the introduction of the substitutivity axiom $P: x = y \rightarrow (P(x) \rightarrow P(y))$ (represented as the column $\{x = y, P(x), \neg P(y)\}$), while Fig. 9(ii) presents the same connection in an abridged way.

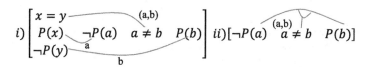

Fig. 9. (*i*) A connection using the substitutivity axiom; (*ii*) an equality connection [4]

This subject naturally leads to the representation of number restrictions connections in the abridged form, deployed in the next subsection.

5.2 Abridged Form - Representation and Reasoning

(Qualified) number restrictions can be in *abridged form* ($\geq | \leq nr(.C)$ with $n \in \mathbb{N}^*$). In this case, one should note that $\neg(\geq nr) = \leq(n-1)r$ and $\neg(\leq nr) = \geq(n+1)r$.

Definition 10 (Number restriction literal). *Number restriction literals* are literals representing (qualified) number restrictions. They can be negated and/or instantiated, and/or under- or sidelined or with no line. In case a restriction involves more than one clause, literals are top indexed with a same new column index number.

Definition 11 (Number restriction valid interval). Two number restrictions form a *valid interval* iff their numerical restrictions share an intersection, e.g. $>5r$, $<8 \neg r$.

Definition 12 (Number restriction θ-substitution, θ-complementary number restriction connection). Let A and B be two number restriction literals, $\leq | \geq nr$ and $\geq | \leq m \neg r$, instantiated or not, representing role instance sets $\langle r(x, y_1), \ldots, r(x, y_n) \rangle$ and $\langle r(z, w_1), \ldots, r(z, w_m) \rangle$, with a valid interval between them (vi). A *number restriction θ-substitution* for the pair is a mapping θ, s.t. $\theta(x) = \theta(y), \theta(y_i) = \theta(w_i)$, with $i = 1$ to min(vi). A *θ-complementary number restriction connection* is a pair of number restriction literals over a same role in the form $\{ \leq | \geq nr, \geq | \leq m \neg r \}$, that, under a number restriction θ-substitution, share a valid interval vi.

A connection represents a tautology, e.g. $E \sqcup \neg E$. For number restrictions, this means a valid interval, as, for example, any individual possessing any number of role instances (including 0) with r satisfies the restriction $>5r \sqcup <8r$. If there is a "hole", for instance, $>8r \sqcup <5r$, then individuals with 5 to 8 role instances of r would not satisfy the restriction, and the latter cannot be a tautology. Recall that $<8r$ is represented as $<8 \neg r$, only to facilitate the connections to be settled.

Example 6 ($\mathcal{ALCHQ}^=$ connection calculus, abridged form). Figures 10 and 11 display the proof from Example 2 in the abridged form, using the graphical matrix representation and the formal calculus. Note that min$(> 1 \text{hasPart}, < 3 \neg \text{hasPart}) = 2$.

The abridged form can easily accommodate number restrictions with role hierarchies, if connections between number restrictions and role axioms exist.

Fig. 10. Proof of Example 2 in the abridged form. $\langle (a, v_i) \rangle$, $i = 1, 2$ is a set of two role instances and $v_i, i = 1, 2$ is a set of two instances (of concept Wheel).

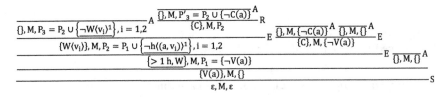

Fig. 11. The proof of Example 2 using the calculus, with $M = \{\{ > 1 \text{hasPart}, \text{Wheel}, \neg \text{Vehicle}\}$, $\{\text{Car}, \underline{<3 \neg \text{hasPart}^1}\}, \{\text{Car}, \underline{\neg \text{Wheel}^1}\}, \{\text{Vehicle(a)}\}, \{\neg \text{Car(a)}\}\}$ (literals are abbreviated)

Example 7 (Number restrictions, role hierarchies). $O = \{ > 2\,\text{hasPart.Wheel} \sqsubseteq$
Car, hasComponent $\subseteq$ hasPart, Truck $\sqsubseteq\ \geq 6\,\text{hasPart.Wheel}\}$, $\alpha = \text{Truck} \sqsubseteq \text{Car}$.

This query is represented by $M = \{\{ > 2\ \text{hasPart, Wheel}, \neg\text{Car}\}, \{\text{hasComponent},$
$\neg\text{hasPart}\}, \{\text{Truck}, <5\ \neg\text{hasComponent}^1\}, \{\text{Truck}, \underline{\neg\text{Wheel}^1}\}, \{\neg\text{Truck(a)}\}, \{\text{Car(a)}\}$.

Figure 12 brings the proof for M, with $\min(> 2\,\text{hasPart}, <5\,\text{hasPart}) = 3$.

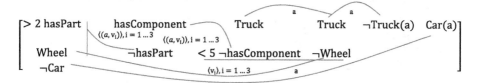

Fig. 12. Proof with number restrictions and a role hierarchy axiom

6 Discussion

Matricial inference methods, such as the CM, presents a few advantages over other methods, as well as some drawbacks. We will discuss our method, at first in the light of memory handling and existent solutions to solve equality equations in the context of FOL. Next, we briefly comment some recent comparative performance of our $\mathcal{ALC}$ reasoner, RACCOON (ReAsoner based on the Connection Calculus Over ONtologies) against well-known DL reasoners [7], and existent solutions for number restrictions within the DL scenario, followed by a small discussion on next steps.

As for memory usage, in the CM, matrices require only a copy of the matrix and data structures to store the current path, the pending clauses and literals, the unifier and literal's indices. It does not generate any intermediary results; this constitutes an interesting benefit in terms of memory usage over *generative* methods such as resolution or tableaux, which create intermediary clauses and sub-formulae.

Indeed, dealing efficiently with memory with cyclic ontologies is crucial for a DL reasoner, since a number of fragments (including $\mathcal{ALCN}$-Aboxes) have been proven PSpace-complete [1]. Our calculus processes cycles (thanks to the *Copy rule*), saving memory due to keeping only one copy of the matrix in memory [3, 4]. The other copies are virtual, i.e., only the index μ is created or incremented and stored, together with the θ-substitution and the current path. The next example portraits this case.

Example 8 (Cycles). $O = \{\exists\text{hasSon. (Dr} \sqcup \text{DrAncestor)} \sqsubseteq \text{DrAncestor, hasSon}$
(ZePadre, Moises), hasSon (Moises, Luiz), hasSon (Luiz, Fred), Dr (Fred)$\}$, $\alpha =$
DrAncestor(ZePadre). This cyclic query has its proof represented by both Figs. 13a and b.

Figure 13a brings an explicit copy of the second clause, needed for the proof. On the other hand, Fig. 13b incorporate indices to denote how the only copy was used with different individuals and instantiations. At least in theory, such idea exists in the CM,

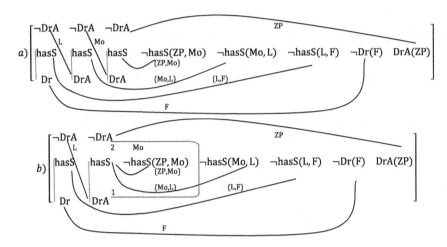

Fig. 13. Proof representations of a cyclic query, with (*a*) explicit and (*b*) implicit copies

called *implicit amplification* [3]; we adopted it in RACCOON with the same notation, and gain memory with its procedure.

Clausal inference methods require normal forms, in which transformations apply over formulae to produce clauses over which the method works. On the one hand, clause manipulation accelerates reasoning in reasonably expressive logics, e.g., FOL. On the other hand, the drawbacks are at least two-fold.

First, literals' redundancy among clauses often constitutes an overhead in large knowledge bases. In the CM, matrix representation minors the problem during reasoning, as the method is non-generative; anyway, it remains if, in an initial query representation in DNF, clauses share too many literals. For the $\mathcal{ALCHQ}^{=}$ θ-CM, the two-lined normal form reduces this type of redundancy at the expense of introducing a small number of new symbols. To sum up, the best solution consists in applying a non-clausal connection method [12], where matrices can be nested.

Another problem for clausal calculi resides on adapting to an increasing set of constructs in DL: each new construct to be inserted into the calculi requires careful analysis, and frequently changes in the existing rules. This problem also plagues equality approaches in clausal systems. Consolidated solutions from saturation-based reasoning, such as paramodulation [13], are hard to be integrated, and the former is not complete for the connection method [11]. Nevertheless, an equality approach based on RUE (Resolution with Unification and Equality) [5] seems plausible for connection calculi but has not been tried yet. Our aim in formalizing our calculus with the Eq system is paving the way for such more efficient solutions.

Although the Eq system is not yet coded in RACCOON, the goal-oriented search embodied by the connection calculus, together with its economical approach to memory, made the reasoner display unexpected fair results for $\mathcal{ALC}$ consistency, compared to Hermit, FacT++ and Konclude. A summary of the benchmarking conducted over the ORE 2014 and 2015 baselines is deployed in Fig. 14 [7].

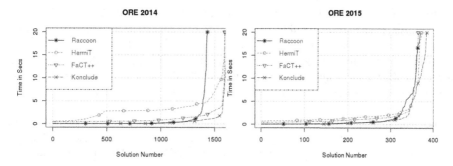

Fig. 14. Comparison of RACCOON and ORE competitors for consistency on the ORE 2014 and 2015 baselines ($\mathcal{AL}, \mathcal{ALE}$ and $\mathcal{ALC}$ ontologies)

In the baselines, ontologies were ranked by size and expressivity. RACCOON exhibited the fastest results (side by side with Konclude) in smaller and less complex ontologies; however, against the larger and more complex set (the last ones), results start to decay (in a graceful fashion), probably due to the lack of DL optimizations. Furthermore, in the first experiment, RACCOON's performance fell short in ontologies in the presence of a certain structure where cycles occur inside other cycles massively. Apart from that, the results seem promising, given the possibility of implementing reductions built in other competitors.

When faced with number restrictions and their equalities, the idea is applying the abridged form first, which demand less steps and memory; only in the cases it does not suffice, the expanded form must be used (comparing two number restrictions has a quadratic complexity in the simpler cases, not to talk about checking the ABox). Besides, with the expanded form, hundreds of substitutivity axioms might need to be added to the matrix. Thus, $\mathcal{ALCHQ}^= \theta$-CM can only be competitive in this DL fragment, when, e.g., solutions based on rewriting [2, 10] can be devised and integrated, i.e., a way to substitute equal individuals by their canonical representative is envisaged. Bibel already suggested term rewriting as a possible technique to solve equality in the CM [4]. Integrating it with the $\mathcal{ALCHQ}^= \theta$-CM represents a challenge for our calculus to remain competitive as more expressive fragments are to be addressed.

7   Conclusions and Future Work

In the current work, $\mathcal{ALCHQ}^= \theta$-CM is presented, a connection method that enhances the $\mathcal{ALC} \theta$-CM, by, mainly, introducing (in)equalities and, as a respective solution to handle them, equality connections with equality predicate substitutivity axioms explicit or implicit, as defined by Bibel. Two new forms of representing number restrictions are also shown: the abridged and the expanded form. In the former, cardinality restrictions are a new type of literals themselves, and this new notion of literal together with its respective new connection type had to be defined. In the latter, number restrictions are replaced by literals and (in)equalities that correspond to the number restriction's semantic definition.

As for theoretical future work, we aim to create more sophisticated blocking schemes for dynamic and double blocking for DL constructs like inverses, union, intersection and complement of roles [9], transitivity, role chains and value maps, complex role axioms and dealing with nominals. As for practical future work, we intend to enhance the fragment currently dealt by RACCOON to include $\mathcal{ALCHQ}^=$, as well as the future new solutions mentioned as theoretical future work.

Acknowledgements. This work was partially supported by the project Reconciling Description Logics and Non-Monotonic Reasoning in the Legal Domain (PRC CNRS–FACEPE France–Brazil) and the anonymous reviewers. Fred Freitas also thanks Jens Otten, Evandro and Patty Travassos, for the personal support.

References

1. Baader, F., Calvanese, D., McGuinness, D., Nardi, D., Patel-Schneider, P. (eds.): The Description Logic Handbook. Cambridge University Press, Cambridge (2003)
2. Bate, A., Motik, B., Cuenca Grau, B., Simancik, F., Horrocks, I.: Extending consequence-based reasoning to $\mathcal{SHIQ}$. In: Workshop on Description Logics (DL), CEUR, pp. 34–46 (2015)
3. Bibel, W.: Matings in matrices. Commun. ACM **26**, 844–852 (1983)
4. Bibel, W.: Deduction – Automated Logic. Academic Press, London (1993)
5. Digricoli, V., Harrison, M.: Equality-based Binary Resolution. J. ACM **33**(2), 253–289 (1986)
6. Freitas, F.: A connection calculus over the description logic $\mathcal{ALC}$. In: Canadian Conference on Artificial Intelligence (AI), Victoria, Canada (2016)
7. Freitas, F., Melo, D., Otten, J.: RACCOON: a connection reasoner for $\mathcal{ALC}$. In: Proceedings of International Conference on Logic for Programming, Artificial Intelligence and Reasoning (LPAR) (2017)
8. Glimm, B., Horrocks, I., Motik, B., Stoilos, G., Wang, Z.: HermiT: an OWL 2 reasoner. J. Autom. Reason. **53**(3), 245–269 (2014)
9. Horrocks, I., Sattler, U.: A description logic with transitive and inverse roles and role hierarchies. J. Logic Comput. **9**(3), 385–410 (1999)
10. Motik, B., Nenov, Y., Piro, R., Horrocks, I.: Combining rewriting and incremental materialisation maintenance for datalog programs with equality. In: IJCAI, pp. 3127–3133 (2015)
11. Otten, J.: Restricting backtracking in connection calculi. AI Commun. **23**(2–3), 159–182 (2010)
12. Otten, J.: nanoCoP: natural non-clausal theorem proving. In: Proceedings of IJCAI, pp. 4924–4928 (2017)
13. Robinson, G., Wos, L.: Paramodulation and Theorem Proving in First-Order Theories with Equality. Mach. Intell. **4**, 135–150 (1969)
14. Schmidt, R., Tishkovsky, D.: Analysis of blocking mechanisms for description logics. In Proceedings of the Workshop on Automated Reasoning (2007)
15. Steigmiller, A., Liebig, T., Glimm, B.: Konclude: system description. J. Web Semant. Sci. Serv. Agents World Wide Web **27**(1), 78–85 (2014)
16. Tsarkov, D., Horrocks, I.: FaCT++ description logic reasoner: system description. In: Furbach, U., Shankar, N. (eds.) IJCAR 2006. LNCS (LNAI), vol. 4130, pp. 292–297. Springer, Heidelberg (2006). https://doi.org/10.1007/11814771_26

A First Order Logic Benchmark
for Defeasible Reasoning Tool Profiling

Abdelraouf Hecham[1(✉)], Madalina Croitoru[1], and Pierre Bisquert[2]

[1] LIRMM, University of Montpellier, Montpellier, France
`hecham@lirmm.fr`
[2] INRA, Montpellier, France

Abstract. In this paper we are interested in the task of a data engineer choosing what tool to use to perform defeasible reasoning with a first order logic knowledge base. To this end we propose the first benchmark in the literature that allows one to classify first order defeasible reasoning tools based on their semantics, expressiveness and performance.

1 Introduction

Used in many practical domains [3,14,21], defeasible reasoning allows to reason with incomplete or inconsistent knowledge where conclusions can be challenged by additional information. An inherent characteristic of defeasible reasoning is its systematic reliance on a set of intuitions and rules of thumb, which have been long debated between logicians [1,17,20,23]. For example, should an information that is derived from a contested claim be used to contest another claim (i.e. ambiguity handling)? Or, can different 'chains' of reasoning for the same claim be combined to defend against challenging statements (i.e. reinstatement)? It appears that no single approach is appropriate in all situations, or for all purposes. When it comes to the defeasible reasoning tools in the literature, confusingly, each follows different subsets not clearly stated in the tool description or companion papers.

We are interested in the task of a data engineer *looking to select what tool to use* to perform defeasible reasoning. To facilitate this task we propose **the first benchmark in the literature for first order logic defeasible reasoning tools profiling**. We show how to use the proposed benchmark **in order to categorize existing tools** based on their *semantics* (e.g. ambiguity handling), logical language (e.g. existential rules) and *expressiveness* (e.g. priorities). We stress that we do *not want to compare* the tools amongst themselves but to be able to provide *an informative benchmark* to allow understanding the *strengths and intuitions of available tools*.

After introducing in Sect. 2 the logical language and defeasible reasoning, in Sect. 3 we enumerate the various criteria for analysing defeasible reasoning tools. In Sect. 4 we present the proposed benchmark and show how the structure of the benchmark corresponds to the various tools criteria. Finally, in Sect. 5, we run a set of available tools on the benchmark and discuss the results.

© Springer Nature Switzerland AG 2018
C. Benzmüller et al. (Eds.): RuleML+RR 2018, LNCS 11092, pp. 81–97, 2018.
https://doi.org/10.1007/978-3-319-99906-7_6

2   Background Notions

Language. We consider[1] a first order language L composed of formulas built with the usual quantifiers ($\exists, \forall$) and the connectors: implication ($\rightarrow, \Rightarrow, \rightsquigarrow$) and conjunction ($\wedge$). An *atom* is of the form $p(t_1, \cdots, t_k)$ and its complement is of the form $\neg p(t_1, \cdots, t_k)$, where p is a predicate and t_i are variables or constants[2]. $\top, \bot$ are also allowed and considered themselves atoms. A *rule* r is a formula of the form $\forall \boldsymbol{X}, \boldsymbol{Y} \left(\mathscr{B}(\boldsymbol{X}, \boldsymbol{Y}) \Rightarrow \exists \boldsymbol{Z} \; \mathscr{H}(\boldsymbol{X}, \boldsymbol{Z}) \right)$ such that $\Rightarrow \in \{\rightarrow, \Rightarrow, \rightsquigarrow\}$, where $\boldsymbol{X}, \boldsymbol{Y}$ are tuples of variables, $\boldsymbol{Z}$ is a tuple of *existential variables*, and $\mathscr{B}, \mathscr{H}$ are finite non-empty conjunctions of atoms respectively called *body* and *head* of r and denoted $Body(r)$ and $Head(r)$. A rule r can be of three types: (1) strict rules ($\rightarrow$) express undeniable implications i.e. if $Body(r)$ then definitely $Head(r)$; (2) defeasible rules ($\Rightarrow$) express a weaker implication i.e. if $Body(r)$ then generally $Head(r)$ and (3) defeater rule ($\rightsquigarrow$) are used to prevent the complement of a conclusion from being drawn i.e. if $Body(r)$ then the complement of any atom in $Head(r)$ should not be concluded. It does not imply that $Head(r)$ is concluded.

A defeasible knowledge base is a tuple $\mathscr{K} = (\mathscr{F}, \mathscr{R}, \succ)$ where $\mathscr{F}$ is a set of 'fact' rules of the form $\top \rightarrow \mathscr{B}(\boldsymbol{a})$ or $\top \Rightarrow \mathscr{B}(\boldsymbol{a})$, $\mathscr{R}$ is a finite set of rules (strict rules are denoted by $\mathscr{R}_\rightarrow$, defeasible rules by $\mathscr{R}_\Rightarrow$, and defeater rules by $\mathscr{R}_\rightsquigarrow$), and $\succ$ is an acyclic superiority relation over rules. A rule r_1 is said to be *superior* to another rule r_2 iff $r_1 \succ r_2$ and $r_2 \not\succ r_1$ (r_2 is said to be inferior to r_1). This expresses that r_1 may override r_2. Since defeasible reasoning is mostly concerned by whether a conclusion is entailed or not, we only consider boolean queries. A boolean query is an existentially closed conjunction of atoms of the form $Q = \exists \boldsymbol{X} \Phi(\boldsymbol{X}, \boldsymbol{a})$? (where Φ is a conjunction of atoms, $\boldsymbol{X}$ is a set of existential variables, and $\boldsymbol{a}$ is a set of constants). A ground boolean query is a conjunction of ground atoms of the form $Q = \Phi(\boldsymbol{a})$?.

Inference Mechanisms. Reasoning can be achieved using inference mechanisms that fall under two main approaches. *Forward chaining* (also called *chase*) is the exhaustive application of the set of rules over the set of facts. *Backward chaining* consists in using the rules to rewrite the query. Reasoning with existential rules is not always guaranteed to stop. Decidable abstract classes of rules have been defined [6]: (1.) Finite Expansion Set (FES) where forward chaining is guaranteed to stop, (2.) Finite Unification Set (FUS) where backward chaining is guaranteed to stop, and (3.) Bounded Treewidth Set (BTS) which ensures decidability although no algorithm is currently available for this class. Greedy BTS (GBTS) is an expressive subclass of BTS that is provided with a forward-chaining-like algorithm. Concrete classes that may specialize one or several of the above abstract classes are recognizable by syntactic properties (e.g. transitive rules for FES class) [5], online tools such as KIABORA[3] can output if the knowledge base is decidable (i.e FES, FUS, GBTS or their combination).

---

[1] The minimal superset of the languages used in first order logic defeasible reasoning.

[2] Variables are denoted by uppercase letters $X, Y, Z, etc.$, constants by lowercase letters $a, b, c, etc.$, and unknown constants (nulls) by $null_1, null_2, etc.$

[3] http://graphik-team.github.io/graal/kiabora.

Cyclicity on rules poses additional decidability problems [5]. The Graph of Rule Dependencies (GRD) is a directed graph that encodes the interactions between rules: nodes represent rules and there is an edge from r_1 to r_2 iff an application of the rule r_1 may create a new application of the rule r_2. A GRD is acyclic when it has no circuit.

Reasoning. To reason defeasibly about a conclusion, all chains of rule applications reaching that conclusion must be evaluated along with any conflict that arises from other chains of rules. This can be achieved using two kinds of approaches: First, using the idea of extensions, where reasoning chains (arguments) are built then evaluated at a later stage; this encapsulates argumentation-based techniques such as grounded semantics [12] and dialectical trees [13]. Other approaches are based on the evaluation of arguments during their construction, such as defeasible logics [9,22].

3   Defeasible Reasoning Features

Let us concretely discuss the various **features** concerning *semantics, expressiveness* and *performance* based on the different **intuitions** behind defeasible reasoning [1,17,20,23]. Please note that we do not discuss what intuitions are better to adopt, as these often conflict. Our aim is to facilitate the task of selecting what defeasible reasoning tool to use based on the reasoning requirements and the data at hand.

Semantics. Different intuitions impact what conclusions are accepted or rejected in a defeasible reasoning setting:

1. *Ambiguity Handling:* As illustrated in Example 1 information derived from an ambiguous (i.e. contested) claim should be used to contest another claim [25].

Example 1. *The defeasible knowledge base $\mathcal{K}$ describes that evidence "a" suggests that the defendant 'jack' is responsible of the crime while evidence "b" indicates that he is not. According to the underlying legal system, a defendant is presumed not guilty unless responsibility has been proven. $\mathcal{K} = (\mathcal{F}, \mathcal{R}, \varnothing)$:*

- $\mathcal{F} = \{\top \Rightarrow evid(a, incriminating, jack), \top \Rightarrow evid(b, absolving, jack), \top \Rightarrow defendant(jack)\}$.
- $\mathcal{R} = \{\forall X, defendant(X) \Rightarrow \neg guilty(X), \forall X, Y, evid(X, incriminating, Y) \Rightarrow responsible(Y), \forall X, Y, evid(X, absolving, Y) \Rightarrow \neg responsible(Y), \forall X, responsible(X) \Rightarrow guilty(X)\}$.

Is jack not guilty? Given both evidence "a" and "b", the fact "responsible(jack)" is ambiguous and it is used to derive "guilty(jack)". The question is "Should guilty(jack) be used to contest $\neg$guilty(jack) and make it ambiguous?". In an **ambiguity blocking** *setting, the ambiguity of "responsible(jack)" blocks (forbids) any ambiguity derived from it. Therefore "$\neg$(guilty(jack))" is uncontested* and the answer to the query $Q = \neg guilty(jack)$? is 'true'. On the other hand, in an **ambiguity propagating** setting, the ambiguity of "responsible(jack)" is propagated to "$\neg guilty(jack)$" because its complement "guilty(jack)" can be derived, hence, the answer to the query Q is 'false'.

Ambiguity propagation results in fewer conclusions (since more ambiguities are allowed), which might make it preferable when the cost of an incorrect conclusion is high, whereas *ambiguity blocking* might be more intuitive in situations where contested claims cannot be used to contest other claims (e.g. in the legal domain) [17].

2. *Team Defeat (Direct Reinstatement):* The absence of team defeat means that a rule r_1 implying an atom f attacked by another rule r_2 implying $\neg f$ can only be defended by r_1 itself (meaning that for r_1 to 'survive' it has to be superior to r_2 i.e. $r_1 \succ r_2$ and $r_2 \not\succ r_1$). However, if we allow team defeat, r_1 can be successfully defended by another rule r_3 for f that is superior to r_2 (even if r_1 is inferior to r_2), as illustrated in Example 2.

Example 2. *Generally, animals do not fly unless they are birds. Also, penguins do not fly except magical ones. "Tweety" is an animal, a bird, and a magical penguin.* $\mathcal{K} = (\mathcal{F}, \mathcal{R}, \succ)$:

- $\mathcal{F} = \{\top \Rightarrow animal(tweety) \wedge bird(tweety) \wedge penguin(tweety) \wedge magical(tweety)\}$.
- $\mathcal{R} = \{r_1 : \forall X, animal(X) \Rightarrow \neg fly(X), r_2 : \forall X, bird(X) \Rightarrow fly(X), r_3 : \forall X, penguin(X) \Rightarrow \neg fly(X), r_4 : \forall X, magical(X) \wedge penguin(X) \Rightarrow fly(X)\}$.
- $(r_2 \succ r_1), (r_4 \succ r_3)$.

The query is $Q = fly(tweety)$ *(i.e. can "Tweety" fly?). In the absence of team defeat, the answer to Q is* **'false'** *because there is no chain of reasoning for "fly(tweety)" that can defend itself from all attacks: even if r_2 defends itself from r_1 (because $r_2 \succ r_1$), it does not defend against r_3 (since $r_2 \not\succ r_3$), and the same applies for r_4: it defends against r_3 but fails against r_1 because $r_4 \not\succ r_1$. If team defeat is allowed then the answer to Q is* **'true'** *("Tweety" can fly) because all attacks are defeated: r_1 is defeated by r_2 ($r_2 \succ r_1$) and r_3 is defeated by r_4 ($r_4 \succ r_3$).*

3. *Floating Conclusions:* Sometimes two conflicting and equally strong arguments might lead to the same conclusion down the line. These conclusions are called 'floating conclusions' [20].

Example 3. *A first witness says that "Jack" killed "John" by stabbing him while a second witness says that he shot him. Both testimonies are of equal strength and both imply that "Jack" killed "John", however they are conflicting.* $\mathcal{K} = (\mathcal{F}, \mathcal{R}, \emptyset)$:

- $\mathcal{F} = \{\top \Rightarrow stabbed(jack, john) \land shot(jack, john).$
- $\mathcal{R} = \{r_1 : \forall X, Y, stabbed(X, Y) \Rightarrow \neg shot(X, Y),$
  $r_2 : \forall X, Y \ shot(X, Y) \Rightarrow \neg stabbed(X, Y), \ r_3 : \forall X, Y \ stabbed(X, Y) \Rightarrow killed(X, Y), \ r_4 : \forall X, Y \ shot(X, Y) \Rightarrow killed(X, Y)\}.$

The query is $Q = killed(jack, john)$ *(i.e. did "Jack" kill "John"?). "killed(jack, john)" is a floating conclusion. One might argue that regardless if the witnesses disagree on the details, the conclusion is the same and therefore the answer to* Q *is* **'true'** *(i.e. floating conclusions should be accepted). However, one can also argue that the two witnesses undermine each other's credibility, and therefore the answer to the query* Q *should be* **false** *(i.e. floating conclusions should be rejected).*

4. *Handling of Strict Rules:* In some defeasible reasoning tools, such as the ones based on Defeasible Logics, facts that are not in direct conflict, and that are defeasibly derived from non ambiguous ones, are accepted (even if the application of strict rules and facts generates conflict). Other formalisms reject any fact that leads to conflict when strict rules and facts are applied.

Example 4 (Consistent Answers). *Consider the following* $\mathcal{K} = (\mathcal{F}, \mathcal{R}, \emptyset)$:

- $\mathcal{F} = \{\top \Rightarrow incrim(e1, alice), \top \Rightarrow absolv(e2, alice)\}$
- $\mathcal{R} = \{r_1 : \forall X, Y \ incrim(X, Y) \rightarrow resp(Y), \ r_2 : \forall X, Y \ absolv(X, Y) \rightarrow \neg resp(X)\}$

The facts $incrim(e1, alice)$ *and* $absolv(e2, alice)$ *are entailed in some formalisms because there is no direct attack on them, however other formalisms consider that these facts are not entailed because they lead to a conflict if strict rules are applied.*

Expressiveness. Reasoning tools can be classified w.r.t. the expressiveness of their underlying language:

1. *Rules with Existential Variables:* They are logical fragments useful in applications such as Ontology Based Data Access (OBDA) [18] and Semantic Web [11]. Detecting support for existential rules is tricky since most defeasible reasoning tools omit *quantifiers* which might lead to unwanted results. Variables appearing in the head of rules are sometimes considered existential variables, for example the rule $p(X) \rightarrow q(X, Y)$ can be either interpreted as $\forall X p(X) \rightarrow \exists Y q(X, Y)$ or $\forall X, Y p(X) \rightarrow q(X, Y)$. Example 5 shows how this affects reasoning.

Example 5. *Consider the following situation where "jack" is a murderer and "john" is a victim. A murderer is a person who killed someone. This situation is described in* $\mathcal{K} = (\mathcal{F}, \mathcal{R}, \emptyset)$ *with* $\mathcal{F} = \{\top \Rightarrow murderer(jack) \wedge victim(john)\}$ *and* $\mathcal{R} = \{murderer(X) \rightarrow killed(X,Y)\}$. *If we run the query* $Q = killed(jack, john)$? *(did jack kill john?) using a tool that does not take into account existential variables the answer would be "**true**" because it assumes that all known constants (persons) are killed by all murderers (i.e.* $\forall X, Y \, murderer(X) \wedge \top(Y) \rightarrow killed(X,Y)$*). In fact, it will also consider that* $killed(jack, jack)$ *is "true".*

However if we run the query Q *using a tool that supports existential variables, the answer would be "**false**" since it is not possible to make the link between the generated null and the constant "john".*

2. *Rules with cycles:* We consider two types of cycles: Support cycles (when the Graph of Rule Dependency is cyclic) and Attack cycles. In presence of a *cyclic GRD* some inference mechanisms (such as SLD resolution [4]) might loop infinitely as it might lead to an infinite cycle of evaluating the conclusion then the premise then the conclusion and so on as shown in the following example.

Example 6 (Support Cycle). *Consider the following knowledge base* $\mathcal{K} = (\mathcal{F}, \mathcal{R}, \emptyset)$ *for representing legal contracts. A person is generally an individual and an individual is a person. "bob" is a person. Is "bob" an individual* $Q = individual(bob)$?

- $\mathcal{F} = \{\top \rightarrow person(bob)\}$
- $\mathcal{R} = \{r_1 : \forall X \, person(X) \Rightarrow individual(X), \, r_2 : \forall X \, individual(X) \Rightarrow person(X)\}$

Evaluating Q *would require evaluating the application of* r_1 *generating* *individual(bob), which would require evaluating* $person(bob)$*, this in turn might require evaluating individual(bob) given* r_2 *and continue on and on.*

Cyclic conflict happens when two chains of reasoning attack each other at different levels as shown in Example 7. Some logics (such as Defeasible Logics) would loop infinitely in such situations.

Example 7 (Attack Cycle). *Let* $\mathcal{K} = (\mathcal{F}, \mathcal{R}, \succ)$:

- $\mathcal{F} = \{\top \Rightarrow p(a), \top \Rightarrow q(a)\}$.
- $\mathcal{R} = \{\forall X \, p(X) \Rightarrow \neg q(X), \forall X \, q(X) \Rightarrow \neg p(X)\}$.

Evaluating the query $Q = \neg p(a)$ *would result in an infinite cycle if the arguments are evaluated on construction. Otherwise the answer to* Q *is '**false**'.*

3. *Rule Application Block:* Some situations require that rules are prevented from being applied, to express that a conclusion should not be derived and at the same time its complement is not necessarily derived either. This solves some non-intuitive results of certain logics [23]. Blocking rule applications can be achieved either by giving rules labels and considering them as atoms, or by using defeater rules.

Example 8 *Birds generally fly. We cannot say that birds with broken wings can fly or not. Let* $\mathscr{K} = (\mathscr{F}, \mathscr{R}, \emptyset)$:

- $\mathscr{F} = \{\top \Rightarrow bird(tweety) \wedge brokenWings(tweety)\}$.
- $\mathscr{R} = \{r_1 : \forall X\ bird(X) \Rightarrow fly(X),\ r_2 : \forall X\ brokenWings(X) \rightsquigarrow \neg fly(X)\}$.

Or, if we use rule labels:

- $\mathscr{F} = \{\top \Rightarrow bird(tweety) \wedge brokenWings(tweety)\}$.
- $\mathscr{R} = \{r_1 : \forall X\ bird(X) \Rightarrow fly(X),\ r_2 : \forall X\ brokenWings(X) \Rightarrow \neg r_1\}$.

The answer to the query $Q = fly(tweety)$ *is* **"false"**.

4. *Priority Relation:* used to resolve ambiguities, can be variously expressed (cardinal, ordinal or implicitly - such as generalized specificity [13]).
5. *Type of Queries:* All defeasible tools support at least boolean ground queries, some allow for boolean existentially closed (non ground) queries.

4   Benchmark Description

The benchmark provides indications on how defeasible reasoning tools are handling the previously described features (their support and subsequent scaling up).

Benchmarking Methodology. We build upon the *propositional* defeasible logic performance oriented benchmark from [19] that generates various parameterized knowledge bases (also known as theories). We *adapt existing theories for the first order language* and *extend them with twelve additional theories* to account for features listed in the previous section. These theories serve two purposes: first, to test the tools' ability to handle the features (especially when these features are not explicitly stated in the companion paper of the tools). Second, to test their performance when faced with gradually complex situations requiring these features. For example: does the tool allow for team defeat? How does it perform when there are larger and larger instances requiring team defeat? Before defining the benchmark, two key notions must be kept in mind:

1. To test the support for a semantics feature, this feature must be "isolated", meaning that the result of the query must only depend on the feature and no other external factor. That is why most theories use only defeasible rules (to avoid the disruptive effect of handling strict rules) and no preferences.
2. While negative results (i.e. situations where tools are not able to give the results required by a certain feature) are definitive, positive results (i.e. situations where tools do provide the intended results of a feature) on the other hand *do not prove the feature is fully supported*.

Benchmark Theories. Figures 1 and 2 give a representation of the benchmark theories, dashed lines represent conflict, $\Rightarrow$ and $\rightsquigarrow$ are defeasible and defeater rules respectively.

- **Ambiguity:** (denoted $ambiguity(n)$) contains a chain of n rules $s_{i-1}(a) \Rightarrow s_i(a)$, and two chains of $2n$ rules $q_{i-1}(a) \Rightarrow q_i(a)$ and $p_{i-1}(a) \Rightarrow p_i(a)$, plus the rules $s_n(a) \Rightarrow \neg q_n(a)$ and $q_{2n}(a) \Rightarrow \neg p_{2n}(a)$, and the defeasible facts $s_0(a)$, $q_0(a)$, $p_0(a)$. The query $Q = p_{2n}(a)$? is not entailed (false) in ambiguity propagating, but is entailed (true) in ambiguity blocking. The parameter n allows the scaling of the theory to longer and longer chains where conflicts appear further down the line.
- **Team Defeat:** (denoted $team(n)$) each conclusion is supported by a team of two defeasible rules and attacked by another team of two defeasible rules. Preferences ensure that each attacking rule is inferior to one of the supporting rules. The antecedents of these rules are in turn supported and attacked by cascades (n levels) of teams of rules. The query $Q = p_0(a)$? is entailed if team defeat is allowed.
- **Floating Conclusions:** (denoted $floating(n)$) contains n couples of conflicting rules $\top \Rightarrow p_i(a)$ and $\top \Rightarrow \neg p_i(a)$, and n rules $p_i(a) \Rightarrow q(a)$. The query $Q = q(a)$? is entailed if floating conclusions are allowed.
- **Consistent Derivation:** (denoted $consistent(n)$) contains two defeasible facts $p_0(a)$, $q_0(a)$ and two chains of n strict rules of the form $p_{i-1}(a) \to p_i(a)$ and $q_{i-1}(a) \to q_i(a)$ that lead to a conflict down the line because of the rules $p_n(a) \to p_{n+1}(a)$ and $q_n(a) \to \neg p_{n+1}(a)$. The query $Q = p_0(a)$ is not entailed if atoms need to be consistent w.r.t. strict rules (indirectly consistent derivation), otherwise it is entailed.
- **Existential Rules:** (denoted $exist(n)$) composed of n rules $\top \Rightarrow p(a_i)$, and the rule without quantifiers $p(X) \Rightarrow q(X, Y)$. $Q = q(a_0, a_n)$? is not entailed if existential rules are supported.

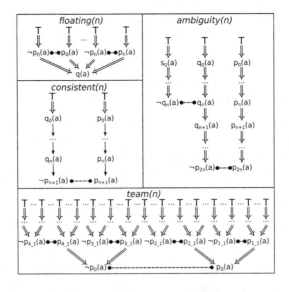

Fig. 1. Representation of semantics theories

- **FES:** (denoted $transitive(n)$) contains the rule $\top \Rightarrow p_0(a,b) \wedge p_0(b,c)$, and a chain of n *transitive rules* of the form $\forall X, Y, Z, \; p_{i-1}(X,Y) \wedge p_{i-1}(Y,Z) \Rightarrow p_{i-1}(X,Z) \wedge p_i(X,Y) \wedge p_i(Y,Z)$. Evaluating $Q = p_n(a,c)$? would result in an infinite loop if FES rules are not supported.
- **FUS:** (denoted $chainAtomB(n)$) contains the rule $\top \Rightarrow p_0(a,b)$, and a chain of n *atomic body rules* of the form $\forall X, Y, \; p_{i-1}(X,Y) \Rightarrow \exists Z, \; p_{i-1}(X,Z) \wedge p_{i-1}(Z,Y) \wedge p_i(X,Y)$. The query $Q = p_n(a,b)$? would result in an infinite loop if FUS existential rules are not supported.
- **GBTS:** (denoted $chainFrG(n)$) contains the rule $\top \Rightarrow p_0(a,b) \wedge p_0(b,c)$, and a chain of n *frontier-guarded rules* of the form $\forall X, Y, Z, \; p_{i-1}(X,Y) \wedge p_{i-1}(Y,Z) \Rightarrow \exists W, \; p_{i-1}(X,W) \wedge p_{i-1}(W,Y) \wedge p_i(X,Y) \wedge p_i(Y,W)$. Evaluating the query $Q = p_n(a,b)$? would result in an infinite loop if GBTS existential rules are not supported.
- **Cyclic GRD:** (denoted $cyclic(n)$) contains the rule $\top \Rightarrow p_1(a)$ and a cyclic chain of n defeasible rules as $p_i(X) \rightsquigarrow p_{i \bmod n}(X)$. Evaluating $Q = p_0(a)$? results in a loop.
- **Circular Reasoning:** (denoted $circular(n)$) consists of a defeasible fact $\neg p_0(a)$ and a cycle of rules of the form $p_i(a) \Rightarrow p_{i \bmod n}(a)$. Evaluating the query $Q = \neg p_0(a)$ might result in an infinite loop due to circular reasoning.
- **Cyclic Conflict:** (denoted $cyclicConf(n)$) composed of n cyclic conflict of the form $p_i(a) \Rightarrow \neg q_i(a)$ and $q_i(a) \Rightarrow \neg p_i(a)$. Evaluating $Q = p_{n+1}(a)$? might loop infinitely.
- **Rule Block:** (denoted $ruleBlock(n)$) contains n rules $\top \Rightarrow p_i(a)$ and $p_i(a) \Rightarrow q(a)$, and a single defeater rule $\top \rightsquigarrow \neg q(a)$ that blocks all other rules. The queries $Q = q(a)$? is not entailed. The parameter n determines how many rules have to be blocked. This theory tests performance with regards to handling rule applications blocking.
- **Priority:** (denoted $levels(n)$) is a cascade of n disputed conclusions $p_i(a)$. For each i, there are rules $r_i \colon \top \Rightarrow p_i(a)$ and $r_i' \colon p_{i+1} \Rightarrow \neg p_i(a)$. For each *odd* $i \geq 1$ a priority asserts that $r_i' \succ r_i$. A final rule $\top \Rightarrow p_{n+1}(a)$ gives uncontested support for $p_{n+1}(a)$. $Q = p_0(a)$? is entailed if priorities are respected.
- **Queries:** (denoted $query(n)$) composed of n rules $\top \Rightarrow p(a_i)$, and the rule $\forall X, \; p(X) \Rightarrow q(X)$. The query $Q = \exists X q(X)$? is entailed if existentially closed queries are supported (as there are n atoms of the form $q(a_i)$).
- **Chain Theory** (denoted $chain(n)$) contains the rule $\top \Rightarrow p_0(a)$ and a chain of n defeasible rules of the form $p_{i-1}(X) \Rightarrow p_i(X)$. Evaluating the query $Q = p_n(a)$? would test performance when faced with a long chain of rules.
- **Tree Theory** (denoted $tree(n,k)$) is a k-branching tree of depth n in which every atom occurs once and $p_0(a)$ is its root. The query $Q = p_0(a)$? would test performance w.r.t. a large number of short arguments.
- **Directed Acyclic Graph Theory** (denoted $dag(n,k)$) is a k-branching tree of depth n in which every literal occurs k times. The query $Q = p_0(a)$? would test performance when faced with many arguments for the same atom.

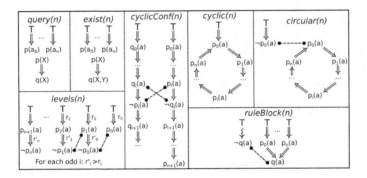

Fig. 2. Representation of some expressiveness theories

The generated knowledge bases have to be adapted to the format of each tool. For example, rules can be transformed into an equivalent set of rules with atomic head, priority relation can be transformed into a number based priority, negation can be represented with negative constraints, etc. We conclude this section by an important remark. Benchmark support for abstract classes of existential rules such as FES, FUS and GBTS is achieved via concrete decidable classes. Not satisfying a concrete class (e.g. transitive rules) implies not satisfying the corresponding abstract class (e.g. FES rules). However, please note that the inverse is not necessarily true. More generally, while negative results (i.e. situations where tools are not able to give the results required by a certain feature) are definitive, positive results on the other hand (i.e. situations where tools do provide the intended results of a feature) *do not prove the feature is fully supported.*

5   Running the Benchmark on Tools

Let us start by presenting the main defeasible reasoning implementations we used in this paper to illustrate how the proposed benchmark can be used for tool profiling (that are, to the best of our knowledge, the only still functioning, publicly available tools for first order defeasible reasoning as of the time of writing of this paper). **ASPIC+** [24] is a framework for specifying systems in structured argumentation used for defeasible reasoning thanks to its grounded semantics (equivalent to defeasible reasoning with ambiguity propagation [15]). We use a prototype implementation available online[4] (denoted here by $ASPIC^*$). Other implementations use a propositional language only. **DEFT**[5] [16] is a first-order defeasible reasoning tool for existential rules that uses the $Datalog^{\pm}$ language. It relies on a dialectical tree mechanism (that can correspond to ambiguity propagation [13]). **DeLP** [13] (Defeasible Logic Programming) is a formalism that relies on dialectical trees to allow for defeasible reasoning with ambiguity

---

[4] http://aspic.cossac.org.
[5] https://github.com/hamhec/DEFT.

propagation. We use the implementation in Tweety1.7 libraries [26] (denoted here by $DeLP^*$). An online tool called DeLP client[6] is also available. **Flora-2** [27, 28] is a rule-based knowledge base system designed for a variety of automated tasks on the Semantic Web, ranging from meta-data management to intelligent agents. It has a commercial version called Ergo with additional functionalities.

Table 1. Execution time in seconds (selected results). 'true' and 'false' indicate query entailment and are used to check support of the feature (the best time is shown in bold)

Theory		$ASPIC^*$	$DeLP^*$	SPINdle	Flora-2	DEFT
$ambiguity(n)$	$n=50$	0.44 (false)	148.17 (false)	**0.11 (false)** | **0.09 (true)**	1.06 (true)	**0.11 (false)**
	$n=1800$	∞	T.O.	∞	17.237 (true)	12.503 (false)
	$n=2000$	∞	T.O.	∞	18.942 (true)	∞
$team(n)$	$n=4$	**0.227 (false)**	301.19 (true)	0.289 (true)	4.358 (true)	**0.287 (true)**
	$n=7$	T.O.	T.O.	**109.46 (true)**	T.O.	201.917(*true*)
$floating(n)$	$n=100$	0.270 (false)	209.45 (false)	**0.332 (false)**	2.143 (false)	1.345 (false)
	$n=5000$	198.861 (false)	T.O.	**150.144 (false)**	T.O.	203.18 (false)
$consistent(n)$	$n=1000$	0.193 (true)	269.984 (false)	**0.703 (true)**	5.292 (true)	**2.969 (false)**
	$n=8000$	8.321 (true)	T.O.	**8.854 (true)**	36.821 (true)	239.504(*false*)
$exist(n)$	$n=100$	0.09 (true)	0.93	284.39 (true)	1.28 (true)	**0.01 (false)**
$transitive(n)$	$n=100$	N.A.	N.A.	N.A.	N.A.	**253.62 (true)**
$chainAtomB(n)$	$n=1$	N.A.	N.A.	N.A.	N.A.	T.O.
$chainFrG(n)$	$n=1$	N.A.	N.A.	N.A.	N.A.	T.O.
$cyclicSupp(n)$	$n=1000$	∞	291.37 (true)	**0.35 (true)**	5.712 (true)	0.44 (true)
	$n=10000$	∞	T.O.	**26.61 (true)**	51.72 (true)	288.71 (true)
$circular(n)$	$n=1000$	∞	284.90 (true)	0.31 (true)	4.38 (true)	**0.04 (true)**
$cyclicConf(n)$	$n=5$	0.627 (true)	55.89 (true)	0.903 (true)	0.922 (true)	**0.106 (true)**
	$n=1000$	T.O.	T.O.	T.O.	T.O.	**79.525 (true)**
$ruleBlock(n)$	$n=500$	19.23 (true)	N.A.	**1.41 (true)**	12.99 (true)	N.A.
$levels(n)$	$n=100$	**0.20 (true)**	4.61 (true)	0.33 (true)	5.17 (true)	0.81 (true)
$query(n)$	$n=100$	N.A.	N.A.	N.A.	**1.25 (true)**	N.A.
$chain(n)$	$n=600$	108.05 (true)	99.46 (true)	**0.24 (true)**	2.35 (true)	0.33 (true)
	$n=10000$	∞	T.O.	**16.04 (true)**	45.44 (true)	288.71 (true)
$tree(n,5)$	$n=2$	0.04 (true)	193.64 (true)	**0.03 (true)**	0.83 (true)	0.022 (true)
	$n=7$	∞	T.O.	∞	211.94 (true)	**182.83 (true)**
$dag(n,10)$	$n=1$	∞	239.75 (true)	**7.51 (true)**	18.41 (true)	19.53 (true)
	$n=10$	∞	T.O.	**60.82 (true)**	113.53 (true)	73.05 (true)

A key notion to keep in mind is that we are not comparing the formalisms themselves, we are comparing the tools based on those formalisms. A formalism might allow for more than what the tool presents. That is one of the reasons that justify having a dedicated benchmark to better analyze and understand the implementation of the tools. Furthermore, some of the tools considered are prototypes, therefore they might not have been developed with performance in mind. All experiments presented in this section were performed on an Intel core i7

---

[6] http://lidia.cs.uns.edu.ar/delp_client.

Table 2. Classification results (✓indicates the tool supports the feature).

Feature		$ASPIC^*$	$DeLP^*$	SPINdle	Flora-2	DEFT
Ambiguity	Prop.	✓	✓	✓	-	✓
	Block.	-	-	✓	✓	-
Team Defeat	TD	-	✓	✓	✓	✓
	noTD	✓	-	-	-	-
Floating	FC	-	-	-	-	-
Conclusions	noFC	✓	✓	✓	✓	✓
Consistent	Direct	-	✓	-	-	✓
Derivation	Indirect	✓	-	✓	✓	-
Existential Rules	S-FES	-	-	-	-	✓
	FUS	-	-	-	-	-
	GBTS	-	-	-	-	-
Cycles	Support	-	✓	✓	✓	✓
	Attack	✓	✓	✓	✓	✓
Rule Block		✓	-	✓	✓	-
Preference	$\succ$	-	✓	✓	✓	✓
	$\mathbb{R}$	✓	-	-	-	-
Non-gound Queries		-	-	-	✓	-

2.60 GHz quad core Linux machine with 8 GB of RAM and a Java heap of 2 GB. To avoid random performance fluctuations each test is performed five times for each tool and we record the average *in-CPU* execution time. The experiments are reproducible[7].

Tools Benchmark Results. Table 1 presents the time (in CPU seconds) required for each tool to answer the query according to the size and type of the query (the execution time includes the time needed for parsing the knowledge base and answering the query). ∞ denotes a stack overflow, *T.O.* denotes a timeout (set to 5 minutes), and *N.A.* indicates that a test theory is not applicable for that tool.

Results Discussion. The main objective of the proposed benchmark is to help with the tools profiling according to the defeasible knowledge base and reasoning they can handle. To this end, from the results in Table 1, we can draw the following conclusions (summarised in Table 2):

---

[7] https://github.com/anoConf/Benchmark.

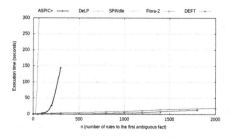
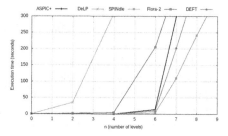

Fig. 3. Response time for $ambiguity(n)$ **Fig. 4.** Response time for $team(n)$

– **Semantics:** The underlying theoretical and practical choices affect the semantics the tools can handle: *Ambiguity Handling: ASPIC**, DEFT and *DeLP**
cannot express ambiguity blocking and correspond to ambiguity propagation
due to the underlying formalisms. Flora corresponds only to ambiguity blocking while SPINdle is the only tool that can handle both blocking and propagating. Performance wise (Fig. 3), $DeLP^*$ has a timeout at $n = 10$, $ASPIC^*$
stops at $n = 300$, SPINdle at $n = 1400$, and DEFT $n = 1800$ due to stack
overflow. Flora-2, DEFT, and SPINdle can scale to longer chain of rules for
ambiguous facts with significantly low response time. *Team Defeat:* Most tools
allow only for team defeat except $ASPIC^*$ that does not allow for it. While
Defeasible Logics can represent the presence and absence of team defeat, SPIN-
dle and Flora-2 only implement the presence of team defeat. SPINdle has the
best performance, followed by DEFT, $ASPIC^*$, Flora-2, then $DeLP^*$ (Fig. 4).
Floating Conclusions: None of the considered tools support floating conclusions
due to their underlying formalisms (Fig. 5). *Handling Strict Rules:* DEFT and
$DeLP^*$ use indirectly consistent derivations while $ASPIC^*$, Flora and SPINdle
do not. This directly impacts performance results (as seen in Fig. 6).

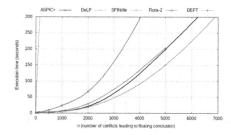
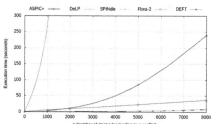

Fig. 5. Response time for $floating(n)$ **Fig. 6.** Response time for $consistent(n)$

- **Expressiveness:** The choice of the inference mechanism affects the expressiveness the tool can handle: *Existential rules:* $ASPIC^*$, $DeLP^*$, SPINdle, and Flora were not designed to account for existential rules. As supported by the results of the Existential theory, FES, FUS and GBTS are not applicable in their context. DEFT can handle existential rules in general, and SkolemFES rules in particular (due to its use of forward chaining), however it loops infinitely in FUS and GBTS fragments. *Cycles:* DEFT, $DeLP^*$, and Flora can handle cyclic GRDs and circular reasoning (*support cycle*) contrary to ASPIC+. This is due to the fact that $ASPIC^*$ relies on SLD resolution (which loops infinitely in presence of cycles in the GRD), while DEFT uses a chase mechanism (which is guaranteed to stop when no existential rule is used). $DeLP^*$, SPINdle and Flora rely on resolution with a grounding phase and cycle checks (Fig. 7). All considered tools can handle cyclic conflicts (*attack cycles*). However, the attack cycle checks are not needed for DEFT since arguments are evaluated after construction, that is why it outperforms other tools (e.g. $n = 1000$ in Fig. 8). *Rule Application Block:* $ASPIC^*$ uses negated labels of rules to block their application, SPINdle uses defeater rules, while Flora uses the predicate '$\backslash cancel(label)$'. DEFT and $DeLP^*$ have no support for such feature. As seen in Table 1, SPINdle has the best performance followed by Flora-2 and $ASPIC^*$. *Preference between rules:* $ASPIC^*$ uses decimal values to express priority on rules (this priority relation is total and might lead to unwanted behavior as it is hard to express incomparability between rules). $DeLP^*$, SPINdle, Flora, and DEFT use a partial priority relation based on labeled rules. *Non-ground queries:* Only Flora supports non ground queries.
- **Performance:** In case of a tie in expressiveness or semantics, one can use performance to make an informed choice on the tool to be used. From Table 1 we can see that each tool makes trade-offs between performance and expressiveness. In general, SPINdle has the best performance compared to other tools, followed by DEFT and Flora-2. $ASPIC^*$ is as fast as SPINdle on small knowledge bases but it does not scale well. DEFT has the best performance when there are attack cycles. These differences in performance are due to three main factors. First, *grounding phase is costly*. DEFT, for instance, achieves its performance results thanks to its forward chaining algorithms that ground rules on the fly, contrary to the other tools. Second, *handling cycles is costly*. $ASPIC^*$ is faster than $DeLP^*$ for example because the latter relies on cycle checks to avoid infinite loops. DEFT does not need to check loops contrary to all other tools. Third, *expressiveness is costly*, DEFT and $DeLP^*$ has to perform consistency checks using strict rule. Flora also provides very powerful syntactic features (dynamic rule labels, higher order syntax, etc.) which might affect its performance.

Tool Profiling. let us show how a data engineer could make practical use of our benchmark in order to chose the appropriate defeasible reasoning tool.

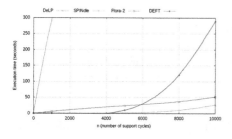
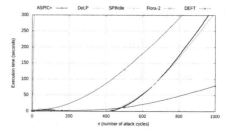

Fig. 7. Response time for $cyclicSupp(n)$ **Fig. 8.** Response time for $cyclicConf(n)$

Example 9 *Consider the following decision scenario of an emergency response team that wants to determine if a person victim of an accident is an organ donor. A person being hurt in an accident is considered a victim. Legally any victim is assumed not to be an organ donor. A person that gives her consent is considered an organ donor. A person in a critical condition generally cannot give her consent. The legal tutor of a person can give his consent for her being an organ donor. The following KB describes this use case. $\mathcal{K} = (\mathcal{F}, \mathcal{R}, \emptyset)$ where:*

- *$\mathcal{F} = \{\top \Rightarrow hurt(john)\}$.*
- *$\mathcal{R} = \{r_1 : \forall X\ hurt(X) \Rightarrow victim(X), r_2 : \forall X, victim(X) \Rightarrow \neg OrganDonor(X), r_3 : \forall X, consentFor(X, X) \Rightarrow organDonor(X), r_4 : \forall X, critical(X) \Rightarrow \neg ConsentFor(X, X)\ r_5 : \forall X, Y, legalTutor(X, Y) \wedge consentFor(X, Y) \Rightarrow organDonor(Y), \}$.*

*This knowledge base does not use existential rules and is acyclic. Therefore, given the results of the benchmark, all considered tools can be applied. If the data engineer wants to use ambiguity blocking with team defeat then she can either use SPINdle or Flora-2 (SPINdle is in this case recommended given the performance results), if she does not want to allow for team defeat then **no tool can be used**. If on the other hand the data engineer wants to use ambiguity propagation then she can either use DeLP* or DEFT if she needs team defeat (DEFT is in this case recommended given the performance results) or ASPIC* if she does not. Let us add the rule that a victim is probably someone who is hurt ($\forall X, victim(X) \Rightarrow hurt(X)$). In this case the knowledge base becomes cyclic. Therefore ASPIC* cannot be used (cf. Table 2). Let us now add a new existential rule stating that if someone is an organ donor then somebody gave his consent (the person or her tutor i.e. $\forall X\ organDonor(X) \rightarrow \exists Y\ consentFor(Y, X)$). In this case, according to the Table 2 results, only DEFT can be used.*

6   Discussion

We proposed an informative benchmark allowing to shed light on the capabilities of existing tools for defeasible reasoning. This paper presents an exhaustive list of operational first order defeasible reasoning tools; other implementations such as DR-Device [7] and DR-Prolog [8] are not maintained and propositional defeasible reasoning tools of [10] are not available. Our study provides insights about current gaps in the state of the art. For instance, we can observe in Table 2 that some features such as floating conclusions are not supported by any tool, or that support for some desirable combinations of features (such as ambiguity propagating with team defeat) is lacking.

The list of features does not consider (1) expressing conflicting literals using negative constraint, (2) implicit priority relations, and (3) negation-as-failure. The former is due to the fact that conflicts can easily be translated between the two representations [1], e.g. $\neg p(\boldsymbol{X})$ is transformed into $np(\boldsymbol{X})$ and the negative constraint $p(\boldsymbol{X}) \wedge np(\boldsymbol{X}) \rightarrow \bot$ is added to the rules). Regarding implicit priorities, they sometimes can be represented using explicit ones [23]. Negation-as-failure can be treated by theory rewriting [2].

References

1. Antoniou, G.: Defeasible reasoning: a discussion of some intuitions. Int. J. Intell. Syst. **21**(6), 545–558 (2006)
2. Antoniou, G., Billington, D., Governatori, G., Maher, M.J.: Representation results for defeasible logic. ACM Trans. Comput. Logic (TOCL) **2**(2), 255–287 (2001)
3. Antoniou, G., Billington, D., Maher, M.J.: On the analysis of regulations using defeasible rules. In: Proceedings of the 32nd Annual Hawaii International Conference on Systems Sciences, HICSS-32, pp. 7–23. IEEE (1999)
4. Apt, K.R., Van Emden, M.H.: Contributions to the theory of logic programming. J. ACM (JACM) **29**(3), 841–862 (1982)
5. Baget, J.-F., Garreau, F., Mugnier, M.-L., Rocher, S.: Extending acyclicity notions for existential rules. In: ECAI, pp. 39–44 (2014)
6. Baget, J.-F., Leclère, M., Mugnier, M.-L., Salvat, E.: On rules with existential variables: walking the decidability line. Artif. Intell. **175**(9–10), 1620–1654 (2011)
7. Bassiliades, N., Antoniou, G., Vlahavas, I.: A defeasible logic reasoner for the semantic web. Int. J. Semant. Web Inf. Syst. (IJSWIS) **2**(1), 1–41 (2006)
8. Bikakis, A., Antoniou, G.: DR-Prolog: a system for reasoning with rules and ontologies on the semantic web. In: AAAI, vol. 5, pp. 1594–1595 (2005)
9. Billington, D.: Defeasible logic is stable. J. Logic Comput. **3**(4), 379–400 (1993)
10. Bryant, D., Krause, P.: A review of current defeasible reasoning implementations. Knowl. Eng. Rev. **23**(03), 227–260 (2008)
11. Cali, A., Gottlob, G., Pieris, A.: Advanced processing for ontological queries. Proce. VLDB Endowment **3**(1–2), 554–565 (2010)
12. Dung, P.M.: On the acceptability of arguments and its fundamental role in non-monotonic reasoning, logic programming and n-person games. Artif. Intell. **77**(2), 321–357 (1995)
13. García, A.J., Simari, G.R.: Defeasible logic programming: an argumentative approach. Theor. Pract. Logic programm. **4**(1 + 2), 95–138 (2004)

14. Garcia, D.R., Garcia, A.J., Simari, G.R.: Planning and defeasible reasoning. In: Proceedings of the 6th International Joint Conference on Autonomous Agents and Multiagent Systems, pp. 856–858. ACM (2007)
15. Governatori, G., Maher, M.J., Antoniou, G., Billington, D.: Argumentation semantics for defeasible logic. J. Logic Comput. **14**(5), 675–702 (2004)
16. Hecham, A., Croitoru, M., Bisquert, P.: Argumentation-based defeasible reasoning for existential rules. In: Proceedings of the 16th Conference on Autonomous Agents and MultiAgent Systems, pp. 1568–1569 (2017)
17. Horty, J.F., Touretzky, D.S., Thomason, R.H.: A clash of intuitions: the current state of nonmonotonic multiple inheritance systems. In: Proceedings of the Tenth International Joint Conference on Artificial Intelligence, pp. 476–482 (1987)
18. Lenzerini, M.: Data integration: a theoretical perspective. In: Proceedings of the Twenty-First ACM SIGMOD-SIGACT-SIGART Symposium on Principles of Database Systems, pp. 233–246. ACM (2002)
19. Maher, M.J., Rock, A., Antoniou, G., Billington, D., Miller, T.: Efficient defeasible reasoning systems. Int. J. Artif. Intell. Tools **10**(04), 483–501 (2001)
20. Makinson, D., Schlechta, K.: Floating conclusions and zombie paths: two deep difficulties in the "directly skeptical" approach to defeasible inheritance nets. Artif. Intell. **48**(2), 199–209 (1991)
21. Morgenstern, L.: Artificial intelligence inheritance comes of age: applying non-monotonic techniques to problems in industry. Artif. Intell. **103**, 237–271 (1998)
22. Nute, D.: Defeasible reasoning: a philosophical analysis in prolog. In: Fetzer, J.H. (ed.) Aspects of Artificial Intelligence. Studies in Cognitive Systems, vol. 1, pp. 251–288. Springer, Dordrecht (1988). https://doi.org/10.1007/978-94-009-2699-8_9
23. Prakken, H.: Intuitions and the modelling of defeasible reasoning: some case studies. In: Ninth International Workshop on Nonmonotonic Reasoning, pp. 91–99. Toulouse (2002)
24. Prakken, H.: An abstract framework for argumentation with structured arguments. Argument Comput. **1**(2), 93–124 (2010)
25. Stein, L.A.: Resolving ambiguity in nonmonotonic inheritance hierarchies. Artif. Intell. **55**(2–3), 259–310 (1992)
26. Thimm, M.: Tweety - a comprehensive collection of java libraries for logical aspects of artificial intelligence and knowledge representation. In: Proceedings of the 14th International Conference on Principles of Knowledge Representation and Reasoning (KR 2014) (2014)
27. Wan, H., Kifer, M., Grosof, B.N.: Defeasibility in answer set programs with defaults and argumentation rules. Semant. Web **6**(1), 81–98 (2015)
28. Yang, G., Kifer, M., Zhao, C.: $\mathscr{F}$LORA-2: a rule-based knowledge representation and inference infrastructure for the semantic web. In: Meersman, R., Tari, Z., Schmidt, D.C. (eds.) OTM 2003. LNCS, vol. 2888, pp. 671–688. Springer, Heidelberg (2003). https://doi.org/10.1007/978-3-540-39964-3_43

Restricted Chase Termination: A Hierarchical Approach and Experimentation

Arash Karimi[1]($\boxtimes$), Heng Zhang[2], and Jia-Huai You[1]

[1] Department of Computing Science, University of Alberta, Edmonton, Canada
akarimi@ualberta.ca

[2] School of Software Engineering, Tianjin University, Tianjin, China

Abstract. The chase procedure for existential rules is an indispensable tool for several database applications, where its termination guarantees decidability of these tasks. Most previous studies have focused on the Skolem chase variant and its termination analysis. It is known that the restricted chase variant is more powerful in termination analysis provided a database is given. But all-instance termination presents a challenge since the critical database and similar techniques do not work. We develop a novel technique to characterize the activeness of all possible cycles of a certain length for restricted chase, which leads to the formulation of a parameterized class of finite restricted chase, called $k\text{-safe}(\Phi)$. This approach is applicable to any class of finite Skolem chase identified with a condition of acyclicity. More generally, we show that the approach can be applied to the entire hierarchy of *bounded rule sets* previously only defined for Skolem chase. Experiments on a collection of ontologies from the web show the applicability of the proposed methods on real-world ontologies.

1 Introduction

The advent of emerging applications of knowledge representation and ontological reasoning have been the motivation of recent studies on existential rule languages, known as *tuple-generating dependencies* (*TGDs* [6], also called *existential rules*) or Datalog$^\pm$ [7], which have been considered a powerful modeling language for applications in data exchange, data integration, ontological querying, and so on. A major advantage of this approach is that the formal semantics based on first-order logic facilitates reasoning in an application, where answering conjunctive queries over a database extended with a set of existential rules is a primary task, but unfortunately an undecidable one in general [5]. The *chase procedure* is a bottom-up algorithm that extends a given database by applying specified rules. If such a procedure terminates, given an input database I, a finite rule set R and a conjunctive query, we can answer the query against R and I by deciding whether the result of chase based on R and I entails the query.

© Springer Nature Switzerland AG 2018
C. Benzmüller et al. (Eds.): RuleML+RR 2018, LNCS 11092, pp. 98–114, 2018.
https://doi.org/10.1007/978-3-319-99906-7_7

Four variants of chase procedure have been considered in the literature, which are called *oblivious, semi-oblivious (Skolem), restricted* (aka *standard*) and *core* chase. With oblivious chase being a weaker version of Skolem chase and core chase as a parallel, wrapping procedure of the restricted chase, the main interests have been on Skolem [15] and restricted chase [11]. In particular, given a rule set and a database, we know that whenever Skolem chase terminates so does the restricted chase, but the reverse does not hold in general. Thus, restricted chase is more powerful in termination analysis.

In spite of existence of many notions of acyclicity in the literature (cf. [10] for a survey), there are natural examples from the real world ontologies that are non-terminating under Skolem chase but terminating under restricted chase. However, finding a suitable characterization to assure restricted chase termination is a challenging task, and in the last decade, to the best of our knowledge only a few conditions have been discovered. In [8], the classes of *restricted joint acyclicity (RJA), restricted model-faithful acyclicty (RMFA)* and *restricted model-summarizing acyclicty (RMSA)* of finite all-instance, all-path restricted chase are introduced which generalize the classes of JA [14], MFA and MSA [10], respectively. Intuitively, their classes introduce a *blocking criterion* to check if the head of each rule is already entailed by the derivations when constructing the arena for checking the corresponding acyclicity conditions for JA, MFA, and MSA, respectively. Here, we extend their work in two different ways. First, we provide a highly general theoretical framework to identify strict super classes of all existing classes of finite Skolem chase that we are aware of, and second, we show a general critical database technique, which works uniformly for all bounded finite chase classes.

The main contributions of this paper are as follows:

1. We introduce a novel characterization of derivations under restricted chase and show that while the traditional critical database technique [15] does not work for restricted chase, a kind of "critical databases" exist by which the non-termination behavior of a derivation sequence can be captured. This is shown in Theorem 1.
2. We define a hierarchy of decidable classes of finite restricted chase, called k-safe(Φ), which, when given a definition of acyclicity, is instantiated to a concrete class of finite chase. This is achieved by Theorem 2 based on which various acyclicity conditions under Skolem chase can be generalized to introduce classes of finite chase beyond finite Skolem chase.
3. We show that the entire hierarchy of δ-bounded rule sets under Skolem chase [17] can be generalized by introducing δ-bounded sets under restricted chase, and as shown in Theorem 6, this extension does not increase the reasoning complexity under Skolem chase.
4. Our experimental results on selected ontologies from the web show practical applications of our approach to real-world ontologies. In particular, in contrast with the current main focus of the field on acyclicity conditions for termination analysis, our experiments show that many ontologies in the real-world involve cycles of various kinds but indeed fall into finite chase.

Proofs are removed from this paper due to space restriction and can be found in the full version of this paper [13].

2   Preliminaries

We assume the following pairwise disjoint sets of symbols: C a countably infinite set of constants, N a countably infinite set of (labeled) nulls, and V a countably infinite set of variables. A *schema* is a finite set $\mathcal{R}$ of relation (or predicate) symbols, where each $Q \in \mathcal{R}$ is assigned a positive integer as its arity which is denoted by $arity(Q)$. *Terms* are elements in $C \cup N \cup V$. *Ground terms* are terms involving no variables. An atom is an expression of the form $Q(\mathbf{t})$, where $\mathbf{t} \in (C \cup V \cup N)^{arity(Q)}$ and Q is a predicate symbol from $\mathcal{R}$. A *general instance* (or simply an *instance*) I is a set of atoms over the schema $\mathcal{R}$; $term(I)$ denotes the set of terms occurring in I. A *database* is a finite instance I where terms are constants from C. Given two instances I and J (over the same schema), a *homomorphism* $h : I \mapsto J$ is a mapping on terms which is identity on constants and for every atom $Q(\mathbf{t})$ of I we have that $Q(h(\mathbf{t}))$ (which we may write alternatively by $h(Q(\mathbf{t}))$) is an atom of J.

A tuple-generating dependency (also called a rule) is a first-order sentence r of the form: $\phi(\mathbf{x}, \mathbf{y}) \rightarrow \exists \mathbf{z} \, \psi(\mathbf{x}, \mathbf{z})$, where $\mathbf{x}$ and $\mathbf{y}$ are sets of universally quantified variables (with the quantifier omitted) and ϕ and ψ are conjunctions of atoms constructed from relation symbols from $\mathcal{R}$, constants from C, and variables from $\mathbf{x} \cup \mathbf{y}$ and $\mathbf{x} \cup \mathbf{z}$, respectively. The formula ϕ (resp. ψ) is called the *body* of r, denoted $body(r)$ (resp. the *head* of r, denoted $head(r)$).

Given a rule r, a *Skolem function* f_z^r is introduced for each variable $z \in \mathbf{z}$ where $arity(f_z^r) = |\mathbf{x}|$. Terms constructed from Skolem functions and constants are called *Skolem terms*. In this paper, we will regard Skolem terms as a special class of labeled nulls. *Ground terms* in this context are constants from C or Skolem terms, and atoms in a general instance may contain Skolem terms as well. The *functional transformation* of r, denoted $sk(r)$, is the formula obtained from r by replacing each occurrence of $z_i \in \mathbf{z}$ with $f_{z_i}^r(\mathbf{x})$. The *Skolemized version* of a rule set R, denoted $sk(R)$, is the union of $sk(r)$ for each rule $r \in R$. In this paper, a rule set is a finite set of rules.

Given a rule $r = \phi(\mathbf{x}, \mathbf{y}) \rightarrow \exists \mathbf{z} \, \psi(\mathbf{x}, \mathbf{z})$, we use $var_u(r)$, $var_{fr}(r)$, $var_{ex}(r)$, and $var(r)$, respectively, to refer to the set of *universal* ($\mathbf{x} \cup \mathbf{y}$), *frontier* ($\mathbf{x}$), *existential* ($\mathbf{z}$), and *all* variables appearing in r. An *extension* h' of a homomorphism h, denoted $h' \supseteq h$, assigns, in addition to mapping h, ground terms to existential variables. A *position* is an expression of the form $P[i]$, where P is an n-ary predicate and i ($1 \leq i \leq n$) is an integer. We are interested only in positions associated with frontier variables - for each $x \in var_{fr}(r)$, $pos_B(x)$ (resp. $pos_H(x)$) denotes the set of positions of $body(r)$ (resp. $head(r)$) in which x occurs.

We further define: a *path* $(r_1, r_2, \dots)$ (based on R) is a nonempty (finite or infinite) sequence of rules from R; a *cycle* $(r_1, \dots, r_n)$ ($n \geq 2$) is a finite path whose first and last elements coincide (i.e., $r_1 = r_n$); a *k-cycle* ($k \geq 1$) is a cycle in which at least one rule has $k+1$ occurrences and all other rules have $k+1$ or less occurrences. Given a path π, $\mathsf{Rule}(\pi)$ denotes the set of distinct rules in π.

We assume all rules are *standardized apart* so that no variables are shared by more than one rule. For a set or a sequence W, the cardinality $|W|$ is defined as usual. Given a rule set R, with $||R||$, we denote the number of symbols occurring in R.

2.1 Skolem and Restricted Chase Variants

Chase is a construction that accepts as input a database I and a rule set R and adds atoms to I. In this paper, our main focus is on the Skolem and restricted chase variants.

We first define triggers, active triggers and their applications. In this paper, when we define a homomorphism $h : I \mapsto J$, if I and J are clear from the context, we may just define such a homomorphism as a mapping from variables to terms.

Definition 1. Let R be a rule set, I an instance, and $r \in R$. A pair (r, h) is called *a trigger for R on I* (or simply *a trigger on I*) if h is a homomorphism such that $h(body(r)) \subseteq I$. If in addition there is no extension $h' \supseteq h$, where $h' : var(r) \mapsto term(I)$, such that $h'(head(r)) \subseteq I$, then (r, h) is called *an active trigger on I*.

An *application* of a trigger or an active trigger (r, h) on I returns $I' = I \cup h(sk(head(r)))$. We write a trigger application by $I\langle r, h\rangle I'$.

Intuitively, a trigger (r, h) is active if given h, the implication in r cannot be satisfied by any extension $h' \supseteq h$ that maps existentially quantified variables to terms in I. In other words, to satisfy the implication, the application of an active trigger must derive at least one new instance of head atoms.

Definition 2. Given a database I and a rule set R, we define Skolem chase based on a breadth-first fixpoint construction as follows: we let $\mathsf{chase}^0_{sk}(I, R) = I$ and, for all $i > 0$, let $\mathsf{chase}^i_{sk}(I, R)$ be the union of $\mathsf{chase}^{i-1}_{sk}(I, R)$ and $h(head(sk(r)))$ for all rules $r \in R$ and all homomorphisms h such that (r, h) is a trigger on $\mathsf{chase}^{i-1}_{sk}(I, R)$. Then, we let $\mathsf{chase}_{sk}(I, R)$ be the union of $\mathsf{chase}^i_{sk}(I, R)$, for all $i \geq 0$.   .

On the other hand, restricted chase is known to be order sensitive.

Definition 3. Let R be a rule set and I_0 a database.

- A finite sequence, $I_0, I_1, \ldots, I_n$, is called *a terminating (or finite) restricted chase sequence (based on R)*, if for each $0 \leq i < n$, there exists an active trigger (r, h) on I_i such that $I_i\langle r, h\rangle I_{i+1}$ and there exists no active trigger on I_n. The result of the chase is I_n.
- An infinite sequence, $I_0, I_1, \ldots$, is called *a non-terminating (or infinite) restricted chase sequence (based on R)* if

(i) for each $i \geq 0$, there exists an active trigger (r, h) on I_i such that $I_i \langle r, h \rangle I_{i+1}$, and

(ii) it satisfies the *fairness condition*: for all $i \geq 1$ and for all active triggers (r, h) on I_{i-1}, where $r \in R$, there exists $j \geq i$ such that either $I_{j-1} \langle r, h \rangle I_j$ or the trigger (r, h) is not active on I_{j-1}. The result of the chase is $\bigcup_{i \geq 0} I_i$.

We say that a rule set R *has finite restricted chase*, or *is terminating under restricted chase*, if there are only finite restricted chase sequences based on R, for all databases.

The classes of rule sets whose chase terminates on all paths (all possible derivation sequences of chase steps) independent of the given databases (thus all instances) is denoted by $CT_{\forall\forall}^{\triangle}$, where $\triangle \in \{sk, res, core\}$ (sk for Skolem chase; res for restricted chase and $core$ for core chase). Note that $CT_{\forall\forall}^{core}$ is also known as *finite expansion sets* or *fes* [4].

A conjunctive query (CQ) Q is a formula of the form $Q(\mathbf{x}) := \exists \mathbf{y} \, \Phi(\mathbf{x}, \mathbf{y})$, where $\mathbf{x}$ and $\mathbf{y}$ are tuples of variables; $\Phi(\mathbf{x}, \mathbf{y})$ is a conjunction of atoms with variables in $\mathbf{x} \cup \mathbf{y}$. A boolean conjunctive query (BCQ) is a CQ of the form $Q()$. It is well-known that, for all BCQs q and for all database I, $I \cup R \models q$ (under the semantics of first-order logic) iff $\text{chase}_{sk}(I, R) \models q$ and iff $\bigcup_{\forall P, H} \text{chase\_p}_{res}(I, P, H) \models q$ [11].

Finally, to illustrate the practical relevance of restricted chase, let us consider modeling a secure communication protocol where two different signal types can be transmitted: *type A* for inter-zone communication and *type B* for intra-zone communication. Let us consider a scenario where a transmitter from one zone requests to establish a secure communication with a receiver from another zone in this network. There are an unknown number of *trusted servers*. Before a successful communication between two users can occur, following a handshake protocol, the transmitter must send a type A signal to a trusted server in the same zone and receive an acknowledgment back. Then, that trusted server sends a type B signal to a trusted server in the receiver zone.

Below, we use existential rules to model the required communication (the modeling here does not include the actual process of transmitting signals).

Example 1. Consider the rule set R_1 below, where $S(x, y)$ denotes a request to send a type A signal from x to y and $D(x, y)$ a request to send a type B signal from x to y.

$$D(x, y) \rightarrow \exists u \, S(x, u), S(u, x). \quad D(x, y), S(x, z), S(z, x) \rightarrow \exists v \, D(z, v).$$

Note that u is assumed to be a trusted server in the zone where x is located; Similarly for v and y. With s_1 and s_2 as Skolem functions, we have $sk(R_1)$:

$$r_1 : D(x, y) \rightarrow S(x, s_1(x)), S(s_1(x), x). \quad r_2 : D(x, y), S(x, z), S(z, x) \rightarrow D(z, s_2(z)).$$

With database $I_0 = \{D(t, r)\}$, after applying r_1 and r_2, we get $I_0 \cup \{S(t, s_1(t)), S(s_1(t), t), D(s_1(t), s_2(s_1(t)))\}$. Clearly, there are homomorphisms (h_1, h_2) such that the path (r_1, r_2) leads to a restricted chase sequence. But this is not the case for the path (r_1, r_2, r_1), since the trigger for applying the last rule on the path is not active - the head can be satisfied by already derived atoms $S(s_1(t), t)$ and $S(t, s_1(t))$.

Now let us consider a related rule set $R_2 = \{r_1, r_2\}$. The difference is that we use a predicate $B(a)$ to specify that a is a trusted server.

$$r_1 : D(x, y) \rightarrow \exists u\, B(u), S(x, u), S(u, x)$$
$$r_2 : D(x, y), S(x, z), S(z, x), B(z) \rightarrow \exists v\, B(v), D(z, v)$$

With the same input database I_0, it can be verified that any non-empty prefix of $\sigma = (r_1, r_2, r_1, r_2, r_1)$ leads to a restricted chase sequence except σ itself. Note that σ is a 2-cycle.

3   Previous Development and Related Work

Since our technical development is often related to, or compared with, the state-of-the-art, let us introduce some key finite classes of chase here.

Weakly-acyclic (WA) [11], roughly speaking, tracks the propagation of terms in different positions. A rule set is WA if there is no position in which Skolem terms including Skolem functions can be propagated cyclically, possibly through other positions.

Joint-acyclic (JA) [14] generalizes WA as follows. Let R be a rule set. For each variable $y \in var_{ex}(R)$, let $Move(y)$ be the smallest set of positions such that (i) $pos_H(y) \subseteq Move(y)$ and (ii) for each rule $r \in R$ that $var_{ex}(r) \neq \emptyset$ and for all variables $x \in var_u(r)$, if $pos_B(x) \subseteq Move(y)$, then $pos_H(x) \subseteq Move(y)$. Then the *JA dependency graph* $JA(R)$ of R is defined as: the set of vertices of $JA(R)$ is $var_{ex}(R)$ and there is an edge from y_1 to y_2 whenever the rule that contains y_2 also contains a variable $x \in var_u(R)$ such that $pos_H(x) \neq \emptyset$ and $pos_B(x) \subseteq Move(y_1)$. $R \in JA$ if $JA(R)$ does not have a cycle.

A rule set R belongs to the *acyclic graph of rule dependencies* (aGRD) class of acyclic rules if there is no cyclic dependency relation between any two (not necessarily different) rules of R, possibly through other dependent rules of R.

Model-faithful acyclic (MFA) [10] is a semantic acyclicity class of Skolem chase which generalizes all the Skolem acyclicity classes mentioned above. A rule set R is MFA if in the Skolem chase of R w.r.t. the critical database of R, there is no cyclic Skolem term (a term with at least two occurrences of some Skolem function). Also, *restricted model-faithful acyclicity (RMFA)* [8] generalizes MFA as follows. Let R be a non-disjunctive rule set. For each rule $r \in R$ and each homomorphism h such that h is a homomorphism on $body(r)$, $C_{h,r}$ is defined as the union of the $h(body(r))$, where each occurrence of a constant renamed so that no constant occurs more than once, and the set of facts F_t for each Skolem term t in $h(body(r))$, where F_t is the set of ground facts involved in the derivation of facts containing t. Let RMFA(R) be the least set of facts such that it contains the critical database of R and let $r \in R$ be a rule and h a homomorphism such that $body(r) \subseteq$ RMFA(R). Let $v \in var_{ex}(r)$ be some existential variable of r. If $\exists v.h(head(r))$ is not logically entailed by the exhaustive application of non-generating rules (the rules with no existential variables in the head) on the set of atoms $C_{h,r}$, then $h(sk(head(r))) \subseteq \mathrm{RMFA}(R)$. We define $R \in \mathrm{RMFA}$ if $\mathrm{RMFA}(R)$ contains no cyclic Skolem terms.

4   Finite Restricted Chase by Activeness

A primary tool for termination analysis of Skolem chase is the technique of critical database [15]. Recall that a critical database is one that contains a ground atom for each relation symbol filled with exactly one fresh constant. The critical database can be used to faithfully simulate the termination behavior of Skolem chase - a rule set is all-instance terminating if and only if it is terminating with the critical database. However, this technique does not apply to restricted chase.

Example 2. With $R = \{E(x_1, x_2) \rightarrow \exists z E(x_2, z)\}$ and the critical database $I^c = \{E(*, *)\}$, where $*$ is a fresh constant, the Skolem chase does not terminate w.r.t. I^c, which is a faithful simulation of the termination behavior of R under Skolem chase. But the restricted chase of R and I^c terminates in zero step, as no active triggers exist. However, the restricted chase of R and database $\{E(a, b)\}$ does not terminate.

Given a path, our goal is to simulate a sequence of restricted chase steps with an arbitrary database by a sequence of restricted chase steps with a fixed database. By running this simulation with a fixed database for pre-specified paths, we will be able to use its termination to conclude the termination of restricted chase for all databases.

Note that, since in general we can only expect sufficient conditions for termination, such a simulation should at least capture all infinite derivations by a rule set with an arbitrary database.[1] On the other hand, we only need to consider the type of paths that potentially lead to cyclic applications of chase.

Example 3. Consider the singleton rule set R with rule $r : T(x, y), P(x, y) \rightarrow \exists z T(y, z)$. With $I_0 = \{T(a, b), P(a, b)\}$, we have: $\mathrm{chase}_{sk}(I_0, R) = I_0 \cup \{T(b, f(b))\}$, where f is a Skolem function. After one application of r, no more triggers exist and thus the Skolem chase of R and I_0 terminates (so does the restricted chase of R and I_0).

Note that r in Example 3 depends on itself based on the classic notion of unification. With the aim of ruling out similar false dependencies, we consider a dependency relation under which the cycle (r, r) in the above example is not identified as a dangerous cycle. Towards this goal, we adopt the notion of rule dependencies as introduced in [1], which is based on *piece unification*.

---

[1] By the coRE-completeness upper bound established by Grahne [12], there does not exist a faithful simulation of the termination behavior under restricted chase by using a fixed database.

Definition 4. (Piece unification [3]) Given a pair of rules (r_1, r_2), a *piece unifier* of $body(r_2)$ and $head(r_1)$ is a unifying substitution θ of $var(B) \cup var(H)$ where $B \subseteq body(r_2)$ and $H \subseteq head(r_1)$ which satisfies the following conditions: (a) $\theta(B) = \theta(H)$, and (b) variables in $var_{ex}(H)$ are unified only with those occurring in B but not in $body(r_2) \setminus B$. We call each piece unifier defined by some pair of (B, H), (B, H)-*induced piece unifier* of $body(r_2)$ and $head(r_1)$.

Condition (a) gives a sufficient condition for rule dependency, but it may be an overestimate, which is constrained by condition (b). Note that in Example 3, condition (a) holds for $B = \{T(x, y)\}$ and $H = \{T(y, z)\}$ where $\theta = \{x/y, y/z\}$,[2] and condition (b) does not, since $var_{ex}(H) = \{z\}$ and z is unified with y which occurs in both B and $body(r) \setminus B = \{P(x, y)\}$. Therefore, no piece unifier of $body(r)$ and $head(r)$ exists.

Piece unification is known to provide a tight condition on rule dependencies in that for any two rules r and r', if $body(r)$ and $head(r')$ are not piece unifiable, then no trigger (r, h) exists that relies on some atom derived from $head(r')$.

Below, given a substitution θ, $dom(\theta)$ denotes the domain of θ, which is the set of substituted variables, and $codom(\theta)$ denotes the co-domain of θ, which is the set of substitutes in θ. For technical reasons, if θ is a piece unifier of $body(r)$ and $head(r')$, then $dom(\theta)$ refers to the subset of substituted variables which also appear in $body(r)$ and $codom(\theta)$ refers to the subset of substitutes which appear in $body(r)$ as well.[3]

Definition 5. Let r and r' be two rules and h a homomorphism from $var_u(body(r'))$ to ground terms. We say that r' *depends on* r w.r.t. h, if there is a piece unifier θ of $body(r')$ and $head(r)$ and a homomorphism $g : codom(\theta) \mapsto codom(h)$ such that $\forall x \in dom(\theta), g(\theta(x)) = h(x)$.

Intuitively, that "r' depends on r w.r.t. h" says that there is a piece unifier θ of $body(r')$ and $head(r)$ that is "*consistent with* h", in the sense that there exists a homomorphism $g : codom(\theta) \mapsto codom(h)$ such that $\forall x \in dom(\theta)$, g maps $\theta(x)$ to what h maps x to. E.g., if $h(x)$ and $\theta(x)$ are distinct constants, such a homomorphism g does not exist.

Terminology: Given a tuple $V = (v_1, \ldots, v_n)$ where $n \geq 2$, a *projection of V preserving end points*, denoted $V' = (v'_1, \ldots, v'_m)$, is a projection of V (as defined in usual way), with the additional requirement that the end points are preserved, i.e., $v'_1 = v_1$ and $v'_m = v_n$. By abuse of terminology, V' above will simply be called a *projection* of V.

Definition 6. Let R be a rule set and $\pi = (r_1, \ldots, r_n)$ a path with $n \geq 2$. A tuple of homomorphisms $H = (h_1, \ldots, h_n)$ is called *chained* for π if there is a projection $H' = (h'_1, \ldots, h'_m)$ of H and the corresponding path projection $\pi' = (r'_1, \ldots, r'_m)$ of π such that for all $1 \leq i < m$, r'_{i+1} depends on r'_i w.r.t. h'_i.

---

[2] In the literature of unification, $\theta = \{x/y, y/z\}$ would have been written as $\{x/z, y/z\}$. Following [3] we keep the substitutes like x/y for technical reasons.

[3] These variables play a critical role in the construction of critical databases (cf. Definition 8).

We are ready to define the notion of activeness.

Definition 7 (Activeness). Let R be a rule set and I_0 a database. A path $\pi = (r_1 \ldots, r_n)$ where $r_i \in R$ for $1 \leq i \leq n$ is said to be *active* w.r.t. I_0, if there exists a sequence $I_0, \ldots, I_n$ and a chained tuple of homomorphisms $H = (h_1, \ldots, h_n)$ for π such that, for all $i > 0$, (r_i, h_i) is an active trigger on I_{i-1} and $I_{i-1}\langle r_i, h_i \rangle I_i$. In this case, H is called a *witness* of the activeness of π w.r.t. I_0.

Intuitively, the definition says that a path π is active w.r.t. a database I_0 if there is an active trigger for each rule application on the path, and the application of the last rule depends on some earlier ones and eventually on the first on the path. In other words, if π is not active w.r.t. I_0, either some rule in π does not apply due to lack of an active trigger, or the last rule in π does not depend on the first in π. In either case, π does not pose as a "dangerous cycle" even if it is a cycle.

We are now ready to address the issue of which databases to check against for termination analysis of restricted chase. In what follows, we introduce a technique to construct what we call a *restricted critical database*, denoted I^π, for each given path $\pi = (r_1, \ldots, r_n)$ "on the fly" to simulate all possible derivation sequences generated by the sequence of rules on the path w.r.t. arbitrary databases.

Roughly speaking, I^π consists of certain body atoms of rules in π, where variables are replaced with *fresh constants*, which are called *indexed constants*. Notationally, given a variable x and an integer j, we use $\langle x, j \rangle$ to denote an indexed constant. The goal is to provide necessary triggers for the traversal of π based on piece unification.

Since in I^π we must provide atoms to trigger r_1 in path π above, for ease of presentation, let us define a special mapping for that purpose, $f_0 : var_u(body(r_1)) \mapsto \langle var_u(body(r_1)), 1 \rangle$, such that $f_0(x) = \langle x, 1 \rangle$. That is, to trigger r_1 in π, we will include in I^π the body atoms of $body(r_1)$ with each variable x therein replaced by fresh constant $\langle x, 1 \rangle$. We are then ready to define I^π as follows.

Definition 8 (Restricted critical database). Let R be a rule set and $\pi = (r_1, \ldots, r_n)$ a path. For each (B, H)-induced piece unifier θ_i^l of $body(r_{i+1})$ and $head(r_j)$ $(1 \leq j \leq i < n, 1 \leq l \leq m)$, where m is the number of piece unifiers of $body(r_{i+1})$ and $head(r_j)$, let $B' = \{\beta \mid \beta \in body(r_{i+1}) \setminus B$ and $var(\beta) \cap var(B) \neq \emptyset\}$. We define a function $f_i^l : dom(\theta_i^l) \mapsto \langle codom(\theta_i^l), \mathbb{N} \rangle$ such that for each $x \in var(B') \cap dom(\theta_i^l)$ where $\theta_i^l(x)$ is a variable, we have $f_i^l(x) = \langle \theta_i^l(x), j \rangle$. We then define $I^\pi = f_0(body(r_1)) \cup \bigcup_{i=1}^n \bigcup_{l=1}^m \tilde{f}_i^l(B')$ and call it *the restricted critical database of π*, where $\tilde{f}_i^l$ extends f_i^l by mapping each variable $x \in var(B') \setminus dom(\theta_i^l)$ and each variable x that does not occur in $var(B) \cup var(B')$ for all (B, H)-induced piece unifiers of $body(r_{i+1})$ and $head(r_j)$ to $\langle x, i + \kappa \rangle$, where $i + \kappa$ is a number that makes $\langle x, i + \kappa \rangle$ distinct.[4]

---

[4] For example, $\langle x, i + \kappa \rangle$ is distinct if $i + \kappa$ is a fresh number.

Above, two kinds of indexed constants are generated, either by function f_i^l or by $\tilde{f}_i^l$. The latter is for two different purposes. The goal is to avoid the possibility that two distinct variables incidentally become identical (See Example 5).

Example 4. Let $R = \{r\}$ where

$$r: \ P(x,y), E(y,w), N(s,t), Q(r,s) \rightarrow \exists u \exists v P(u,w), N(t,v)$$

Given the path $\pi = (r, r)$, there are two piece unifiers of $body(r)$ and $head(r)$. Let $B_1 = \{P(x,y)\}$, $H_1 = \{P(u,w)\}$, $B_2 = \{N(s,t)\}$, and $H_2 = \{N(t,v)\}$. The (B_1, H_1)-induced piece unifier is $\theta_1^1 = \{x/u, y/w\}$ and (B_2, H_2)-induced is $\theta_1^2 = \{s/t, t/v\}$. The restricted critical database of π is:

$$
\begin{aligned}
I^\pi &= f_0(body(r)) \cup \{E(w^1, w^2), Q(r^2, t^1)\} \\
&= \{P(x^1, y^1), E(y^1, w^1), N(s^1, t^1), Q(r^1, s^1)\} \cup \{E(w^1, w^2), Q(r^2, t^1)\}
\end{aligned}
$$

where we write x^i instead of $\langle x, i \rangle$ for simplicity. In this example, the set $f_0(body(r))$ is straightforward. Let us consider how $E(w^1, w^2)$ is constructed. By definition, $B_1' = \{E(y, w)\}$, and as $y \in var(B_1') \cap dom(\theta_1^1)$ where $\theta_1^1(y) = w$ is a variable, we have $f_1^1(y) = \langle w, 1 \rangle = w^1$. Since $w \in var(B_1') \setminus dom(\theta_1^1)$, we have $\tilde{f}_i^l(w) = \langle w, 2 \rangle = w^2$, where 2 is a number that makes $\langle w, 2 \rangle$ a distinct constant (the same applies to r^2).

Example 5. In this example, we illustrate the mapping $\tilde{f}_i^l(.)$ of Definition 8. Consider a simple rule $r: \ P(x,y), E(y,w) \rightarrow \exists u P(u,w)$ and the path $\pi = (r, r)$. Let $B = \{P(x,y)\}$ and $H = \{P(u,w)\}$. The (B, H)-induced piece unifier is $\{x/u, y/w\}$. Now $B' = \{E(y, w)\}$, and the critical database of π is $I^\pi = f_0(body(r)) \cup \{E(w^1, w^2)\} = \{P(x^1, y^1), E(y^1, w^1)\} \cup \{E(w^1, w^2)\}$. It is not hard to verify that π is active w.r.t. I^π. However, let $I' = (I^\pi - \{E(w^1, w^2)\}) \cup \{E(w^1, w^1)\}$. The coincidence of the two occurrences of w^1 was not intended by the original rule; as a result, π is not active w.r.t. I'. Thus, we would have failed to capture derivations of restricted chase with an arbitrary database. This example shows that $\tilde{f}_1^1(.)$ is needed to induce distinct atoms by using appropriate numbers $i + \kappa$.

The theorem below serves as the basis for our approach of this paper.

Theorem 1. *Let R be a rule set and $\pi = (r_1, \ldots, r_n)$ a path based on R. Then, π is active w.r.t. some database if and only if π is active w.r.t. the critical database I^π.*

By the contrapositive of the only-if statement of the theorem, if π is not active w.r.t. I^π, then π is not active w.r.t any database. Thus, for restricted chase termination, we only need to test, for each k-cycle π with a fixed k, whether the chase fails to apply at some rule in π starting from database I^π. If this is the case for all k-cycles of the same k, we then conclude that the given rule set R is terminating; otherwise, for some k-cycle of the fixed k, restricted chase can reach the last rule and apply it; in this case we do not know whether R is terminating or not. We can then use larger values of k to conduct more powerful termination analysis, but with more cost.

Note that the termination of all k-cycles for a fixed k automatically guarantees the termination of all k'-cycles with $k' \geq k$.

5 K-Safe(Φ) Rules

We now apply the results of the previous section to define classes of finite restricted chase. The idea is to introduce a parameter of *cycle function* to generalize various acyclicity notions in the literature, and we will test a path only when it fails to satisfy the given acyclicity condition.

Definition 9. Let R be a rule set and Σ the set of all finite cycles based on R. A *cycle function* is a mapping $\Phi^R : \Sigma \mapsto \{T, F\}$, where T and F denote *true* and *false*, respectively.

Let Φ be a binary function from rule sets and cycles of which Φ^R is the projection function on its first parameter, i.e. $\Phi(R, \sigma) = \Phi^R(\sigma)$, where R is a rule set and σ is a cycle. By overloading, the function Φ is also called a cycle function.

Definition 10. (k-safe(Φ) rule sets)

- Let R be a rule set and σ a k-cycle where $k \geq 1$. σ is *safe* if for all databases I, σ is not active w.r.t. I.
- R is said to be in k-safe(Φ), or belong to k-safe(Φ) (under cycle function Φ), if for every k-cycle σ which is mapped to T under Φ^R, σ is safe.

For example, it can be verified that the rule set R_1 in Example 1 is in k-safe(Φ_Π) for any $k \geq 1$ and any cycle function Φ_Π based on some Skolem acyclicity condition Π in the literature such as WA, JA, and MFA, etc.

Algorithm 1 gives a procedure to determine whether a rule set belongs to the class k-safe(Φ_Π) - the procedure returns *true* if it is and *false* otherwise, where when $k = 0$, 0-safe(Φ_Π) $= \Pi$ is the class of rule sets that satisfy the acyclicity condition Π.

Algorithm 1. k-safe(Φ)

Input: A set of rules R; An integer $k \geq 0$; A cycle function Φ
Output: Boolean value *IsAcyclic*;

1: **procedure** k-safe(R, Φ)
2:    *IsAcyclic* = *true*;
3:    **for each** k-cycle σ based on R **do**
4:        Find the restricted critical database I^σ of σ;
5:        **if** $\Phi(R, \mathrm{Rule}(\sigma)) = T$ **then**
6:            **if** σ is active w.r.t. I^σ **then**
7:                *IsAcyclic* = *false*;
8:                **return** *IsAcyclic*;
9:        **else**
10:            **return** *IsAcyclic*

Below, we show how to define a cycle function from any arbitrary rule-based acyclicity condition of finite Skolem chase such as JA [14], aGRD [1], MFA [10], etc.

Definition 11. Let Π be an arbitrary condition of acyclicity of finite Skolem chase. For convenience, let us also denote by Π the class of rule sets that satisfy this acyclicity condition. A cycle function Φ_Π is defined as follows: for each rule set R and each cycle σ based on R if the condition for checking whether Π holds for rules in $\mathsf{Rule}(\sigma)$, then Φ_Π maps (R, σ) to F; otherwise Φ_Π maps (R, σ) to T.

Example 6. Considering the rule set R_1 from Example 1, and assuming $\Pi = $ aGRD in Definition 11, Φ_Π maps cycles $\sigma_1 = (r_1, r_2)$ and $\sigma_2 = (r_2, r_1)$ to T.

We can show the following theorem.

Theorem 2. *Let Π be a class of finite Skolem chase that is defined by a condition of acyclicity and Φ_Π be the corresponding cycle function as defined above. Then, for all $k \geq 1$, (i) $\Pi \subseteq k\text{-safe}(\Phi_\Pi)$, (ii) $k\text{-safe}(\Phi_\Pi) \subseteq CT_{\forall\forall}^{res}$, and (iii) $(k-1)\text{-safe}(\Phi_\Pi) \subseteq k\text{-safe}(\Phi_\Pi)$. In addition, for non-disjunctive rule sets, $RMFA \subset k\text{-safe}(\Phi_{aGRD})$, where $k = \|R\|^{(m+1)}$, in which m is the number of existential variables occurring in different rules of R, one for each rule $r \in R$ in which $var_{ex}(r) \neq \emptyset$. and $\|R\|$ is the number of symbols occurring in R.*

Example 7. It is not difficult to check that the rule set R_1 in Example 1 is in 1-safe(Φ_{aGRD}), and the rule set R_2 in the same example belongs to 2-safe(Φ_{aGRD}) as well as 2-safe(Φ_{WA}), but it does not belong to any known class of acyclicity including RMFA.

6   Extension of Bounded Rule Sets

In [17], a family of existential rule languages with finite (Skolem) chase based on the notion of δ-*boundedness* has been introduced and the data and combined complexities of reasoning with those languages for specific bound functions (namely, k-*exponentially bounded functions*) have been derived. Our aim in this section is to provide an effective method to extend bounded languages to introduce all-instance terminating restricted chase classes. First, let us introduce some notions.

A *bound function* is a function from positive integers to positive integers. A rule set R is called δ-*bounded under Skolem chase* for some bound function δ, if for all databases I, $ht(\mathsf{chase}_{sk}(I, R)) \leq \delta(\|R\|)$, where $\|R\|$ is the number of symbols occurring in R, and $ht(A)$ is the maximum height (maximum nesting depth) of Skolem terms that have at least one occurrence in A, and ∞ otherwise. Let us denote by δ-$\mathcal{B}^{sk}$ the class of δ-*bounded rule sets under Skolem chase*. The class of δ-*bounded rule sets under restricted chase*, denoted δ-$\mathcal{B}^{res}$, is defined as follows.

Definition 12. Given a bound function δ, a rule set R is called δ-*bounded under the restricted chase variant* if, for all databases I, R is in k-safe(Φ_{aGRD}), where $k = \|R\|^{\mathcal{O}(\delta(\|R\|))}$.

The next result states the relationship between δ-$\mathcal{B}^{res}$ and δ-$\mathcal{B}^{sk}$.

Theorem 3. *For any bound function δ, δ-$\mathcal{B}^{res} \supsetneq \delta$-$\mathcal{B}^{sk}$.*

Membership Complexity: We consider the membership problem in δ-$\mathcal{B}^{res}$ languages. Given a rule set R and a bound function δ, whether R is δ-bounded under the restricted chase variant.

Proposition 4. *Let δ be a bound function computable in $\mathrm{DTime}(T(n))$[5] for some function $T(n)$. Then, it is in*

$$\mathrm{DTime}(\mathsf{C}_\delta + ||R||^{||R||^{\mathcal{O}(\delta(||R||))}} \times \mathsf{C}_c)$$

to check if a rule set R is δ-bounded under the restricted chase variant, where $\mathsf{C}_\delta = T(log||R||)^{\mathcal{O}(1)}$ and $\mathsf{C}_c = ||R||^{2^{\mathcal{O}(\delta(||R||))}} \times 2^{||R||^{\mathcal{O}(\delta(||R||))}}$.

The first term in the above bound gives the complexity of computing the bound function. The second computes cycles which are mapped to T under δ-cycle function w.r.t. R and C_c is the complexity of checking the chained property defined in Definition 6.

Now consider what we call *exponential tower functions*: $\mathsf{exp}_\kappa(n) =$
$$\begin{cases} n & \kappa = 0 \\ 2^{\mathsf{exp}_{\kappa-1}(n)} & \kappa > 0 \end{cases}$$
Then, we have the following corollary from Proposition 4:

Corollary 5. *Checking if a rule set is exp_κ-bounded under restricted chase variant is in $(\kappa + 2)$-$\mathrm{ExpTime}$.*

The corollary implies that, for any exponential tower function δ, the extra computation for checking δ-boundedness under restricted chase stays within the same complexity upper bound for δ-boundedness under Skolem chase, as reported in [17].

Data and Combined Complexity

Since the size of the tree generated by restricted chase has the same upper bound as that generated by Skolem chase, it is not difficult to show that the complexity upper bound for checking $R \cup I \models q$ for exp_κ-bounded rule sets is the same for the restricted and Skolem chase variants. It then follows from [17] that we have

Theorem 6. *The problem of Boolean conjunctive answering for exp_κ-bounded rule sets under restricted chase variant is $(\kappa + 2)$-$\mathrm{ExpTime}$-complete for combined complexity and PTime-complete for data complexity.*

Remark 1. Based on Theorem 6, it can be observed that the entire hierarchy of δ-bounded rule sets under Skolem chase introduced in [17] can be extended with no increase in combined and data complexity of reasoning. This holds even for individual syntactic classes of finite Skolem chase (such as WA, JA, SWA, etc.).

---

[5] The set of all decision problems solvable in $T(n)$ using a deterministic Turing machine.

7 Experimentation

To evaluate the performance of our proposed methods for termination analysis, we implemented our algorithms on top of the GRAAL *rule engine* [2]. Our goal is two-fold. 1) To understand the relevance of our theoretical approach with real-world applications, and 2) to see that even though the problem of checking semantic acyclicity conditions is notorious for their high complexities, they may be a valuable addition to the tools of termination analysis in real-world scenarios.

We looked into a random collection of 500 ontologies from The Manchester OWL Corpus (MOWLCorp) [16], a large corpus of ontologies on the web. After standard transformation into rules (see [10] for details),[6] based on the number of existential variables occurring in transformed rules, we picked rules from two categories of up to 5 and 5–200 existential variables with equal probability (250 from each). We ran all tests on a Macintosh laptop with 1.7 GHz Intel Core i7 processor, 8 GB of RAM, and a 512 GB SSD, running macOS High Sierra.

In our experiments, we performed the following steps: 1. transforming ontologies into the normal form using standard techniques (cf. [9]); 2. forming all k-cycles and for each k-cycle σ, constructing the restricted critical database I^{σ} and checking if $\mathsf{Rule}(\sigma) \in \Pi$, for each Π from {WA, JA, aGRD}; 3. for each Π from {WA, JA, aGRD} and for each $\mathsf{Rule}(\sigma) \notin \Pi$, checking the activeness of σ w.r.t. I^{σ}. For each ontology, we allowed 2.5 hours to complete all of these tasks; in case of running out of time or memory, we report no terminating result.

For the first experiment, we considered k-safe(Φ) rule sets for different cycle functions Φ based on WA, JA and aGRD acyclicity conditions for different values of k. In Table 1, the results of these experiments are summarized where a number is the number of terminating rule sets for its corresponding class. As can be seen in Table 1, in all of the considered classes by increasing k, the number of terminating ontologies increases.[7] In particular, there is a big jump of the number of terminating ontologies under restricted chase for any acyclicity condition when changing k from 4 to 5. Furthermore, it is interesting to observe that among 500 ontologies, the three syntactic methods (when $k = 0$) identify only a small subset of terminating ontologies. Second, in theory we know WA $\subset$ JA. For our collection of practical ontologies, the gap between the terminating classes under the two cycle functions, one for WA and the other for JA, is nontrivial. Third, though in theory aGRD $\cap$ JA $\neq \emptyset$, we see that for our collection the recognized classes under WA and JA are much larger than the one under aGRD. One possible explanation is that since in all experiments the considered cycles are connected through the chained property, considering cycle functions to be those of aGRD does not add much. However, the WA and JA cycle functions recognize more terminating ontologies.

---

[6] Due to the limitation of this transformation, our collection does not include ontologies with nominals, number restrictions or denial constraints.

[7] We did not manage to complete the test for the cases with $k \geq 7$, due to limited resources. Thus, we are uncertain about whether more terminating ontologies may exist in this collection.

For the second experiment, we performed time analysis for the tested ontologies for different cycle functions by fixing k to 6. The results are reported in Table 2, where the average running time, as well as the number of ontologies *terminating within the average running time* (abbreviated as T.W.A.T) for that particular cycle function, are reported. It can be seen that around half of the terminating ontologies are determined within the average time in each of the three cycle functions. Furthermore, the number of ontologies for which our experiments halted with timeout/memory failures are also shown in the table. Overall, we found 24 terminating ontologies under restricted chase but non-terminating under Skolem chase. Among those that were tested, 5 do not belong to RMFA nor RJA.

Table 1. Number of terminating ontologies for different cycle functions and values of k.

Membership among 500 ontologies from the MOWLCorp			
k	k-safe(Φ_{aGRD})	k-safe(Φ_{WA})	k-safe(Φ_{JA})
$k = 0$	15	25	40
$k = 1$	21	48	66
$k = 2$	55	82	100
$k = 3$	79	106	124
$k = 4$	95	122	140
$k = 5$	170	197	215
$k = 6$	179	206	224

Table 2. Time and memory analysis for membership testing of terminating ontologies.

Classes	Time/Memory analysis				
	Avg. time (s)	T.W.A.T (#)	Timeout failure (#)	Memory failure (#)	Terminating (%)
6-safe(Φ_{aGRD})	4342	86	2	25	35.8
6-safe(Φ_{WA})	3755	124	1	11	41.2
6-safe(Φ_{JA})	3470	132	1	7	44.8

8   Conclusion

In this work we introduced a technique to characterize finite restricted chase which can be applied to extend any class of finite Skolem chase identified by a condition of acyclicity. Then, we showed how to apply our techniques to extend δ-bounded rule sets. Our complexity analyses showed that this extension does not increase the complexities of membership checking, nor the complexity of combined and data reasoning tasks for δ-bounded rule sets under restricted chase compared to Skolem chase. Our experimental results discovered a growing number of practical ontologies with finite restricted chase by increasing k as well as changing the underlying cycle function. We will next investigate conditions for subclasses with a reduction of cost for membership testing. One idea is to find syntactic conditions under which triggers to a rule are necessarily active. We anticipate that position graphs could be useful in these analyses.

References

1. Baget, J.-F.: Improving the forward chaining algorithm for conceptual graphs rules. In: Proceedings KR 2004, pp. 407–414 (2004)
2. Baget, J.-F., Leclère, M., Mugnier, M.-L., Rocher, S., Sipieter, C.: Graal: a toolkit for query answering with existential rules. In: Bassiliades, N., Gottlob, G., Sadri, F., Paschke, A., Roman, D. (eds.) RuleML 2015. LNCS, vol. 9202, pp. 328–344. Springer, Cham (2015). https://doi.org/10.1007/978-3-319-21542-6_21
3. Baget, J.-F., Michel, M., Mugnier, M.-L., Salvat, E.: Extending decidable cases for rules with existential variables. In: Proceedings IJCAI 2009, pp. 677–682 (2009)
4. Baget, J.-F., Mugnier, M.-L.: Extensions of simple conceptual graphs: the complexity of rules and constraints. J. Artif. Intell. Res. **16**, 425–465 (2002)
5. Beeri, C., Vardi, M.Y.: The implication problem for data dependencies. In: Even, S., Kariv, O. (eds.) ICALP 1981. LNCS, vol. 115, pp. 73–85. Springer, Heidelberg (1981). https://doi.org/10.1007/3-540-10843-2_7
6. Beeri, C., Vardi, M.Y.: A proof procedure for data dependencies. JACM **31**(4), 718–741 (1984)
7. Calì, A., Gottlob, G., Lukasiewicz, T., Marnette, B., Pieris, A.: Datalog+/-: a family of logical knowledge representation and query languages for new applications. In: Proceedings LICS 2010, pp. 228–242 (2010)
8. Carral, D., Dragoste, I., Krötzsch, M.: Restricted chase (non) termination for existential rules with disjunctions. In: Proceedings IJCAI 2017, pp. 922–928 (2017)
9. Carral, D., Feier, C., Cuenca Grau, B., Hitzler, P., Horrocks, I.: $\mathcal{EL}$-ifying ontologies. In: Demri, S., Kapur, D., Weidenbach, C. (eds.) IJCAR 2014. LNCS (LNAI), vol. 8562, pp. 464–479. Springer, Cham (2014). https://doi.org/10.1007/978-3-319-08587-6_36
10. Grau, B.C., et al.: Acyclicity notions for existential rules and their application to query answering in ontologies. J. Artif. Intell. Res. **47**, 741–808 (2013)
11. Fagin, R., Kolaitis, P.G., Miller, R.J., Popa, L.: Data exchange: semantics and query answering. Theor. Comput. Sci. **336**(1), 89–124 (2005)
12. Grahne, G., Onet, A.: The data-exchange chase under the microscope. CoRR, abs/1407.2279 (2014)
13. Karimi, A., Zhang, H., You, J.-H.: A hierarchical approach to restricted chase termination for existential rules. Technical report, University of Alberta, Edmonton, AB, Canada (2018)
14. Krötzsch, M., Rudolph, S.: Extending decidable existential rules by joining acyclicity and guardedness. In: Proceedings AAAI 2011 (2011)
15. Marnette, B.: Generalized schema-mappings: from termination to tractability. In: Proceedings PODS 2009, pp. 13–22. ACM (2009)

16. Matentzoglu, N., Parsia, B.: The Manchester OWL Corpus (MOWLCorp), original serialisation, July 2014
17. Zhang, H., Zhang, Y., You, J.-H.: Existential rule languages with finite chase: complexity and expressiveness. In Proceedings AAAI 2015, pp. 1678–1684. AAAI Press (2015)

On Horn Conjunctive Queries

Enrique Matos Alfonso$^{(\boxtimes)}$ and Giorgos Stamou

National Technical University of Athens (NTUA), Athens, Greece
`gardero@image.ntua.gr`

Abstract. Most query rewriting systems focus on answering Conjunctive Queries that have only positive atoms because the use of negation can easily make the entailment problem undecidable. However, restricting the way we use negation on Conjunctive Queries can make the entailment problem decidable and can also ensure the existence of algorithms based on Query Rewriting that find their answers. In this paper, we propose a definition of Horn Conjunctive Queries to denote queries that have one negated atom. We also present an algorithm based on query rewriting that finds the answers of a Union of Horn Conjunctive Queries with respect to a set of Existential Rules. Additionally, we conduct some experiments to compare the performance with other state of the art systems that are able to answer conjunctive queries with negation using tableaux algorithms. The experimental data confirms that our system performs better than the other systems we considered when dealing with big ontologies.

1 Introduction

Description Logics (DLs) [1] and Existential Rules [4] are both fragments of First-Order Logic (FOL) where the expressive power is restricted. Some of the restrictions ensure decidability of the *query entailment* problem and provide the conditions for the implementation of efficient algorithms that take into account the restrictions of the fragment and introduce optimizations on the reasoning process.

When the entailment problem is decidable we can also perform *query answering* to find the set of tuples defining the assignments for the free variables in the query that make query to be entailed from the available data. *Query Rewriting* is a popular method to do query answering based on *Backward Chaining*.

Most of the research published on the mentioned FOL fragments and the implemented systems focus on the entailment of Conjunctive Queries (CQ), where no use of negation is allowed. The use of very restricted forms of negation in conjunctive queries drops the decidability results even for very restricted fragments like *DL-Lite*$_{core}^{\mathcal{H}}$ [11]. On the contrary, the entailment of conjunctive queries that use guarded negation is proven to be decidable [5] over frontier-guarded existential rules. Nevertheless, state of the art query rewriting systems mainly focus on providing implementations for answering conjunctive queries without negation. Having an efficient way to entail queries with negated atoms

© Springer Nature Switzerland AG 2018
C. Benzmüller et al. (Eds.): RuleML+RR 2018, LNCS 11092, pp. 115–130, 2018.
https://doi.org/10.1007/978-3-319-99906-7_8

could become very useful when it comes to checking the consistency of a system with respect to new rules. Because the counter examples of rules can be expressed using negation inside of conjunctive queries.

In this paper, we introduce the concept of *Horn conjunctive queries* ($\mathsf{CQ}^{\neg h}$), a type of conjunctive queries that allows the negation of one atom and corresponds semantically to the negation of a rule on the Existential Rules framework. We reduce the entailment problem of such queries, with respect to a set of Existential Rules, to the entailment of conjunctive queries without negated atoms. Restricted forms of Existential Rules where such reduction ensures decidability of the entailment problem are also presented. Additionally, the proposed approach is implemented into COMPLETO [14] allowing us to perform query rewriting and query answering for Horn UCQs. The implementation is compared to other systems that use *tableaux* algorithms to find the answers of OWL concepts that allow the use of negation. The experimental results show that the system we implemented performs better than the other systems that were considered for the case of ontologies with a large number of ABox assertions.

In our previous work [14], we proposed a method that was able to find UCQ-rewritings for conjunctive queries with negated atoms. However, the method was complete only for a specific kind of queries. The method did not consider FOL resolution steps between clauses corresponding to queries and would only provide a complete UCQ-rewriting when such resolution steps were not possible or not required (*strongly disconnected* queries). Our current approach transforms queries into rules and uses rewriting approaches that consider all possible interactions between those rules. Thus, the current approach provides a complete solution for queries that our previous approach was not able to answer in a complete way.

The following Section introduces some basic concepts related to Existential Rules. Next, Conjunctive Queries with Negation, Horn Conjunctive Queries and Horn UCQs ($\mathsf{UCQ}^{\neg h}$) are defined. In Sect. 4, a rewriting approach to answer $\mathsf{UCQ}^{\neg h}$ is presented. Section 5 provides the experiments carried out and their results. We finish with some conclusions derived from the results in Sect. 6.

2   Preliminaries

We assume readers to be familiar with the syntax and semantics of First-Order Logic. Regarding the *entailment* of formulas, it can be transformed by changing the *hypotheses* and *consequences* in the following way:

$$\Sigma \models F \quad \text{iff} \quad \Sigma, \neg F \models \bot. \tag{1}$$

As a consequence, when the formula F is a disjunction of sub-formulas F_1 and F_2, we have that:

$$\Sigma \models F_1 \vee F_2 \quad \text{iff} \quad \Sigma, \neg F_1 \models F_2. \tag{2}$$

An *atom* is of the form $a(e_1, \ldots, e_k)$ where a is a predicate symbol of *arity* $k \geq 1$ and each *argument* e_i is a variable or a constant. A *conjunctive query* CQ is a conjunction of atoms:

$$\exists \boldsymbol{X} \; a_1(\boldsymbol{x_1}) \wedge \ldots \wedge a_n(\boldsymbol{x_n})$$

denoted by:

$$q(\boldsymbol{X^+}) :- a_1(\boldsymbol{x_1}), \ldots, a_n(\boldsymbol{x_n}),$$

where $\boldsymbol{X^+} = \bigcup_i var(\boldsymbol{x_i}) \setminus \boldsymbol{X}$ is the set of free variables in the query and it is referred to as the *answer variables* of the query and $var(\boldsymbol{x_i})$ denotes the set of variables in the tuple of the arguments $\boldsymbol{x_i}$. If $\boldsymbol{X^+} = \emptyset$, the query is called *boolean conjunctive query* BCQ and it is denoted simply by q instead of $q()$. A *union of conjunctive queries* UCQ is a set of conjunctive queries and it is semantically equivalent to the disjunction of all the queries in it. All the queries in a UCQ share the same answer variables and it is denoted as $Q(\boldsymbol{X}) :- q_1(\boldsymbol{X}) \vee \ldots \vee q_n(\boldsymbol{X})$. From a query, we could be interested in removing atoms involving some specific predicate symbol p, the operation is denoted by $| \, . \, |^{-p}$ and it results in the following query:

$$|q(\boldsymbol{X^+})|^{-p} = a_{s_1}(\boldsymbol{x_{s_1}}), \ldots, a_{s_m}(\boldsymbol{x_{s_m}}) \quad \text{where } \{\ldots, s_i, \ldots\} = \{j \mid a_j \neq p\}.$$

For the sake of simplicity, we define a *fact* as a ground atom, even if in the field of Existential Rules sometimes it is also defined as an existentially closed conjunction of atoms. An *existential rule* (ER) is a closed formula:

$$\forall \boldsymbol{X} \exists \boldsymbol{Y^+} a_1(\boldsymbol{x_1}), \ldots, a_n(\boldsymbol{x_n}) \to h(\boldsymbol{y})$$

denoted as

$$a_1(\boldsymbol{x_1}), \ldots, a_n(\boldsymbol{x_n}) \to h(\boldsymbol{y}),$$

where $\boldsymbol{X} = \bigcup_i var(\boldsymbol{x_i})$ and $\boldsymbol{Y^+} = var(\boldsymbol{y}) \setminus \boldsymbol{X}$. The variables in $\boldsymbol{X} \cap var(\boldsymbol{y})$ are called *frontier variables*. The *body* (*head*) of the rule is the formula to the left (right) of the implication symbol. The body of a rule is a conjunction of atoms and the head is an atom. A (*negative*) *constraint* is a rule where the head corresponds to $\bot$. Semantically, constraints can be seen as queries (the body atoms) that cannot be satisfied in order to keep consistency. A positive (not negated) atom $a_i(\boldsymbol{x_i})$ is a *guard* for a set of variables $\boldsymbol{x}$ iff $\boldsymbol{x} \subseteq var(\boldsymbol{x_i})$. A set of variables $\boldsymbol{x}$ is *guarded* in a formula F (we could also limit it to a sub-formula) if there is a guard for $\boldsymbol{x}$ in F. A rule is *guarded* if the set of variables in the head is guarded by one of the atoms in the body of the rule and it is *frontier guarded* if the set of variables in the frontier of the rule is guarded by an atom in the body of the rule.

A *Knowledge Base* $\mathcal{K}$ is a finite set of formulas. They are frequently used to entail another formula of interest. In the Existential Rules framework, the knowledge base $\mathcal{K}$ consists of existential rules $\mathcal{R}$, constraints $\mathcal{C}$ and facts $\mathcal{D}$.

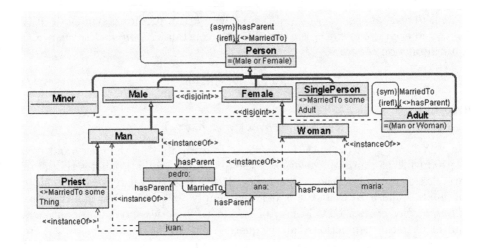

Fig. 1. UML diagram of an ontology example generated with OWLGrEd.

Example 1. Figure 1 shows a knowledge base with all the elements described previously. The diagram was generated with the OWLGrEd[1] software that uses UML diagrams to represent the elements of the ontology and includes some additional notation to express properties like symmetry (sym), asymmetry(asym) and irreflexivity (irefl). Equivalences are expressed with equality sign and disjointness is expressed with the "<>" symbol. It is straightforward to understand which elements represent rules, constraints and facts with the basic knowledge of UML but still we could mention some of them:

– Rules
  - $Adult(X) \rightarrow Person(X)$ (Subclass)
  - $hasParent(X, Y) \rightarrow Person(X)$ (Domain)
  - $MarriedTo(X, Y) \rightarrow MarriedTo(Y, X)$ (Symmetry)
– Constraints
  - $Adult(X), Minor(X) \rightarrow \bot$ (Disjoint Classes)
  - $hasParent(X, Y), MarriedTo(X, Y) \rightarrow \bot$ (Disjoint Object Properties)
  - $Priest(X), MarriedTo(X, Y) \rightarrow \bot$
– Facts
  - $Woman(ana)$ (Class Assertion)
  - $hasParent(maria, pedro)$ (Object Property Assertion)

Notice that Fig. 1 refers to an ontology with elements of the Web Ontology Language (OWL). The ontology was translated into a knowledge base in the fragment of Existential Rules. However, not all the ontologies in OWL format can be translated to Existential Rules. Although, we can focus on the OWL 2 ER [2] fragment, for which it is possible to translate all the axioms of the ontology into a ER knowledge base. A partial translation of more expressive ontologies

---

[1] http://owlgred.lumii.lv/.

can also be done, but in these cases the reasoning processes might not be sound or complete with respect to the original ontology.

The *conjunctive query entailment problem* is defined as the decision problem of whether a boolean conjunctive query q is entailed from a knowledge base $\mathcal{K}$ i.e.

$$\mathcal{R}, \mathcal{C}, \mathcal{D} \models q. \tag{3}$$

An *answer* of a conjunctive query $q(\boldsymbol{X}^+)$ with respect to a knowledge base $\mathcal{K}$, is a tuple $\boldsymbol{t}$ such that the corresponding query $q(\boldsymbol{t})$, is entailed by $\mathcal{K}$. The query $q(\boldsymbol{t})$ is obtained by applying the substitution $\boldsymbol{X}^+ \leftarrow \boldsymbol{t}$ to $q(\boldsymbol{X}^+)$, i.e. the answer variables are substituted with the corresponding components of the tuple $\boldsymbol{t}$. In case of boolean queries the answer is denoted by ().

Conjunctive query answering is defined as the problem of finding the set of answers of a conjunctive query $q(\boldsymbol{X}^+)$ with respect to a knowledge base. It is common in the literature to focus only on boolean conjunctive queries because they can also represent conjunctive queries with answer variables by adding *dummy atoms* with the answer variables of the query. For this reason, we focus on boolean conjunctive queries from now on.

For general existential rules and CQs, the entailment problem (3) is not decidable [4]. Nevertheless, for some fragments with restricted expressivity we can ensure the decidability of (3).

In general, the approaches to entail a query fall in two major categories. *Forward chaining* approaches infer new facts from the existing ones applying the rules until no new facts can be inferred. On the contrary, *backward chaining* approaches apply rules in the reverse order and produce e.g. new conjunctive queries. Both families of approaches aim to reduce the original problem to the entailment of a union of conjunctive queries with respect to a set of facts i.e.

$$\mathcal{D} \models q. \tag{4}$$

Problem (4) focuses on finding a substitution σ for the variables in q such that for every atom $a_i(\boldsymbol{x}_i)$ in q holds that $a_i(\boldsymbol{x}_i)\sigma \in \mathcal{D}$. The problem belongs to the *NP*-Complete complexity class [7].

In the *rewriting approach* [6,13], the query and the rules are transformed so that the answers can be computed in a much easier way with respect to the data. Usually, the resulting expression can be a datalog program or a union of conjunctive queries. For a given set of rules $\mathcal{R}$, a set of *UCQ-rewritings* of a conjunctive query (or UCQ) q is defined as a UCQ $\mathcal{R}_q^*$ such that for all sets of facts $\mathcal{D}$:

$$\exists \, q_i \in \mathcal{R}_q^* \text{ such that } \mathcal{D} \models q_i \text{ implies that } \mathcal{R}, \mathcal{D} \models q. \tag{5}$$

If the converse of (5) holds i.e.

$$\mathcal{R}, \mathcal{D} \models q \text{ implies that } \exists \, q_i \in \mathcal{R}_q^* \text{ such that } \mathcal{D} \models q_i,$$

the set $\mathcal{R}_q^*$ is a *complete* UCQ-rewriting of q with respect to $\mathcal{R}$. Each element of a UCQ-rewriting set is called a *rewriting* (or $\mathcal{R}$-rewriting) of the original query with respect to the set of rules $\mathcal{R}$.

In the knowledge base of Example 1, if we rewrite the query $Q(X)$:−
$Person(X)$ we will obtain the following complete UCQ-rewriting:

$$Q(X) :- Adult(X) \lor Female(X) \lor Male(X) \lor Man(X) \lor Minor(X) \lor$$
$$Person(X) \lor Priest(X) \lor SinglePerson(X) \lor Woman(X) \lor$$
$$MarriedTo(Y, X) \lor MarriedTo(X, Y) \lor hasParent(Y, X) \lor$$
$$hasParent(X, Y),$$

with answers $\{ana, maria, juan, pedro\}$.

A set of rules $\mathcal{R}$ is called a *finite unification set* (*fus*) iff for all conjunctive queries q there exists a sound, complete and finite UCQ-rewriting Q of q with respect to $\mathcal{R}$ such that, for any $\mathcal{R}$-rewriting q' of q, there is a $\mathcal{R}$-rewriting q'' in Q that maps to q' i.e. $q' \rightarrow q''$.

Knowing whether a set of rules $\mathcal{R}$ is a *fus* is undecidable [4]. However, several classes of existential rules are known to be *fus* [4]:

- *Linear or atomic-hypothesis rules*: Rules with one atom in the body.
  - $DL\text{-}Lite_{core}^{\mathcal{H}}$ is a special case of linear rules.
- *Domain-restricted rules*: Rules where the atoms in the head contain all or none of the variables in the body.
- *Weakly acyclic rules*: A set of rules where the *graph of dependencies* between rules is acyclic.

In general, the concept of dependency between rules is very important to detect fragments in the framework of Existential Rules for which the entailment problem is decidable. We say a conjunction of atoms Q *depends* on a rule r iff there is a conjunction of atoms F such that $F \nvDash Q$ and $F, r \models Q$. A rule r_i depends on a rule r_j iff the body of r_i depends on the rule r_j. Furthermore, the concept of dependency allows us to define the *graph of dependencies* between rules by building a graph where the rules are the nodes and a directed edge between two nodes represents the existence of a dependency between the corresponding rules. A *cut* $\{\mathcal{R}_1, \mathcal{R}_2\}$ is a partition of the set of rules $\mathcal{R}$ and it is a *directed cut* $\mathcal{R}_1 \triangleright \mathcal{R}_2$ if none of rules in $\mathcal{R}_1$ depends on a rule of $\mathcal{R}_2$.

Property 1. Given a set of rules $\mathcal{R}$ with a directed cut $\mathcal{R}_1 \triangleright \mathcal{R}_2$, for all queries q and set of facts $\mathcal{D}$:

$$\mathcal{D}, \mathcal{R} \models q \text{ if there is a query } P \text{ such that } \mathcal{D}, \mathcal{R}_1 \models P \text{ and } P, \mathcal{R}_2 \models q.$$

Proof. The proof is based on being able to organize the application of rules from $\mathcal{R}$. The existing dependencies ensure that rules of $\mathcal{R}_1$ are never depending on rules from $\mathcal{R}_2$. For a detailed proof check [4].   □

Property 1 [4] allows us to study the decidability of entailment when we combine two sets of rules for which the entailment problem is decidable.

3   Queries with Negated Atoms

Let us consider the entailment problem of conjunctive queries with negated atoms (CQ¬) in the context of a knowledge base composed by facts $\mathcal{D}$, existential rules $\mathcal{R}$ and negative constraints $\mathcal{C}$.

In Example 1, we might want to know whether there is "a pair of people that cannot be married":

$$\exists X \exists Y \, Person(X) \wedge Person(Y) \wedge \neg MarriedTo(X,Y).$$

The negation used in CQ¬ is based on Open-World Assumptions (OWA) and in natural language it is usually expressed with "cannot be". Variables present in positive literals are, as usual, existentially quantified.

We could also be interested in knowing if there is a person that cannot be married at all:

$$\exists X \forall Y \, Person(X) \wedge \neg MarriedTo(X,Y).$$

Variables that are only present in negated literals cannot be existentially quantified, because this makes the expression *unsafe*.

Definition 1. *A conjunctive query with negated atoms* (CQ¬) *is a conjunction of literals, either positive* $a_i(\boldsymbol{x}_i)$ *or negated* $\neg p_j(\boldsymbol{y}_j)$:

$$\exists \boldsymbol{X} \forall \boldsymbol{Y} \, a_1(\boldsymbol{x}_1) \wedge \ldots, a_n(\boldsymbol{x}_n) \wedge \neg p_1(\boldsymbol{y}_1) \wedge \ldots \wedge \neg p_m(\boldsymbol{y}_m),$$

represented by:

$$q(\boldsymbol{X}^+) :- a_1(\boldsymbol{x}_1), \ldots, a_n(\boldsymbol{x}_n), \neg p_1(\boldsymbol{y}_1), \ldots, \neg p_m(\boldsymbol{y}_m),$$

where $\boldsymbol{X} \subseteq \bigcup var(\boldsymbol{x}_i)$, $\boldsymbol{X}^+ = \bigcup var(\boldsymbol{x}_i) \setminus \boldsymbol{X}$ *and* $\boldsymbol{Y} = \bigcup var(\boldsymbol{y}_j) \setminus \boldsymbol{X}$. *The set* $\boldsymbol{X}^+$ *contains the answer variables of the query.*

If the knowledge base does not have constraints ($\mathcal{C} = \emptyset$), any interpretation I of $\mathcal{D}, \mathcal{R}$ could be extended in order to map the negated atoms $p_i(\boldsymbol{y}_i)$ in q to true. Hence, there will always be some interpretations of $\mathcal{D}, \mathcal{R}$ where q does not hold i.e. $\mathcal{R}, \mathcal{D} \not\models q$.

When we have constraints in the knowledge base, we can easily transform the decision problem $\mathcal{D}, \mathcal{R}, \mathcal{C} \models q$ into a consistency check of $\mathcal{D}, \mathcal{R}, \mathcal{C}, \neg q$. Hence, we have that:

$$\mathcal{D}, \mathcal{R}, \mathcal{C} \models q \quad \text{iff} \quad \mathcal{D}, \mathcal{R}, \mathcal{C}, \neg q \models \bot \text{ (is inconsistent).} \qquad (6)$$

A conjunctive query with negated atoms is based on *safe* negation (CQ¬ˢ) if all the variables in negated atoms are also present in positive atoms of the query. The entailment problem for CQ¬ˢ is undecidable even with respect to a $DL\text{-}Lite_{core}^{\mathcal{H}}$ knowledge base [11]. Conjunctive queries with *guarded* negated atoms (CQ¬ᵍ) have guards for the variables that appear in every negated atom. For a UCQ¬ᵍ with a set of frontier-guarded rules the consistency check of our system (6) is in the *coNP* complexity class [5].

The consistency check approach (6) is useful to study the decidability of the problem, yet finding answers for a query in this way is too inefficient. Basically, one would need to solve problem (6) for all possible tuples that one can build using the constants in $\mathcal{D}$.

3.1   Horn Queries with Negation

The problem of deciding whether a query is entailed, for a given set of rules, constraints and data:

$$\mathcal{R}, \mathcal{C}, \mathcal{D} \models q \tag{7}$$

can be transformed into an equivalent problem by changing the hypotheses and consequences of the equation:

$$\mathcal{R}, \mathcal{D}, \neg q \models \neg \mathcal{C}. \tag{8}$$

In Eq. (8), the term $\neg \mathcal{C}$ is a union of BCQ $\{\ldots q_i \ldots\}$ with boolean queries q_i corresponding to the bodies of the constrains in $\mathcal{C}$ i.e.

$$q_i = a_1(\boldsymbol{x_1}), \ldots, a_n(\boldsymbol{x_n})$$

for each constraint

$$a_1(\boldsymbol{x_1}), \ldots, a_n(\boldsymbol{x_n}) \rightarrow \bot \in \mathcal{C}.$$

On the other hand, $\neg q$ depends on the shape of q but if it contains only one negated atom it will be translated into a rule i.e. $\neg(\exists \boldsymbol{X} \forall \boldsymbol{Y}, a_1(\boldsymbol{x_1}), \ldots, a_n(\boldsymbol{x_n}), \neg p(\boldsymbol{y}))$ is transformed into

$$r_q = \forall \boldsymbol{X} \exists \boldsymbol{Y} a_1(\boldsymbol{x_1}), \ldots, a_n(\boldsymbol{x_n}) \rightarrow p(\boldsymbol{y}).$$

Conjunctive queries with a negated atom are called *Horn Conjunctive Queries* ($\mathsf{CQ}^{\neg h}$).

Consequently, in order to find the answers of a Horn query we can rewrite the bodies of the constraints by using an additional rule r_q corresponding to q.

The rule r_q remains inside the framework of Existential Rules, with the variables $\boldsymbol{Y}$ that are not present in positive literals as existential variables. On the other hand, for Horn $\mathsf{CQ}^{\neg g}$ or even Horn $\mathsf{CQ}^{\neg s}$ we can ensure that r_q will not have any existential variables. Additionally, when we perform UCQ rewriting with the new set of rules, it is convenient to keep track of when the rule r_q was applied in order to identify the rewritings that were obtained using that rule. Thus, we can add a dummy atom $q()$ to the body of r_q. The queries with the predicate q in their atoms will be obtained by applying at least one rewriting step using r_q. Notice that the predicate q cannot be present in the knowledge base in order to avoid changing the semantics of Eq. (7).

The resulting set of rules $\mathcal{R} \cup \{r_q\}$ also needs to be a *fus* in order to guarantee the existence of a rewriting of the bodies of the constraints in the knowledge base. Therefore, by rewriting the bodies of the constraints we cannot ensure that all Horn queries can be answered. Nevertheless, depending on the rules in $\mathcal{R}$ and r_q we can check some of the sufficient conditions ensuring that the resulting set of rules is also a *fus*.

The final UCQ rewriting of the bodies of the constraints will contain (i) queries obtained using only rules from $\mathcal{R}$ and (ii) queries that were obtained by applying r_q at least once. The queries from (i) will allow us to express the inconsistencies of the original knowledge base and queries from (ii) will contain the rewritings of q (removing the dummy atoms).

The intuition behind Eq. (8) is that Eq. (7) will be satisfied when the application of the rule r_q introduces inconsistencies with respect to the constraints of the system.

Performing Forward Chaining with the resulting set of rules $\mathcal{R} \cup \{r_q\}$ could also be used to answer the bodies of the constraints in $\mathcal{C}$. However, there needs to be a way to tell apart the inconsistencies introduced by using r_q and those that do not depend on the presence of r_q. Basically, we have two problems to solve:

$$\mathcal{R}, \mathcal{D} \models \neg\mathcal{C} \text{ (consistency of the knowledge base)}$$

and

$$\mathcal{R} \cup \{r_q\}, \mathcal{D} \models \neg\mathcal{C} \text{ (consistency of the knowledge base if the new rule is added).}$$

Forward Chaining algorithms could also be modified in order to flag the facts that can only be obtained due to an application of r_q. We will then be interested if one of the flagged atoms is involved in triggering a constraint in $\mathcal{C}$. This would avoid computing the forward chaining saturation of both knowledge bases, considering that one of them is a subset of the other.

3.2   Union of Horn CQs

For conjunctive queries without negated atoms, the entailment of a UCQ $\{q_1, \ldots, q_n\}$ is a matter of considering the entailment problem of each query q_i separately and then taking the disjunction of the results:

$$\mathcal{K} \models \bigvee_{i=1}^{n} q_i \quad \text{iff}$$

$$\mathcal{K} \models q_1 \text{ or } \ldots \text{ or } \mathcal{K} \models q_i \text{ or } \ldots \text{ or } \mathcal{K} \models q_n.$$

In the presence of a union of conjunctive queries with negation (UCQ$^\neg$), we can consider the reduction in Eq. (6) and notice that it is possible to perform resolution between two clauses corresponding to negation of queries q_i. Therefore, considering entailment of each of the queries separately would not be a complete approach.

Example 2. Consider an empty set of rules and constraints with a UCQ$^\neg$:

$$\models a(\boldsymbol{x}) \vee b(\boldsymbol{y}), \neg a(\boldsymbol{y}).$$

By reasoning with each of the queries separately we obtain:

$$\models a(\boldsymbol{x})$$

and

$$\models b(\boldsymbol{y}), \neg a(\boldsymbol{y})$$

but we would not be able to infer that $b(\boldsymbol{x})$ is a rewriting of the initial UCQ⁻ i.e.

$$\mathcal{D} \models b(\boldsymbol{y})$$

implies

$$\mathcal{D} \models a(\boldsymbol{x}) \vee b(\boldsymbol{y}), \neg a(\boldsymbol{y}),$$

but $b(\boldsymbol{y}) \not\models a(\boldsymbol{x})$ and $b(\boldsymbol{y}) \not\models b(\boldsymbol{y}), \neg a(\boldsymbol{y})$.

A possible approach to follow can be to convert the Horn queries into rules and perform rewriting on the remaining queries plus the constraints of the system:

$$\mathcal{R} \cup \{r_{q_i} \mid horn(q_i)\} \models \neg \mathcal{C} \vee (\bigvee_{pos(q_i)} q_i), \tag{9}$$

where $horn(q_i)$ is true iff q_i is a Horn query and $pos(q_i)$ is true iff the query q_i contains no negated atom. Properties $horn/1$ and $pos/1$ can be checked syntactically over the queries. Union of conjunctive queries that contain either Horn conjunctive queries or conjunctive queries are called union of Horn conjunctive queries (UCQ⁻ʰ).

Property 2. For a finite unification set $\mathcal{R}$ and a UCQ⁻ʰ q, if the set of rules corresponding to the Horn queries is also a *fus* and together they define a directed cut i.e. $\mathcal{R} \triangleright \{r_{q_i} \mid horn(q_i)\}$, then the entailment problem for q is decidable for any set of constraints and facts.

Proof. If we consider Property 1 and the reduction of the entailment problem in Eq. (9) we can see that the resulting set of rules $\mathcal{R} \cup \{r_{q_i} \mid horn(q_i)\}$ is a *fus* of existential rules. □

Property 2 helps us knowing beforehand if the UCQ rewriting of the initial UCQ⁻ʰ exists. Besides checking the *fus* property for the set of rules corresponding to the Horn queries, we also need to make sure that the rules in $\mathcal{R}$ do not depend on the set of rules corresponding to the Horn queries. Nevertheless, if our Horn queries are translated to rules that have the same property of the rules in $\mathcal{R}$ i.e. $\mathcal{R} \cup \{r_{q_i} \mid horn(q_i)\}$ are linear rules or domain restricted rules, then we don't need to check the dependencies between both set of rules to ensure decidability.

4   Rewriting a Union of Horn CQs

Horn conjunctive queries with answer variables

$$q(\boldsymbol{X}) :- a_1(\boldsymbol{x_1}), \ldots, a_n(\boldsymbol{x_n}), \neg p(\boldsymbol{y})$$

are transformed into Horn boolean conjunctive queries:

$$q :- q(\boldsymbol{X}), a_1(\boldsymbol{x_1}), \ldots, a_n(\boldsymbol{x_n}), \neg p(\boldsymbol{y})$$

with a corresponding existential rule r_q:

$$r_q = q(\boldsymbol{X}), a_1(\boldsymbol{x_1}), \dots, a_n(\boldsymbol{x_n}) \rightarrow p(\boldsymbol{y}).$$

Atoms $q(\boldsymbol{X})$ will help identifying the rewritings obtained by applying r_q and the answers $\boldsymbol{X}$ of the query.

To find the answers of a $\mathsf{UCQ}^{\neg h}$ q, we rewrite the positive queries in q and also the constraint queries in $\neg\mathcal{C}$. Then, we keep those rewritings that contain atoms with the predicate q. The rest of the queries in the final UCQ-rewriting will express the inconsistencies of our knowledge base. When the initial query q is a BCQ, it is easy to transform a rewriting q_i of the constraints that used r_q into a rewriting of q. We just need to remove those q atoms we find in the query

$$q :- |q_i|^{-q}.$$

On the contrary, if answer variables are present in q and r_q was applied more than once, defining the answer tuples can be more complicated. The rewriting will possibly contain more than one atom with the predicate q i.e. $q(\boldsymbol{X_1}), \dots, q(\boldsymbol{X_k})$. This implies that we can have k possibly different tuples when the query $|q_i|^{-q}$ is entailed from the facts:

$$q(\boldsymbol{X_1}) :- |q_i|^{-q}$$

$$\dots$$

$$q(\boldsymbol{X_k}) :- |q_i|^{-q}.$$

The algorithm in Fig. 2 defines the general procedure to find the rewritings of a $\mathsf{UCQ}^{\neg h}$. For simplicity, queries $q(\boldsymbol{X})$:- $l_1, \dots, l_n$ in the initial Union of Horn CQs are transformed (**reshape/1**) into boolean queries q :- $q(\boldsymbol{X}), l_1, \dots, l_n$ that help us keep track of the rewritings of the original queries in the input $\mathsf{UCQ}^{\neg h}$. The **positive/1** function returns those queries that do not have negated atoms. With the boolean function **hasHorn/1** we can check if there are any Horn conjunctive queries and with **horn/1** we can obtain them. The constraints $a_1(\boldsymbol{x_1}), \dots, a_n(\boldsymbol{x_n}) \rightarrow \bot$ are transformed (**to_cqueries/1**) into queries () :- $a_1(\boldsymbol{x_1}), \dots, a_n(\boldsymbol{x_n})$ in order to rewrite them. The queries are rewritten using an external rewriting algorithm **rewrite_ext/2**. Finally, the rewritings are filtered (**to_rewritings/2**), selecting those that have the predicate 'q' and also transformed into answers of the original queries in q.

On Example 1 we could rewrite $q(X)$:- $Person(X), \neg MarriedTo(X, Y)$ and obtain the following UCQ-rewriting:

$$q(X) :- Priest(X) \vee$$

$$Minor(X) \vee$$

$$SinglePerson(X).$$

Notice that r_q has an existential variable and it cannot produce rewritings from the following constraints:

$$MarriedTo(X, Y), hasParent(X, Y) \rightarrow \bot$$

$$MarriedTo(X, X) \rightarrow \bot.$$

```
function rewrite (R , C , q)
         q := reshape (q)
         ucq := {}
         ucq.addAll(positive(q))
         if (hasHorn(q)) then
                      for q' in horn(q) do
                              R.add(r_q')
                      end for
                      ucq.addAll(to_cqueries(C))
         end if
         ucq := rewrite_ext(ucq, R)
         ucq := to_rewritings(ucq, 'q')
         return ucq
end function
```

Fig. 2. Function to rewrite Horn UCQs.

On the other hand, if we include Y as answer variable i.e.

$$q'(X,Y) :- Person(X), Person(Y), \neg MarriedTo(X,Y),$$

we are asking for pairs of people that cannot be married. The rewriting has 81 queries but basically the approach is to introduce the rule

$$q'(X,Y), Person(X), Person(Y) \rightarrow MarriedTo(X,Y)$$

and to rewrite the constraints:

$$MarriedTo(X,Y), Minor(X) \rightarrow \perp$$
$$MarriedTo(X,Y), Priest(X) \rightarrow \perp$$
$$MarriedTo(X,Y), SinglePerson(X) \rightarrow \perp$$
$$MarriedTo(X,Y), hasParent(X,Y) \rightarrow \perp$$
$$MarriedTo(X,X) \rightarrow \perp.$$

5   Experiments

Our system COMPLETO was upgraded with respect to the version presented in [14]. We now use the GRAAL [3] rewriting system that is able to rewrite CQs using existential rules. We also changed the MySQL database to H2 database for representing the ABox assertions in the ontology. The OWL 2 ER fragment of the TBox and the rules corresponding to the Horn queries are used to rewrite the constraints of the system. Then, the ABox assertions that could be encoded initially in OWL format are translated to a H2 database. Finally, the consistency check and instance retrieval processes can be carried out by using the constraints rewriting, the database of assertions and the queries that need to be rewritten and answered. A description of the system and how it can be installed and used is available online[2]. Additionally, we used the interfaces provided in the OWL API for the FACT++ [15] and HERMIT [9] solvers. Both systems perform reasoning using tableau techniques. However, they are designed to deal with ontology languages that are more expressive than OWL 2 ER.

The experiments were carried out on an Intel® Core™ i7-5930K CPU @ 3.50 GHz x 6, with 32 Gb of RAM memory and a SSD running Ubuntu 16.04 64-bit. We used ontologies that have both constraints and assertions. Additionally, they also belong to the OWL 2 ER fragment. The benchmark is composed by one of the groups of ontologies used in [8], the one from the Lehigh University Benchmark (LUBM) [10]. Additionally, constraints stating that sibling atomic concepts are disjoint were added. The group of LUBM ontologies consists of the same set of axioms and different number of assertions associated to different

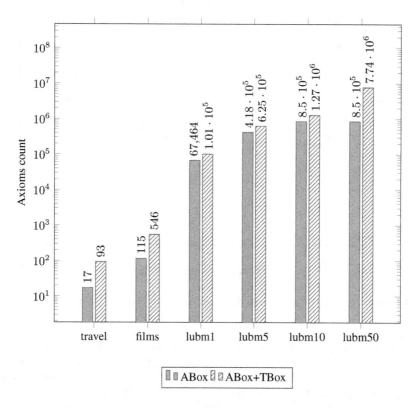

Fig. 3. Axiom counts of the ontologies of the benchmark

---

[2] http://image.ntua.gr/~gardero/completo2.0/usermanual.pdf.

number of universities (1, 5, 10, and 50) given as a parameter to the LUBM generator [10]. Additionally we tested the system using two small ontologies travel[3] and films[4]. Figure 3 shows the axioms count of the ABox and ABox+TBox for the ontologies of the benchmark.

The queries for the experiments were obtained by applying Association Rules techniques implemented using the Weka software [12]. Rules that describe hidden relations between the concepts of the ontology were obtained and we rewrote the counter examples expressions corresponding to the rules in order to check when it is consistent to add the new rules to the ontologies. A total of 86 queries were used for the travel ontology, 14 for the films ontology and 7 for the LUBM ontologies group.

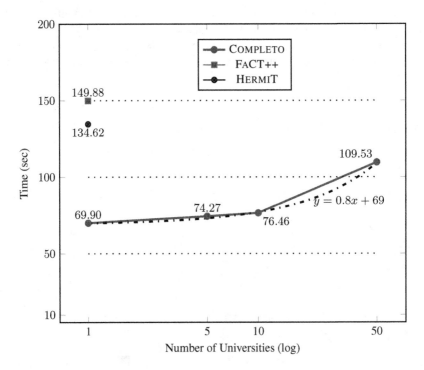

Fig. 4. Comparison of the average runtime per query for the LUBM group of ontologies

Figure 4 shows the average runtime per query for the LUBM group of ontologies. The runtime for COMPLETO increases with the size of the ABox and one can notice that it describes a linear relation ($y = 0.8x + 69$) to the number of universities in the ABox. On the other hand, FACT++ and HERMIT were only able to provide answers for the ABox containing only one university and

---

[3] http://www.owl-ontologies.com/travel.owl.

[4] https://www.irit.fr/recherches/MELODI/ontologies/FilmographieV1.owl.

they both took on average approximately twice as longer than COMPLETO for answering each query. For the rest of the LUBM ontologies, the systems reached the timeout of one hour per query defined for the experiments.

For the films ontology, COMPLETO takes 28.9 s per query while HERMIT and FACT++ take less than 0.2 s per query. In the case of the travel ontology, HERMIT and FACT++ take both 0.03 s per query while COMPLETO takes 0.48 s per query. Both Films and travel ontology have a very small number of assertions compared to the group of LUBM ontologies.

The RAM memory used by COMPLETO is not strongly affected by the size of the ABox and the average is 2,480 MB. The other systems used more than 5,800 MB for the only case where they were able to give answers.

6   Conclusions

In this paper, we proposed the definition of Horn queries and union of Horn conjunctive queries. We also provide a way to check the decidability of the entailment problem for these queries, by using a reduction to the entailment problem of conjunctive queries. The reduction also allows to answer Horn conjunctive queries using classic query answering methods developed on conjunctive queries.

We propose the use of conjunctive query rewriting approach to provide a UCQ rewriting for a union of Horn conjunctive queries. The method is implemented in the version 2.0 of the system COMPLETO. The GRAAL system was used as an external rewriter and a connection to a H2 database allowed efficient instance retrieval for the obtained rewriting.

COMPLETO was compared to FACT++ and HERMIT for rewriting Horn queries. The experimental results showed that COMPLETO is faster than the other systems for big ontologies. For ontologies with more than half a million axioms FACT++ and HERMIT were not able to find the answers of the queries on time. For very small ontologies COMPLETO is still fast, yet FACT++ and HERMIT outperform it.

Finally, we are very glad with the satisfactory performance of COMPLETO but we believe that the principal result in this investigation is the definition of Horn queries and the way we can answer them. We can use the system to improve the consistency check for the ontologies.

In the future, we want to propose a method that is able to rewrite more expressive queries, especially those containing more than one negated atom.

References

1. Baader, F., Calvanese, D., McGuinness, D.L., Nardi, D., Patel-Schneider, P.F. (eds.): The Description Logic Handbook: Theory, Implementation, and Applications. Cambridge University Press, New York (2003)
2. Baget, J.F., Gutierrez, A., Leclère, M., Mugnier, M.L., Rocher, S., Sipieter, C.: Datalog+, RuleML and OWL 2: formats and translations for existential rules. In: RuleML: Web Rule Symposium, Berlin, Germany, August 2015. https://hal.archives-ouvertes.fr/hal-01172069

3. Baget, J.-F., Leclère, M., Mugnier, M.-L., Rocher, S., Sipieter, C.: Graal: a toolkit for query answering with existential rules. In: Bassiliades, N., Gottlob, G., Sadri, F., Paschke, A., Roman, D. (eds.) RuleML 2015. LNCS, vol. 9202, pp. 328–344. Springer, Cham (2015). https://doi.org/10.1007/978-3-319-21542-6_21

4. Baget, J.F., Leclére, M., Mugnier, M.L., Salvat, E.: On rules with existential variables: Walking the decidability line. Artif. Intell. **175**(9), 1620–1654 (2011). http://www.sciencedirect.com/science/article/pii/S0004370211000397, https://doi.org/10.1016/j.artint.2011.03.002

5. Bárány, V., ten Cate, B., Otto, M.: Queries with guarded negation (full version). CoRR abs/1203.0077 (2012). http://arxiv.org/abs/1203.0077

6. Calvanese, D., Giacomo, G., Lembo, D., Lenzerini, M., Rosati, R.: Tractable reasoning and efficient query answering in description logics: the DL-Lite family. J. Autom. Reason. **39**(3), 385–429 (2007). http://dx.doi.org/10.1007/s10817-007-9078-x

7. Chandra, A.K., Merlin, P.M.: Optimal implementation of conjunctive queries in relational data bases. In: Proceedings of the Ninth Annual ACM Symposium on Theory of Computing, STOC 1977, pp. 77–90. ACM, New York (1977). http://doi.acm.org/10.1145/800105.803397

8. Du, J., Pan, J.Z.: Rewriting-based instance retrieval for negated concepts in description logic ontologies. In: Arenas, M., et al. (eds.) ISWC 2015. LNCS, vol. 9366, pp. 339–355. Springer, Cham (2015). https://doi.org/10.1007/978-3-319-25007-6_20

9. Glimm, B., Horrocks, I., Motik, B., Stoilos, G., Wang, Z.: HermiT: an OWL 2 reasoner. J. Autom. Reason. **53**(3), 245–269 (2014). https://doi.org/10.1007/s10817-014-9305-1

10. Guo, Y., Pan, Z., Heflin, J.: LUBM: a benchmark for OWL knowledge base systems. Web Semant. **3**(2–3), 158–182 (2005). http://dx.doi.org/10.1016/j.websem.2005.06.005

11. Gutiérrez-Basulto, V., Ibañez-García, Y., Kontchakov, R., Kostylev, E.V.: Conjunctive queries with negation over DL-lite: a closer look. In: Faber, W., Lembo, D. (eds.) RR 2013. LNCS, vol. 7994, pp. 109–122. Springer, Heidelberg (2013). https://doi.org/10.1007/978-3-642-39666-3_9

12. Hall, M., Frank, E., Holmes, G., Pfahringer, B., Reutemann, P., Witten, I.H.: The WEKA data mining software: an update. SIGKDD Explor. Newsl. **11**(1), 10–18 (2009). http://doi.acm.org/10.1145/1656274.1656278

13. König, M., Leclère, M., Mugnier, M., Thomazo, M.: Sound, complete and minimal UCQ-rewriting for existential rules. Semant. Web **6**(5), 451–475 (2015). https://doi.org/10.3233/SW-140153

14. Alfonso, E.M., Stamou, G.: Rewriting queries with negated atoms. In: Costantini, S., Franconi, E., Van Woensel, W., Kontchakov, R., Sadri, F., Roman, D. (eds.) RuleML+RR 2017. LNCS, vol. 10364, pp. 151–167. Springer, Cham (2017). https://doi.org/10.1007/978-3-319-61252-2_11

15. Tsarkov, D., Horrocks, I.: FaCT++ description logic reasoner: system description. In: Furbach, U., Shankar, N. (eds.) IJCAR 2006. LNCS (LNAI), vol. 4130, pp. 292–297. Springer, Heidelberg (2006). https://doi.org/10.1007/11814771_26

CHR.js: A CHR Implementation in JavaScript

Falco Nogatz[1](✉), Thom Frühwirth[2], and Dietmar Seipel[1]

[1] Department of Computer Science, University of Würzburg,
Am Hubland, D-97074 Würzburg, Germany
{falco.nogatz,dietmar.seipel}@uni-wuerzburg.de
[2] Institute of Software Engineering and Programming Languages,
Ulm University, D-89069 Ulm, Germany
thom.fruehwirth@uni-ulm.de

Abstract. Constraint Handling Rules (CHR) is usually compiled to logic programming languages. While there are implementations for imperative programming languages such as C and Java, its most popular host language remains Prolog. In this paper, we present CHR.JS, a CHR system implemented in JavaScript, that is suitable for both the server-side and interactive client-side web applications. CHR.JS provides (i) an interpreter, which is based on the asynchronous execution model of JavaScript, and (ii) an ahead-of-time compiler, resulting in synchronous constraint solvers with better performances. Because of the great popularity of JavaScript, CHR.JS is the first CHR system that runs on almost all and even mobile devices, without the need for an additional runtime environment. As an example application we present the CHR.JS Playground, an offline-capable web-interface which allows the interactive exploration of CHRs in every modern browser.

Keywords: Constraint handling rules · JavaScript · Compiler

1 Introduction

Constraint Handling Rules (CHR) [7] has its origins in the field of constraint logic programming. However, today's applications cover many different areas, ranging from traditional reasoning and time tabling problems to data mining, compiler construction, and computational linguistics [8]. Although it is usually used together with a hosting language, CHR has been evolved to a general-purpose programming language since its creation in the early 1990s. One reason for this development has been the implementation of CHR systems in different programming languages. Among others, there are CHR systems for most popular languages, including Java [1,18,22] and C [23]. While these implementations in imperative programming languages are typically faster, CHR's most popular host language remains Prolog. As a result, CHR is more common in the research community than for commercial applications that could benefit from its forward-chaining rewrite rules.

© Springer Nature Switzerland AG 2018
C. Benzmüller et al. (Eds.): RuleML+RR 2018, LNCS 11092, pp. 131–146, 2018.
https://doi.org/10.1007/978-3-319-99906-7_9

As today's applications increasingly become interactive, one of the main challenges is the handling of state and its mutations. The handling and coordination of multiple events (e.g., mouse clicks, sensor data) could be described using CHRs, modelling the program's state as the actual content of the constraint store. From this point of view, the combination of CHR with the increasingly interactive environment of web applications seems promising. Besides this, the programming language and field of constraint logic programming could benefit from a web-based implementation that can be easily run on most of the current devices, without the need for an additional installation step. JavaScript seems like an intended target to be a CHR host language: measured against dissemination and popularity, it is currently one of the most popular programming languages. Douglas Crockford, who developed the JavaScript Object Notation (JSON), once stated that every personal computer in the world had at least one JavaScript interpreter installed on it and in active use [3].

JavaScript is already a popular target language for compilation, too. There are currently more than 300 languages that compile to JavaScript.[1] By porting CHR to JavaScript, we can benefit from this broad distribution of runtime environments. For the implementation of CHR.JS, we define some design goals:

Resemblance to existing CHR systems. The CHR.JS syntax should feel natural for users with experience in other CHR systems.

Syntax based on JavaScript. The definition of CHRs should conform to design patterns in JavaScript. We strive for a natural integration of both languages.

Support for different runtime environments. CHR.JS should be portable across multiple runtime environments, including all modern web browsers and the server-side JavaScript framework node.js [2].

Extensible tracing options. By being executable on the web, CHR can be opened to the public. We want to improve the understanding of CHR programs by providing various tracing options.

Efficiency. The CHR system should be efficient. But unlike most of the other hosting languages of existing CHR implementations, JavaScript is an interpreted programming language and compiled just-in-time (JIT), so it might not be possible to compete with C or Java implementations.

Overview. The remainder of the paper is organised as follows. In Sect. 2, we shortly introduce the syntax and semantics of CHR. As a motivational example and to emphasise the usefulness of the CHR.JS system, we present the web-based CHR tracer called CHR.JS *Playground* in Sect. 3. In Sect. 4, existing approaches on the compilation of CHR into imperative programming languages are introduced. We define the integration of CHR with the JavaScript language in Sect. 5. The compilation scheme for asynchronous CHRs, which is used by the interpreter of CHR.JS, is presented in Sect. 6. Next, Sect. 7 introduces the compilation

---

[1] List of languages that compile to JS, https://github.com/jashkenas/coffeescript/wiki/list-of-languages-that-compile-to-js.

scheme for synchronous CHRs, used by the AOT compiler. The performance of CHR.JS is compared to several other CHR systems in Sect. 8. Finally, we conclude with a summary and discussion of future work in Sect. 9.

2 Constraint Handling Rules

In this section, the syntax and semantics of CHR are shortly summarised. For a more detailed introduction, we refer to [7].

Constraints are expressions of the form $c(t_1, \ldots, t_n)$ with $n \geq 0$, where c is an n-ary constraint symbol and $t_1, \ldots, t_n$ are terms of the host language. In addition to these *CHR constraints*, there are *built-in constraints*, which are data structures of usually the same form but which are defined in the host language. E.g., in Prolog these are predicates – either defined by the user or built-in –, and functions in JavaScript.

All CHR constraints that are known to be true are placed in a multi-set which is called the *constraint store*. By defining rules, it is possible to manipulate its contents. There are three types of rewrite rules which are applied until a final state is reached:

- the *propagation rule* is of the form $K_1, \ldots, K_n \Rightarrow G_1, \ldots, G_m \mid B_1, \ldots, B_l$,
- the *simplification rule* is of the form $R_1, \ldots, R_n \Leftrightarrow G_1, \ldots, G_m \mid B_1, \ldots, B_l$,
- the *simpagation rule* is a combination of both and of the form $K_1, \ldots, K_k \setminus R_{k+1}, \ldots, R_n \Leftrightarrow G_1, \ldots, G_m \mid B_1, \ldots, B_l$,

with K_i and R_i CHR constraints, G_i built-in constraints, and B_i built-in or CHR constraints. The CHR constraints denoted by K_i are kept in the constraint store, the R_i are removed, and the B_i are added. A rule is only applied if there are constraints in the constraint store which match with K_i resp. R_i, and if the *guard* specified by the built-in constraints G_i is satisfied. A rule is optionally preceded by *Name* @, where *Name* is its identifier.

Unlike its most popular host language Prolog, CHR is a committed-choice language and consists of multi-headed and guarded rules. There are multiple operational semantics for CHR. CHR.JS is based on the refined operational semantics ω_r as defined in [4], like most current CHR implementations. Most importantly, our implementation fixes the execution order of the given rules, while there remains non-determinism in the search of partner constraints.

Running Example. Figure 1 shows the classical *gcd/1* handler. Its two rules with the identifiers *gcd1* and *gcd2* define a constraint solver that calculates the greatest common divisor (GCD) of all positive integers specified as *gcd/1* constraints. Given the two constraints $gcd(36)$ and $gcd(8)$, the rule *gcd2* is applied, replacing $gcd(36)$ by $gcd(28)$. After five more steps, the constraint $gcd(0)$ is created and removed by the rule *gcd1*. The only remaining constraint $gcd(4)$ is the result.

$$gcd1 @ gcd(0) \Leftrightarrow true$$
$$gcd2 @ gcd(N) \setminus gcd(M) \Leftrightarrow 0 < N, N \leq M \mid gcd(M - N)$$

Fig. 1. CHR rules to calculate the greatest common divisor given as $gcd/1$ constraints.

3   CHR.js Playground: Web-Based Tracing for CHR

In our experience, there are two typical scenarios when working with a CHR system, both with different requirements: either one wants to simply (i) use the constraint solving mechanism, then with its best performance; or the user's aim is (ii) to interact with the rules and the constraint store. The latter is often the case when developing and tracing CHRs, or for educational purposes.

Fig. 2. Screenshot of the CHR.JS Playground at chrjs.net run in the Google Chrome browser with tracing enabled.

As an example application, our contribution contains an interactive web-based tracer for CHR. Figure 2 presents a screenshot of the created web application. It is inspired by collaborative code sharing platforms like JSFiddle[2] and SWISH[3] [21]. On the left-hand side, the source code editor is used to edit CHRs and to define built-in constraints (i.e. functions) in native JavaScript. In the right panel, queries can be specified, there is an optional tracer with step-by-step execution, and the current constraint store is visualised. A public, hosted instance is available online at http://chrjs.net/playground.

Although it is a web application, the CHR.JS Playground can be used standalone offline, because unlike SWISH no remote Prolog server is needed to run the specified queries. The stated CHRs are compiled on the fly. The CHR.JS Playground provides a persistent mode, so it is also possible to define CHRs that work on an already existing constraint store. To the best of our knowledge, this is the first CHR implementation that runs on mobile devices.

4   Related Work

Several approaches to compile CHR have already appeared in the literature. Since it was created as a language extension for Prolog in the first place [11–13], Prolog is the target language predominantly discussed. The implicit execution stack of Prolog maps very well to the ordered execution stack of the refined operational semantics ω_r: if a new constraint is added, all of its occurrences are handled as a conjunction of Prolog goals and are therefore executed before any other added constraint.

For imperative target languages, there are two major CHR systems: (i) K.U. Leuven JCHR [18], a CHR system for Java, and (ii) CCHR [23], a CHR system for C, which is currently the fastest implementation of CHR. Both implementations are discussed in [19]. A historical overview of CHR implementations can be found in [17].

Basic Compilation Scheme for Imperative Languages and Optimisations. The compilation scheme of CHR for logic programming languages as presented in [13] can be adopted to a procedural computation style by replacing Prolog predicates with methods or function calls. The resulting basic compilation scheme for imperative programming languages is presented in [19] and independent from the actual target language.

Although this general scheme is conform to the refined operational semantics ω_r, it is fairly inefficient. Multiple optimisations have been proposed in the past with [19] providing an exhaustive overview. These optimisations have been categorised into general ones (e.g., indexing, avoiding loop invariants, and guard simplifications) and optimisations in respect of recursions. Since JavaScript does not – unlike, for example, C and some implementations of the Java Virtual Machine – support tail call optimisations (TCO), they are of special interest

---

[2] JSFiddle, https://jsfiddle.net/.
[3] SWISH, https://swish.swi-prolog.org/.

for the implementation of CHR.JS.[4] Most non-trivial CHR programs contain recursions, and the discussed basic compilation scheme adds even more layers of recursive function calls due to its use of helper functions for each occurrence handler. On the other hand, the maximum call stack size is very limited in all major JavaScript systems, ranging from about 10k to 50k. Van Weert et al. present an adapted compilation scheme using a technique called *trampoline* [10] to avoid stack overflows for CHRs with tail calls. For the CHR.JS compiler we make use of the *explicit stack*, where the host language's stack is replaced by a self-maintained continuation queue on the host's heap.

5   Seamless Integration of CHR into JavaScript

Following our design goals, CHR.JS should be easy to use and adapt for both JavaScript and CHR experts. However, JavaScript has a different syntax than CHR and the well-known hosting language Prolog. In this section, we present how CHR can be embedded into JavaScript code and used together with JavaScript's synchronous and asynchronous functions. Even though this is discussed in particular for CHR, this section is useful for any reader interested in the seamless integration of a rule-based language into JavaScript.

5.1   Embed CHR in JavaScript Using Tagged Template Strings

The syntax of rule definitions is very similar to most existing CHR systems. Simple rules can be specified the same way as in CHR for Prolog (i.e. $\Rightarrow$ is encoded as ==>, and $\Leftrightarrow$ as <=>), as long as one uses the JavaScript equivalents of Prolog operators.[5] Moreover, different rules are either separated by a newline or a semicolon instead of a period. Unlike K.U. Leuven JCHR, CCHR and CHR systems for Prolog, CHR constraints do not need to be declared in advance. CHR.JS goes the other way round and uses a special syntax for the built-ins in the guard and body which must be enclosed by a dollar sign followed by curly brackets ${...}. As of now, there is no support for logical variables.

JavaScript and Prolog have a thing common: both lack easy support for multiline strings. With SWI-Prolog since version 6.3.17 this has been addressed using *quasi-quotations* [20]. They provide a special syntax to directly embed text that spawns multiple lines, which makes them suitable to embed external domain–specific languages (DSL) into Prolog source code without any

---

[4] The JavaScript language is standardised as *ECMAScript* [5]. The most recent version of the ECMAScript specification is the sixth version, often referred to as *ES6* or *ES2015* or by its codename *Harmony*. Although it defines TCO, it has not yet been implemented by the major browsers.

[5] For example the equality check in JavaScript is performed using == or === (type-safe), instead of the often used unification = in Prolog.

modification [16]. A similar technique has been recently added to JavaScript. So called *tagged template strings* allow to embed a DSL directly into JavaScript using the following syntax:

```
tag`text with ${ embedded_expr } even across multiple lines`
```

where `tag` is a user-defined function (the *template handler*) and expressions can be embedded using the `${...}` notation. Figure 3 presents the *gcd/1* handler as introduced in Sect. 2 in CHR.JS syntax. Since in JavaScript the backslash \ is an escape character in strings, it has to be escaped by a second backslash.

```
var chr = new CHR()
chr` gcd1 @ gcd(0) <=> true
     gcd2 @ gcd(N) \\ gcd(M) <=> 0 < N, N <= M | gcd(M-N)`
```

Fig. 3. CHR.JS rules to calculate the greatest common divisor.

The CHR.JS constructor `CHR()` creates the template handler `chr`, which can be used to embed the CHRs in JavaScript as a tagged template string. The template handler generates an abstract syntax tree (AST) for the given CHR program. In order to parse the rules, we have formalised their structure using a Parsing Expression Grammar (PEG) [6] and its JavaScript parser generator *PEG.js*[6]. PEG's syntax is similar to Definite Clause Grammars (DCG). Since the template string contains JavaScript fragments (e.g., the guard $0 < N$), we extended the JavaScript meta-grammar shipped with PEG.js to be able to parse CHR rules, too. A more detailed presentation of these PEG rules, the rule grammar, and the generation of the AST is given in [15, Sect. 4.3].

5.2 Synchronous and Asynchronous Execution

For each constraint c/n in the rule head a caller function $\texttt{chr}.c(arg_1, \ldots, arg_n)$ is created by CHR.JS. This way, the calculation of the GCD of the numbers 36 and 8 can be invoked by calling `chr.gcd(36)` and `chr.gcd(8)`. Because JavaScript has no static typing, the same caller function `chr.c` is used for all n, i.e. gcd/2 is invoked by simply specifying two arguments.

In most traditional imperative programming languages there is a strict stack-based execution cycle. To avoid blocking functions, concurrency models based on multiple threads have been established. Since JavaScript is single-threaded, this has been solved using the *event loop*. For functions taking long to execute it is possible to define a callback which is invoked once the function has been finished. These functions are called *asynchronous*.

The GCD of our running example can be calculated without any blocking function. However, if the application of a rule depends, e.g., on the result of a possibly long-running database query, we can make use of CHR.JS' support for

---

[6] PEG.js, https://pegjs.org/.

asynchronous functions. The caller function chr.c $(arg_1, \ldots, arg_n)$ provides a method .then(callback) to specify the callback function which is used once the constraint solving process has been completely finished. It is realised using the increasingly more popular approach of using *Promises* [9]:

```
chr.gcd(36).then(function () {     // call when finished handling gcd(36)
  chr.gcd(8).then(function () {     // call when finished handling gcd(8)
    console.log(chr.Store.toString()) // prints constraint store
  }) })                            // output:    gcd(4)
```

In JavaScript, a Promise represents the eventual completion or failure of an asynchronous operation. Once it is created, a callback function cb can be attached via .then(cb). It is called as soon as the asynchronous function has been finished and takes the computed value as its first argument.

If there is only a single asynchronous function in one of the rule's guard or body, the complete CHR.JS constraint solver becomes asynchronous. Due to JavaScript's execution model using the event loop, there is simply no way to wrap an asynchronous function inside another function and make it synchronous, that means blocking, again. So we have to categorise two kinds of CHR programs that we want to use with CHR.JS: those which contain asynchronous functions, and those which do not. This is reflected also in our two compilation schemes: CHR.JS provides an interpreter, which uses and supports asynchronous functions. Its compilation scheme is presented in Sect. 6. On the other hand we provide an AOT compiler which only supports synchronous functions. Both have their justifications: the asynchronous version is flexible and avoids stack overflows by design, because only a single stack frame is generated per message in the event loop. On the other hand, the synchronous version is faster and more natural for users already familiar with CHR.[7]

6   An Asynchronous CHR Interpreter Using Promises

While an asynchronous function can not be brought back into a synchronous form, the other way round is always possible. JavaScript's Promise.resolve(v) creates a Promise object that always immediately resolves to the specified value v:

```
var p = Promise.resolve([1,2,3]) // creates a new Promise p
p.then(function (ret) {          // p is "then-able" now like chr.gcd(8)
  console.log(ret) })            // output:    [1,2,3]
```

We have modified the basic compilation scheme of [19, Sect. 5.2] to use Promises, i.e. to use asynchronous callbacks specified via .then(). The constraints in the rule body and guard must be called asynchronously. The modified loop variant in the compilation scheme for a single occurrence occurrence_c_i_j_i($\ldots$) is presented in Fig. 4.

---

[7] A more detailed discussion on using synchronous or asynchronous functions is given in [15, Sect. 3.4].

```
if (!Store.allAlive(constraintIds))      // = nested check of still alive ids   [l. 8]
  return resolve()
if (!Store.allDifferent(constraintIds))  // = pairwise comparison               [ll. 9-11]
  return resolve()
if (History.has(ruleId, constraintIds))  // = notInHistory()                    [l. 13]
  return resolve()
var guards = [                           // = g_1 and ... and g_ng              [l. 12]
  new Promise(function(s, j) { return g_1 ? s() : j() }),
  ...
  new Promise(function(s, j) { return g_ng ? s() : j() })
]
Promise.all(guards)                      // prove all guards
  .then(function () {                    // all guards satisfied
    History.add(ruleId, constraintIds)   // = addToHistory()                    [l. 14]
    Store.kill(constraintIds[r])         // = kill()                            [ll. 15-17]
    ...
    Store.kill(constraintIds[h])
    Promise.resolve()
      .then(function() { return b_1() }) // invoke Promise for body 1           [ll. 18-20]
    . ...
      .then(function() { return b_nb() })// invoke Promise for body nb
      .then(function() { resolve() })
      .catch(function() { reject() })
  }).catch(function() { reject() })      // could not be fulfilled
```

Fig. 4. The modified loop variant for the compilation of a single occurrence. The bracketed line numbers refer to the original compilation scheme of [19].

The functions `resolve()` resp. `s()` successfully conclude the current Promise, similar to a `return` statement in synchronous function calls. With the functions `reject()` resp. `j()` the Promise gets rejected, similar to a `throw` statement in synchronous function calls.

`Promise.all(arrayOfPromises)` executes a given array of Promises in parallel. Note that due to CHR's refined operational semantics ω_r this is only allowed for the guards. The body constraints have to be handled sequentially instead. In [15, Sect. 4.5], we began to examine the parallel execution of constraints, which remains an interesting field for future improvements and research.

Support for Event Listeners and Breakpoints. Similar to the CHR reference implementation by Christian Holzbaur [13], CHR.JS provides a runtime environment which is reused by all instances. For example, the global constraint store referenced in Fig. 4 as `Store` can be accessed as part of the created `chr` object using `chr.Store`. During program execution it emits events for the addition and removal of a constraint. As usual in JavaScript, they can be received by adding event listeners as follows:

```
chr.Store.on('add', function (c) { /* added constraint c */ })
chr.Store.on('remove', function (c) { /* removed constraint c */ })
```

We use traditional callbacks instead of Promises for the event listeners, since Promises can be executed only once, whereas it is a reasonable use-case to fetch the removal of several constraints with multiple event listeners.

Similar to the constraint store, the defined CHR rules can be accessed and modified using `chr.Rules`. It holds an object for every defined CHR rule, for instance `chr.Rules['gcd1']` and `chr.Rules['gcd2']`. They have a special `Breakpoints` property which allows the binding of a Promise that will be called once the rule is tried to be applied. Unlike for event listeners, the further application of the CHR.JS program is paused until this Promise is resolved.

7   Ahead-of-Time Compilation with an Explicit Stack

Having to wait for the event loop for every single Promise, the compilation scheme presented in Sect. 6 does not result in fast constraint solvers. However, without the use of asynchronous functions, the constraint solver easily ends in a stack overflow because of the heavy use of recursion in the basic compilation scheme. This can be avoided using an optimising technique which is introduced in [19] as *explicit stack*. Instead of directly calling, e.g., the body constraints of a rule, an appropriate *continuation* is returned by the occurrence handler and pushed to the global list `stack`. The continuations are then handled by a global loop, similar to the event loop:

```
function trampoline() {
  while (constraint = stack.pop()) // pull first element
    constraint.continue() } // might push new continuations to the stack
```

We push the constraints that have been added in the rule's body to `stack` and add the continuation as the property `cont` of this particular constraint, so the call of `constraint.continue()` simply invokes it. Working with continuations is common in JavaScript, because functions are first-class citizens.

The initial caller function of a constraint, for instance `chr.gcd()`, generates the constraint object and initialises the `constraint.cont` property with the first occurrence handler `__gcd_1_0`:

```
function gcd() {
  var args = Array.prototype.slice.call(arguments)
  var arity = arguments.length, functor = "gcd/" + arity
  var constraint = new Constraint("gcd", arity, args);
  constraint.cont = [__gcd_1_0, 0]; stack.push(constraint)
  trampoline() }
```

The occurrence functions are of the form $\_c_i\_a_i\_j_i$, with c_i the current constraint name, a_i its arity and j_i an increasing number which identifies the occurrence. At the end, we add a generic handler with the occurrence number $(j_i + 1)$, which simply takes the constraint c from the stack and adds it to the constraint store:

```
function __gcd_1_3(c,n) { c.cont = null; chr.Store.add(c) }
```

If, for instance, a constraint $c/0$ occurs only in a rule's body but in no head, there is no rule that can be applied when c is added. So the only occurrence handler is the generic $\_c\_0\_0$, which adds c to the constraint store.

Instead of directly using the caller functions of the body constraints, we now add these constraints to the stack and assign their first occurrence handler as their first continuation. Therefore, a typical generated code fragment looks like this:

```
if (condition)
  c.cont = [nextOccurrenceHandler, 0]; stack.push(c); return
```

For instance, this is used with the rule's guard as the `condition`: if they are not satisfied, the next occurrence handler is called. As seen in the previous code fragments, we not only specify the continuation but also a number n which is initialised with 0. It is used to effectively iterate through all possible combinations of partner constraints in rules where the active constraint is kept. Instead of using a (possibly nested) loop, we can simply add the current occurrence handler as the next continuation but with an incremented n, so the next combination of partner constraints is used.

8   Experimental Evaluation

CHR.JS has been developed in a test-driven approach. Currently its compliance to the refined operational semantics ω_r is ensured by more than 420 functional tests. The correctness of CHR.JS is discussed in [15, Sect. 4.2.2]. Our implementation closely resembles the basic compilation scheme proposed in [19], whose completeness and correctness is shown in the same place. The functional tests has been used in a continuous integration environment with *Travis CI*[8].

8.1   Used Benchmarks and Systems

In order to compare our implementation to existing CHR systems, we used four benchmarks based on [23] and the CCHR implementation[9]:

- *gcd* calculates the greatest common divisor of 5 and $1000 \times N$ using the subtraction-based Euclidean algorithm as presented in our running example. It is a linear program involving at most two constraints.
- *fib* calculates the N'th Fibonacci number by bottom-up evaluation. This involves at most three constraints: an `upto/1` and the last two `fib/2`.
- *primes* generates all prime numbers upto N using the sieve of Eratosthenes.
- *ram* is a RAM simulator which counts down from N.

---

[8] Travis Continuous Integration service, https://travis-ci.org/.
[9] Copy available at https://svn.ulyssis.org/repos/sipa/cchr/.

The original CCHR benchmarks specify two more problems, *tak* and *leq*. We do not make use of them, because both require logical variables.

Basically, our benchmark suite executes a given command as often as possible within a 10 s time slot. It measures the number of iterations as well as the average execution time. We do not consider the used memory.[10]

All benchmarks are run on an Intel Core i7 9xx Dual Core CPU with 8 GB of RAM, using Ubuntu Server 16.04.3 64bit (Linux Kernel 4.4.0) with low load. We compare with three other CHR implementations: K.U. Leuven JCHR (v1.5.1) in Java (OpenJDK v1.8.0), CCHR (no version number provided, GCC v5.4.0), and K.U. Leuven CHR in SWI-Prolog (v7.6.4). For reference we provide a native JavaScript solution run with node.js (v9.5.0). CHR.JS has been used in v3.3.1 and with node.js (v9.5.0).

The asynchronous CHR.JS interpreter as presented in Sect. 6 makes great use of JavaScript's Promises. In [15, Sect. 6.2], we have shown that this technique is not even competitive to equivalent synchronous, iterative implementations. For every Promise, the JavaScript systems in all of today's browsers add a latency of four milliseconds. We therefore only use AOT-compiled CHR.JS programs in the benchmarks.[11]

8.2 Benchmark Results

Figure 5 shows the results of the benchmarks. Table 1 lists the geometric averages to complete the calculations. The averages for JavaScript have been set to 1 and those of the other systems have been scaled relatively. For the average calculation we consider only problem sizes that (i) have been successfully finished by all four systems and the native JavaScript implementation within 10 s, and (ii) the overall completion time for every system is not lower than 0.1 ms.

All benchmarks have in common that CCHR is the fastest CHR implementation. CHR.JS will not be able to compete with CCHR, since even the native JavaScript implementation of the problems is one order of magnitude slower than the C constraint solver.

The *gcd* and *fib* problems are similar in kind: both are actively working on only two constraints and one important CHR rule. By the use of a simpagation rule in both cases one of the constraints is removed and another gets added. But while for the *fib* problem it is guaranteed that always the older constraint is removed, this is not necessarily for *gcd*. In fact, the problem to solve gcd(5), gcd(1000*N) always removes the just now created gcd/1 constraint.

In the CHR.JS AOT compiler we already have implemented the *late storage* optimisation as suggested in [19, Sect. 5.3]. So, the problem to solve gcd(5), gcd(1000*N) stores only a single constraint at all, since a constraint gcd(P) immediately invokes the continuation for gcd(P-5), and so on.

---

[10] Benchmarks available at https://github.com/fnogatz/CHR-Benchmarks.

[11] CHR.JS provides a command line utility to pre-compile CHR programs: chrjs --optimized program.in.

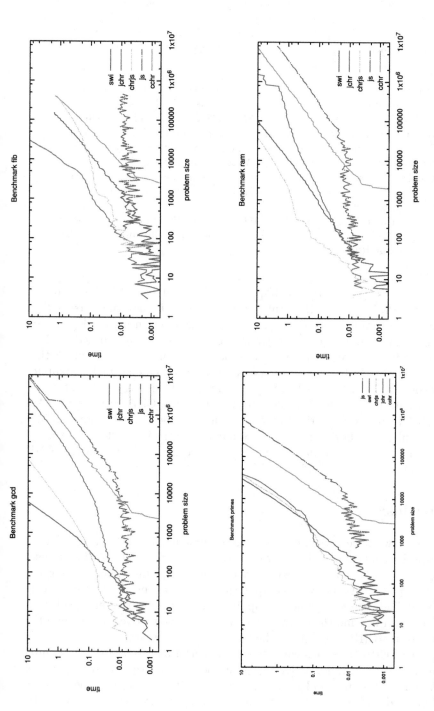

Fig. 5. Results for the benchmarks *gcd*, *fib*, *primes*, and *ram*. Further annotations are given in Table 1. Note that all benchmarks have in common that the native JavaScript implementation is not linear as expected. Because the start-up time for node.js scripts is about 10ms, the linear dependence can be seen only for big enough problem sizes.

Table 1. Relative geometric averages of benchmark results

Program	SWI-Prolog	K.U. Leuven JCHR	Chr.js	JavaScript	CCHR
gcd	280	6.8	53	[a]1.0	.08
fib	3.3	39	[b]9.9	[c]1.0	.05
primes	16	18	19	1.0	.03

[a]For very large $N \times 1000$, the problem exceeds the largest safe integer number in JavaScript, `Number.MAX_SAFE_INTEGER`. The calculation therefore needs more iterations due to the imprecision of the input value.

[b]For $N = 1470$ the N'th Fibonacci number exceeds the largest possible number in JavaScript, `Number.MAX_VALUE`. From there on the results are simply stated as `Infinity`. The Chr.js program finishes but the addition `Infinity + Infinity` is faster than the additions before, resulting in a faster overall execution.

[c]To avoid exceeding `Number.MAX_VALUE` we reset the numerical sequence every 1470th loop pass. For $N \approx 2 \cdot 10^9$ the JavaScript implementation takes about 10 s.

In the *primes* benchmark, our implementation is at par with the CHR systems in SWI-Prolog and JCHR, but still two orders of magnitude slower than the native JavaScript implementation. The *primes* problem highly depends on an efficient way to find partner constraints. To the best of our knowledge, there is no JavaScript standard implementation of an efficient in-memory index that works with node.js and all major browsers. In the worst case, a single lookup for partner constraints in Chr.js has to loop through all existing constraints.

The results in Fig. 5 and Table 1 suggest that the CHR systems in SWI-Prolog, JCHR and our contribution Chr.js have implemented various optimisations, resulting in fairly similar performances. There is no clear ranking of all the four systems – except for CCHR, whose claim to be the fastest CHR implementation could be verified.

9   Conclusion

In this work, we have presented Chr.js, the first implementation of CHR in JavaScript. It is published at https://github.com/fnogatz/CHR.js (MIT License) and supports synchronous and asynchronous JavaScript functions in the rules' guards and bodies. As an example application, we have presented the Chr.js Playground. This offline-capable web application uses event listeners and breakpoints, so that rules and the constraint store can be interactively edited and the execution of the CHR program can be traced in the browser.

To achieve CHR programs with reasonable performances, we have presented the compilation scheme for CHR to synchronous JavaScript. It makes use of continuation-passing to avoid recursions. Although the generated programs are at least one order of magnitude slower than their native JavaScript counterparts, there are several promising open optimisation ideas.

The presented approach of embedding CHR into JavaScript using tagged template strings might be useful for the integration of other rule-based DSLs, too. In particular, we would like to adapt the existing JavaScript interface of SWI-Prolog's Pengines [14] library, which allows the definition of remote procedure calls from web applications to Prolog engines, to also use a similar mechanism.

References

1. Abdennadher, S., Krämer, E., Saft, M., Schmauss, M.: JaCK: a Java Constraint Kit. Electr. Notes Theoret. Comput. Sci. **64**, 1–17 (2002)
2. Cantelon, M., Harter, M., Holowaychuk, T.J., Rajlich, N.: Node.js in Action. Manning Publications, Shelter Island (2017)
3. Crockford, D.: JavaScript: the world's most misunderstood programming language. Douglas Crockford's Javascript (2001)
4. Duck, G.J., Stuckey, P.J., de la Banda, M.G., Holzbaur, C.: The refined operational semantics of constraint handling rules. In: Demoen, B., Lifschitz, V. (eds.) ICLP 2004. LNCS, vol. 3132, pp. 90–104. Springer, Heidelberg (2004). https://doi.org/10.1007/978-3-540-27775-0_7
5. ECMAScript ECMA-Kommittee: A general purpose, cross-platform programming langugage, Standard ECMA-262 (1997)
6. Ford, B.: Parsing expression grammars: a recognition-based syntactic foundation. In: ACM SIGPLAN Notices, vol. 39, pp. 111–122. ACM (2004)
7. Frühwirth, T.: Constraint Handling Rules. Cambridge University Press, Cambridge (2009)
8. Frühwirth, T.: Constraint handling rules - what else? In: Bassiliades, N., Gottlob, G., Sadri, F., Paschke, A., Roman, D. (eds.) RuleML 2015. LNCS, vol. 9202, pp. 13–34. Springer, Cham (2015). https://doi.org/10.1007/978-3-319-21542-6_2
9. Gallaba, K., Mesbah, A., Beschastnikh, I.: Don't call us, we'll call you: characterizing callbacks in JavaScript. In: 2015 ACM/IEEE International Symposium on Empirical Software Engineering and Measurement (ESEM), pp. 1–10. IEEE (2015)
10. Ganz, S.E., Friedman, D.P., Wand, M.: Trampolined style. In: ACM SIGPLAN Notices, vol. 34, pp. 18–27. ACM (1999)
11. Holzbaur, C., Frühwirth, T.: Compiling constraint handling rules. In: ERCIM/COMPULOG Workshop on Constraints, CWI, Amsterdam (1998)
12. Holzbaur, C., Frühwirth, T.: Compiling constraint handling rules into prolog with attributed variables. In: Nadathur, G. (ed.) PPDP 1999. LNCS, vol. 1702, pp. 117–133. Springer, Heidelberg (1999). https://doi.org/10.1007/10704567_7
13. Holzbaur, C., Frühwirth, T.: A prolog constraint handling rules compiler and runtime system. Appl. Artif. Intell. **14**(4), 369–388 (2000)
14. Lager, T., Wielemaker, J.: Pengines: web logic programming made easy. Theor. Pract. Logic Programm. **14**(4–5), 539–552 (2014)
15. Nogatz, F.: CHR.js: compiling constraint handling rules to JavaScript. Master thesis, Ulm University, Germany (2015)
16. Nogatz, F., Seipel, D.: Implementing GraphQL as a query language for deductive databases in SWI-prolog using DCGs, quasi quotations, and dicts. In: Proceedings of 30th Workshop on Logic Programming (WLP 2016) (2016)
17. Schrijvers, T.: Analyses, optimizations and extensions of constraint handling rules. Ph.D. thesis, K.U. Leuven, Belgium, June 2005

18. Van Weert, P., Schrijvers, T., Demoen, B.: K.U. Leuven JCHR: a user-friendly, flexible and efficient CHR system for Java, pp. 47–62
19. Van Weert, P., Wuille, P., Schrijvers, T., Demoen, B.: CHR for imperative host languages. In: Schrijvers, T., Frühwirth, T. (eds.) Constraint Handling Rules. LNCS (LNAI), vol. 5388, pp. 161–212. Springer, Heidelberg (2008). https://doi.org/10.1007/978-3-540-92243-8_7
20. Wielemaker, J., Hendricks, M.: Why it's nice to be quoted: quasiquoting for prolog. In: Proceedings of 23rd Workshop on Logic-based Methods in Programming Environments (WLPE) (2013)
21. Wielemaker, J., Lager, T., Riguzzi, F.: SWISH: SWI-prolog for sharing. In: Proceedings of the International Workshop on User-Oriented Logic Programming (IULP 2015) (2015)
22. Wolf, A.: Adaptive constraint handling with CHR in Java. In: Walsh, T. (ed.) CP 2001. LNCS, vol. 2239, pp. 256–270. Springer, Heidelberg (2001). https://doi.org/10.1007/3-540-45578-7_18
23. Wuille, P., Schrijvers, T., Demoen, B.: CCHR: the fastest CHR implementation. In: Proceedings of 4th Workshop on Constraint Handling Rules (CHR07), pp. 123–137 (2007)

Complex Event Processing Under Uncertainty Using Markov Chains, Constraints, and Sampling

Romain Rincé[1,2(✉)], Romain Kervarc[1], and Philippe Leray[2]

[1] ONERA – The French Aerospace Lab, Palaiseau, France
romain.rince@onera.fr
[2] LS2N – Laboratoire des Sciences du Numérique de Nantes,
UMR CNRS 6004 Université de Nantes, Nantes, France

Abstract. For the last two decades, complex event processing under uncertainty has been widely studied, but, nowadays, researchers are still facing difficult problems such as combinatorial explosion or lack of expressiveness while inferring about possible outcomes. Numerous approaches have been proposed, like automaton-based methods, stochastic context-free grammars, or mixed methods using first-order logic and probabilistic graphical models. Each technique has its own pros and cons, which rely on the problem structure and underlying assumptions. In our case, we want to propose a model providing the probability of a complex event from long data streams produced by a simple, but large system, in a reasonable amount of time. Furthermore, we want this model to allow considering prior knowledge on data streams with a high degree of expressiveness.

1 Introduction

Since the end of the last century, the explosion of computerisation leads to growing amount of data to monitor. Detecting interesting or suspicious behaviours along data streams is a key goal on safety-critical systems. As those systems might be composed of numerous agents, their behaviours might be hidden by the interwine data produced by each agent. Complex Event Processing (CEP) focuses on analysing these data streams to detect interesting behaviours along the whole duration of a system execution. We usually call the information produced by a system Low Level Events (LLEs) and the behaviours complex events (CEs), as they are LLEs compositions.

Many CEP techniques allow monitoring events from a data stream, but, as most information on a system is detected through sensors or human knowledge, it may contain errors, mostly erroneous detections (e.g. missing an event, leading to a specific behaviour not being recognized), or false detections (e.g. an event that actually never occurred) leading to false recognitions. Uncertainty may also appear when CEs are designed, since they are usually defined based on human knowledge or through statistical analysis, which may miss specific cases where

© Springer Nature Switzerland AG 2018
C. Benzmüller et al. (Eds.): RuleML+RR 2018, LNCS 11092, pp. 147–163, 2018.
https://doi.org/10.1007/978-3-319-99906-7_10

the desired behaviour emerges. Many authors address uncertainty in various ways. [1,2] use Non Deterministic Finite Automata associated to probabilities to compute the likelihood of a CE. Other authors represent CEP as a logical problem and use specific Probabilistic Graphical Models (PGMs) to calculate probabilities, such as Markov Logic Networks (MLNs) [3,4], or Problog [5]. [6] represent CEs as stochastic context-free grammars. These techniques will be discussed in deeper detail later, are roughly divided between exact inference (all possible outcomes are evaluated to compute the probabilities as in [5,7]) and approximate inference (relying on PGMs and sampling to compute the probabilities like in [3,8]).

The way uncertainty is dealt with in CEP also depends on system specifics: long time relation, kind of uncertainty (on events, attributes, time, model design...,) online inference, attributes with continuous values, discrete or continuous time, computational speed, exact or approximate evaluation, etc. Addressing all possible cases in a single method seems unachievable, so each work focuses on its own specific constraints. Consequently, literature offers a wide variety of approaches, not only technically but also conceptually. Some focus on event attribute uncertainties but without considering long time relations, while others do the opposite.

In this paper, we propose a method to estimate CE recognition likelihood in a reasonable amount of time from a potentially erroneous data-stream of LLEs produced by a system. We consider uncertainty on events, i.e. event detection is not guaranteed (they may be missed or incorrectly detected). More formally, we aim at producing probability estimations of CEs, even with long term relations, close to methods preforming exact computation, but with a better scalability to larger problems. We want prior knowledge to be provided to constrain possible executions of the system and taken into account for the probability computation. This knowledge might be expressed as LLEs or CEs.

On our model, we use the chronicle formalism [9,10], which describes CEs by association of LLEs or previously defined CE using interval operators. Probability estimation will be computed using Markov Chain Monte-Carlo (MCMC) on a non-homogenous Markov process (NHM) constructed using an initial Markov chain (MC) M that describes the system producing the events of our stream. The noisy data stream is considered as prior knowledge on the execution of our system and hence as constraints on M. Regarding all constraints and M, we define the NHM as the representation of all possible executions. It produces samples for the MCMC using random walk. Creating the NHM requires prior knowledge that is all the LLEs observed in the data stream, but we want to extend our method to be able to use an external information represented as a CE to constrain the NHM. This CE would be a chronicle representing a specific behaviour that as be observed during the production of the data stream.

Section 2 presents the techniques and CEP representation that we use. Sections 3 and 4 show how we estimate the likelihood of a chronicle on a stream and how we express knowledge at a high level. Performance comparison with Problog and MLNs is provided in Sects. 5 and 6 discusses our solution and compare it with other approaches.

2   Background

Here, we provide insight of the necessary background for our contribution. First, we present the chronicles which is the CEP system that we used for recognitions, then we remind basic knowledge on NHM and Deterministic Finite Automata (DFA).

2.1   The Chronicle Model

Many CEP techniques exist like SASE+, T-REX, Dousson's chronicles, Event Calculus. [11–14], but for our method we will focus on *Chronicles* [9,10].

Like all the above methods, chronicles aim at detecting meaningful information within temporal data flows. This information is usually a behaviour or a specific activity that will be model into a CE. Many of these methods have been modified to deal, on their own way, with uncertainty and we aim to extend the Chronicle model too.

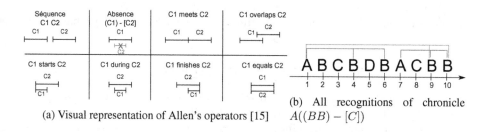

(a) Visual representation of Allen's operators [15]

(b) All recognitions of chronicle $A((BB) - [C])$

Fig. 1. Chronicle formalism

For the chronicle model, data is composed of LLEs, i.e. events with their detection times, upon which logical formulae, the chronicles (i.e. CEs) are built inductively using Allen's operators[1] [15] (cf. Fig. 1a). Two events might be associated together, based on their time points, to compose a chronicle. Regarding the operator used, a chronicle describe a behaviour or activity on a time interval. As the operators associate intervals, it is possible to compose more complex chronicles using previously defined chronicles. These operators allow the chronicles to define long-term relations between events, since they represent more the positioning of events relative to each other than a specific duration of time. Consequently, it is possible to recognise CEs taking place on the full duration of a data stream. Figure 1b presents the recognitions of a chronicle where an event A precedes two events B, without any event C between the two B, which is denoted $A((BB) - [C])$. Here, $(BB) - [C]$ is a sub-chronicle.

---

[1] Chronicles use over 15 interval operators: Allen's and duration-related constraints – cf. [9].

CEP techniques commonly manage attributes associated with LLEs and CEs, which may be used to compose specific recognition rules, but for our approach, we will ignore attributes i.e. consider only nullary events. We first want to focus on a method performing inference in relative short amount of time, even with numerous different types of event along relatively quite long data streams. Dealing with attributes under uncertainty is an additional subject that we will certainly study in future work but is not addressed here. To avoid confusion below, *events* will refer to LLE and *chronicles* to CEs.

2.2 Discrete Non-Homogeneous Markov Chains from Markov Process

An important part of our method consists in producing a NHM that represents a system modelled by a Markov process and constraints on its execution. We now outline the creation of the NHM as proposed by [16].

The method aims to produce sequences of states from a Markov process M defined over a finite set of states $\mathcal{A}$. Given a length L, S is the set of all sequences of length L that may be produced by M with non-zero probabilities. For a sequence $s = s_1, \ldots, s_L, s \in S, s_i \in \mathcal{A}$:

$$p_M(s) = p_M(s_1) \cdot p_M(s_2|s_1) \cdots p_M(s_L|s_{L-1})$$

We now consider a subset of sequences $S_C \subseteq S$ that should follow a set of constraints C. These constraints are unary, describing a set of states possible at a given time, or binary, describing a set of transitions between two consecutive times. The constraints are embedded into a NHM represented by a set $\tilde{M}$ of transition matrices $\tilde{M}^{(i)}, i = 1, \ldots, L$ where $p_{\tilde{M}}(s_i|s_{i-1}) = \tilde{M}^{(i)}$ and $\tilde{M}$ verifies the two properties:

- $p_{\tilde{M}}(s) = 0$ for $s \notin S_C$
- $p_{\tilde{M}}(s) = p_M(s|S_C)$ otherwise

Briefly, computation of the NHM works as follows: compute the intermediate matrices $Z^{(0)}, \ldots, Z^{(t)}, \ldots, Z^{(L-1)}$ that are the equals to M but with all the impossible transitions between $t - 1$ et t, regarding the constraints, set to 0. Then $\tilde{M}$ is computed using the following formula:

$$
\begin{aligned}
\tilde{m}_{j,k}^{(L-1)} &= \frac{z_{j,k}^{(L-1)}}{\alpha_j^{(L-1)}}, \quad \alpha_j^{(L-1)} = \sum_{k=1}^{n} z_{j,k}^{(L-1)} \\
\tilde{m}_{j,k}^{(i)} &= \frac{\alpha_k^{(i+1)} z_{j,k}^{(i)}}{\alpha_j^{(i)}}, \quad \alpha_j^{(i)} = \sum_{k=1}^{n} \alpha_k^{(i+1)} z_{j,k}^{(i)} \quad 0 < i < L-1 \\
\tilde{m}_k^{(0)} &= \frac{\alpha_k^{(1)} z_{j,k}^{(0)}}{\alpha_j^{(0)}}, \quad \alpha_j^{(1)} = \sum_{k=1}^{n} \alpha_k^{(1)} z_k^{(0)}
\end{aligned}
\tag{1}
$$

where n is the number of states. As shown by Pachet *et al.* [16] $\tilde{M}$ generates exactly the sequences $s \in S_C$ and that these sequences have the same probabilities in M and $\tilde{M}$ up to a constant factor.

2.3   Deterministic Finite Automaton

In this paper, we use DFA to represent a set of event sequences S of same length L. This set may be considered as a language $\mathcal{L}$ over the alphabet Σ which is the set of all the events appearing on S. As all sequences have the same length L, $\mathcal{L}$ might be represented as an acyclic DFA and minimized in linear time [17]. As a reminder, a DFA $\mathcal{A} = (\mathcal{Q}, \Sigma, \delta, q_0, \mathcal{F})$ is defined with $\mathcal{Q}$ a finite set of states, Σ an alphabet, $\delta : \mathcal{Q} \times \Sigma \mapsto \mathcal{Q}$ a transition function, $q_0 \in \mathcal{Q}$ an initial state, and $\mathcal{F} \subseteq \mathcal{Q}$ the set of final states.

3   Probability Estimation of a Chronicle on Noisy Data Stream

3.1   Process

Our goal is to define a model able to estimate the probability of a given chronicle ch on a specific data stream. This chronicle might be seen as a query on the stream. In this paper, we will focus on calculating the likelihood that at least one recognition of the chronicle appears on the stream, but we could ask for any specific number of recognitions. We also assume that the stream results from sensor observations of an actual system composed of sub-systems changing their states during time. We consider time as discrete and events are subsets of the current state of the sub-systems at given times. We suppose that our system may be described as a discrete, stationary, first-order MC M whose states are the cartesian product of sub-systems states.

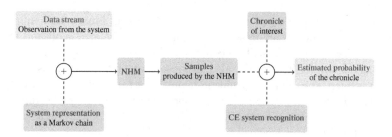

Fig. 2. Probability estimation process

Information provided on streams is supposed to be our observations and may be erroneous or noisy regarding the system observed. For instance, imagine that a system is observed using sensors sensible to errors. Note that this modelling handles missing or erroneous detections but not incorrect detection times: two state change detections swapped in time may not be represented.

Our process to estimate probability (Fig. 2) consists in transforming the data stream into a set of unary and binary constraints and used them with the Markov model, as presented in Sect. 2.2, to construct the corresponding NHM $\tilde{M}$. Using random walk on this NHM, we generate a sufficient amount of possible streams of states that explains the prior data stream. With a sufficient amount of samples, the probability of each sequence should be close to the distribution provided by the NHM. Each sample produced may be analysed through a CE recognition system that provides the number of recognitions of ch. Estimating its probability just consists in counting the number of samples that recognise ch among all.

3.2 Toy Example: An Hurricane Alarm

In this section, we illustrate our process with a toy example. Suppose that we use the system described at Fig. 3a. The model is composed of two subsystems, Hurricane and Alarm, having different possible states. The Hurricane part might be on state Hurr or Calm meaning respectively that there is currently a hurricane or not. The Alarm part might be on state On or Off meaning respectively that the hurricane alarm is triggered or not. The alarm is not completely safe and might trigger without hurricane or reciprocally not triggering during a hurricane. It represents the behaviour of a hurricane alarm regarding the weather and its own state. Transition probabilities are provided in Fig. 3a. The alarm may be considered as the sensor used to detect a hurricane. So the data stream provides the timely state of the alarm, whilst the state of the weather might almost never be provided.

For now, we transform our model into a simple MC M where its states are combinations of the states of the two sub-systems. The resultant matrix is given on Fig. 3b.

According to [16], we can constrain the MC using binary and unary constraints at given times: to express e.g. that at $t = 2$ the alarm is off and at $t = 3$ a hurricane rises, the NHM will be constructed by removing inconsistent transitions at corresponding times. We also suppose that at $t = 0$ there is neither an alarm nor a hurricane. This information is our constraint set S_C. Regarding constraints, the dependency graph of states between instants might be represented as Fig. 4. The probabilities are re-evaluated using back-propagation as presented in Sect. 2.2 (cf. Eq. 1).

Sampling is performed by random-walk, selecting a path regarding the probabilities given by the NHM. Each sample produced should then be parsed through a CEP engine. After enough samples, we will be able to estimate chronicle likelihood by counting the number of recognitions over all samples. This method provides the likelihood of a given chronicle but prior knowledge may only be represented as a succession of possible states at given times. But it could be interesting to express it as a behaviour. In our toy example, we might e.g. know that between two times a hurricane rised but the alarm never triggered. The next section provides a method to estimate a chronicle likelihood regarding this kind of knowledge.

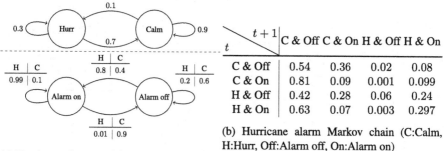

(b) Hurricane alarm Markov chain (C:Calm, H:Hurr, Off:Alarm off, On:Alarm on)

(a) Hurricane alarm model and transition probabilities

Fig. 3. Hurricane alarm model representation

	1	$\tilde{M}_1$	2	$\tilde{M}_2$	3	$\tilde{M}_3$	4
	C & Off		C & Off		C & Off		C & Off
	C & On		C & On		C & On		C & On
	H & Off		H & Off		H & Off		H & Off
	H & On		H & On		H & On		H & On

Fig. 4. Graphical representation of the NHM from instant 1 to 4. Constraints: Alarm off at t = 1 & t = 2, Hurricane at t = 3

4   Chronicle Probability Estimation Under High-Level Constraints

We described a method to approximate using sampling the probability of a chronicle recognition under unary and binary constraints, and now want to extend it to constraints expressed in a higher formalism, namely chronicles. Formally, it means that we do not provide the exact time of a known event but an interval where a CE appears.

In this section, we show how to express these constraints as a sub-stream set, which we then regroup into graphs to reduce the samples needed, and a method to construct graphs. These transformations from chronicles as constraints to a constraint sub-graph are detailed on Fig. 6, which focuses on a part of the full process (on Fig. 5).

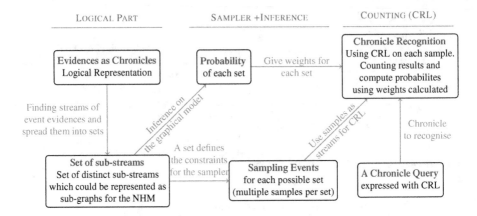

Fig. 5. Architecture of the sampling model

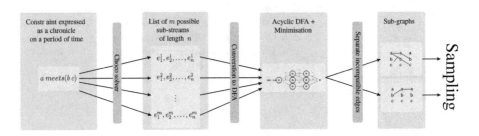

Fig. 6. Process road map to transform high-level constraints

4.1 Constraint Sub-streams to Represent Behaviours

Expressing a chronicle as a constraint over an interval is equivalent to consider as constraints all possible sub-streams Φ producing a recognition of this chronicle on this interval. In this paper, Φ will represent all the possible execution of the system regarding the constraints during two instants of time. Consequently, one sub-stream is a possible execution of the system on this interval of time. Finding all the sub-streams is not our main purpose here, and may be defined as a Constraint Satisfaction Problem (CSP) handled by a solver. To avoid combinatorial explosion of the solving, the chronicle is used as a constraint over a restricted time interval and not over the whole stream. For instance, specifying a sequence of two states as a constraint in a time interval gathers all the possible outcomes of stream where this chronicle should be recognised.

Considering that we have Φ, a naive approach would be to sample over each of these sub-streams $\varphi \in \Phi$, since each could be expressed with unary and binary constraints. Given the set Φ of sub-streams, the probability of a sample s on these constraints would be equal to:

$$P(s|\Phi) = \sum_{\varphi_i \in \Phi} P_M(\varphi_i|\Phi) \times P_{\tilde{M}_{\varphi_i}}(s) \qquad (2)$$

where $P_{\tilde{M}_{\varphi_i}}(s) = P_M(s|\varphi_i)$ is the probability that the sample is generated by the model $\tilde{M}$ under the constraint φ_i.

But, as no φ_i is included in another φ_j, the sequences that they might generate are independent. Consequently, if a stream s follows the constraints Φ, it can be generated by only one $\varphi' \in \Phi$, meaning only one $P_{\tilde{M}_{\varphi'}}(s)$ has a non-zero probability. Furthermore, because of the independence:

$$P_M(\varphi_i|\Phi) = \frac{P_M(\varphi_i)}{P_M(\Phi)} \qquad (3)$$

if φ' is the sub-stream producing s, Eq. 2 may be rewritten:

$$P(s|\Phi) = \frac{P_M(\varphi')}{P_M(\Phi)} \times P_{\tilde{M}_{\varphi'}}(s) \qquad (4)$$

However, this approach requires sampling over all sub-streams and their number grows exponentially on their length (depending of course on the chronicle: the more it is constraining, the less possible outcomes), it could lead to a drastic amount of sampling even using parallel computing.

4.2   Representing Constraint Sub-streams as Sub-graphs

To reduce the number of necessary samplings, we take advantage of the NHM structure to represent the constraint streams: using local binary constraints, more than one sub-stream may be represented in an accepting sub-graph of the NHM.

Definition 1. A constraint sub-graph is *accepting* for the constraint sub-streams if all paths are in bijection with them.

For instance, we define a constraint Φ from the streams $\varphi_w, \varphi_x, \varphi_y$ in Fig. 7a which maybe represented in one sub-graph. This could reduce drastically the number of needed sampling as the three streams are now embedded in only one sub-graph. But if we want to add a fourth constraint φ_z to Φ directly (dashed in Fig. 7b), the graph is no longer accepting as it recognizes sub-stream $((a,1)(a,2)(a,3))$ as a valid constraint. In that case, it is necessary to split the set of constrained streams into two sub-graphs (Fig. 7c). Indeed, conditions to split are highly correlated with the full set of constraint streams. E.g., assuming that we consider the three streams in Fig. 7d as constraints in Φ, the graph in Fig. 7b is accepting.

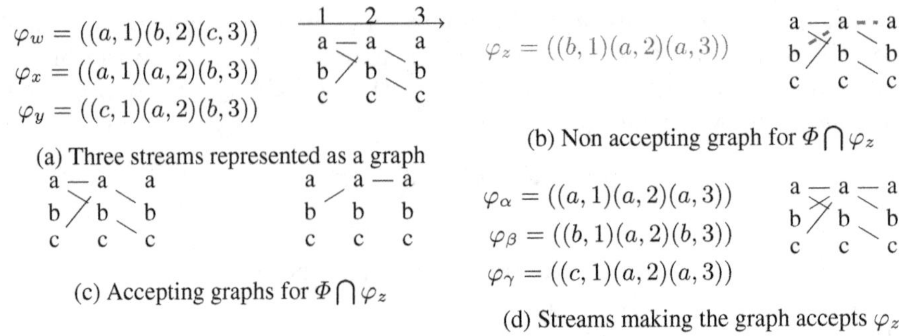

$\varphi_w = ((a,1)(b,2)(c,3))$
$\varphi_x = ((a,1)(a,2)(b,3))$
$\varphi_y = ((c,1)(a,2)(b,3))$

(a) Three streams represented as a graph

(c) Accepting graphs for $\Phi \bigcap \varphi_z$

$\varphi_z = ((b,1)(a,2)(a,3))$

(b) Non accepting graph for $\Phi \bigcap \varphi_z$

$\varphi_\alpha = ((a,1)(a,2)(a,3))$
$\varphi_\beta = ((b,1)(a,2)(b,3))$
$\varphi_\gamma = ((c,1)(a,2)(a,3))$

(d) Streams making the graph accepts φ_z

Fig. 7. Examples of accepting/not accepting sub-graphs

4.3 Finding a Set of Constraint Sub-graphs

To perform the transformation, we will define our set of constraint sub-streams as a language $\mathcal{L} \subseteq \Sigma^n$ on the alphabet $\Sigma = \{a, b, c\}$ defined as the set of states $\mathcal{A}$ from a corresponding NHM, and n the length of the streams. As we pointed out, $\mathcal{L}$ might be represented as an acyclic DFA. E.g., the streams $\varphi_w, \varphi_x, \varphi_y, \varphi_z$ might be represented as the DFA in Fig. 8. Using this automaton, it is possible to identify streams that could not appear on the same sub-graph.

Definition 2. Two edges of the DFA are incompatible if they are at the same depth, share the same transition from Σ leading to two distinct states in $\mathcal{Q}$. Two sub-streams are incompatible if they each contain one of two incompatible edges.

In our DFA in Fig. 8, transitions between q_1, q_5 and q_4, q_5 lead to the same state and thus are not incompatible. By contrast, transitions between q_4, q_5 and q_6, q_7 are incompatible as they are at the same depth from the initial state, depend on the same symbol a, and lead to different states. It is now possible to separate streams according to the incompatibility expressed through the DFA (cf. an example in Fig. 8 where each set is dashed differently), which is performed by Algorithm 1, a breadth-first recursive algorithm on depth: from the initial node it separates at each level incompatible edges into sets and creates for each a new automaton with all accessible ancestors and descendants, until reaching all final states. This algorithm does not necessarily provide a minimal splitting in terms of set number, but ensures that the resultant sets are indeed independent, and is sufficient for our purpose.

4.4 Sampling with Constraint Sub-graph

The likelihood has to be estimated differently, but is still similar to Eq. 2, as we do not sample over a simple constraint sub-stream but over a set of sub-streams. The marginal probability of a set $P_M(\Phi)$ is the product of the unnor-

---

Algorithm 1. Split_automaton

---

    inputs : $\mathcal{A}$, the automaton associated to the language
              $C_{\mathcal{A}}$, a set of pairs of constrained edges in $\mathcal{A}$
              d, depth of a layer
    outputs: *sol*, a set of automata without inside incompatible edges
1 *edges_sets* $\leftarrow$ separate incompatible edges at depth d into sets regarding $C_{\mathcal{A}}$
2 **for** *set* $\in$ *edges_sets*
3   Create new automaton $\mathcal{A}' \leftarrow$ from *set*, descendants of *set* and ancestor of *set*
4   Minimize $\mathcal{A}'$
5   **if** $C_{\mathcal{A}'}$ *is empty*
6   add $\mathcal{A}'$ in sol
7   **else**
8   add $Split\_automaton(\mathcal{A}', d+1)$ in sol
9 **return** *sol*

---

malized constrained matrices of the NHM, which is easily evaluated during back-propagation. Given a sub-set $\Phi_s \subseteq \Phi$ that can produce a sequence s, the probability of s regarding Φ_s:

$$P(s|\Phi) = \frac{P_M(\Phi_s)}{P_M(\Phi)} \times P_{\tilde{M}_{\Phi_s}}(s) \tag{5}$$

5   Experimentations

In this section, we will compare our approach with Problog [18], which has been used successfully to manage uncertainty in CEP and produces exact results. As Problog is based on first order logic, it is relatively easy to model the hurricane system, design the chronicle, and set constraints. We compare our method with Problog as it provides the exact likelihood regarding the problem and the constraints, so it would be possible to estimate how close our approximate method is from exact computation.

Furthermore, we provide a comparison of inference times between our method, Problog, and an approach using MLNs [19]. MLNs have been quite often used in literature to represent uncertainty in CEP, particularly from the

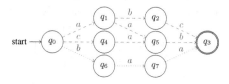

Fig. 8. Minimal automaton for the streams $\varphi_w, \varphi_x, \varphi_y, \varphi_z$ and resulting separation.

computer vision domain [8,20,21]. We do not provide a comparison of estimations between our method and MLN approach. Indeed, MLNs were not able to produce coherent results due to the sampling method used with MLNs and the size of the problem when converted into the MLN structure. In brief, computational issues rise when a model is design with circumscription which implies many loopy relationships between predicates making the MLN sampler inefficient. More details about this subject is addressed in [22].

For our experimentations, we used the hurricane model described above in Fig. 3a and b. We want to perform an inference on this model with the following chronicle as a query:

$$((H\ H) - [C])\ equals\ ((\textit{off off}) - [on]) \tag{6}$$

This chronicle describes a period, during which a hurricane strikes but the alarm is never raised. As observation, we state that for $t \in [2,5]$ the alarm was never on, but meanwhile a hurricane happened, as formalised by this chronicle:

$$H\ during\ ((\textit{off off}) - [on]) \tag{7}$$

To constraint our model regarding this prior knowledge, we turn Eq. 7 into a set of sub-graphs as described in Sect. 4 by using *Choco* as constraint solver[2].

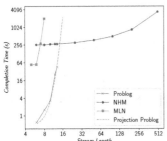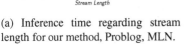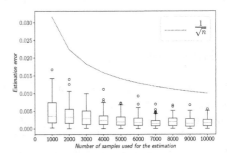

(a) Inference time regarding stream length for our method, Problog, MLN.

(b) Estimation errors compared to the exact evaluation regarding the number of samples created.

Fig. 9. Inference time and estimation errors of our approach.

We set the number of samples to 10 000 per sub-graph and compared the inference time of our method with Problog, and a MLN-based approach. The results are shown in Fig. 9a. Due to a lack of memory, we could not produce results for Problog streams of length above 13, but computation time was clearly exponential[3]. Even if our sampling method is slower to perform on really small

---

[2] http://www.choco-solver.org/ [23].

[3] It was to be expected, as Problog computes all possible solutions, the set of which grows exponentially.

problems, it appears clearly that problem dimension has less impact on the computation time of our method than Problog and MLN approach. It is noteworthy that the stream is in fact weakly constrained, so Problog might have performed better with more constraints. But it remains true that the maximum number of free events is quite low in comparison with our method. Moreover, we compare our estimation with the results provided by Problog on streams of length 13. Figure 9b shows the results of the relative error of one hundred estimations when different amount of samples are used. As expected for a sampling approach, our error is decreasing in $O(\sqrt{n})$.

6 Discussion

Our results are promising and indicate that the approach scales for larger problems and long data streams. But it does not solve every problem that uncertainty may bring. Consequently, we present in this discussion a brief overview of the state of the art and the differences with our method.

Automata-Based Methods. Those approaches are usually extensions of the SASE model or Cugola's work which use (N)DFA as pattern model. Given a stream, the recognition of a pattern corresponds to the termination of its associated automaton. The uncertainty computation depends on assumptions and goals; e.g., [24] calculates the marginal probability of a pattern by enumerating all possible recognitions and summing their probabilities, with events assumed independent. Other approaches ([1]) relax the independence assumption and use a MC to describe the dependencies between events.

Usually, complex temporal constraints are not used or permitted with these methods, but some exceptions exist as [2], where the authors calculate the most probable explanation for activities using probabilities associated to the transitions of the automaton. In that case, the stochastic automaton allows specification of such temporal constraints. A similar approach from Fazzinga, Flesca, Furfaro, *et al.* [25] exists that uses a forward-backward algorithm to construct iteratively all the explanations into a tree structure where irrelevant explanations regarding the constraints are cut.

Automata-based methods provide a large spectrum of approaches but often tend to focus on representations of CE as sequences of LLEs with sometimes Kleene operator. Absence operator is a rare to be found. On uncertainty, three categories emerge: those assuming LLEs independence assumptions, those using first order Markovian assumptions and those using ad-hoc approaches of uncertainty (for instance [25] uses a bounded explorations of inconsistent explanations associate to a confidence approximation).

First-Order Logic (FOL) and PGMs. Those methods usually rely on logic to describe models and rules, and on PGM to represent uncertainty. Two main graphical models are used to handle uncertainty: MLNs and Bayesian networks. Large amount of research has been produced around CEP and MLNs [3,4] especially for human activity recognition. MLNs were introduced by [19] and use a

FOL semantic to describe a Markov random field where a specific query on the model can be approximated using MCMC. The sampling relies on finding possible worlds with respect to the FOL problem. The FOL expressiveness made this model quite popular but, in practice, it has high computation costs on complex problems [22, 26].

Although less common, Bayesian approaches produced interesting results. They are generally used to describe the uncertainty on the relation between events in a defined complex event [27]. But some research [28] proposes solutions for dealing efficiently with uncertainty on simple events[4] and not just their relationship using a probability distribution on each event. However, these probability distributions should be given by an expert and the approach does not allow them to change over time. Moreover, the probability of events and the probability of the relation are just multiplied since they are supposed to be independent, but not all the system would satisfy this hypothesis. Anyway, this approach focused on a different uncertainty problem than ours, since it offers a representation of the confidence we have on CE modelling.

Another approach describes a CE system with Problog [29]. Problog does not rely on graphical models, but uses the knowledge from FOL domain to find all possible outcomes of a system described with a set of Horn clauses. all used Horn clauses might be associated with a probability that describes the chance that under the assumption the clause body is asserted, the head will be too. This approach was used with event calculus [3] and showed its efficiency. But, even if it provides the exact probability of the designed problem using Sentential Decision Diagram, it comes with expensive computation costs on large structures. An equivalent approach proposed by [7] used the MLN structure.

Grammars. Grammars are an interesting way to represent CE. [6] uses stochastic context free grammars from [30] to describe complex event regarding a data stream. Each transition rule from the grammar is associated to a probability and the algorithm tries to explain the outcome data stream by looking at all the successions of rules matching it. The stream probability is the sum of the probabilities of each succession of rules.

This method has some drawbacks, as it does not manage attributes and could be overwhelmed when the number of possible explanations grows, but nonetheless the expressiveness of this approach remains really interesting.

Overview. As we explained in the introduction, comparing these methods is not an easy task since each approach might focus on different aspects of uncertainty or CEP representation. But, we think our approach to be an interesting contribution as it proposes to efficiently estimate event uncertainty using long time relations to describe CEs in reasonable time compared to MLNs, that are though widely used. Furthermore, using CE as complementary prior knowledge has, to our knowledge, never been proposed in previous works of the community. Nonetheless we want to address some restrictions that should be pointed out.

---

[4] In particular, they propose an interesting first approach for the uncertainty on event attributes.

In our method, as we said in Sect. 2.1, we consider only systems with 0-ary events but many systems do not satisfy this condition. It is still possible to adapt systems with finite discrete attributes by defining a 0-ary event for each attribute combination. But it may lead on huge numbers of events and thus on massive transition matrices, hence storage issues. Furthermore, this simple approach is not convenient for attributes with continuous values. Another interest point is the number of matrices used to create the NHM. The analysis of really long data streams could lead to store a considerable amount of matrices, which could be easily reduced by an interleave process that calculate the NHM while producing the samples.

The high constraint expressiveness (cf. Sect. 4) is limited by the need to find all possible streams. This leads to pick small intervals where the chronicle should appear to avoid a combinatorial explosion. It would be interesting to have a more straight-forward way to find the corresponding automaton. As chronicles are expressed with a context-free grammar it might be possible to find incompatible sub-streams using push-down automata instead of DFA. Incidentally, it may let us express really strong constraints along the full stream.

7   Conclusion and Perspectives

In this paper, we introduce a method performing CE recognition and analysis under uncertainty detection of LLE more scalable on long data streams, with high-level knowledge description. The approach is in two steps: first, we estimate the probability of a chronicle recognition on an uncertain data stream. The observed data stream is used as a constraint on the system allowing a NHM to describe the system. This NHM is then used to perform a MCMC sampling, where each sample is analysed through a CE recognition system, thus leading to the estimation the likelihood of a chronicle. Second, we use chronicles as a prior knowledge on the system. Chronicles are transformed using an automaton representation into constraint sub-graphs for the NHM, which reduce substantially the needed sample amount, since a sub-graph embeds many possible sub-streams according to the chronicle used.

Our results showed that our techniques performed good probability estimations, scalable on long data streams to analyse regarding our criteria, whereas other approaches tend to be intractable or inaccurate. In future work, we plan to investigate three improvement axes. First, we plan to avoid sampling by using model checking approaches, thus reducing computation time, even if such an approach would reduce the expressiveness of query (e.g. it would not be possible to express a query that looks for a certain number of CE recognitions per streams). Second, the current structure of our method might be easily adapt to a Map/Reduce approach and might have an important impact on computation time. Third, we aim at representing our constraint automata directly from the chronicle representation without solving a CSP. Regarding some preliminary experimentations, this method, combined with the model checking approach, might provide an efficient solution, fast enough for online computation even with high level constraints.

References

1. Wang, Y., Cao, K., Zhang, X.: Complex event processing over distributed probabilistic event streams. Comput. Math. Appl. **66**(10), 1808–1821 (2013)
2. Albanese, M., et al.: Finding "Unexplained" activities in video. In: IJCAI 2011, pp. 1628–1634 (2011)
3. Skarlatidis, A.: Probabilistic event calculus for event recognition. ACM Trans. Comput. Logic (TOCL) **16**(2), 11 (2015)
4. Liu, F., Deng, D., Li, P.: Dynamic context-aware event recognition based on Markov logic networks. Sensors **17**(3), 491 (2017)
5. Skarlatidis, A.: A probabilistic logic programming event calculus. Theory Pract. Logic Program. **15**(02), 213–245 (2015)
6. Ivanov, Y.A., Bobick, A.F.: Recognition of visual activities and interactions by stochastic parsing. IEEE Trans. Patt. Anal. Mach. Intell. **22**(8), 852–872 (2000)
7. Morariu, V., Davis, L.S., et al.: Multi-agent event recognition in structured scenarios. In: 2011 IEEE Conference on Computer Vision and Pattern Recognition (CVPR), pp. 3289–3296. IEEE (2011)
8. Song, Y.C., et al.: A Markov logic framework for recognizing complex events from multimodal data. In: Proceedings of the 15th ACM on International Conference on Multimodal Interaction, Series ICMI 2013, pp. 141–148. ACM (2013)
9. Piel, A.: Reconnaissance de comportements complexes par traitement en ligne de flux d'evenements. Ph.D. thesis, University of Paris 13 (2014)
10. Carle, P., Choppy, C., Kervarc, R.: Behaviour recognition using chronicles. In: 5th International Symposium on Theoretical Aspects of Software Engineering (TASE), pp. 100–107. IEEE (2011)
11. Diao, Y., Immerman, N., Gyllstrom, D.: Sase+: An agile language for Kleene closure over event streams. UMass Technical report (2007)
12. Cugola, G., Margara, A.: Complex event processing with T-REX. J. Syst. Softw. **85**(8), 1709–1728 (2012)
13. Dousson, C., Le Maigat, P.: Chronicle recognition improvement using temporal focusing and hierarchization. In: IJCAI, vol. 7, pp. 324–329 (2007)
14. Artikis, A., Sergot, M., Paliouras, G.: Run-time composite event recognition. In: Proceedings of the 6th ACM International Conference on Distributed Event-Based Systems, pp. 69–80. ACM (2012)
15. Allen, J.F.: Maintaining knowledge about temporal intervals. Commun. ACM **26**(11), 832–843 (1983)
16. Pachet, F., Roy, P., Barbieri, G.: Finite-length Markov processes with constraints. In: IJCAI (2011)
17. Bubenzer, J.: Minimization of acyclic DFAs. In: Stringology 2011, pp. 132–146 (2011)
18. Dries, A., et al.: ProbLog2: probabilistic logic programming. In: Bifet, A. (ed.) ECML PKDD 2015. LNCS (LNAI), vol. 9286, pp. 312–315. Springer, Cham (2015). https://doi.org/10.1007/978-3-319-23461-8_37
19. Richardson, M., Domingos, P.: Markov logic networks. Mach. Learn. **62**(1–2), 107–136 (2006)
20. Tran, S.D., Davis, L.S.: Event modeling and recognition using Markov logic networks. In: Forsyth, D., Torr, P., Zisserman, A. (eds.) ECCV 2008. LNCS, vol. 5303, pp. 610–623. Springer, Heidelberg (2008). https://doi.org/10.1007/978-3-540-88688-4_45

21. Skarlatidis, A., Paliouras, G., Vouros, G.A., Artikis, A.: Probabilistic event calculus based on Markov logic networks. In: Olken, F., Palmirani, M., Sottara, D. (eds.) RuleML 2011. LNCS, vol. 7018, pp. 155–170. Springer, Heidelberg (2011). https://doi.org/10.1007/978-3-642-24908-2_19

22. Rincé, R., Kervarc, R., Leray, P.: On the use of WalkSAT based algorithms for MLN inference in some realistic applications. In: Benferhat, S., Tabia, K., Ali, M. (eds.) IEA/AIE 2017. LNCS (LNAI), vol. 10351, pp. 121–131. Springer, Cham (2017). https://doi.org/10.1007/978-3-319-60045-1_15

23. Prud'homme, C., Fages, J.-G., Lorca, X.: Choco Documentation (2017)

24. Kawashima, H., Kitagawa, H., Li, X.: Complex event processing over uncertain data streams. In: 2010 International Conference on P2P, Parallel, Grid, Cloud and Internet Computing (3PGCIC), pp. 521–526 (2010)

25. Fazzinga, B.: Efficiently interpreting traces of low level events in business process logs. Inf. Syst. **73**, 1–24 (2018)

26. Alevizos, E.: Probabilistic complex event recognition: a survey. ACM Comput. Surv. **50**(5), 1–31 (2017)

27. Wang, X., Ji, Q.: Context augmented dynamic Bayesian networks for event recognition. Patt. Recogn. Lett. **43**, 62–70 (2014)

28. Cugola, G.: Introducing uncertainty in complex event processing: model, implementation, and validation. Computing **97**(2), 103–144 (2015)

29. Fierens, D.: Inference in probabilistic logic programs using weighted CNF's. Theory Pract. Logic Program. **15**(03), 258–401 (2012)

30. Stolcke, A.: An efficient probabilistic context-free parsing algorithm that computes prefix probabilities. Comput. Linguist. **21**(2), 165–201 (1995)

On the Impact and Proper
Use of Heuristics in Test-Driven
Ontology Debugging

Patrick Rodler[(✉)][iD] and Wolfgang Schmid

Alpen-Adria Universität Klagenfurt, 9020 Klagenfurt, Austria
{patrick.rodler,wolfgang.schmid}@aau.at

Abstract. Given an ontology that does not meet required properties
such as consistency or the (non-)entailment of certain axioms, Ontology
Debugging aims at identifying a set of axioms, called diagnosis, that
must be properly modified or deleted in order to resolve the ontology's
faults. As there are, in general, large numbers of competing diagnoses and
the choice of each diagnosis leads to a repaired ontology with different
semantics, Test-Driven Ontology Debugging (TOD) aims at narrowing
the space of diagnoses until a single (highly probable) one is left. To this
end, TOD techniques automatically generate a sequence of queries to an
interacting oracle (domain expert) about (non-)entailments of the correct
ontology. Diagnoses not consistent with the answers are discarded. To
minimize debugging cost (oracle effort), various heuristics for selecting
the best next query have been proposed. We report preliminary results
of extensive ongoing experiments with a set of such heuristics on real-
world debugging cases. In particular, we try to answer questions such
as "Is some heuristic always superior to all others?", "On which factors
does the (relative) performance of the particular heuristics depend?" or
"Under which circumstances should I use which heuristic?".

Keywords: Ontology debugging · Test-driven debugging
Query selection · Heuristics · User interaction · Active learning

1 Introduction

With the advent and growing popularity of semantic web technologies in the last
two decades, the number of applications relying on knowledge specified in terms
of ontologies has considerably increased. One example of a vital field extensively
adopting ontologies for highly critical applications is biomedicine.[1] As the size
(up to hundreds of thousands of axioms) and complexity of the used ontologies is

---

This work is supported by Carinthian Science Fund (KWF), contract KWF-
3520/26767/38701.

[1] See, e.g., OBO project (http://obo.sourceforge.net) or NCI-Thesaurus (http://ncit.
nci.nih.gov).

© Springer Nature Switzerland AG 2018
C. Benzmüller et al. (Eds.): RuleML+RR 2018, LNCS 11092, pp. 164–184, 2018.
https://doi.org/10.1007/978-3-319-99906-7_11

constantly growing, the likeliness of faults, e.g. wrong entailments or logical contradictions, in these ontologies is significant. However, such defectiveness could have severe consequences, e.g. in health-related applications, on the one hand, and its root cause may be extremely hard to identify for humans on the other hand.

As a remedy, *ontology debugging (OD)* approaches [8,25], based on the general *model-based diagnosis* framework [15], have been developed. Given an ontology that does not satisfy requirements such as consistency, coherency or the (non-)entailment of certain axioms, the goal of OD is to find an explanation of the ontology's faultiness in terms of a set of incorrect axioms. Such an axiom set is called a *diagnosis*. However, the mere use of OD tools assisting a human by the generation (and ranking [9]) of diagnoses often does not solve the problem due to a couple of reasons. First [29], such (non-interactive) approaches often suggest unnecessarily large diagnoses (*non-parsimony*), neglect some solutions (*incompleteness*), return wrong explanations (*unsoundness*) or exhibit *poor performance*. Second, even if such a system overcomes all the said issues, it does unavoidably (due to a lack of additional information) suffer from the problem of generally large solution spaces (comprising up to thousands [27]) of competing diagnoses. Although the deletion or adequate modification of any diagnosis enables to formulate an ontology where all (initially present) faults are repaired, each diagnosis' choice leads necessarily to a solution ontology with different semantics [16]. Even if they are ranked, opting for (one of) the top-ranked diagnoses does not give any guarantees regarding the semantics of the resulting repaired ontology.

Addressing this issue, inspired by [3,11], (interactive) *test-driven ontology debugging (TOD)* techniques [16,24,27] were proposed and their general feasibility, scalability and practical efficiency was demonstrated by various conducted studies [21,22,27,28]. TOD techniques build on an idea well known from software engineering, which is the specification of test cases to successively narrow down the possible causes of fault. In the context of ontology engineering, a *positive (negative) test case* represents a set of axioms that must (not) be entailed by the intended ontology. The process of formulating test cases can be pursued until one diagnosis has overwhelming probability or, ultimately, until a single one remains. As the manual formulation of meaningful test cases – in the sense that they distinguish well between diagnoses – might be a hard task due to the involved mental reasoning with expressive logics (such as OWL 2 [6]), state-of-the-art TOD systems undertake the task of test case formulation and quality assessment. The workload for an *oracle*, usually a domain expert, interacting with the system thus reduces to classifying these automatically generated test cases, called *queries*, as positive or negative. This means answering questions whether presented axioms are or are not entailments of the intended ontology. Since oracle consultations are usually very costly, the practicality and efficiency of TOD approaches is inextricably linked to the number (and, e.g., the difficulty) of queries asked in order to pin down the *actual diagnosis*, i.e. the actually faulty axioms.

Unfortunately, the global minimization of the oracle costs (i.e. finding a cost-minimal *sequence of queries* revealing the actual diagnosis) is NP-hard [7]. As a result, TOD methods have to confine themselves to a local optimization (i.e. computing the best *next* query). To this end, a one-step lookahead evaluation of queries (i.e. how favorable is the expected situation after asking *one* query?) proved to be a very good trade-off between gained information and required effort [10], and is thus state-of-the-art in TOD.

However, there is not a unified view of what it means for a query to be "good", but several (one-step lookahead) heuristics [11,18,22,27], many of them inspired by active learning research [26]. These heuristics are expressed in terms of quantitative *query selection measures (QSMs)* that assign a real-valued goodness estimate to each query. A few empirical studies of QSMs in the domain of TOD exist, where [27,28] focus on two "traditional" QSMs [11,12] and [22] suggest and evaluate a novel QSM. Moreover, there are the theoretical analyses [17,18,21] which derive a range of new QSMs as well as equivalences and superiorities between new and traditional QSMs, and introduce efficient (heuristic) computation methods for optimal queries wrt. QSMs. Complementary to these researches, we shed light on the performance (in terms of oracle cost throughout a TOD session) of and relationships between *both the traditional and the new* QSMs in the present work. For this purpose, we are currently conducting extensive evaluations where we investigate the particular QSMs under varying conditions, similar to [27], regarding **(a)** diagnoses probability distributions, **(b)** quality (meaningfulness) of the probabilities, **(c)** available evidence (size of the diagnoses sample) for query computation, and **(d)** diagnostic structure (ontology size; # and size of diagnoses; reasoning complexity) using real-world debugging problems. The data of the (so-far finished) experiments shall be exploited to approach i.a. the following questions:

- Do the factors (a)–(d) affect the (relative) performance of the QSMs?
- Which QSM is preferable under which circumstances?
- Is there a (clear) winner among the QSMs?
- How far do the QSM performances differ under different conditions?

The rest of the paper is organized as follows. Section 2 briefly introduces technical basics wrt. TOD. Section 3 recaps the QSMs used in the experiments. The evaluation setting is described in Sect. 4, and results discussed in Sect. 5. Finally, Sect. 6 concludes.

2   Preliminaries

In this section we briefly characterize the basic technical concepts used throughout this work, based on the framework of [16,27] which is originally based on [15] (cf. [19]).

Ontology Debugging Problem Instance. An ontology to be debugged is given by $\mathcal{O} \cup \mathcal{B}$, where $\mathcal{O}$ includes the possibly faulty axioms and $\mathcal{B}$ the correct background knowledge axioms. That is, one can lay the debugging focus on just a subset $\mathcal{O}$ of the entire ontology, putting certain axioms, e.g. assertions, to $\mathcal{B}$. The pragmatics is that faults will only be sought within $\mathcal{O}$, i.e. the considered search space is restricted. Requirements to the intended ontology are captured by sets of positive (P) and negative (N) test cases [3]. Each test case is a set (interpreted as conjunction) of axioms; positive ones $p \in P$ must be and negative ones $n \in N$ must not be entailed by the intended ontology. We call $\langle \mathcal{O}, \mathcal{B}, P, N \rangle$ an *(ontology) debugging problem instance (DPI)*.

Example 1. Consider the following ontology with the terminology $\mathcal{T}$:

$$\{ \quad ax_1 : ActiveResearcher \sqsubseteq \exists writes.(Paper \sqcup Review) ,$$
$$ax_2 : \exists writes.\top \sqsubseteq Author , \quad ax_3 : Author \sqsubseteq Employee \sqcap Person \quad \}$$

and assertions $\mathcal{A} : \{ax_4 : ActiveResearcher(ann)\}$. To debug the terminology while accepting as correct the assertion and stipulating that Ann is not necessarily an employee (negative test case $n_1 : \{Employee(ann)\}$), one can specify the following DPI: $dpi_{ex} := \langle \mathcal{T}, \mathcal{A}, \emptyset, \{n_1\} \rangle$.   □

Diagnoses. Let $\mathbf{C}_\perp := \{C \sqsubseteq \perp \mid C \text{ class name in } \mathcal{O}\}$ and $U_P := \bigcup_{p \in P} p$. Given that the ontology to be debugged, along with the positive test cases, is inconsistent or incoherent, i.e. $\mathcal{O} \cup \mathcal{B} \cup U_P \models x$ for some $x \in \{\perp\} \cup \mathbf{C}_\perp$, or some negative test case is entailed, i.e. $\mathcal{O} \cup \mathcal{B} \cup U_P \models n$ for some $n \in N$, some axioms in $\mathcal{O}$ must be accordingly modified or deleted to enable the formulation of the intended ontology. We call such a set of axioms $\mathcal{D} \subseteq \mathcal{O}$ a *diagnosis* for the DPI $\langle \mathcal{O}, \mathcal{B}, P, N \rangle$ iff $(\mathcal{O} \setminus \mathcal{D}) \cup \mathcal{B} \cup U_P \not\models x$ for all $x \in N \cup \{\perp\} \cup \mathbf{C}_\perp$. $\mathcal{D}$ is a *minimal diagnosis* iff there is no diagnosis $\mathcal{D}' \subset \mathcal{D}$. We call $\mathcal{D}^*$ *the actual diagnosis* iff all $ax \in \mathcal{D}^*$ are faulty and all $ax \in \mathcal{O} \setminus \mathcal{D}^*$ are correct. For efficiency and to suggest minimally-invasive repairs, modern TOD systems restrict the focus to the computation of minimal diagnoses.

Example 2. For $dpi_{ex} = \langle \mathcal{O}, \mathcal{B}, P, N \rangle$ from Example 1, $\mathcal{O} \cup \mathcal{B} \cup U_P$ entails the negative test case $n_1 \in N$, i.e. that Ann is an employee. The reason is that according to $ax_1(\in \mathcal{O})$ and $ax_4(\in \mathcal{B})$, Ann writes some paper or review since she is an active researcher. Due to the additional $ax_2(\in \mathcal{O})$, Ann is also an author because she writes something. Finally, since Ann is an author, she must be both an employee and a person, as postulated by $ax_3(\in \mathcal{O})$. Hence, $\mathcal{D}_1 : [ax_1]$, $\mathcal{D}_2 : [ax_2]$, $\mathcal{D}_3 : [ax_3]$ are (all the) minimal diagnoses for dpi_{ex}, as the deletion of any $ax_i \in \mathcal{O}$ breaks the unwanted entailment n_1.   □

Diagnoses Probabilities. If axiom fault probabilities $p(ax_i)$ for $ax_i \in \mathcal{O}$ are available, e.g. by considering common fault patterns [14,23] or other heuristic information [9], probabilities of diagnoses $\mathcal{D} \in \mathbf{D}$ (of being the actual diagnosis) can be computed [11,27] as $p(\mathcal{D}) = \prod_{ax \in \mathcal{D}} p(ax) \prod_{ax \in \mathcal{O} \setminus \mathcal{D}} (1 - p(ax))$ and updated by means of Bayes' Rule (see [16, p. 130]) each time a new test case

is added. Sometimes however $p(ax)$ for $ax \in \mathcal{O}$ might not be directly given, but derivable from the structure of the axioms. For instance, fault probabilities regarding logical (e.g. $\neg, \sqcap, \forall$) [27] or non-logical (e.g. class names) [16] symbols occurring in axioms might be available. Regarding the former, the axiom author might not properly use or fully understand these constructs from the logical perspective; as to the latter, the axiom author, say an orthopedist, might not possess the required (domain) expertise regarding certain concepts, say *Acne* or *Basalioma*. Such fault information may originate from, e.g., experience, a subjective or expert guess, or through the analysis of relevant logs or past debugging sessions. Let $p(s_i)$ be the probability that a (non-)logical symbol s_i is faulty and n_i be the number of occurrences of s_i in ax. Then [27]:
$p(ax) = 1 - \prod_{s_i \text{ occurs in } ax}(1 - p(s_i))^{n_i}$.

Example 3. Reconsider dpi_{ex} from Example 1. Suppose that the ontology author knows from past debugging sessions to make quite many mistakes using quantifiers, some using negation, conjunction and disjunction, but almost none using subsumption. This could lead to the fault probabilities $\langle p(\exists), p(\sqcap), p(\sqcup), p(\sqsubseteq)\rangle = \langle 0.25, 0.05, 0.05, 0.01\rangle$ relevant to dpi_{ex}. Using these, the fault probability of axiom ax_1 (including the symbols $\sqsubseteq, \exists, \sqcup$) computes as $p(ax_1) = 1 - (1 - 0.01)(1 - 0.25)(1 - 0.05) \approx 0.29$. Similarly, we obtain $p(ax_2) \approx 0.26$ and $p(ax_3) \approx 0.06$. Hence, we can derive $p(\mathcal{D}_1) = (0.29)(1 - 0.26)(1 - 0.06) \approx 0.21$, $p(\mathcal{D}_2) \approx 0.17$ and $p(\mathcal{D}_3) \approx 0.03$. □

Queries and Q-Partition. Let $\mathbf{D}$, called the *leading diagnoses*, be a set of at least two (precomputed) minimal diagnoses for $dpi = \langle \mathcal{O}, \mathcal{B}, P, N \rangle$. Usually, the diagnoses with highest probability or minimum cardinality are used for this purpose. A *query* (wrt. $\mathbf{D}$) is a set of axioms q that rules out at least one diagnosis in $\mathbf{D}$, both if q is classified as a positive test case $(P \leftarrow P \cup \{q\})$, and if q is classified as a negative test case $(N \leftarrow N \cup \{q\})$. That is, at least one $\mathcal{D}_i \in \mathbf{D}$ is not a diagnosis for $\langle \mathcal{O}, \mathcal{B}, P \cup \{q\}, N \rangle$ and at least one diagnosis $\mathcal{D}_j \in \mathbf{D}$ is not a diagnosis for $\langle \mathcal{O}, \mathcal{B}, P, N \cup \{q\} \rangle$. The classification of a query q to either P or N is accomplished by an oracle, e.g. a domain expert, answering the question "Is (each axiom in) q an entailment of the intended (correct) ontology?". Thus, the *oracle* is a function $\mathsf{class} : \mathbf{Q} \rightarrow \{P, N\}$ where $\mathbf{Q}$ is the query space; $\mathsf{class}(q) = P$ if the answer to the question is positive, else $\mathsf{class}(q) = N$.

An expedient tool towards the verification and goodness estimation of query candidates q is the notion of a q-partition. Namely, every set of axioms q partitions any set of diagnoses $\mathbf{D}$ into three subsets:

- $\mathbf{D}_q^+$: includes all $\mathcal{D} \in \mathbf{D}$ where $\mathcal{D}$ is not a diagnosis for $\langle \mathcal{O}, \mathcal{B}, P, N \cup \{q\} \rangle$ (diagnoses predicting that q is a positive test case)
- $\mathbf{D}_q^-$: includes all $\mathcal{D} \in \mathbf{D}$ where $\mathcal{D}$ is not a diagnosis for $\langle \mathcal{O}, \mathcal{B}, P \cup \{q\}, N \rangle$ (diagnoses predicting that q is a negative test case)
- $\mathbf{D}_q^0 = \mathbf{D} \setminus (\mathbf{D}_q^+ \cup \mathbf{D}_q^-)$: includes all $\mathcal{D} \in \mathbf{D}$ where $\mathcal{D}$ is a diagnosis for both $\langle \mathcal{O}, \mathcal{B}, P \cup \{q\}, N \rangle$ and $\langle \mathcal{O}, \mathcal{B}, P, N \cup \{q\} \rangle$ (*uncommitted diagnoses*, no prediction about q)

A partition $\mathfrak{P}$ of $\mathbf{D}$ into three sets is called *q-partition* iff there is a query q wrt. $\mathbf{D}$ such that $\mathfrak{P} = \langle \mathbf{D}_q^+, \mathbf{D}_q^-, \mathbf{D}_q^0 \rangle$. According to the definition of a query, it holds that q is a query iff both $\mathbf{D}_q^+$ and $\mathbf{D}_q^-$ are non-empty sets. This fact can be taken advantage of for *query verification*. Coupled with diagnoses probabilities, the q-partition provides useful hints [18] about the *query quality* in that it enables to

(1) test whether q is a *strong query*, i.e. one without uncommitted diagnoses ($\mathbf{D}_q^0 = \emptyset$),
(2) estimate the impact q's classification $\mathsf{class}(q)$ has in terms of diagnoses elimination (potential a-posteriori change of the diagnoses space), and
(3) assess the probability of q's positive and negative classification (e.g. to compute the uncertainty of q).

For given $\mathbf{D}$, we estimate [11]: $p(\mathsf{class}(q) = P) = p(\mathbf{D}_q^+) + \frac{1}{2}p(\mathbf{D}_q^0)$ and $p(\mathsf{class}(q) = N) = p(\mathbf{D}_q^-) + \frac{1}{2}p(\mathbf{D}_q^0)$ where $p(\mathbf{D}_q^X) = \sum_{\mathcal{D} \in \mathbf{D}_q^X} p(\mathcal{D})$ for $X \in \{+,-,0\}$ and $p(\mathcal{D})$ for $\mathcal{D} \in \mathbf{D}$ is the probability of $\mathcal{D}$ normalized over $\mathbf{D}$ (i.e. $\sum_{\mathcal{D} \in \mathbf{D}} p(\mathcal{D}) = 1$).

Example 4. Let the computed leading diagnoses for dpi_{ex} be $\mathbf{D} = \{\mathcal{D}_1, \mathcal{D}_2, \mathcal{D}_3\}$. One query wrt. $\mathbf{D}$ is, e.g., $q_1 := \{ActiveResearcher \sqsubseteq Author\}$. Because, (a) adding q_1 to P yields that the removal of $\mathcal{D}_1$ or $\mathcal{D}_2$ from $\mathcal{O}$ no longer breaks the unwanted entailment $Employee(ann)$, i.e. $\mathcal{D}_1, \mathcal{D}_2$ are no longer minimal diagnoses, (b) moving q_1 to N means that $\mathcal{D}_3$ is not a minimal diagnosis anymore, as, to prevent the entailment of (the new negative test case) q_1, at least one of ax_1, ax_2 must be deleted. The resulting q-partition for q_1 is thus $\langle \mathbf{D}_{q_1}^+, \mathbf{D}_{q_1}^-, \mathbf{D}_{q_1}^0 \rangle = \langle \{\mathcal{D}_3\}, \{\mathcal{D}_1, \mathcal{D}_2\}, \emptyset \rangle$. Consequently, q_1 is a strong query ($\mathbf{D}_{q_1}^0 = \emptyset$) and the estimated probability of q_1's positive (negative) classification, based on the normalized diagnoses probabilities $\langle p(\mathcal{D}_1), \ldots, p(\mathcal{D}_3) \rangle = \langle 0.5, 0.42, 0.08 \rangle$, is 0.08 (0.92). Note, e.g., $q_2 := \{Author \sqsubseteq Person\}$, having the partition $\langle \{\mathcal{D}_1, \mathcal{D}_2\}, \emptyset, \{\mathcal{D}_3\} \rangle$, is not a query since no leading diagnoses are invalidated after assigning q_2 to P, i.e. a positive answer does not bring along any useful information for diagnoses discrimination. Intuitively, this is because q_2 does not contribute to the violation of n_1 (in fact, the other "part" $Author \sqsubseteq Employee$ of ax_3 does so). $\square$

Test-Driven Ontology Debugging. Formally, the (optimal) test-driven ontology debugging problem (TOD) can be stated as follows:

Problem 1 ((Optimal) TOD). **Given:** DPI $\langle \mathcal{O}, \mathcal{B}, P, N \rangle$. **Find:** (Lowest-cost) set of test cases $P' \cup N'$ such that there is only one minimal diagnosis for $\langle \mathcal{O}, \mathcal{B}, P \cup P', N \cup N' \rangle$.

Example 5. Let the actual diagnosis be $\mathcal{D}_3$, i.e. ax_3 is the (only) faulty axiom in $\mathcal{O}$ (intuition: an author is not necessarily employed, but might be, e.g, a free-lancer). Then, given dpi_{ex} as an input, solutions to the TOD problem, yielding the final diagnosis $\mathcal{D}_3$, are, e.g., $P' = \emptyset, N' = \{\{\exists writes.\top \sqsubseteq Employee\}, \{Author \sqsubseteq Employee\}\}$ or $P' = \{\{ActiveResearcher \sqsubseteq Author\}\}, N' = \emptyset$. Measuring the TOD cost by the number of test cases, the latter solution (cost: 1) is optimal, the former (cost: 2) not. $\square$

Note, TOD is a *symptom-driven* approach to *fault localization*. That is, given some discrepancies (symptom), such as inconsistency or unwanted entailments, between the actual and the intended ontology, the goal is to (efficiently) collect sufficient information to locate the faulty axioms (actual diagnosis) *that explain the observed problems*. TOD must be distinguished from, but can nevertheless be profitably combined with, other techniques, e.g. ones addressing *ontology repair* [8,30] (how to correct the faulty axioms?), *ontology revision* [13] (find *all* faulty axioms) or *ontology enrichment* [5] (find missing axioms; can help to detect problems/symptoms).

Query Selection Measures (QSMs). The said query properties (1)–(3) characterized by the q-partition are essentially what QSMs take into account to quantitatively rate the query quality. Formally, a QSM is a function $m : \mathbf{Q} \to \mathbb{R}$ that assigns a value $m(q)$ to each query $q \in \mathbf{Q}$. All QSMs are heuristics towards Optimal TOD (Problem 1). That is, their goal is to minimize the expected cost $\sum_{\mathcal{D}} p(\mathcal{D})\mathsf{cost}(\mathcal{D})$ of locating the actual diagnosis $\mathcal{D}^*$. At this, $\mathsf{cost}(\mathcal{D})$ is usually conceived of as the sum of individual query (answering) costs over all queries required to unambiguously isolate $\mathcal{D}$. For the purpose of this paper we assume $\mathsf{cost}(\mathcal{D})$ represents the number of queries to isolate $\mathcal{D}$ (all queries assumed equally costly).

Table 1. ([18, Table 2]) QSM designators (column 1) and according functions $m(q)$ (column 2). Column 3 indicates whether the QSM is optimized by maximizing ($\nearrow$) or minimizing ($\searrow$) the function m.

QSM m	$m(q)$	opt.
ENT	$\sum_{c \in \{P,N\}} p(\mathsf{class}(q) = c) \log_2 p(\mathsf{class}(q) = c)$	$\searrow$
SPL	$\left\| \|\mathbf{D}_q^+\| - \|\mathbf{D}_q^-\| \right\|$	$\searrow$
KL	$-\sum_{X \in \{\mathbf{D}_q^+, \mathbf{D}_q^-\}} \frac{\|X\|}{\|\mathbf{D}_q^+ \cup \mathbf{D}_q^-\|} \log_2 \frac{p(X)}{p(\mathbf{D}_q^+ \cup \mathbf{D}_q^-)}$	$\nearrow$
EMCb	$p(\mathsf{class}(q) = P)\|\mathbf{D}_q^-\| + p(\mathsf{class}(q) = N)\|\mathbf{D}_q^+\|$	$\nearrow$
MPS	$p(\mathbf{D}_{q,\min})$ if $\|\mathbf{D}_{q,\min}\| = 1$, 0 else 1)	$\nearrow$
BME	$\|\mathbf{D}_{q,p,\min}\|$ 2)	$\nearrow$
RIO'	$\frac{\mathsf{ENT}(Q)}{2} + \mathbf{D}_{q,n}$ 3)	$\searrow$

Key:

1): $\mathbf{D}_{q,\min} := \arg\min_{X \in \{\mathbf{D}_q^+, \mathbf{D}_q^-\}}(\|X\|)$

2): $\mathbf{D}_{q,p,\min} :=$
$$\begin{cases} \mathbf{D}_q^- & \text{if } p(\mathbf{D}_q^-) < p(\mathbf{D}_q^+) \\ \mathbf{D}_q^+ & \text{if } p(\mathbf{D}_q^+) < p(\mathbf{D}_q^-) \\ 0 & \text{else} \end{cases}$$

3): $\mathbf{D}_{q,n} := \begin{cases} c_q - n & \text{if } c_q \geq n \\ \|D\| & \text{else} \end{cases}$

where $c_q := \min\{\|\mathbf{D}_q^+\|, \|\mathbf{D}_q^-\|\}$ and n denotes the minimal number of diagnoses the selected query must eliminate [22]

3   The Evaluated Heuristics

In this section we briefly revisit and explain the QSMs – originally introduced in other works – we use in our experiments. These include the "classical" frequently used ones [11,27] and the newer ones proposed in [18,22] and discussed in-depth in [17]. Since we employ a query computation and selection method [21] that guarantees to produce only (the more favorable, cf. [20, Sect. 2.4.1]) strong queries, [18, Table 3] tells us that we have to deal with seven (non-equivalent) QSMs in this case. We next illustrate the rough idea behind these heuristics, listed in Table 1. Note, we also mention a random QSM which we used as a baseline in our evaluations.

Information Gain ENT: [11,27] Chooses a query with the highest expected information gain or, equivalently, with the lowest expected posterior entropy wrt. the diagnoses set $\mathbf{D}$. As derived in [11], $\mathsf{ENT}(q)$ is the better, the closer the probabilities for positive and negative classification of q are to 0.5 (cf. formula in Table 1).

Split-In-Half SPL: [12,27] Chooses a query q whose q-partition best splits the diagnoses set $\mathbf{D}$ in half, i.e. where both $|\mathbf{D}_q^+|$ and $|\mathbf{D}_q^-|$ are closest to $\frac{1}{2}|\mathbf{D}|$. Intuitively, an optimal q wrt. SPL guarantees that a half of the (known) diagnoses are eliminated by querying q's classification.

Kullback-Leibler Divergence KL: [17,18,26] Chooses a query with largest average disagreement between query-classification predictions of single diagnoses $\mathcal{D} \in \mathbf{D}$ and the consensus (prediction) of all $\mathcal{D} \in \mathbf{D}$, based on an information-theoretic measure of the difference between two probability distributions [26]. As demonstrated in [17, Prop. 26], this QSM can be represented in terms of the formula given in Table 1.

Expected Model Change EMCb: [17,18,26] Chooses a query for which the expected number of invalidated diagnoses in $\mathbf{D}$ is maximized.

Most Probable Singleton MPS: [17,18] Chooses a query q for which the minimum-cardinality set among $\{\mathbf{D}_q^+, \mathbf{D}_q^-\}$ is a singleton $\{\mathcal{D}\}$ where $\mathcal{D}$ has maximal probability. Intuitively, MPS seeks to eliminate, with a maximal probability, the maximal possible number of $|\mathbf{D}| - 1$ diagnoses in $\mathbf{D}$.

Biased Maximal Elimination BME: [17,18] Chooses a query with a bias (probability >0.5) towards one classification (P or N) such that this more likely classification rules out an as high as possible number of diagnoses in $\mathbf{D}$.

Risk Optimization RIO': [17,22] Chooses a query with optimal information gain (ENT-value) among those that, in the worst case, eliminate (at least) $n \leq \frac{1}{2}|\mathbf{D}|$ diagnoses in $\mathbf{D}$. At this, the parameter n is learned by reinforcement based on the diagnoses elimination performance achieved so far during a TOD session.[2]

---

[2] We consider the slightly modified version RIO' of the original RIO [22], as suggested in [18].

Table 2. q-partitions for the queries $q_i := \{ax_i\}$ in Example 6.

q	$\mathbf{D}_q^+$	$\mathbf{D}_q^-$	$p(\mathbf{D}_q^+)$	$p(\mathbf{D}_q^-)$
$\{ax_1\}$	$\{\mathcal{D}_1, \mathcal{D}_2, \mathcal{D}_3, \mathcal{D}_4, \mathcal{D}_6\}$	$\{\mathcal{D}_5\}$	0.59	0.41
$\{ax_2\}$	$\{\mathcal{D}_5, \mathcal{D}_6\}$	$\{\mathcal{D}_1, \mathcal{D}_2, \mathcal{D}_3, \mathcal{D}_4\}$	0.45	0.55
$\{ax_3\}$	$\{\mathcal{D}_2, \mathcal{D}_3, \mathcal{D}_4, \mathcal{D}_5\}$	$\{\mathcal{D}_1, \mathcal{D}_6\}$	0.95	0.05
$\{ax_4\}$	$\{\mathcal{D}_1, \mathcal{D}_2, \mathcal{D}_3, \mathcal{D}_4\}$	$\{\mathcal{D}_5, \mathcal{D}_6\}$	0.55	0.45
$\{ax_5\}$	$\{\mathcal{D}_1, \mathcal{D}_3, \mathcal{D}_4, \mathcal{D}_5, \mathcal{D}_6\}$	$\{\mathcal{D}_2\}$	0.67	0.33
$\{ax_6\}$	$\{\mathcal{D}_1, \mathcal{D}_2, \mathcal{D}_4, \mathcal{D}_5, \mathcal{D}_6\}$	$\{\mathcal{D}_3\}$	0.86	0.14
$\{ax_7\}$	$\{\mathcal{D}_1, \mathcal{D}_2, \mathcal{D}_3\}$	$\{\mathcal{D}_4, \mathcal{D}_5, \mathcal{D}_6\}$	0.48	0.52

Random RND: Samples one element uniformly at random from the query space **Q**.

Example 6. To illustrate these different selection principles, let us consider a DPI (cf. [17, Table 1 + 2]) with $\mathcal{O} = \{1, \ldots, 7\}$ (where numbers i denote axioms ax_i) which gives rise to the minimal diagnoses **D** and associated diagnoses probabilities given by

$$\mathbf{D} = \{\mathcal{D}_1, \ldots, \mathcal{D}_6\} = \{[2,3], [2,5], [2,6], [2,7], [1,4,7], [3,4,7]\}$$
$$\{p(\mathcal{D}_1), \ldots, p(\mathcal{D}_6)\} = \{0.01, 0.33, 0.14, 0.07, 0.41, 0.04\}$$

Let, for simplicity, the query space **Q** consist (only) of all single axiom sets $q_i := \{ax_i\}$ for $ax_i \in \mathcal{O}$. The q-partitions of these queries are shown in Table 2. Now, the query choice made by the discussed QSMs in this case is as given in Table 3.   □

Table 3. Query choice made by the different QSMs in Example 6.

QSM	best query	explanation
ENT:	q_7	$p(\mathbf{D}_{q_7}^+)$ and $p(\mathbf{D}_{q_7}^-)$ are closest to 0.5 over all queries q_i
SPL:	q_7	$|\mathbf{D}_{q_7}^+|$ and $|\mathbf{D}_{q_7}^-|$ are equal to $\frac{|\mathbf{D}|}{2} = 3$
KL:	q_3	$KL(q_3) = 1.48$ is maximal over all queries q_i
EMCb:	q_7	the expected number of eliminated diagnoses is 3 (and lower for all other queries q_i)
MPS:	q_1	$|\mathbf{D}_{q_1}^-| = |\{\mathcal{D}_5\}| = 1$ and $p(\mathcal{D}_5) = 0.41 > 0.33(\text{cf. } q_5) > 0.14(\text{cf. } q_6)$
BME:	q_7	$BME(q_7) = 3$ is maximal over all queries q_i
RIO' (with $n = 2$):	q_2 or q_4	these are the queries with best ENT-value among all queries ($q2, q3, q4$) which eliminate n diagnoses in **D** in the worst case

4   Experimental Settings

The Dataset. Table 4 depicts the (part of the overall) dataset investigated in the so-far[3] finished experiments. The tested ontologies U,M,T,E are inconsistent real-world cases; these were also examined in [8,27]. The DPI dpi_j we extracted from $\mathcal{O}_j$ was $\langle \mathcal{O}_j, \emptyset, \emptyset, \emptyset \rangle$ $(j = 1, \ldots, 4)$, i.e. the background $\mathcal{B}$, positive (P) and negative (N) test cases were (initially) empty. Moreover, Table 4 shows the diagnostic structure of the used debugging problems in terms of the ontology size, the number and size of minimal diagnoses, and the logical expressivity which influences the reasoning complexity.

The Factors. To test the behavior and robustness of the discussed QSMs under various scenarios, we – in addition to the DPI – varied the following factors in our experiments:

(F1) the type of probability distribution (concerning faults wrt. logical symbols) (*non-biased, moderately biased, strongly biased*),

(F2) 3 different random choices of assigned probabilities for each distribution type (to average out potential peculiarities of a specific probability assignment),

(F3) the plausibility of the probabilities (simulated by *plausible, random, implausible* oracle behavior),

(F4) the amount of information available for query selection (number of leading diagnoses $ld \in \{6, 10, 14\}$), and

(F5) the actual diagnosis $\mathcal{D}^*$ (i.e. the target solution of the TOD sessions).

Ad (F1): Let S be the set of all logical symbols (cf. Sect. 2) occurring over all $ax \in \mathcal{O}_j$ and $E_\lambda(x) = \lambda e^{-\lambda x}$ the probability density function of the exponential distribution. Three probability distribution types were modeled, by assigning to each symbol in S ...

- *all-equal (EQ):* ... a fixed equal (random) value $r \in [0, 1]$
- *moderately biased (MOD):* ... the probability $E_\lambda(x_i)$ for a random $x_i \in [i - \frac{1}{2}, i + \frac{1}{2})$ where i is randomly chosen (without replacement) from $\{1, \ldots, |S|\}$ and $\lambda := 0.5$ (same λ as used in [27])
- *strongly biased (STR):* ... the probability $E_\lambda(x_i)$ for a random $x_i \in [i - \frac{1}{2}, i + \frac{1}{2})$ where i is randomly chosen (without replacement) from $\{1, \ldots, |S|\}$ and $\lambda := 1.75$ (same λ as used in [27])

---

[3] Note, due to the comprehensiveness (large number of factor combinations tested) of our evaluations, experiments are very time-consuming (up to several weeks for one ontology).

Table 4. Dataset used in the experiments.

j	KB $\mathcal{O}_j$	$|\mathcal{O}_j|$	expressivity [1]	#D/min/max [2]	Key:
					1): Description Logic expressivity [1, p. 525ff.].
1	University (U) [3]	50	$\mathcal{SOIN}^{(D)}$	90/3/4	**2):** #D, min, max denote the number, the min. and
2	MiniTambis (M) [3]	173	$\mathcal{ALCN}$	48/3/3	max. size of minimal diagnoses for the DPI.
3	Transportation (T) [3]	1300	$\mathcal{ALCH}^{(D)}$	1782/6/9	**3):** Sufficiently complex cases (#D $\geq$ 40) used in
4	Economy (E) [3]	1781	$\mathcal{ALCH}^{(D)}$	864/4/8	[27].

Intuitively, one can view both MOD and STR to (1) precompute a sequence $p_1 > \cdots > p_{|S|}$ of values in $(0, 1)$ where, on average, the ratio between each value p_i and the next smaller one p_{i+1} is $p_i/p_{i+1} = e^\lambda$, i.e. ≈ 1.6 for MOD and ≈ 5.8 for STR, and (2) assign to each $s \in S$ a randomly chosen probability p_i from this sequence without replacement. Hence, if sorted from large to small, the fault probabilities assigned to logical symbols occurring in $\mathcal{O}_j$ are completely uniform for EQ (*no bias*), moderately descending for MOD (*moderate bias*) and steeply descending for STR (*strong bias*).

Example 7. Returning to Example 3, note the strong bias (STR) in the fault probabilities of the symbols $\exists, \sqcap, \sqsubseteq$, i.e. each probability is five times as high as the next one. □

For instance, EQ could model a situation where a novice knowledge engineer or domain expert obtains a faulty ontology, and there is no relevant information about their faults at hand. On the other hand, MOD can be interpreted to simulate a moderate tendency in the fault information, i.e. a non-negligible number of symbols have a non-negligible fault probability. For example, an ontology author might extract from logs of her past debugging sessions that she were misusing a range of different symbols, but some more often than others. STR reflects cases where the differences in fault likeliness are substantial, i.e. very few symbols have a non-negligible probability of being faulty, whereas most of the symbols are practically always correct. An example is a knowledge engineer that, in the past, has made almost only errors regarding quantifiers.

Ad (F3): Let q be a query with $p(\mathsf{class}(q) = P) = x$ (cf. Sect. 2). The plausibility of the given probabilistic information was modeled by different oracle functions class, simulating different strategies of query classification:

- *plausible*: classify q to P with probability x
- *random*: classify q to P with probability 0.5
- *implausible*: classify q to P with probability $1 - x$

Recall (Sect. 2), $p(\mathsf{class}(q) = N) = 1 - p(\mathsf{class}(q) = P)$. The idea is that, given (un)reasonable fault information, the estimated query classification probabilities should be good (bad) approximations of the real likelihood of getting a respective outcome. The plausible scenario reflects the case where given probabilities are useful and provide a rational bias, e.g. when different (reliable) sources of fault information are integrated or the user knows their strengths and weaknesses well. The random strategy aims at estimating the average number of queries needed to pin down $\mathcal{D}^*$, assuming we cannot make useful predictions about the oracle. The implausible strategy represents a misleading fault model, where probabilities turn out to be opposite to what the given information suggests, e.g., when using subjective estimates or historical data that do not apply to the present scenario. As QSMs utilize fault information for query suggestion, we want to assess their robustness under changing fault information quality [22,27].

Example 8. Intuitively, given the actual diagnosis $\mathcal{D}_3$ in our running example (Examples 1–5) and the diagnoses probability distribution in Example 3 (assigning $\mathcal{D}_3$ only a value of 0.03), the fault information $p(.)$ would fall into the category "implausible". □

Ad (F5): We specified the target solution $\mathcal{D}^*$ in the different TOD sessions implicitly through the oracle answer strategies, see (F3). That is, each TOD session continued until positive (P') and negative (N') test cases were collected such that there was just a single minimal diagnosis for the DPI $\langle \mathcal{O}_j, \emptyset, P', N' \rangle$ (resulting from the initial DPI by adding P' and N', cf. Problem 1). This implicit definition of $\mathcal{D}^*$ has the advantage of higher generality and closeness to reality over a prior explicit fixation of some $\mathcal{D}^*$ among the minimal diagnoses for the initial DPI $dpi_j^0 := \langle \mathcal{O}_j, \emptyset, \emptyset, \emptyset \rangle$ [27]. Because, in the latter case only one specific class of TOD problems is considered, namely those where the actual solution $\mathcal{D}^*$ is already a minimal diagnosis for dpi_j^0. In practice, this assumption might often not hold. The reason is that the DPI changes throughout TOD, i.e. dpi_j^i becomes dpi_j^{i+1} after the incorporation of a new test case; this transformation generally gives rise to "new" diagnoses (minimal diagnoses for dpi_j^{i+1}) that are proper supersets of ruled out "original" ones (minimal diagnoses for dpi_j^i inconsistent with the added test case) [15,16].

The Tests. For each of the DPIs $dpi_1, \ldots, dpi_4$, for each of the 8 QSMs explicated in Sect. 3, and for each of the 3^4 factor level combinations of factors (F1) – (F4) we performed 20 TOD sessions, adopting the algorithms for query computation presented in [20,21]. Factor (F5) was implicitly varied in these 20 runs through the randomized oracle behavior (F3), yielding in most cases a different $\mathcal{D}^*$. When some $\mathcal{D}^*$ happened to occur repeatedly in the 20 sessions, we discarded such duplicate runs.[4]

---

[4] To reproduce the experiments or access logs see http://isbi.aau.at/ontodebug/ evaluation.

5   Experimental Results

5.1   Representation

The obtained experimental results are shown by Figs. 1, 2, 3 and 4 which graph the number of queries required by the tested QSMs until $\mathcal{D}^*$ could be isolated. At this, the green/yellow/red bars depict the situation of a plausibly/randomly/implausibly answering oracle (F3). Each bar represents an average over (up to) 20 TOD sessions (F5) and 3 random choices of probabilities (F2). Each figure summarizes the results for one ontology in Table 4; the plots for the U and T cases are more comprehensive, including all combinations of factor levels for (F1), (F3) and (F4), whereas the depictions of M and E are kept shorter due to space restrictions, showing only the $ld = 10$ case of (F4) for all settings of (F1) and (F3). Along the x-axes of the figures we have the 8 different QSMs, grouped by manifestations of factor (F4) in Figs. 1 and 3, and by instantiations of factor (F1) in Figs. 2 and 4.

5.2   Observations

Gained insights from the study of the experimental data are discussed next.

Is there a Clear Winner? This question can be answered negatively pretty clearly. For instance, have a look at the MOD, $ld = 14$ case in Fig. 1. Here we see that MPS performs really good compared to all other QSMs for all oracle types. In fact, it is better than all others in the plausible and random configurations, and loses just narrowly against RND given implausible answers. However, if we draw our attention to, e.g., the EQ case in the same figure, we recognize that MPS comes off significantly worse than other heuristics under a plausible oracle behavior. Similar argumentations apply for all other potential winner QSMs. For $ld = 10$, Table 5, which lists the best QSMs in all the different settings we investigated, confirms that there is no single best QSM.

Sensitivity to Fault Information. That there is no QSM which always outmatches all others is not a great surprise, as we evaluate under various types of given probabilistic information $p(.)$ and the different measures exploit $p(.)$ to a different extent when selecting a query. As a result, we can observe probability-independent QSMs such as SPL outperform (lose against) strongly probability-reliant ones such as ENT in situations where the fault information is wrongly (reasonably) biased, e.g., see the implausible (plausible) cases for MOD and STR in Figs. 1 and 3. So, e.g., SPL can never benefit from high-quality meta information about faults, but cannot effect a significant overhead given low-quality probabilities either. The behavior of, e.g., ENT, is diametrically opposite. To verify this, check the difference between the green and red bars for both SPL and ENT for MOD and STR; for SPL they are hardly different at all, whereas for ENT they diverge rapidly as we raise the bias (EQ → MOD → STR) in the underlying distribution. In contrast to these extreme cases, there is, e.g., RIO′ which incorporates both the diagnoses elimination rate and fault probabilities in its calculations. The consequence is a behavior that mostly lies in between the performances of SPL and ENT. Based on the data in the figures, which is quite consistent in this regard, the following *qualitative ordering from most to least probability-sensitive* can be imposed on QSMs:

$$\langle \mathsf{EMCb}, \mathsf{BME}, \mathsf{ENT}, \mathsf{KL}, \mathsf{MPS}, \mathsf{RIO}', \mathsf{RND}, \mathsf{SPL} \rangle \tag{1}$$

Impact of the DPI/Diagnostic Structure. Trivially, the overall number of (minimal) diagnoses to discriminate between impacts the average number of queries required. Thus, for M (48 minimal diagnoses initially), U (90), E (864) and T (1782), respectively, the min/avg/max number of queries over all QSMs and sessions is (rounded) 3/7/18, 4/8/19, 6/10/19 and 4/12/29. The difference between M and E, for instance, can be quite well seen by comparing the length of the bars in Figs. 2 and 4 which are placed side by side. On the contrary and as one would expect, there are no indications of the ontology size $|\mathcal{O}_j|$ (3rd column, Table 4) having a remarkable influence on QSM performance (as the ontology size has generally no bearing on the number of minimal diagnoses). The reasoning complexity (4th column, Table 4), in contrast, albeit not relevant to the QSM performance, is known to affect the query computation time [20]. The latter was quite constant over all runs and QSMs and amounted to maximally 0.18/0.14/0.18/0.13 sec (per query) for the cases M/U/E/T. The relative behavior of the QSMs under varying DPI (but otherwise same conditions) appears to be quite stable. To see this, compare, e.g., the EQ, the MOD and the STR cases between Figs. 1 and 3, or Figs. 2 and 4. From the pragmatic point of view, if this consistency of QSM performances irrespective of the particular DPI generalizes (as needs to be verified using a larger dataset), a nice implication thereof would be the possibility to recommend (against) QSMs independently of (the structure of) the problem at hand.

Impact of the Leading Diagnoses. As Figs. 1 and 3 indicate quite well, and numbers confirm, there is no significant average difference in the numbers of queries for varying $ld \in \{6, 10, 14\}$. This is in line with the findings of [2]. What we can realize, though, is an exacerbation of the discrepancy between the plausible (green bars) and implausible (red bars) cases when ld increases. The random case (yellow bars), on the other hand, is mostly stable. The reason for this intensification of the effect of good or bad bias with larger diagnoses samples is that more extreme decisions might be made in this case. A simple illustration of this is to compare a "risky" [22] query (one that might invalidate very few diagnoses) wrt. a sample of 3 and 100 diagnoses; in the former case, this would be one eliminating either 1 or 2, in the latter one ruling out either 1 or 99 known hypotheses. We see that the former query is similar to a "risk-less" split-in-half choice, while the latter is far off being that conservative. A practical consequence of this is that it might make sense to try generating a higher number of diagnoses per iteration (if feasible in reasonable time) if a probability-based measure, e.g. EMCb or ENT, is used and the trust in the given (biased) fault information is high (e.g. if reliable historical data is available). Verify this by considering

Table 5. Shows which QSM(s) exhibited best performance in the various scenarios in (F1) × (F3) for all DPIs (1st column) in Table 4 and the setting $ld = 10$ of (F4). The QSM(s) with lowest # of queries (per scenario) are underlined. All stated non-underlined QSMs lay within 3% of the best QSM wrt. # of queries. The number below the QSM(s) gives the possible overhead $(\#q_{worstQSM(S),S}/\#q_{bestQSM(S),S} - 1) * 100$ in % incurred by using a non-optimal QSM in a scenario S, where $\#q_{X,S}$ refers to the # of required queries of QSM X in scenario S, and $bestQSM(S)$ / $worstQSM(S)$ denote the best/worst QSM in scenario S. The colors indicate criticality of QSM choice based on the overhead, from lowest = green to highest = red.

		PLAUSIBLE			RANDOM			IMPLAUSIBLE	
	EQ	MOD	STR	EQ	MOD	STR	EQ	MOD	STR
M	KL	RIO', ENT, BME	MPS, ENT	MPS	MPS	MPS	MPS	RND	RND
	63	176	144	46	47	48	118	131	277
U	BME	BME	MPS, BME	MPS	MPS	MPS	RND	RND	RND, KL
	59	129	151	42	50	53	67	149	220
E	BME	ENT	EMCb, RIO', BME	ENT, MPS	MPS	ENT, RIO', BME, MPS	MPS	KL	RND
	64	93	90	30	33	37	121	191	93
T	EMCb	EMCb, RIO', ENT	ENT, BME, EMCb, MPS	MPS	MPS	MPS	MPS	RND	RND
	62	125	174	45	40	38	93	102	123

Table 6. Number of times each QSM is (among) the best in Table 5.

		ENT	SPL	KL	EMCb	MPS	BME	RIO'	RND
	among best	7	0	3	4	18	8	4	8
ALL	the best	4	0	2	4	16	4	2	8
	among best	5	0	1	4	3	7	3	0
PLAUSIBLE	the best	2	0	1	4	3	4	1	0

EMCb and ENT in the MOD and STR cases for $ld \in \{6, 14\}$ in Figs. 1 and 3. By contrast, when adopting a probability-insensitive QSM, say SPL, one seems to be mostly better off when relying on a smaller ld. That is, when the meta information is vague, a good option is to rely on a "cautious" [22] measure such as SPL *and* a small diagnoses sample. Note, the latter is doubly beneficial as it also decreases computation times.

Importance of Using a Suitable QSM. To quantify the importance of QSM choice we compute the *degree of criticality of choosing the right QSM in a scenario* as the overhead in oracle cost (number of queries) when employing the worst instead of the best QSM in this scenario, see (the caption of) Table 5. At this, a *scenario* refers to one factor level combination in (F1) × (F3). We learn from Table 5 that, even in the least critical cases (green-colored), we might experience a worst-case overhead in oracle effort of at least 30% when opting for the wrong QSM. This overhead is drastically higher in other cases and reaches figures of over 250%. That is, more than triple the effort might be necessary to locate a fault under an inopportune choice of QSM heuristic. However, we emphasize that even a 30% overhead must be considered serious given that usually oracle inquiries are very costly. Hence, appropriate QSM selection *is* an important issue to be addressed in all scenarios.

As a predictor of the criticality, the scenario (columns in Table 5) appears to be a reasonable candidate, as the colors already suggest. In fact, the coefficients of variation, one computed for each column in Table 5, are fairly low, ranging from 3% to 26% (except for the last column with 47%). So, the negative effect of a bad QSM choice is similar in equal scenarios, and does not seem to be dependent on the DPI.

Which QSM to use in which Scenario? To approach this question, we have, for all four DPIs, analyzed all the nine settings in (F1) × (F3) wrt. the optimal choice of a QSM. The result is presented in Table 5. We now discuss various insights from this analysis.

Overall Picture. SPL is never a (nearly) optimal option. This is quite natural because, intuitively, going for no "risk" at all means at the same time excluding the chance to perform extraordinarily well. All other QSMs appear multiple times among those QSMs which are ≤3% off the observed optimal number of queries. Table 6 (rows 1 + 2) lists how often each QSM is (among) the best. It shows that MPS is close to the optimum in a half of the cases, significantly more often than all other heuristics. However, blindly deciding for MPS is not a rational way to go. Instead, one must consider the numbers at a more fine-grained level, distinguishing between the quality of the given fault distribution (blocks in Table 5), to get a clearer and more informative picture.

The Implausible Cases: Here RND distinctly prevails. It occurs in all but four optimal QSM sets, and is often *much* better than other measures, e.g., see the STR setting in Fig. 2. At first sight, it might appear counterintuitive that a random selection outweighs all others. One explanation is simply that the randomness prevents RND from getting misled by the (wrong) fault information. Remarkable is, however, that in quasi all cases RND significantly outperforms SPL, which acts independently of the given probabilities as well. The conclusion from this is that, whenever the prior distribution is wrongly biased, introducing randomness into the query selection procedure saves oracle effort.

The Random Cases: These cases are strongly dominated by MPS which occurs in each set of best QSMs per scenario. Therefore, whenever the given fault information does neither manifest a tendency towards nor against the actual diagnosis, MPS is the proper heuristic. Moreover, the benefit of using MPS seems to increase the more leading diagnoses are available for query selection (see Figs. 1 and 3). Since MPS, in attempt to invalidate *a maximal number of diagnoses*, suggests very "risky" queries (see above), a possible explanation for this is that acting on a larger diagnoses sample allows to guarantee a higher risk than when relying on a smaller sample (cf. discussion above). However, as all Figs. 1, 2, 3 and 4 clearly reveal, MPS is definitely the wrong choice in any situation where we have a plausible, but unbiased probability distribution. In such cases it manifests sometimes significantly worse results than other heuristics do. But, as soon as a bias is given, the performance of MPS gets really good.

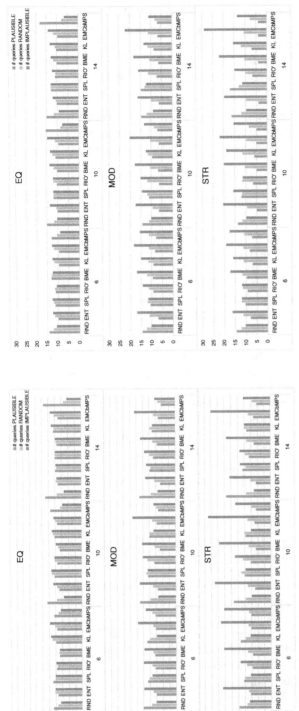

Fig. 1. Results for the University (U) case. (Color figure online)

Fig. 2. Results for the MiniTambis (M) case with $ld = 10$ (F4). (Color figure online)

Fig. 3. Results for the Transportation (T) case. (Color figure online)

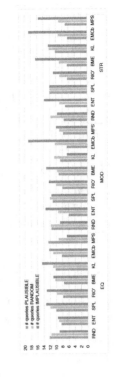

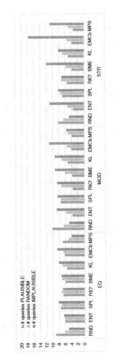

Fig. 4. Results for the Economy (E) case with $ld = 10$ (F4). (Color figure online)

The Plausible Cases: Throughout these cases we have the highest variation concerning the optimal QSM. Actually, all QSMs except for RND and SPL do appear as winners in certain cases. The distribution of the number of appearances as (or among) the best QSM(s) over all QSMs is displayed by Table 6 (rows 3 + 4). That, e.g., ENT is rather good in these cases and RND is no good choice (see also Figs. 1, 2, 3 and 4) is in agreement with the findings of [27]. However, we realize that BME is (among) the best QSMs more often than ENT. Comparing only these two, we find that BME outdoes ENT 7 times, ENT wins against BME 4 times, and they are equally good once. A reason for the strength of BME could be the fact that it will in most cases achieve only a minor bias towards one query outcome, as the maximization of the diagnoses elimination rate requires an as small as possible number of diagnoses with a probability sum >0.5. Thus, there is on the one hand a bias increasing the expected diagnoses invalidation rate, and on the other hand a near 50-50 outcome distribution implying a good entropy value. Unsurprisingly, if we sort the QSMs from most to least times being (among) the best based on Table 6 (rows 3 + 4), the resulting order coincides quite well with Eq. (1). In other words, in the plausible scenarios, probability-sensitive heuristics perform best.

Towards New QSMs/Meta-Heuristics. Exploiting the discussed results, one could endeavor to devise new QSMs that are superior to the investigated ones. For instance, in the implausible cases, only RND, MPS and KL occur as best QSMs. Thus, an optimal heuristic for these cases should likely adopt or unify selection principles of these three QSMs. One idea could be, e.g., to sample a few queries using RND and then choose the best one among them using (a weighted combination of) MPS and/or KL. Generally, one could use a meta heuristic that resorts to an appropriately (possibly dynamically re-)weighted sum of the QSM-functions (Table 1, 2nd column). Also, a QSM selecting queries based on a majority voting of multiple heuristics is thinkable, e.g., in Example 6 the query selected by such a QSM would be q_7 (cf. Table 3).

6   Conclusions and Future Work

Results of extensive evaluations on both classical and recently suggested query selection measures (QSMs) for test-driven ontology debugging (TOD) are presented. Main findings are: Using an appropriate QSM is essential, as otherwise TOD cost overheads of over 250% are possible. The one and only best QSM does not exist (or has not yet been found). Besides the size of the solution space of diagnoses, main factors influencing TOD cost are the bias in and the quality of the fault probability distribution, but not the ontology (debugging problem) as such or the size of the diagnoses sample used for query selection. Different QSMs prevail in the various probability distribution scenarios. Interestingly, the quite popular and frequently adopted entropy measure only manifested good (albeit not best) behavior in a single set of scenarios.

Future work topics include in-depth analyses of the (full) results and the design of new QSMs, e.g. meta-heuristics, based on the lessons learned. Moreover, machine learning techniques could be adopted to recommend optimal QSMs based on a classification of a debugging scenario wrt. the QSM-relevant factors we found. And, we plan to integrate the investigated QSMs into our Protégé ontology debugging plug-in [24].[5] From the application point of view – since the discussed techniques are not only applicable to ontologies, but to any monotonic knowledge representation formalism [16] – we intend to explore other use cases of the method. One example could be the adoption in the context of knowledge-based recommender systems [4] where model-based diagnosis is applied for relaxing user selection filters for avoiding empty result sets. Our gained insights could be profitably exploitable for guiding the relaxation process.

References

1. Baader, F., Calvanese, D., McGuinness, D.L., Nardi, D., Patel-Schneider, P.F. (eds.): The Description Logic Handbook. Cambridge University Press, Cambridge (2007)
2. De Kleer, J., Raiman, O.: Trading off the costs of inference vs. probing in diagnosis. In: IJCAI 1995, pp. 1736–1741 (1995)
3. Felfernig, A., Friedrich, G., Jannach, D., Stumptner, M.: Consistency-based diagnosis of configuration knowledge bases. Artif. Intell. **152**(2), 213–234 (2004)
4. Felfernig, A., Mairitsch, M., Mandl, M., Schubert, M., Teppan, E.: Utility-based repair of inconsistent requirements. In: Chien, B.-C., Hong, T.-P., Chen, S.-M., Ali, M. (eds.) IEA/AIE 2009. LNCS (LNAI), vol. 5579, pp. 162–171. Springer, Heidelberg (2009). https://doi.org/10.1007/978-3-642-02568-6_17
5. Ferré, S., Rudolph, S.: Advocatus Diaboli – Exploratory Enrichment of Ontologies with Negative Constraints. In: ten Teije, A., et al. (eds.) EKAW 2012. LNCS (LNAI), vol. 7603, pp. 42–56. Springer, Heidelberg (2012). https://doi.org/10.1007/978-3-642-33876-2_7
6. Grau, B.C., Horrocks, I., Motik, B., Parsia, B., Patel-Schneider, P.F., Sattler, U.: OWL 2: The next step for OWL. JWS **6**(4), 309–322 (2008)
7. Hyafil, L., Rivest, R.L.: Constructing optimal binary decision trees is NP-complete. Inf. Process. Lett. **5**(1), 15–17 (1976)
8. Kalyanpur, A.: Debugging and repair of OWL ontologies. Ph.D. thesis, University of Maryland, College Park (2006)
9. Kalyanpur, A., Parsia, B., Sirin, E., Cuenca-Grau, B.: Repairing unsatisfiable concepts in OWL ontologies. In: Sure, Y., Domingue, J. (eds.) ESWC 2006. LNCS, vol. 4011, pp. 170–184. Springer, Heidelberg (2006). https://doi.org/10.1007/11762256_15
10. de Kleer, J., Raiman, O., Shirley, M.: One step lookahead is pretty good. In: Readings in Model-Based Diagnosis, pp. 138–142 (1992)

---

[5] http://isbi.aau.at/ontodebug.

11. de Kleer, J., Williams, B.C.: Diagnosing multiple faults. Artif. Intell. **32**(1), 97–130 (1987)
12. Moret, B.M.: Decision trees and diagrams. ACM Comput. Surv. (CSUR) **14**(4), 593–623 (1982)
13. Nikitina, N., Rudolph, S., Glimm, B.: Reasoning-supported interactive revision of knowledge bases. In: IJCAI 2011, pp. 1027–1032 (2011)
14. Rector, A., et al.: OWL pizzas: practical experience of teaching OWL-DL: common errors & common patterns. In: Motta, E., Shadbolt, N.R., Stutt, A., Gibbins, N. (eds.) Engineering Knowledge in the Age of the Semantic Web, EKAW 2004. LNCS, vol. 3257, pp. 63–81. Springer, Heidelberg (2004). https://doi.org/10.1007/978-3-540-30202-5_5
15. Reiter, R.: A theory of diagnosis from first principles. Artif. Intell. **32**(1), 57–95 (1987)
16. Rodler, P.: Interactive debugging of knowledge bases. Ph.D. thesis, University of Klagenfurt (2015). http://arxiv.org/pdf/1605.05950v1.pdf
17. Rodler, P.: Towards better response times and higher-quality queries in interactive knowledge base debugging. Technical report, University of Klagenfurt (2016). http://arxiv.org/pdf/1609.02584v2.pdf
18. Rodler, P.: On active learning strategies for sequential diagnosis. In: International Workshop on Principles of Diagnosis (DX 2017), pp. 264–283 (2018)
19. Rodler, P., Schekotihin, K.: Reducing model-based diagnosis to knowledge base debugging. In: International Workshop on Principles of Diagnosis (DX 2017), pp. 284–296 (2018)
20. Rodler, P., Schmid, W., Schekotihin, K.: A generally applicable, highly scalable measurement computation and optimization approach to sequential model-based diagnosis (2017). http://arxiv.org/abs/1711.05508
21. Rodler, P., Schmid, W., Schekotihin, K.: Inexpensive cost-optimized measurement proposal for sequential model-based diagnosis. In: International Workshop on Principles of Diagnosis (DX 2017), pp. 200–218 (2018)
22. Rodler, P., Shchekotykhin, K., Fleiss, P., Friedrich, G.: RIO: minimizing user interaction in ontology debugging. In: Faber, W., Lembo, D. (eds.) RR 2013. LNCS, vol. 7994, pp. 153–167. Springer, Heidelberg (2013). https://doi.org/10.1007/978-3-642-39666-3_12
23. Roussey, C., Corcho, O., Vilches-Blázquez, L.M.: A catalogue of OWL ontology antipatterns. In: K-CAP 2009, pp. 205–206 (2009)
24. Schekotihin, K., Rodler, P., Schmid, W.: OntoDebug: interactive ontology debugging plug-in for Protégé. In: Ferrarotti, F., Woltran, S. (eds.) FoIKS 2018. LNCS, vol. 10833, pp. 340–359. Springer, Cham (2018). https://doi.org/10.1007/978-3-319-90050-6_19
25. Schlobach, S., Huang, Z., Cornet, R., Harmelen, F.: Debugging incoherent terminologies. J. Autom. Reason. **39**(3), 317–349 (2007)
26. Settles, B.: Active Learning. Morgan and Claypool Publishers (2012)
27. Shchekotykhin, K., Friedrich, G., Fleiss, P., Rodler, P.: Interactive ontology debugging: two query strategies for efficient fault localization. JWS **12–13**, 88–103 (2012)

28. Shchekotykhin, K., Friedrich, G., Rodler, P., Fleiss, P.: Sequential diagnosis of high cardinality faults in knowledge-bases by direct diagnosis generation. In: ECAI 2014, pp. 813–818 (2014)
29. Stuckenschmidt, H.: Debugging OWL ontologies - a reality check. In: EON 2008, pp. 1–12 (2008)
30. Troquard, N., Confalonieri, R., Galliani, P., Penaloza, R., Porello, D., Kutz, O.: Repairing ontologies via axiom weakening (2017). http://arxiv.org/abs/1711.03430

Justifications for Description Logic Knowledge Bases Under the Fixed-Domain Semantics

Sebastian Rudolph[1], Lukas Schweizer[1(✉)], and Satyadharma Tirtarasa[2]

[1] Institute of Artificial Intelligence, TU Dresden, Dresden, Germany
{sebastian.rudolph,lukas.schweizer}@tu-dresden.de
[2] Institute of Theoretical Computer Science, TU Dresden, Dresden, Germany
satyadharma.tirtarasa@tu-dresden.de

Abstract. The fixed-domain semantics for OWL and description logic has been introduced to open up the OWL modeling and reasoning tool landscape for use cases resembling constraint satisfaction problems. While standard reasoning under this new semantics is by now rather well-understood theoretically and supported practically, more elaborate tasks like computation of justifications have not been considered so far, although being highly important in the modeling phase. In this paper, we compare three approaches to this problem: one using standard OWL technology employing an axiomatization of the fixed-domain semantics, one using our dedicated fixed-domain reasoner `Wolpertinger` in combination with standard justification computation technology, and one where the problem is encoded entirely into answer-set programming.

1 Introduction

With the success of semantic technologies and its tool support, most notably the OWL language family and its status as W3C standard, more and more people from various application domains create and use ontologies. Meanwhile, ontological modeling is not only well supported by established tools like Protégé, also methodologies such as the usage of ontology design patterns help practitioners to design and deploy ontologies of high quality [9].

Despite these evolutionary improvements in ontology engineering, the resulting ontologies are not free of errors such as unintended entailments (including the case of inconsistency). For that purpose, research has already brought up several techniques to detect the causalities of unintended entailments, and it has been studied for lightweight ontology languages such as $\mathcal{EL}$ [22], as well as for very expressive description logics up to $\mathcal{SROIQ}$ [13,15], which in fact is the logical foundation of OWL 2 DL [10]. These techniques already found their way as built-in functionality into tools like Protégé, or are available stand-alone. In any case, these methods have become an integral part of the semantic development chain.

© Springer Nature Switzerland AG 2018
C. Benzmüller et al. (Eds.): RuleML+RR 2018, LNCS 11092, pp. 185–200, 2018.
https://doi.org/10.1007/978-3-319-99906-7_12

When considering their purpose, ontologies are often divided into two groups: those where the intended use is an (highly axiomatized) expert system focusing on automated reasoning as main use (typically less data driven), or those ontologies that are rather used for data sharing, integration, and reuse with little or no intentions on reasoning (typically data driven) [9]. However in our collaborations with practitioners, we found scenarios exhibiting characteristics of both usages, aiming at ontologies that (a) represent a detailed specification of some product (schema knowledge), (b) include all data and (c) contain axioms that (non-deterministically) specify variable (configurable) parts of the product. In general, these ontologies resemble constraint-type problems, where the purpose of typical automated reasoning tasks is (i) checking satisfiability and (ii) asking for models – solutions of the encoded problem. For both tasks, the natural assumption in this setup is that the domain is explicitly given in the ontology, and thus is finite and fixed a priori.

To accommodate these requirements, the *fixed-domain semantics* has been introduced [6,27], which allows for reasoning over an explicitly given finite domain. A reasoner, named `Wolpertinger`[1], that supports standard reasoning as well as model enumeration under the fixed-domain semantics has been developed [28], based on a translation of DL into answer-set programming.

Our motivation in this paper is to elaborate on possible approaches to compute justifications for ontologies under the fixed-domain semantics. We focus on three approaches that evolved naturally during our investigation. First, it is possible to axiomatize a finite domain and conduct fixed-domain reasoning using standard tools, such that computing explanations can be done via standard tools as well. Second, the `Wolpertinger` reasoner can be coupled with the off-the-shelf justification components of Protégé, and finally we introduce a dedicated encoding of the whole problem into answer-set programming. Our contributions in this paper are:

1. A formal framework for justifications under the fixed-domain semantics.
2. A novel translation for $\mathcal{SROIQ}$ into answer-set programming that allows for standard reasoning and model enumeration.
3. An extended version of the translation enabling to compute justifications where the problem is encoded entirely into answer-set programming.
4. A comparison of three different approaches: one using standard OWL technology employing an axiomatization of the fixed-domain semantics, one using our dedicated fixed-domain reasoner `Wolpertinger` in combination with standard justification computation technology, and one with our novel translation where the problem is encoded entirely into answer-set programming.

The paper is organized as follows. We briefly recall the description logic $\mathcal{SROIQ}$ and a sufficient background on answer-set programming in Sect. 2. In Sect. 3, we introduce the notion of justifications, especially under the fixed-domain semantics. Each possible approach to compute justifications is then depicted in detail in Sect. 4. Finally, we compare the introduced methodologies in Sect. 5.

---

[1] https://github.com/wolpertinger-reasoner.

2   Preliminaries

OWL 2 DL, the version of the Web Ontology Language we focus on, is defined based on description logics (DLs, [1,26]). We briefly recap the description logic $\mathcal{SROIQ}$ (for details see [14]). Let N_I, N_C, and N_R be finite, disjoint sets called *individual names, concept names* and *role names* respectively. These atomic entities can be used to form complex ones as displayed in Table 1.

A $\mathcal{SROIQ}$ *knowledge base* $\mathcal{K}$ is a tuple $(\mathcal{A}, \mathcal{T}, \mathcal{R})$ where $\mathcal{A}$ is an ABox, $\mathcal{T}$ is a TBox and $\mathcal{R}$ is an RBox. Table 2 presents the respective axiom types available in the three parts. The definition of $\mathcal{SROIQ}$ also contains so-called *global restrictions* which prevents certain axioms from occurring together, retaining decidability. They are not necessary for fixed-domain reasoning considered here, hence we omit them for the sake of brevity. We use $N_I(\mathcal{K})$, $N_C(\mathcal{K})$, and $N_R(\mathcal{K})$ to denote the sets of individual names, concept names, and role names occurring in $\mathcal{K}$, respectively.

The semantics of $\mathcal{SROIQ}$ is defined via interpretations $\mathcal{I} = (\Delta^{\mathcal{I}}, \cdot^{\mathcal{I}})$ composed of a non-empty set $\Delta^{\mathcal{I}}$ called the *domain of* $\mathcal{I}$ and a function $\cdot^{\mathcal{I}}$ mapping individual names to elements of $\Delta^{\mathcal{I}}$, concept names to subsets of $\Delta^{\mathcal{I}}$, and role names to subsets of $\Delta^{\mathcal{I}} \times \Delta^{\mathcal{I}}$. This mapping is extended to complex role and concept expressions (cf. Table 1) and finally used to define satisfaction of axioms (see Table 2). We say that $\mathcal{I}$ *satisfies* a knowledge base $\mathcal{K} = (\mathcal{A}, \mathcal{T}, \mathcal{R})$ (or $\mathcal{I}$ is a *model* of $\mathcal{K}$, written: $\mathcal{I} \models \mathcal{K}$) if it satisfies all axioms of $\mathcal{A}$, $\mathcal{T}$, and $\mathcal{R}$. We say that a knowledge base $\mathcal{K}$ *entails* an axiom α (written $\mathcal{K} \models \alpha$) if all models of $\mathcal{K}$ are models of α.

Table 1. Syntax and semantics of role and concept constructors in $\mathcal{SROIQ}$, where $a_1, \ldots a_n$ denote individual names, s a role name, r a role expression and C and D concept expressions.

Name	Syntax	Semantics
Inverse role	s^-	$\{(x,y) \in \Delta^{\mathcal{I}} \times \Delta^{\mathcal{I}} \mid (y,x) \in s^{\mathcal{I}}\}$
Universal role	u	$\Delta^{\mathcal{I}} \times \Delta^{\mathcal{I}}$
Top	$\top$	$\Delta^{\mathcal{I}}$
Bottom	$\bot$	$\emptyset$
Negation	$\neg C$	$\Delta^{\mathcal{I}} \setminus C^{\mathcal{I}}$
Conjunction	$C \sqcap D$	$C^{\mathcal{I}} \cap D^{\mathcal{I}}$
Disjunction	$C \sqcup D$	$C^{\mathcal{I}} \cup D^{\mathcal{I}}$
Nominals	$\{a_1, \ldots, a_n\}$	$\{a_1^{\mathcal{I}}, \ldots, a_n^{\mathcal{I}}\}$
Univ. restriction	$\forall r.C$	$\{x \mid \forall y.(x,y) \in r^{\mathcal{I}} \to y \in C^{\mathcal{I}}\}$
Exist. restriction	$\exists r.C$	$\{x \mid \exists y.(x,y) \in r^{\mathcal{I}} \wedge y \in C^{\mathcal{I}}\}$
Self concept	$\exists r.Self$	$\{x \mid (x,x) \in r^{\mathcal{I}}\}$
Qualified number	$\leqslant n\, r.C$	$\{x \mid \#\{y \in C^{\mathcal{I}} \mid (x,y) \in r^{\mathcal{I}}\} \leq n\}$
Restriction	$\geqslant n\, r.C$	$\{x \mid \#\{y \in C^{\mathcal{I}} \mid (x,y) \in r^{\mathcal{I}}\} \geq n\}$

Table 2. Syntax and semantics of $\mathcal{SROIQ}$ axioms.

Axiom α	$\mathcal{I} \models \alpha$, if	
$r_1 \circ \cdots \circ r_n \sqsubseteq r$	$r_1^{\mathcal{I}} \circ \cdots \circ r_n^{\mathcal{I}} \subseteq r^{\mathcal{I}}$	RBox $\mathcal{R}$
$\mathsf{Dis}(s,r)$	$s^{\mathcal{I}} \cap r^{\mathcal{I}} = \emptyset$	
$C \sqsubseteq D$	$C^{\mathcal{I}} \subseteq D^{\mathcal{I}}$	TBox $\mathcal{T}$
$C(a)$	$a^{\mathcal{I}} \in C^{\mathcal{I}}$	ABox $\mathcal{A}$
$r(a,b)$	$(a^{\mathcal{I}}, b^{\mathcal{I}}) \in r^{\mathcal{I}}$	
$a \doteq b$	$a^{\mathcal{I}} = b^{\mathcal{I}}$	
$a \not\doteq b$	$a^{\mathcal{I}} \neq b^{\mathcal{I}}$	

Answer-Set Programming. We review the basic notions of answer set programming [19] under the stable model semantics [8], for further details we refer to [4,7].

We fix a countable set $\mathcal{U}$ of *(domain) elements*, also called *constants*; and suppose a total order $<$ over the domain elements. An *atom* is an expression $p(t_1, \ldots, t_n)$, where p is a *predicate* of arity $n \geq 0$ and each t_i is either a variable or an element from $\mathcal{U}$. An atom is *ground* if it is free of variables. $B_{\mathcal{U}}$ denotes the set of all ground atoms over $\mathcal{U}$. A *(disjunctive) rule* ρ is of the form

$$a_1, \ldots, a_n \leftarrow b_1, \ldots, b_k, \; not \, b_{k+1}, \ldots, \; not \, b_m.$$

with $m \geq k \geq 0$, where $a_1, \ldots, a_n, b_1, \ldots, b_m$ are atoms, and "*not*" denotes *default negation*. The *head* of ρ is the set $H(\rho) = \{a_1, \ldots, a_n\}$ and the *body* of ρ is $B(\rho) = \{b_1, \ldots, b_k, \, not \, b_{k+1}, \ldots, \, not \, b_m\}$. Furthermore, $B^+(\rho) = \{b_1, \ldots, b_k\}$ and $B^-(\rho) = \{b_{k+1}, \ldots, b_m\}$. A rule ρ is *safe* if each variable in ρ occurs in $B^+(r)$. A rule ρ is *ground* if no variable occurs in ρ. A *fact* is a ground rule with empty body. An *(input) database* is a set of facts. A (disjunctive) *program* is a finite set of disjunctive rules. For a program Π and an input database D, we often write $\Pi(D)$ instead of $D \cup \Pi$. For any program Π, let U_Π be the set of all constants appearing in Π. $Gr(\Pi)$ is the set of rules $\rho\sigma$ obtained by applying, to each rule $\rho \in \Pi$, all possible substitutions σ from the variables in ρ to elements of U_Π.

An *interpretation* $I \subseteq B_{\mathcal{U}}$ satisfies a ground rule ρ iff $H(\rho) \cap I \neq \emptyset$ whenever $B^+(\rho) \subseteq I$, $B^-(\rho) \cap I = \emptyset$. I satisfies a ground program Π, if each $\rho \in \Pi$ is satisfied by I. A non-ground rule ρ (resp., a program Π) is satisfied by an interpretation I iff I satisfies all groundings of ρ (resp., $Gr(\Pi)$). $I \subseteq B_{\mathcal{U}}$ is an *answer set* (also called *stable model*) of Π iff it is a subset-minimal set satisfying the *Gelfond-Lifschitz reduct* $\Pi^I = \{H(\rho) \leftarrow B^+(\rho) \mid I \cap B^-(\rho) = \emptyset, \rho \in Gr(\Pi)\}$. For a program Π, we denote the set of its answer sets by $\mathcal{AS}(\Pi)$.

For a program Π, we denote the set of its answer sets by $\mathcal{AS}(\Pi)$, and might use $\mathcal{AS}(\Pi)_{|P}$ to project on the predicates $P = \{p_1, \ldots, p_n\}$.

We make use of further syntactic extensions, namely integrity constraints and count expressions, which both can be recast to ordinary normal rules as described in [7]. An *integrity constraint* is a rule ρ where $H(\rho) = \emptyset$, intuitively representing an undesirable situation; i.e. it has to be avoided that $B(\rho)$ evaluates positively. Count expressions are of the form $\#count\{l : l_1, \ldots, l_i\} \bowtie u$, where l is an atom and $l_j = p_j$ or $l_j = not\, p_j$, for p_j an atom, $1 \leq j \leq i$, u a non-negative integer, and $\bowtie \in \{\leq, <, =, >, \geq\}$. The expression $\{l : l_1, \ldots, l_n\}$ denotes the set of all ground instantiations of l, governed through $\{l_1, \ldots, l_n\}$. We restrict the occurrence of count expressions in a rule ρ to $B^+(\rho)$ only. Intuitively, an interpretation satisfies a count expression, if $N \bowtie u$ holds, where N is the cardinality of the set of ground instantiations of l, $N = |\{l \mid l_1, \ldots, l_n\}|$, for $\bowtie \in \{\leq, <, =, >, \geq\}$ and u a non-negative integer.

In order to handle (subset) preferences over answer-sets w.r.t. to ground instances of a specific atom, we make use of `asprin` [3]. The framework is designed to support and simplify the incorporation of preferences over answer-sets.

3 Justifications Under Fixed-Domain Semantics

3.1 Fixed-Domain Semantics

The standard semantics of DLs is defined on arbitrary domains. While *finite model reasoning* (a natural assumption in database theory) has become the focus of studies in DLs [5,18,25], where one is interested in models over arbitrary but finite domains, we consider the case where the domain has an *a-priori known* cardinality and use the term *fixed-domain*. This restriction yields an advantage regarding computational complexity for expressive DLs, but it also seems to reflect the intuitive model-theoretic expectations of practitioners in the industrial use cases we were confronted with. Satisfiability checking in $\mathcal{SROIQ}$ under the standard semantics is N2ExpTime-complete [16], while being NP-complete in the fixed-domain setting [6].

Definition 1 (Fixed-Domain Semantics [6]). *Let Δ be a non-empty finite set called fixed domain. An interpretation $\mathcal{I} = (\Delta^{\mathcal{I}}, \cdot^{\mathcal{I}})$ is said to be Δ-fixed, if $\Delta^{\mathcal{I}} = \Delta$, and $a^{\mathcal{I}} = a$ for all $a \in \Delta$. For a DL knowledge base $\mathcal{K}$, we call an interpretation $\mathcal{I}$ a Δ-model of $\mathcal{K}$ (and write $\mathcal{I} \models_\Delta \mathcal{K}$), if $\mathcal{I}$ is a Δ-fixed interpretation and $\mathcal{I} \models \mathcal{K}$. A knowledge base $\mathcal{K}$ is called Δ-satisfiable, if it has a Δ-model. A knowledge base is said to $\mathcal{K}$ Δ-entail an axiom α ($\mathcal{K} \models_\Delta \alpha$), if $\mathcal{I} \models \alpha$ for every $\mathcal{I} \models_\Delta \mathcal{K}$.*

3.2 Justifications

Logical modeling is prone to error, and it is therefore important to provide debugging support. One of the most investigated methods is to determine explanations of certain entailments. These explanations are usually (minimal) subsets of the input knowledge base that suffice to entail the axiom in question. Several terms have been coined to refer to such (sub)sets. In the context of lightweight description logics *Minimal Axiom Sets* (MinAs) is used, while the task of finding them is called Axiom Pinpointing [2, 22]. Instead, for propositional logic, the term *Minimal Unsatisfiable Subformula* (MUS) to explain unsatisfiability was introduced long before [21]. In this paper we use the notion of *justification*, introduced in the context of highly expressive description logics [15].

Definition 2 (Justification [15]). *Let $\mathcal{K}$ be a knowledge base such that $\mathcal{K} \models \alpha$. $\mathcal{J}$ is a justification for α in $\mathcal{K}$ if $\mathcal{J} \subseteq \mathcal{K}$ and $\mathcal{J} \models \alpha$, and for all $\mathcal{J}' \subset \mathcal{J}, \mathcal{J}' \not\models \alpha$.*

Obviously, there may be multiple justifications for an axiom α. Dually to justifications, one might be interested in minimal subsets that can be retracted in order to restore consistency, or remove the unwanted entailment; commonly called *repair*. These two notions are strongly related in the sense that any repair has a non-empty intersection with each justification. However, in this work we restrict ourselves to justifications only.

Regarding the fixed-domain semantics, any justification needs to adhere to the considered fixed domain. Note that fixed-domain reasoning is monotonic, since otherwise, the subset minimality criterion in the definition of justifications would not be reasonable.

Definition 3 (Fixed-Justification). *Let $\mathcal{K}$ be a knowledge base, and Δ a fixed-domain such that $\mathcal{K} \models_\Delta \alpha$. $\mathcal{J}$ is a Δ-justification for α in $\mathcal{K}$ if $\mathcal{J} \subseteq \mathcal{K}$ and $\mathcal{J} \models_\Delta \alpha$, and for all $\mathcal{J}' \subset \mathcal{J}, \mathcal{J}' \not\models_\Delta \alpha$.*

It is the case that, if $\mathcal{K} \models \alpha$, then $\mathcal{K} \models_\Delta \alpha$ for any fixed-domain Δ. However, it does not hold that, if $\mathcal{J}$ is a justification for $\mathcal{K} \models \alpha$, then $\mathcal{J}$ is a Δ-justification for $\mathcal{K} \models_\Delta \alpha$ for any fixed-domain Δ. Due to a stronger restriction on models, there might exist $\mathcal{J}' \subset \mathcal{J}$, such that $\mathcal{J}' \not\models \alpha$ but $\mathcal{J}' \models_\Delta \alpha$. Nonetheless, giving a justification $\mathcal{J}$ under the standard semantics is helpful, since only subsets of $\mathcal{J}$ need to be considered. Formally, if $\mathcal{J}$ is a justification for $\mathcal{K} \models \alpha$, then there exist no Δ-justification $\mathcal{J}' \supset \mathcal{J}$ for $\mathcal{K} \models_\Delta \alpha$, for any fixed-domain Δ. This holds for any restricted reasoning maintaining monotonicity (e.g. finite model reasoning).

We focus on finding justifications for inconsistency, since entailment checking in $\mathcal{SROIQ}$ can be reduced to satisfiability checking. For example, $\mathcal{K} \models_\Delta A \sqsubseteq B$, iff $\mathcal{K} \cup \{(A \sqcap \neg B)(a)\}$ is Δ-inconsistent, where a is a fresh individual not occurring in $\mathcal{K}$. In the same way, justifications for entailments can be reduced to finding justifications for inconsistency. The caveat is that the introduced axiom should be fixed and not be part of candidate subset guessing.

Example 1. We consider a simple assignment problem, encoded in $\mathcal{K}_{as}$. We let the domain be $\Delta = \{p_1, p_2, p_3, l_1, l_2, l_3, t_1, t_2, t_3\}$.

$$Lecture \sqsubseteq \exists teach^-.Prof \quad Prof \sqsubseteq\ \leq 1\ teach.Lecture \qquad (\alpha_{1-2})$$

$$SpecialLecture \sqsubseteq Lecture \quad SpecialLecture \sqsubseteq \forall teach^-.\{p_2\} \qquad (\alpha_{3-4})$$

$$Lecture \sqsubseteq \neg Prof \quad Lecture \sqsubseteq \neg Time \quad Prof \sqsubseteq \neg Time \qquad (\alpha_{5-7})$$

$$\exists heldAt \sqsubseteq Lecture \qquad \top \sqsubseteq \forall heldAt.Time \qquad (\alpha_{8-9})$$

$$teach \circ heldAt \sqsubseteq busyAt \qquad (\alpha_{10})$$

First, we introduce the core of the knowledge base. Axioms α_{1-2} specify that a lecture must be taught by a professor, but one professor teaches at most one lecture. Axioms α_{3-4} introduce special lectures that can only be taught by professor p_2. Pairwise disjointness of the classes of lectures, professors and times is represented by axioms α_{5-7}. The domain and the range of *heldAt* are restricted by α_{8-9}. Finally, axiom α_{10} defines that a professor is busy at a certain time if he teaches a lecture at that time.

We specify the ABox for $\mathcal{K}_{as}$ in Fig. 1. As shown by the graph, this knowledge base is designed to find a suitable *teach* "configuration". Then, we add additional constraints $\neg busyAt(p_1, t_2)$ $[\alpha_{25}]$ and $\{p_3\} \sqsubseteq\ \leq 1\ busyAt.Time$ $[\alpha_{26}]$. It is easy to see that those constraints enforce p_1 and p_3 to teach l_1. However, l_1 is a special lecture that can only be taught by p_2. Consequently, $\mathcal{K}_{as}$ is inconsistent. Then, for example $\mathcal{J}_{as} = \mathcal{K}_{as} \setminus \{\alpha_{11-13}, \alpha_{15}, \alpha_{17-19}, \alpha_{21-22}\}$ is a Δ-justification for $\mathcal{K}_{as}$ inconsistency.

Note that some assertions can be concluded implicitly, i.e. using the axioms in $\mathcal{J}_{as}$, we can infer that p_1, p_2, p_3 must be professors since other elements in the domain are lectures and time points. Thus, we can remove them to get a minimal justification. Besides $\mathcal{J}_{as}$, there are 52 justifications in total. Also note that $\mathcal{K}_{as}$ is consistent under the standard semantics, since new professors can be introduced to teach problematic lectures.

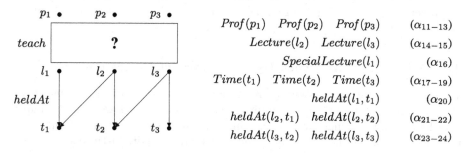

$Prof(p_1)$	$Prof(p_2)$	$Prof(p_3)$	(α_{11-13})
	$Lecture(l_2)$	$Lecture(l_3)$	(α_{14-15})
	$SpecialLecture(l_1)$		(α_{16})
$Time(t_1)$	$Time(t_2)$	$Time(t_3)$	(α_{17-19})
		$heldAt(l_1, t_1)$	(α_{20})
	$heldAt(l_2, t_1)$	$heldAt(l_2, t_2)$	(α_{21-22})
	$heldAt(l_3, t_2)$	$heldAt(l_3, t_3)$	(α_{23-24})

Fig. 1. $\mathcal{K}_{as}$ ABox representation and axioms.

4   Computing Justifications

Algorithms for finding justifications can be categorized coarsely into *black-box* and *glass-box* approaches. *Black-box* approaches use a reasoner to conduct the reasoning tasks it was designed for, i.e. entailment checking. Contrarily, in the *glass-box* approach, reasoners are modified, i.e. the internal reasoning algorithms are tweaked towards justifications. Generally, black-box approaches are more robust and easier to implement, whereas the glass-box approaches provide more potential for optimization. Subsequently, we introduce two black-box approaches, followed by a dedicated glass-box approach.

4.1   Black-Box Approaches

The ontology editor Protégé, has built-in functionality to compute justifications under the standard semantics, which is based on the OWL Explanation Workbench[2] [12]. The underlying algorithm is based on the Hitting-Set Tree (HST) algorithm originating from Reiter's theory of diagnosis [24]. For the details of the implementation we refer to [11].

Axiomatization of Δ-models. Given a knowledge base $\mathcal{K}$ and a fixed domain $\Delta = \{a_1, \ldots, a_n\}$, one can axiomatize the fixed-domain semantics, such that $\mathcal{K} \models_\Delta \alpha$ iff $\mathcal{K} \cup \mathcal{FD}_\Delta \models \alpha$, where $\mathcal{FD}_\Delta = \{\top \sqsubseteq \{a_1, \ldots a_n\}\} \cup \{a_i \not\approx a_j \mid 1 \le i < j \le n\}$. It is easy to see, that those axioms enforce reasoning over Δ. A black-box algorithm for finding justifications merely exploits inconsistency or entailment checking, which is a standard reasoning task, thus standard DL reasoners can be used for fixed-domain standard reasoning. In Sect. 5 we will therefore use the explanation workbench with HermiT as black-box reasoner.

A Fixed-Domain Reasoner as a Black-box. Wolpertinger has been introduced as reasoner adhering to the fixed-domain semantics [28], which can easily be plugged into the explanation workbench. We will evaluate the performance of this approach, and expect the performance to correlate with the performance of entailment checking. With W-black-box we refer to this approach in the subsequent evaluation.

4.2   A Glass-Box Approach Using Answer-Set Programming

We now introduce a glass-box approach for computing justifications using an encoding into answer-set programming. The translation is based on the naïve translation [6], which has already been implemented in Wolpertinger, but some fundamental changes needed to be made in order to compute justifications. Since finding justifications is about finding the corresponding (minimal) subsets of a knowledge base, another "layer" is required, on the top of the model correspondence established in the naïve translation, which is not straightforward to encode

---

[2] Subsequently just called *explanation workbench*.

in ASP. We will therefore avoid negation-as-failure, and hence refer to this new translation as *naff* (negation-as-failure free). Subsequently, the translation is depicted in detail.

Let $\mathcal{K} = (\mathcal{A}, \mathcal{T}, \mathcal{R})$ be a normalized $\mathcal{SROIQ}$ knowledge base, and Δ a fixed domain.[3] With $\Pi(\mathcal{K}, \Delta) = \Pi_{gen}(\mathcal{K}, \Delta) \cup \Pi_{chk}(\mathcal{K}) \cup \Pi_{inc}(\mathcal{K})$, we denote the translation of $\mathcal{K}$ into a logic program w.r.t. Δ. Intuitively, $\Pi_{gen}(\mathcal{K}, \Delta)$ generates candidate interpretations w.r.t. Δ, and each axiom is translated into rules in $\Pi_{chk}(\mathcal{K})$, in such a way, that any violation will cause a dedicated propositional atom to be true. If so, the *Principle of Explosion* (POE) is applied via appropriate rules. For every translated axiom, an additional dedicated propositional activator is added in the body of the resulting rule, allowing to activate or deactivate the rule, thus indicating whether to include or exclude the axiom in a candidate justification. With the disjunctive rules in $\Pi_{gss}(\mathcal{K}, \Delta)$, the generation of extensions for every concept and role name is realized.

$$\Pi_{gss}(\mathcal{K}, \Delta) = \{A(X), not\_A(X) :- \top(X) \mid A \in N_C(\mathcal{K})\} \cup$$
$$\{r(X, Y), not\_r(X, Y) :- \top(X), \top(Y) \mid r \in N_R(\mathcal{K}\} \cup$$
$$\{\top(a) \mid a \in \Delta\}.$$

Atomic clashes need to be detected explicitly, which is done via simple rules in $\Pi_{obv}(\mathcal{K})$. Note that clashes are not represented by constraints, but rules with the dedicated propositional variable *inc* as head.

$$\Pi_{obv}(\mathcal{K}) = \{inc :- A(X), not\_A(X) \mid A \in N_C(\mathcal{K})\} \cup$$
$$\{inc :- r(X, Y), not\_r(X, Y) \mid r \in N_R(\mathcal{K}).$$

Based on the detection of atomic clashes, the rules in $\Pi_{poe}(\mathcal{K})$ encode the POE, that is, every concept and role assertion follows whenever *inc* holds.

$$\Pi_{poe}(\mathcal{K}) = \{A(X) :- inc, \top(X) \mid A \in N_C(\mathcal{K})\} \cup$$
$$\{not\_A(X) :- inc, \top(X) \mid A \in N_C(\mathcal{K})\} \cup$$
$$\{r(X, Y) :- inc, \top(X), \top(Y) \mid r \in N_R(\mathcal{K}\} \cup$$
$$\{not\_r(X, Y) :- inc, \top(X), \top(Y) \mid r \in N_R(\mathcal{K}).$$

Qualified Number Restriction Encoding. One problem that we encountered is the usage of the $<$-operator in the translation of at-least cardinality restrictions. Consider the concept $\geq n\,r.C$, which restricts an individual to have at least n r-neighbors, that are a member of C. The intuitive translation is a constraint that counts how many outgoing r-connections exist, satisfying also the membership in C, thus failing if there are less than n r-neighbors not satisfying the condition. However, this translation does not work anymore due to the rules in $\Pi_{poe}(\mathcal{K})$.

---

[3] We do not provide details on the normalization part, an refer instead to our previous work [6].

We therefore introduce a different view of the semantics of cardinality restrictions in the fixed-domain setting. For simplicity, we define $r.C(a) = \{x \in C^{\mathcal{I}} \mid (a,x) \in r^{\mathcal{I}}\}$. Hence $r.C(a)$ consists of all members of concept C that are connected via r starting in a. The idea is to count individuals which are not a member of the concept where this restriction applies. There are two possibilities that an individual b is not in $r.C(a)$: $(a,b) \notin r$ or $b \notin C$. Let $n = |\Delta^{\mathcal{I}}|$ and $m = |\{b \in \Delta^{\mathcal{I}} \mid b \notin r.C(a)\}|$. Hence, the number of individuals in $r.C(a)$ is $n - m$. This is only possible due to the given fixed domain.

Proposition 1. *Let $\mathcal{K}$ be a $\mathcal{SROIQ}$ knowledge base, Δ be a fixed-domain, and $\mathcal{I}$ a Δ-model of $\mathcal{K}$. Then $(\geq n\, r.C)^{\mathcal{I}} = \{x \in \Delta \mid \#\{y \in \Delta \mid y \notin C^{\mathcal{I}} \text{ or } (x,y) \notin r^{\mathcal{I}}\} \leq |\Delta| - n\}$.*

Hence, we can compute such a relation between two individuals to be used later in the translation of axioms. A new auxiliary predicate is introduced for each pair of concept (and its negation) and role. We define:

$$\Pi_{nra}(\mathcal{K}) = \{not\_r\_C(X,Y) :- not\_C(Y) \mid C \in N_C(\mathcal{K}), r \in N_R(\mathcal{K})\} \cup$$
$$\{not\_r\_C(X,Y) :- not\_r(X,Y) \mid C \in N_C(\mathcal{K}), r \in N_R(\mathcal{K})\} \cup$$
$$\{not\_r\_not\_C(X,Y) :- C(Y) \mid C \in N_C(\mathcal{K}), r \in N_R(\mathcal{K})\} \cup$$
$$\{not\_r\_not\_C(X,Y) :- not\_r(X,Y) \mid C \in N_C(\mathcal{K}), r \in N_R(\mathcal{K})\}.$$

$\Pi_{nra}(\mathcal{K})$ does not change the interpretation built by $\Pi_{gen}(\mathcal{K})$. It merely collects all those individuals satisfying the previously mentioned conditions. Additionally, we have to take care about inverse roles, for which the rules look similar, but variables need to be swapped. Finally, $\Pi_{gen}(\mathcal{K}, \Delta) = \Pi_{gss}(\mathcal{K}, \Delta) \cup \Pi_{obv}(\mathcal{K}) \cup \Pi_{poe}(\mathcal{K}) \cup \Pi_{nra}(\mathcal{K})$.

ABox Translation. The first pruning of the search space originates from ABox assertions. As the input is a normalized knowledge base, each assertion contains only a literal concept, or literal role, respectively. It then straightforward to encode:

$$\Pi_{chk}(\mathcal{A}) = \{inc :- active(i), not\_A(a) \mid A(a) \in \mathcal{A}\} \cup$$
$$\{inc :- active(i), A(a) \mid \neg A(a) \in \mathcal{A}\} \cup$$
$$\{inc :- active(i), not\_r(a,b) \mid r(a,b) \in \mathcal{A}\} \cup$$
$$\{inc :- active(i), r(a,b) \mid \neg r(a,b) \in \mathcal{A}\}.$$

TBox Translation. Each TBox axiom is normalized and of form $\top \sqsubseteq \bigsqcup_{i=1}^{n} C_i$, with each C_i being non-complex, i.e. one of the concept constructors depicted in Table 3. It is then easy to turn normalized axioms into appropriate rules to detect any violation.

$$\Pi_{chk}(\mathcal{T}) = \{inc :- active(j), \tau(C_1), ..., \tau(C_n), \top(X) \mid \top \sqsubseteq \bigsqcup_{i=1}^{n} C_i \in \mathcal{T}\}$$

Table 3. Translation of concept constructors. Note: O_a is a new concept name unique for a, and $m = |\Delta^{\mathcal{I}}|$.

C	$\tau(C)$
A	$not\_A(X)$
$\neg A$	$A(X)$
$\{a\}$	$\{not\_O_a(X)\}, \{O_a(a)\}$
$\forall r.A$	$\{not\_A(Y), r(X,Y)\}$
$\forall r.\neg A$	$\{A(Y), r(X,Y)\}$
$\exists r.Self$	$not\_r(r,X,X)$
$\neg \exists r.Self$	$r(r,X,X)$
$\geq n\ r.A$	$\#count\{Y : not\_r\_A(X,Y)\} > (m-n)$
$\geq n\ r.\neg A$	$\#count\{Y : not\_r\_not\_A(X,Y)\} > (m-n)$
$\leq n\ r.A$	$\#count\{Y : r(X,Y), A(Y)\} > n$
$\leq n\ r.\neg A$	$\#count\{Y : r(X,Y), not\_A(Y)\} > n$

RBox Translation. Since normalized, each axiom in an RBox $\mathcal{R}$ is either a (simplified) role chain, disjointness or role inclusion axiom. As for TBox axioms, each axiom in $\mathcal{R}$ is translated into a rule that enforces the propositional variable inc to be true, whenever the axiom is violated.

$$\Pi_{chk}(\mathcal{R}) = \{inc :- active(i), r(X,Y),\ s(X,Y) \mid \mathsf{Dis}(r,s) \in \mathcal{R}\} \cup$$
$$\{inc :- active(i), r(X,Y),\ not\_s(X,Y) \mid r \sqsubseteq s \in \mathcal{R}\} \cup$$
$$\{inc :- active(i), s_1(X,Y), s_2(Y,Z), not\_r(X,Z) \mid s_1 \circ s_2 \sqsubseteq r \in \mathcal{R}\}.$$

For example, α_2 and α_{10} in Example 1 are encoded as:

```
inc :-  active(2),prof(X),#count{Y:teach(X,Y),lecture(Y)}>1.
inc :-  active(10),teach(X,Y),heldAt(Y,Z),not_busyAt(X,Z).
```

Finally, let $\Pi_{chk}(\mathcal{K}) = \Pi_{chk}(\mathcal{A}) \cup \Pi_{chk}(\mathcal{T}) \cup \Pi_{chk}(\mathcal{R})$, be the translation of all axioms in a knowledge base. It remains to remove any candidate answer-set not including inc, as well as guessing the set of active rules. As a result, any answer-set now indicates which axioms jointly cause the inconsistency. Then, preferring answer-sets that are subset-minimal w.r.t. the set of ground instances of $active$ yield exactly the desired justifications. The following program captures these requirements and completes the translation $\Pi(\mathcal{K}, \Delta) = \Pi_{gen}(\mathcal{K}, \Delta) \cup \Pi_{chk}(\mathcal{K}) \cup \Pi_{inc}(\mathcal{K})$.

$$\Pi_{inc}(\mathcal{K}) = \{ :- not\ inc.$$
$$\{active(X) :- X = 1..n\}.$$
$$\#optimize(p).$$
$$\#preference(p, subset)\{active(C) : C = 1..n\}. \}$$

Theorem 1. *Let* $ACT(\mathcal{K}) = \{active(1), \ldots, active(n)\}$, *where* $n = |\mathcal{K}|$ *and* $\mathcal{K}^X = \{\alpha_i \in \mathcal{K} \mid active(i) \in X\}$. *Then* $\mathcal{AS}(\Pi(\mathcal{K}, \Delta))_{|\{active\}} = \{X \in 2^{ACT(\mathcal{K})} \mid \mathcal{K}^X \text{ is } \Delta\text{-inconsistent}\}$.

Proof sketch. Using the well-known splitting theorem [17], we split $\Pi(\mathcal{K}, \Delta)$ into two parts: axiom (subset) guessing and inconsistency checking. First, we show that each X representing a potential subset can be used to reduce the program to $\Pi(\mathcal{K}^X, \Delta)$. For the second part, we show that if $\mathcal{K}^X$ is Δ-inconsistent, $\mathcal{AS}(\Pi(\mathcal{K}^X), \Delta)$ consists only of exactly one answer set. Combining both arguments via the splitting theorem, it can be concluded that each answer set of $\Pi(\mathcal{K}, \Delta)$ corresponds to a Δ-justification for inconsistency of $\mathcal{K}$. □

We implemented this glass-box approach into `Wolpertinger`. In the evaluation, we refer to this approach as `W-glass-box`. While our translated programs need to be evaluated by `asprin` (which needs `Clingo`), it would be easy to remove the minimality preference, such that each answer set then corresponds to an inconsistent subset of the knowledge base. One could the also define (other) preferences, e.g. prioritizing some axioms to be necessarily included.

5   Evaluation

We introduce several simple constraint-type combinatorial problems that are aligned with our approach. We deliberately make them inconsistent, with a controlled number of justifications. The evaluations were performed on an HPC system with Haswell CPUs using a 4 GB memory limit. Unless stated differently, the timeout for each evaluation was 30 min. We use the hyphen symbol (-) to denote a *timeout*.

We reused an unsatisfiable knowledge base described in [6]. The knowledge base represents a Pigeonhole-type problem. We specified the axioms such that we want a model that depicts an r-chain of length $n+1$, but fixed the domain to n elements, for which a model cannot exist. For $\mathcal{K}_n = (\mathcal{T}_n, \mathcal{A}_n)$, we have:

$$\mathcal{T}_n = \{A_1 \sqsubseteq \exists r.A_2, \ldots, A_n \sqsubseteq \exists r.A_{n+1}\} \cup$$
$$\{A_i \sqcap A_j \sqsubseteq \bot \mid 1 \leq i < j \leq n+1\}$$
$$\mathcal{A}_n = \{A_1(a_1)\}$$
$$\Delta_n = \{a_1, \ldots, a_n\}$$

First, a comparison between the naïve and naff translation as been made. We expected the naff translation to be somewhat slower due to the overhead of computing some auxiliary atoms, which is confirmed as depicted in Table 4 (left). Afterwards, the performance of each approach to compute (Δ)-justifications (of inconsistency) of this knowledge base has been evaluated. In this case, since the only justification is the whole knowledge base, there is no major difference between requesting only one, or all justifications. This would be different if the only justification is a proper subset, because the algorithm has to make sure there

Table 4. Runtimes for checking unsatisfiability of $\mathcal{K}_n$ (left table), and runtimes of each approach for computing one justification.

#	Instance	naff	naïve
1	$\mathcal{K}_5$	0.013 s	0.010 s
2	$\mathcal{K}_6$	0.042 s	0.025 s
3	$\mathcal{K}_7$	0.092 s	0.063 s
4	$\mathcal{K}_8$	0.429 s	0.320 s
5	$\mathcal{K}_9$	5.324 s	3.805 s
6	$\mathcal{K}_{10}$	105.202 s	78.208 s
7	$\mathcal{K}_{11}$	–	1 423.463 s
8	$\mathcal{K}_{12}$	–	–

#	Instances	H-black-box	W-black-box	W-glass-box
1	$\mathcal{K}_5$	6.212 s	6.742 s	0.207 s
2	$\mathcal{K}_6$	7.023 s	6.284 s	0.277 s
3	$\mathcal{K}_7$	8.197 s	7.735 s	0.352 s
4	$\mathcal{K}_8$	9.521 s	9.057 s	2.510 s
5	$\mathcal{K}_9$	25.752 s	23.959 s	17.397 s
6	$\mathcal{K}_{10}$	206.457 s	518.377 s	–
7	$\mathcal{K}_{11}$	2 274.480 s	–	–

is no other justification. Table 4 (right) shows the result. It can be stressed, that for smaller instances, the W-glass-box approach performs best, followed by W-black-box. However, they do not scale well for bigger instances where H-black-box outperforms both of them. For the latter experiment, the timeout was set to one hour.

The second knowledge base $\mathcal{K}_{(m,n)}$ used for evaluation heavily uses cardinality restrictions. Individuals of the source concept C need to be connected with at least n individuals that are each a member of the concept A_i, where $1 \leq i \leq m$. However, we restrict the domain to contain only $n + 1$ elements. Finally, we impose a constraint such that all concepts are disjoint. Obviously, the existence of two such axioms already cause an inconsistency. For $\mathcal{K}_{(m,n)} = (\mathcal{T}_{(m,n)}, \mathcal{A})$ we have:

$$\mathcal{T}_{(m,n)} = \{C \sqsubseteq\, \geq n\, r.A_1, \ldots, C \sqsubseteq\, \geq n\, r.A_m\} \cup$$
$$\{C \sqsubseteq \neg A_1, \ldots, C \sqsubseteq \neg A_m\} \cup$$
$$\{A_1 \sqsubseteq \neg A_2, A_1 \sqsubseteq \neg A_3, \ldots, A_{m-1} \sqsubseteq \neg A_m\}$$
$$\mathcal{A} = \{C(a)\}$$
$$\Delta_n = \{a, x_1, \ldots, x_n\}$$

The result is shown in Table 5. The black-box approach with HermiT failed to compute the justifications for any case within the time limit. This result indicates that standard reasoners struggle in handling cardinality restrictions under the fixed-domain semantics. We suppose that the result originates from the fact that $\geq$-cardinality is handled easily in standard semantics since the reasoner can introduce new individuals satisfying the restriction. While H-black-box is able to solve some of the instances, W-glass-box computes all of them in reasonable time.

The third evaluation is based on the graph-coloring problem. We encode some instances of the Mycielskian graphs[4]. Since the chromatic number of each instance is provided, making them non-colorable is trivial. For a graph with chromatic number n, we only provide $n-1$ colors. The result is shown in Table 6. Each approach exceeded the timeout for the larger instances. Similar to the cardinality evaluation, the W-glass-box approach performs best. For the

---

[4] http://mat.gsia.cmu.edu/COLOR/instances.html.

Table 5. Runtime for individual cardinality.

#	Instances	H-black-box	W-black-box	W-glass-box
1	$\mathcal{K}_{10,10}$	–	94.787 s	3.461 s
2	$\mathcal{K}_{10,20}$	–	75.107 s	5.141 s
3	$\mathcal{K}_{10,30}$	–	104.382 s	8.029 s
4	$\mathcal{K}_{20,10}$	–	448.757 s	45.578 s
5	$\mathcal{K}_{20,20}$	–	–	66.123 s
6	$\mathcal{K}_{20,30}$	–	–	103.721 s
7	$\mathcal{K}_{30,10}$	–	634.572 s	331.576 s
8	$\mathcal{K}_{30,20}$	–	–	476.985 s
9	$\mathcal{K}_{30,30}$	–	–	548.865 s

Table 6. Runtime for n-coloring problems.

#	Instances	#Nodes	#Edges	H-black-box	W-black-box	W-glass-box
1	$\mathcal{K}_{myciel3}$	11	20	43.335 s	71.347 s	1.423 s
2	$\mathcal{K}_{myciel4}$	23	71	–	–	11.327 s
3	$\mathcal{K}_{myciel5}$	47	236	–	–	–

small instance, H-black-box performs better than W-black-box. For the second instance, we find that H-black-box provided merely one justification before the timeout, while W-black-box was able to compute at least five justifications.

As shown in Table 4, H-black-box performs better in some cases. While finding justifications is a hard problem, asking for several of them is more feasible. The necessary adjustments can easily be done for each tool. Another important note to mention is, we only use one thread for evaluation, though the problem itself could be done in parallel.

6   Conclusion

We considered the task of computing justifications for entailments under the fixed-domain semantics, a task of general high importance in the modeling phase of ontologies. We proposed three different approaches to this problem and comparatively evaluated one using standard OWL technology employing an axiomatization of the fixed-domain semantics, one using our dedicated fixed-domain reasoner Wolpertinger in combination with Protégé's explanation workbench, and one where the problem is encoded entirely into answer-set programming. The evaluation suggests that each of the proposed approaches do have their difficulties as well as individual advantages. Hence, it remains imperative to conduct more experiments with different setups. Also, all tools were used in their standard configuration, which gives another optimization angle.

Moreover, other approaches developed to debug answer-set programs need to be considered and compared. For example, Pontelli et al. suggest a method to obtain justifications for the truth value of an atom in an answer-set [23], which might be reused in our setting to obtain an explanation for inconsistency (represented by the propositional atom *inc*). A different approach is the step-wise debugging methodology proposed by Oetsch et al. which allows to identify rules that prohibit a certain (partial) answer-set [20]. However, this approach is designed to answer the question, why some interpretation is actually not an answer-set of the program, thus we see it as future work to identify how this approach can be resembled into our setting. Moreover, it would be a great feature for users if a tool actually recommended automatic repairs in addition to the justifications, which might be realized be using these related approaches.

Acknowledgements. We are grateful for the valuable feedback from the anonymous reviewers, which helped greatly to improve this work. This work is supported by DFG in the Research Training Group QuantLA (GRK 1763) and in the Research Training Group RoSI (GRK 1907).

References

1. Baader, F., Calvanese, D., McGuinness, D., Nardi, D., Patel-Schneider, P.: The Description Logic Handbook: Theory, Implementation, and Applications, 2nd edn., Cambridge University Press (2007)
2. Baader, F., Peñaloza, R., Suntisrivaraporn, B.: Pinpointing in the description logic $\mathcal{EL}^+$. In: Hertzberg, J., Beetz, M., Englert, R. (eds.) KI 2007. LNCS (LNAI), vol. 4667, pp. 52–67. Springer, Heidelberg (2007). https://doi.org/10.1007/978-3-540-74565-5_7
3. Brewka, G., Delgrande, J.P., Romero, J., Schaub, T.: asprin: Customizing answer set preferences without a headache. In: AAAI, pp. 1467–1474. AAAI Press (2015)
4. Brewka, G., Eiter, T., Truszczyński, M.: Answer set programming at a glance. Commun. ACM **54**(12), 92–103 (2011)
5. Calvanese, D.: Finite model reasoning in description logics. In: Proceedings of the 5th International Conference on the Principles of Knowledge Representation and Reasoning (KR 1996), pp. 292–303. Morgan Kaufmann (1996)
6. Gaggl, S.A., Rudolph, S., Schweizer, L.: Fixed-domain reasoning for description logics. In: Kaminka, G.A., et al. (eds.) Proceedings of the 22nd European Conference on Artificial Intelligence (ECAI 2016), Frontiers in Artificial Intelligence and Applications, vol. 285, pp. 819–827. IOS Press, September 2016
7. Gebser, M., Kaminski, R., Kaufmann, B., Schaub, T.: Answer set solving in practice. Synth. Lect. Artif. Intell. Mach. Learn. **6**, 1–238 (2012)
8. Gelfond, M., Lifschitz, V.: Classical negation in logic programs and disjunctive databases. New Gener. Comput. **9**(3/4), 365–386 (1991)
9. Hitzler, P., Gangemi, A., Janowicz, K., Krisnadhi, A., Presutti, V. (eds.): Ontology Engineering with Ontology Design Patterns - Foundations and Applications, Studies on the Semantic Web, vol. 25. IOS Press (2016)
10. Hitzler, P., Krötzsch, M., Parsia, B., Patel-Schneider, P.F., Rudolph, S. (eds.): OWL 2 Web Ontology Language: Primer. W3C Recommendation
11. Horridge, M.: Justification based explanation in ontologies. Ph.D. thesis, University of Manchester (2011)

12. Horridge, M., Parsia, B., Sattler, U.: Explanation of OWL entailments in Protege 4. In: Bizer, C., Joshi, A. (eds.) Proceedings of the Poster and Demonstration Session at the 7th International Semantic Web Conference (ISWC 2008), 28 October 2008, CEUR Workshop Proceedings, vol. 401. CEUR-WS.org (2008)

13. Horridge, M., Parsia, B., Sattler, U.: Explaining inconsistencies in OWL ontologies. In: Godo, L., Pugliese, A. (eds.) SUM 2009. LNCS (LNAI), vol. 5785, pp. 124–137. Springer, Heidelberg (2009). https://doi.org/10.1007/978-3-642-04388-8_11

14. Horrocks, I., Kutz, O., Sattler, U.: The even more irresistible $\mathcal{SROIQ}$. In: Doherty, P., Mylopoulos, J., Welty, C.A. (eds.) Proceedings of the 10th International Conference on Principles of Knowledge Representation and Reasoning, KR 2006, pp. 57–67. AAAI Press (2006)

15. Kalyanpur, A., Parsia, B., Horridge, M., Sirin, E.: Finding all justifications of OWL DL entailments. In: Aberer, K., et al. (eds.) ASWC/ISWC -2007. LNCS, vol. 4825, pp. 267–280. Springer, Heidelberg (2007). https://doi.org/10.1007/978-3-540-76298-0_20

16. Kazakov, Y.: $\mathcal{RIQ}$ and $\mathcal{SROIQ}$ are harder than $\mathcal{SHOIQ}$. In: Brewka, G., Lang, J. (eds.) Proceedings of the 11th International Conference on Principles of Knowledge Representation and Reasoning (KR 2008), pp. 274–284. AAAI Press (2008)

17. Lifschitz, V., Turner, H.: Splitting a logic program. In: ICLP, vol. 94, pp. 23–37 (1994)

18. Lutz, C., Sattler, U., Tendera, L.: The complexity of finite model reasoning in description logics. Inf. Comput. 199(1–2), 132–171 (2005)

19. Niemelä, I.: Logic programs with stable model semantics as a constraint programming paradigm. Ann. Math. Artif. Intell. 25(3–4), 241–273 (1999)

20. Oetsch, J., Pührer, J., Tompits, H.: Stepwise debugging of answer-set programs. TPLP 18(1), 30–80 (2018)

21. Papadimitriou, C.H., Wolfe, D.: The complexity of facets resolved. J. Comput. Syst. Sci. 37(1), 2–13 (1988)

22. Peñaloza, R., Sertkaya, B.: Understanding the complexity of axiom pinpointing in lightweight description logics. Artif. Intell. 250, 80–104 (2017)

23. Pontelli, E., Son, T.C., El-Khatib, O.: Justifications for logic programs under answer set semantics. TPLP 9(1), 1–56 (2009)

24. Reiter, R.: A theory of diagnosis from first principles. Artif. Intell. 32(1), 57–95 (1987)

25. Rosati, R.: Finite model reasoning in DL-Lite. In: Bechhofer, S., Hauswirth, M., Hoffmann, J., Koubarakis, M. (eds.) ESWC 2008. LNCS, vol. 5021, pp. 215–229. Springer, Heidelberg (2008). https://doi.org/10.1007/978-3-540-68234-9_18

26. Rudolph, S.: Foundations of description logics. In: Polleres, A., et al. (eds.) Reasoning Web 2011. LNCS, vol. 6848, pp. 76–136. Springer, Heidelberg (2011). https://doi.org/10.1007/978-3-642-23032-5_2

27. Rudolph, S., Schweizer, L.: Not too big, not too small... complexities of fixed-domain reasoning in first-order and description logics. In: Oliveira, E., Gama, J., Vale, Z., Lopes Cardoso, H. (eds.) EPIA 2017. LNCS (LNAI), vol. 10423, pp. 695–708. Springer, Cham (2017). https://doi.org/10.1007/978-3-319-65340-2_57

28. Rudolph, S., Schweizer, L., Tirtarasa, S.: Wolpertinger: a fixed-domain reasoner. In: Nikitina, N., Song, D., Fokoue, A., Haase, P. (eds.) Proceedings of the ISWC 2017 Posters and Demonstrations and Industry Tracks Co-located with 16th International Semantic Web Conference (ISWC 2017), 23–25 October 2017, CEUR Workshop Proceedings, vol. 1963. CEUR-WS.org (2017)

Technical Communication Papers

Computational Regulation of Medical Devices in PSOA RuleML

Sofia Almpani[1(✉)], Petros Stefaneas[2], Harold Boley[3], Theodoros Mitsikas[1], and Panayiotis Frangos[1]

[1] School of Electrical and Computer Engineering,
National Technical University of Athens, Athens, Greece
salmpani@mail.ntua.gr, {mitsikas,pfrangos}@central.ntua.gr
[2] School of Applied Mathematics,
National Technical University of Athens, Athens, Greece
petrosstefaneas@gmail.com
[3] Faculty of Computer Science, University of New Brunswick, Fredericton, Canada
harold.boley@unb.ca

Abstract. The registration and marketability of medical devices in Europe is governed by the Regulation (EU) 2017/745 and by guidelines published in terms thereof. This work focuses on formalizing the rules for risk-based classification of medical devices as well as the conformity assessment options for each class in Positional-Slotted Object-Applicative (PSOA) RuleML. We tested this open-source knowledge base by querying it in the open-source PSOATransRun system. The aim of this formalization is to create a computational guideline to assist stakeholders.

1 Introduction

In the medical domain there is an increasing interest in AI and computational decision-making approaches. To get maximum technology benefits for people in the medical device industry, it is required to proceed to solutions that integrate 'smart' services and innovative devices in compliance with existing legal frameworks, such as the Regulation (EU) 2017/745 [1] of medical devices. However, while logical reasoning on knowledge representations is rather well-understood, there are no established methods to convert a given medical legal text to an appropriate knowledge representation. For the conversion-reasoning tool chain it will be vital to obtain a high-enough conversion accuracy and to supplement machine-reasoning output with explanations that can be validated by humans.

Medical cases that combine ontologies with rule languages can be used as clinical guidelines [2] or for medical decision support [3]. Description logic-based ontology languages (e.g., OWL-DL) offer a precise semantics, but they can be computationally costly, and are mostly used to express ontology TBoxes about types of entities. Legal-AI models are often rule-based, where a legal text is represented by rules that can express legal definitions, exceptions, arguments,

C. Benzmüller et al. (Eds.): RuleML+RR 2018, LNCS 11092, pp. 203–210, 2018.
https://doi.org/10.1007/978-3-319-99906-7_13

and deductions, and can provide explanations as audit trails of how a particular conclusion was proved.

Many health care procedures are supported by rule-based systems [4] such as for antibiotics prescription [4] and risk assessment of pressure ulcers [5]. In this work, Positional-Slotted Object-Applicative PSOA RuleML [6–8][1] is used for its simplicity and its suitability to express deductions by rules over enriched atoms. Since PSOA RuleML combines object-centered and relational modeling in a unified language, it supports object-relational data facts as well as transformation rules over them [6]. Details about PSOA RuleML syntax, psoa terms[2], and the query system PSOATransRun can be found in [8][3].

The main objectives of our work are (a) to develop a computational rule format of the classification rules and the conformity assessment procedures for EU Regulation 2017/745, (b) to supplement it with object-relational facts about medical devices to form a knowledge base, (c) to build a separately reusable (and further extensible) explicit taxonomy, (d) to test, with PSOATransRun queries [7], (for validation by humans), the accuracy of the developed computational model as well as its interpretability and reliability, and (e) to create a computational guideline to assist regulators, manufacturers, importers, distributors and wholesalers of medical devices in the classification and registration of medical devices. To our knowledge, this is the first attempt to formalize, in a computational manner, a regulation of medical devices. Of course, this can only complement the classification and registration of medical devices by medical experts – it is an informative computational model of the regulation for stakeholders, rather than constituting expert knowledge.

The paper is organized as follows: Sect. 2 describes and evaluates the formalization of the medical devices regulation in PSOA RuleML, and Sect. 3 concludes the paper and outlines future directions.

2   Formalization of Medical Devices Rules in PSOA

The **Regulation (EU) 2017/745** [1] of the European Parliament and of the Council of 5 April 2017 on medical devices presents a framework of risk-based classification, leading to risk-appropriate conformity assessment procedures. Annex VII of the Regulation sets out the classification criteria with 22 rules for the following four classes:

Class I - Generally regarded as low risk[4], e.g. bandages, stethoscopes.
Class IIa - Generally regarded as low-to-medium risk devices, e.g. hearing-aids.

---

[1] PSOA RuleML generalizes F-logic, RIF-BLD, and POSL by a homogeneous integration of relationships and frames into psoa terms.
[2] We use the all-upper-case "PSOA" as a reference to the language and the all-lower-case "psoa" for its terms.
[3] See also the relevant RuleML wiki page http://wiki.ruleml.org/index.php/PSOA_RuleML.
[4] Special cases: *Class Is* for sterile and *Class Im* for measuring function.

Class IIb - Generally regarded as medium-to-high risk, e.g. ventilators.
Class III - Generally regarded as high risk, e.g. prosthetic heart valves.

The **CE marking** on a medical device is a declaration from the manufacturer that the device complies with the essential requirements of the relevant European legislation. The appropriate conformity assessment procedures for the CE marking, depending on the product's class, can be viewed in Fig. 2. Additionally, according to the Unique Device Identification (UDI) directive, medical devices' manufacturers are accountable to ensure complete traceability for their devices.

This use case[5]—Medical Devices Rules—illustrates how PSOA RuleML integrates the data and knowledge representation paradigms of *relationship atoms*[6] with those of *frame atoms*[7]. The formalization consists of five parts:

1. The 22 classification rules of the regulation.
2. The medical device categories in each class.
3. The marketability of medical devices according to the various conformity assessment options.
4. An explicit taxonomy of the medical devices.
5. Representative data (facts) of medical devices.

In the first part, (informal) categories were created to formalize all the **risk-based classification rules** of the regulation. One clause is used for each rule, formed as the example[8] below,

```
% Rule 4: Devices in contact with injured skin.
Forall ?m (:CategoryOfMedicalDevice(?m :N4a) :-
?m#:MedicalDevice(:kind->:NonInvasive
                  :use->:ContactInjuredSkin
                  :specificCase->:MechanicalBarrier))
```

The condition's predicate :MedicalDevice is a frame atom, where the hash infix # denotes *class membership* by typing an OID with its predicate, while the arrow infix, "->", pairs each predicate-independent slot name with its filler. The predicate :CategoryOfMedicalDevices is a relationship that links the medical device with the category it pertains.

An exceptional case is the Rule 5, where time duration is also used for the categorization of the medical device into :Transient, :Shortterm or :Longterm. For this rule we used predicates with math: prefix as defined in the imported mathematics library http://psoa.ruleml.org/lib/math.psoa. They are shortcuts

---

[5] Due to page limitations, the complete code source and queries of the Knowledge Base (KB) can be found in http://psoa.ruleml.org/usecases/MedicalDevices/.

[6] Ordered tuple of positional arguments.

[7] A unique OID typed by a class and described by an unordered collection of slots.

[8] It formalizes the sentence *"All non-invasive devices which come into contact with injured skin or mucous membrane are classified as: class I if they are intended to be used as a mechanical barrier, for compression or for absorption of exudates"* [1, Chap. 3 (4.4) (a)]. The present work is restricted to the English version of the Regulation.

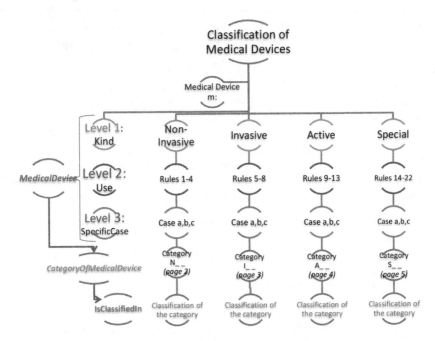

Fig. 1. Visualization of PSOA RuleML decision model for classification rules.

for external built-in calls in PSOA [8]. The specific case :Shortterm is described as follows:

```
% Rule 5 (Time period of usage: Short Term)
Forall ?m ?d (?m#:MedicalDevice(:specificCase ->:ShortTerm) :-
        And(?m#:MedicalDevice(:duration->?d)
        math:lessEq(?d 30)
        math:greaterEq(?d 0.02)))
```

In the second part on the classification of medical devices, the aforementioned categories are connected with the class they reside in, forming an 'Or' branch (disjunction). The generated categories —55 in number— are indicated by three letters which denote the three levels of the categorization (see also Fig. 1), e.g. :N4a, where N denotes a Non-Invasible device, 4 denotes Rule 4, and a denotes the specific case 'a', i.e. mechanical barrier. The categories in Class I are expressed in the following example:

```
%Classification Grouping: Class I
    Forall ?m (:IsClassifiedIn(?m :I) :-
            Or(:CategoryOfMedicalDevice(?m :N1)
            :CategoryOfMedicalDevice(?m :N4a)
            :CategoryOfMedicalDevice(?m :I5a)
            :CategoryOfMedicalDevice(?m :I6b)
            :CategoryOfMedicalDevice(?m :A10a)
            :CategoryOfMedicalDevice(?m :A11c)
            :CategoryOfMedicalDevice(?m :A13)))
```

In the third part, all the different **conformity assessment** routes of each class for the CE marking and the implying **marketability** of medical devices are described. These routes outline the pre-marketability procedure. The post-marketability requirements are out of scope of the current work. In Class I, as described in the example below, all the conditions of the 'And' relation must be fulfilled to obtain the :DeclarationOfConformity.

```
%Requirements for Class I
Forall ?m (:DeclarationOfConformity (?m) :-
      And(:IsClassifiedIn(?m :I)
        :RegisterWithTheECA(?m)
        :AppointingAnEAR(?m)
        :ConformityAssessment(:device->?m :technicalFile->:Yes
            :vigilanceSystem->:Yes :harmonizedStandards->:No)))
```

The PSOA RuleML decision model for Conformity Assessment routes is visualized in Fig. 2, with an object-relational 'And'-'Or' DAG ('And' branches are connected with straight lines, while 'Or' are connected with dashed lines). In 'Or' relations, only one choice from the possible options can be selected, either based on the filler of the slot names, or on the different conditions of the 'And' clauses, so that only one route can be "fully invoked", causing near-deterministic behavior, e.g. for the Quality Assurance only one of the :QualityType can be "fully invoked".

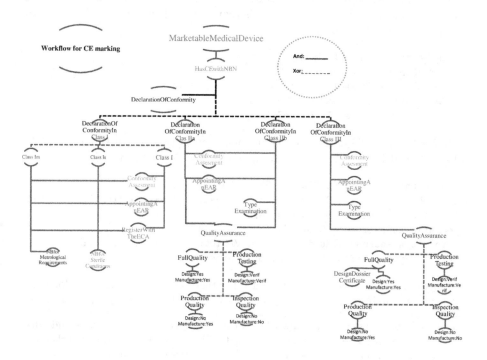

Fig. 2. Marketability requirements for each class.

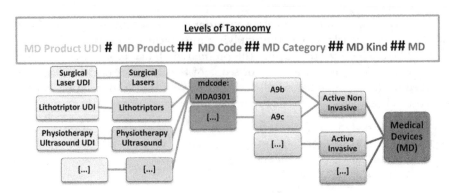

Fig. 3. Visualization of a taxonomy example.

In the fourth part, the Subclass relation (denoted in RIF and PSOA as '##') (e.g., :NonActiveInvasive##:MedicalDevices) is used for building a variable-depth multi-layer **taxonomy**, containing more than 150 different medical device products. The taxonomy consists of five levels as depicted in Fig. 3 starting with the top class to the right and the sub classes to the left. The four levels are 'Subclass of' ##-levels, while the last level is 'Instance of' #-level including individuals for each 'Medical Device Product' subclass with the suffix UDI (e.g., :NerveStimulatorsUDI#:NerveStimulators). In PSOATransRun at least one level 'Instance of' ('witness' instances) is required to allow retrieval. The classes for :NerveStimulatorsUDI are described below:

```
:NonActiveInvasive##:MedicalDevices
:I8b##:NonActiveInvasive
 mdcode:MDN1102##:I8b
:NerveStimulators##mdcode:MDN1102
:NerveStimulatorsUDI#:NerveStimulators
```

In the last part, **Data** for specific medical devices (Facts) were added directly in the Medical Devices KB[9]. An example of a medical device fact is,

```
%Requirements of MDS1006:Class I 2Yes, No ECA
mdcode:MDS1006#:MedicalDevice(:kind->:Invasive :use->:SurgicallyTransient
:specificCase->:ReusableInstruments)
:AppointingAnEAR(mdcode:MDS1006)
:ConformityAssessment(:device->mdcode:MDS1006 :technicalFile->:Yes
:vigilanceSystem->:Yes :harmonizedStandards->:No)
```

The medical devices facts are covering all categories with qualitative slot-filler distinctions. Medical devices facts were developed based on the list of codes

---

[9] The medical devices facts are described with their specific characteristics and with their (randomly chosen) completed marketability requirements. The marketable medical devices in each class can be viewed in: http://psoa.ruleml.org/usecases/MedicalDevices/ClassificationAndMarketability.pdf (p. 8).

(2017/2185) [9] and the corresponding types of devices under Regulation (EU) 2017/745[10]. The predicates with the `mdcode:` prefix are used to describe the medical devices codes of the aforementioned directive.

To test the formalization, we have posed representative queries to the KB and evaluated the answers obtained by PSOATransRun[11]. The Prolog instantiation of PSOATransRun [7], currently in version 1.3.1, is the reference implementation of PSOA RuleML.

In both typical and complex queries the answers provided by PSOA-TransRun were accurate. One limitation for the queries in the taxonomy is that, even though we can ask about all upper classes of a specific level, we can obtain only the instances of the lowest level (without the interme-diate levels). The run-time performance of PSOATransRun has also been evaluated. There was no noticeable delay in the retrieval (for the provided data set, which includes 55 categories in the KB and more than 150 exam-ples of products in the taxonomy), even with queries with three different variables, e.g. `And (:DeclarationOfConformity(?m) :QualityType(?m ?q) :IsClassifiedIn(?m ?c))`.

The KB was additionally validated by a legal expert, corroborating our natural-language-to-logic mapping, as well as the expressiveness, interpretability, and accuracy of the formalization. Therefore, the KB can be considered accurate concerning the classification and marketability parts of the regulation.

3   Conclusions and Future Work

We have demonstrated a formalization of a medical devices regulation as part of a logical KB leading to a computational decision model in PSOA RuleML. The formalization resulted in an object-relational PSOA RuleML rulebase, which was supplemented by object-relational facts about medical devices, also in PSOA RuleML form. The resulting KB is capable of answering queries regarding the classification and marketabitily of medical devices aiming at compliance with the Regulation (EU) 2017/745.

The goal of this formalization is to create a guideline to assist stakeholders in the classification and registration of medical devices. Because the regulation was published recently (still being in a trial period), extensions and improvements of the Medical Devices KB (including UDI/specific types of medical devices) should be of interest. Furthermore, post-marketability and/or clinical evaluation requirements can be added in the Medical Devices Rules.

---

[10] In cases where the codes don't describe specifically a category a random coding is applied (e.g.,`:DeviceR3a`), while in cases where more than one category belongs in the same code, letters a, b, c are used.

[11] Due to page limitations, detailed query examples for the Medical Devices Rules and answers from PSOATransRun can be found in http://wiki.ruleml.org/index.php/Medical_Devices_Rules#Formalization_of_Medical_Devices_Rules_in_PSOA http://psoa.ruleml.org/usecases/MedicalDevices/.

Some proposed longer-term applications of this formalization can be (a) the digital monitoring of (both pre- and post-marketing) traceability and management of medical devices with smart contracts by recording their UDIs on a blockchain, (b) the potential creation of "Healthcare-as-a-service" IT systems, where numerous connected medical devices (e.g. devices with embedded software, wearables, medical assets that generate health data, etc.) are secured in a blockchain-based distributed network pursuant to the legislation, and/or (c) an integration with further robotics-relevant regulations (e.g., wearables) to create a generalized legal framework.

Acknowledgments. We thank Dr. Gen Zou (UNB) for realizing PSOATransRun and for his early comments on this work. Moreover, we thank Dr. Vasileios Aravantinos (Council of State of Greece) for his hints on the expressiveness, interpretability and accuracy of Medical Devices Rules.

References

1. European Parliament: European Parliament. Regulation (EU) 2017/745 of the European Parliament and of the Council of 5 April 2017 on medical devices. Official Journal of the European Union **L 117** (2017)
2. Casteleiro, M.A., Diz, J.J.D.: Clinical practice guidelines: a case study of combining OWL-S, OWL, and SWRL. Knowl.-Based Syst. **21**(3), 247–255 (2008). AI 2007
3. Djedidi, R., Aufaure, M.: Medical domain ontology construction approach: a basis for medical decision support. In: Computer-Based Medical Systems (CBMS 2007), vol. 44, pp. 509–511 (2007)
4. Lezcano, L., Sicilia, M., Rodríguez-Solano, C.: Integrating reasoning and clinical archetypes using OWL ontologies and SWRL rules. J. Biomed. Inform. **44**, 343–353 (2010)
5. Rector, A., Rogers, J.: Ontological and practical issues in using a description logic to represent medical concept systems: experience from GALEN. In: Barahona, P., Bry, F., Franconi, E., Henze, N., Sattler, U. (eds.) Reasoning Web 2006. LNCS, vol. 4126, pp. 197–231. Springer, Heidelberg (2006). https://doi.org/10.1007/11837787_9
6. Boley, H.: PSOA RuleML: integrated object-relational data and rules. In: Faber, W., Paschke, A. (eds.) Reasoning Web 2015. LNCS, vol. 9203, pp. 114–150. Springer, Cham (2015). https://doi.org/10.1007/978-3-319-21768-0_5
7. Zou, G., Boley, H.: PSOA2Prolog: object-relational rule interoperation and implementation by translation from PSOA RuleML to ISO prolog. In: Bassiliades, N., Gottlob, G., Sadri, F., Paschke, A., Roman, D. (eds.) RuleML 2015. LNCS, vol. 9202, pp. 176–192. Springer, Cham (2015). https://doi.org/10.1007/978-3-319-21542-6_12
8. Zou, G., Boley, H., Wood, D., Lea, K.: Port clearance rules in PSOA RuleML: from controlled-english regulation to object-relational logic. In: Proceedings of the RuleML+RR 2017 Challenge, vol. 1875, CEUR, July 2017. http://ceur-ws.org/Vol-1875/paper6.pdf
9. European Parliament: REGULATION (EU) 2017/2185 of 23 November 2017 on the list of codes and corresponding types of devices. Official Journal of the European Union **L 309/7** (2017)

Faceted Answer-Set Navigation

Christian Alrabbaa[1], Sebastian Rudolph[2], and Lukas Schweizer[2(✉)]

[1] Institute of Theoretical Computer Science, TU Dresden, Dresden, Germany
christian.alrabbaa@tu-dresden.de
[2] Institute of Artificial Intelligence, TU Dresden, Dresden, Germany
{sebastian.rudolph,lukas.schweizer}@tu-dresden.de

Abstract. Even for small logic programs, the number of resulting answer-sets can be tremendous. In such cases, users might be incapable of comprehending the space of answer-sets as a whole nor being able to identify a specific answer-set according to their needs. To overcome this difficulty, we propose a general formal framework that takes an arbitrary logic program as input, and allows for navigating the space of answer-sets in a systematic interactive way analogous to faceted browsing. The navigation is carried out stepwise, where each step narrows down the remaining solutions, eventually arriving at a single one. We formulate two navigation modes, one stringent conflict avoiding, and a "free" mode, where conflicting selections of facets might occur. For the latter mode, we provide efficient algorithms for resolving the conflicts. We provide an implementation of our approach and demonstrate that our framework is able to handle logic programs for which it is currently infeasible to retrieve all answer sets.

1 Introduction

Answer-set programming (ASP) is a well-known declarative rule-based programming paradigm, developed for knowledge-representation and problem solving [4,7,13]. It originates from the field of logic programming (thus its syntactic relationship with Prolog) and the field of non-monotonic reasoning. ASP has become popular as generic language for computationally hard problems; that is, problems are encoded as logic programs (rules) and evaluated under the answer-set semantics, such that each answer-set (logical model) yields a solution of the problem. For solvers, such as `Clingo` [8,9] and `DLV` [5], the logic programming community is actively improving usability and interoperability. For example, IDEs have been developed that support users in the same way as it is known for other programming languages [6], or tools able to visualize answer-sets [12]. More recently, both tools were enriched with APIs for a more seamless integration in other programming languages.

We would like to thank the anonymous reviewers for their valuable feedback. This work is partially supported by the German Research Foundation (DFG) within the Research Training Group QuantLA (GRK 1763) and within the Collaborative Research Center SFB 912 – HAEC.

© Springer Nature Switzerland AG 2018
C. Benzmüller et al. (Eds.): RuleML+RR 2018, LNCS 11092, pp. 211–225, 2018.
https://doi.org/10.1007/978-3-319-99906-7_14

However, even if the developed answer-set program behaves in the desired way, i.e. gives rise to all solutions (and only those), it might yield by design a large number of answer-sets, which a user might simply not be able to handle and overview. Even worse, it might even not be possible to compute all solutions in reasonable time. For example, consider the simple encoding of the N-Queens problem in Example 1; it already has 92 solutions for $n = 8$, 724 for $n = 10$, and 14200 solutions for $n = 12$, all computed in just a few seconds; however, $n = 27$ is the largest N-Queens instance for which the number of solutions is known [16]. Answer-sets of a program might be of course parsed, inspected, and visualized individually in some specific way, but this is apparently limited to a small set of answer-sets only and always specific for some application domain.

Certainly, one can (to some extent) formulate a problem in such a way that it becomes an optimization problem, thereby only optimal models are returned. This might suffice in some cases to obtain a limited number of answer-sets, but even then, there might be more optimal models than any user is able to consume.

Our motivation in this paper therefore is to provide a formal framework for *exploring the space of answer-sets* of a logic program in a systematic way by means of a navigation method similar to *faceted browsing*. A facet can be seen as a partial solution that, if activated, is enforced to be present in any answer-set. Intuitively, a successive selection of facets narrows down the remaining answer-sets as well as available facets, thus leading to a manageable amount, or ultimately to one single remaining answer-set. In Example 1, any answer-set consists exactly of those n atoms q(X,Y), where a queen is placed at row X and column Y. Now any of these atoms can act as facet; e.g. under an active facet q(1,1), 4 answer-sets out of 92 are left, and selecting any other facet then yields a unique solution. In contrast to this goal-oriented navigation, we also define *free navigation* where facets can be in conflict with each other. Considering Example 1, the facet q(1,4) would not be available anymore, though enforcing it would require to retract the previous activation of facet q(1,1). We call this retraction of facets *corrections* and provide an efficient approach to compute them, enabling an even more powerful answer-set navigation.

Example 1. Consider the following program Π_1, that is a concise and efficient encoding of the well-known N-Queens problem, taken from [7].

```
(1)                    #const n = 8.
(2)                    { q(I,1..n) } == 1 :- I = 1..n.
(3)                    { q(1..n,J) } == 1 :- J = 1..n.
(4)                    :- { q(D-J,J) } >= 2, D = 2..2*n.
(5)                    :- { q(D+J,J) } >= 2, D = 1-n..n-1.
```

While the first line fixes the value of constant n, each remaining line corresponds to constraints ensuring exactly one queen per column (2), row (3) and diagonals (4–5).

1.1 Related Work

Our framework can be seen as additional layer on top of an ASP solver and is defined purely on the resulting answer-sets of a given program, thus the logic program itself may remain syntactically unknown. In contrast to our motivation, other existing approaches are designed to *debug* an answer-set program in case it does not behave as expected [15]; i.e. one would like to get an answer to the question why a given interpretation is actually not an answer-set of the presumably faulty program, or why some ground atom is not present in any of the answer-sets. In the stepwise approach of Oetsch et al. [15], one starts with a partial interpretation and debugs the program step by step, where a step is an application of a rule acquired from the original program. This is different from our notion of a navigation step, which narrows down remaining answer-sets by adding a constraint rule. In other words, in the suggested navigation scenario, the user's task is to steer the exploration of the answer-set space towards the desired answer-set, which is an answer-set from the beginning, unlike in the debugging setting where the desired answer-set is most likely not an answer-set of the initial program.

Moreover, in databases several approaches have been developed to compute so-called *repairs* [1,11]. In short, a repair denotes the set of tuples that need to be added or retracted from a database instance in order to make it consistent w.r.t. to a set of constraints. Thus, again the initial situation is an inconsistent artifact (here the database) that needs to be repaired somehow in order to regain consistency; i.e. from the beginning we constantly retain consistency; i.e. the initial program is never in an inconsistent state.

We want to emphasize, that our approach is not dedicated to a specific application domain, and generally applicable to arbitrary answer-set programs of any application domain. For example, the framework can also be seen as an engine for product configuration; i.e. the underlying program resembles a specification of a product, where answer-sets then represent configurations of that product. Our contributions in this paper are:

1. A formalization of faceted navigation in the space of answer-sets, based on the notion of brave and cautious consequences.
2. An extended navigational concept, allowing for arbitrary navigation directions and resolving resulting conflicts.
3. An implementation that demonstrates feasibility of the framework even for programs where the total number of answer-sets remains unknown.

2 Answer-Set Programming

We review the basic notions of answer-set programming [14], for further details we refer to [2,7,10].

We fix a countable set $\mathcal{U}$ of *(domain) elements*, also called *constants*; and suppose a total order $<$ over the domain elements. An *atom* is an expression $p(t_1, \ldots, t_n)$, where p is a *predicate* of arity $n \geq 0$ and each t_i is either a variable or an element from $\mathcal{U}$. An atom is *ground* if it is free of variables. $B_{\mathcal{U}}$ denotes the set of all ground atoms over $\mathcal{U}$. A *(disjunctive) rule* ρ is of the form

$$a_1, \ldots, a_n \leftarrow b_1, \ldots, b_k, \ not\,b_{k+1}, \ldots, \ not\,b_m.$$

with $m \geq k \geq 0$, where $a_1, \ldots, a_n, b_1, \ldots, b_m$ are atoms, and *"not"* denotes *default negation*. The *head* of ρ is the set $H(\rho) = \{a_1, \ldots, a_n\}$ and the *body* of ρ is $B(\rho) = \{b_1, \ldots, b_k, not\,b_{k+1}, \ldots, not\,b_m\}$. Furthermore, $B^+(\rho) = \{b_1, \ldots, b_k\}$ and $B^-(\rho) = \{b_{k+1}, \ldots, b_m\}$. A rule ρ is *safe* if each variable in ρ occurs in $B^+(r)$. A rule ρ is *ground* if no variable occurs in ρ. A *fact* is a ground rule with empty body. An *(input) database* is a set of facts. A (disjunctive) *program* is a finite set of disjunctive rules. For a program Π and an input database D, we often write $\Pi(D)$ instead of $D \cup \Pi$. For any program Π, let U_Π be the set of all constants appearing in Π. $Gr(\Pi)$ is the set of rules $\rho\sigma$ obtained by applying, to each rule $\rho \in \Pi$, all possible substitutions σ from the variables in ρ to elements of U_Π.

An *interpretation* $I \subseteq B_{\mathcal{U}}$ *satisfies* a ground rule ρ iff $H(\rho) \cap I \neq \emptyset$ whenever $B^+(\rho) \subseteq I$, $B^-(\rho) \cap I = \emptyset$. I satisfies a ground program Π, if each $\rho \in \Pi$ is satisfied by I. A non-ground rule ρ (resp., a program Π) is satisfied by an interpretation I iff I satisfies all groundings of ρ (resp., $Gr(\Pi)$). $I \subseteq B_{\mathcal{U}}$ is an *answer set* (also called *stable model*) of Π iff it is a subset-minimal set satisfying the *Gelfond-Lifschitz reduct* $\Pi^I = \{H(\rho) \leftarrow B^+(\rho) \mid I \cap B^-(\rho) = \emptyset, \rho \in Gr(\Pi)\}$. For a program Π, we denote the set of its answer sets by $\mathcal{AS}(\Pi)$.

We make use of further syntactic extensions, namely integrity constraints and count expressions, which both can be recast to ordinary normal rules as described in [7]. An *integrity constraint* is a rule ρ where $H(\rho) = \emptyset$, intuitively representing an undesirable situation; i.e. it has to be avoided that $B(\rho)$ evaluates positively. Count expressions are of the form $\#count\{l : l_1, \ldots, l_i\} \bowtie u$, where l is an atom and $l_j = p_j$ or $l_j = not\,p_j$, for p_j an atom, $1 \leq j \leq i$, u a non-negative integer, and $\bowtie \in \{\leq, <, =, >, \geq\}$. The expression $\{l : l_1, \ldots, l_n\}$ denotes the set of all ground instantiations of l, governed through $\{l_1, \ldots, l_n\}$. We restrict the occurrence of count expressions in a rule ρ to $B^+(\rho)$ only. Intuitively, an interpretation satisfies a count expression, if $N \bowtie u$ holds, where N is the cardinality of the set of ground instantiations of l, $N = |\{l \mid l_1, \ldots, l_n\}|$, for $\bowtie \in \{\leq, <, =, >, \geq\}$ and u a non-negative integer.

Consequences We rely on two notions of consequence, given a program Π and an atom α, we say that Π *cautiously entails* α, written $\Pi \models_\forall \alpha$, if for every answer-set $S \in \mathcal{AS}(\Pi)$, $\alpha \in S$. Likewise, we say that Π *bravely entails* α, written $\Pi \models_\exists \alpha$, if there exists and answer-set $S \in \mathcal{AS}(\Pi)$, such that $\alpha \in S$. The set of all cautious consequences of Π is denoted $\mathcal{CC}(\Pi)$ and the set of its brave consequences $\mathcal{BC}(\Pi)$.

3   Faceted Navigation

We distinguish two different modes of faceted navigation for a logic program. In the first one, the facets that can be applied are the ones that are compatible with those previously selected; this is what we call *restricted navigation*. Conversely, in the *free navigation* mode, we drop this restriction and describe a technique that resolves conflicts that can occur due to the unrestricted application of facets.

3.1   Facets and Navigation Step

We first start by defining *facets* of a program, before we introduce the notion *navigation step* as basic navigational building block. If not mentioned otherwise, we use the term *program* to refer to disjunctive programs as introduced in Sect. 2.

Definition 1 (Facet). *Let Π be a disjunctive logic program. Then we denote with $\mathcal{F}^+(\Pi) = \mathcal{BC}(\Pi) \setminus \mathcal{CC}(\Pi)$, the set of inclusive facets, and with $\mathcal{F}^-(\Pi) = \{\overline{p(\bar{t})} \mid p(\bar{t}) \in \mathcal{F}^+(\Pi)\}$, the set of exclusive facets. With $\mathcal{F}(\Pi) = \mathcal{F}^+(\Pi) \cup \mathcal{F}^-(\Pi)$, we denote the set of all facets applicable to Π. We say an answer-set S of Π satisfies an inclusive facet $p(\bar{t}) \in \mathcal{F}^+(\Pi)$ if $p(\bar{t}) \in S$. It satisfies an exclusive facet $\overline{p(\bar{t})} \in \mathcal{F}^-(\Pi)$ if $p(\bar{t}) \notin S$.*

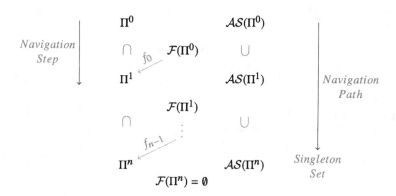

Fig. 1. The interplay of an initial program Π^0, its answer-sets $\mathcal{AS}(\Pi^0)$ and its corresponding facets $\mathcal{F}(\Pi^0)$, for n navigation steps.

With the notion of a facet at hand, we can now start to define the navigation as a sequence of single navigation steps, defined in the following.

Definition 2. *Given a set of facets $\mathcal{F}$, we define the function ic that rewrites every $f \in \mathcal{F}$ into a corresponding integrity constraint. Formally, $ic(f) = {} \leftarrow neg(f)$, with*

$$neg(f) = \begin{cases} not\, p(\bar{t}) & \text{if } f = p(\bar{t}). \\ p(\bar{t}) & \text{if } f = \overline{p(\bar{t})}. \end{cases}$$

We let $ic(\mathcal{F}) := \{ic(f) \mid f \in \mathcal{F}\}$.

Definition 3 (Navigation Step). *A navigation step, written* $\Pi \overset{f}{\Longrightarrow} \Pi'$, *is a transition from one program* Π *to another program* Π', *where* Π' *is obtained by adding the integrity constraint* $ic(f)$ *to* Π, *where* $f \in \mathcal{F}(\Pi)$.

Faceted navigation of Π is possible as long as $\mathcal{BC}(\Pi) \setminus \mathcal{CC}(\Pi) \neq \emptyset$.

Example 2. Consider the following program Π_2:

$$b, a \leftarrow \quad d, e \leftarrow \quad c \leftarrow a$$

Which has the following answer-sets $\mathcal{AS}(\Pi_2) = \{\{b, e\}, \{b, d\}, \{a, e, c\}, \{a, d, c\}\}$, and consequently the facets $\mathcal{F}(\Pi_2) = \{a, b, e, d, c, \bar{a}, \bar{b}, \bar{e}, \bar{d}, \bar{c}\}$. Let $f = a \in \mathcal{F}^+(\Pi)$, then applying $\Pi_2 \overset{a}{\Longrightarrow} \Pi'_2$ yields the answer-sets $\mathcal{AS}(\Pi'_2) = \{\{a, e, c\}, \{a, d, c\}\}$ and facets $\mathcal{F}(\Pi'_2) = \{e, d, \bar{e}, \bar{d}\}$. Continuing, we apply $\Pi'_2 \overset{\bar{e}}{\Longrightarrow} \Pi''_2$, resulting $\mathcal{AS}(\Pi''_2) = \{\{a, d, c\}\}$, and $\mathcal{F}(\Pi''_2) = \emptyset$, thus not allowing any further navigation step.

The following theorem establishes that performing one navigation step by applying a facet has exactly the desired consequence of including or excluding the respective atom from the space of considered answer-sets.

Theorem 1. *Let* Π' *be the program obtained from* Π *by applying one navigation step using some facet* $f \in \mathcal{F}(\Pi)$, *i.e.* $\Pi \overset{f}{\Longrightarrow} \Pi'$. *Then* $\mathcal{AS}(\Pi') = \{S \in \mathcal{AS}(\Pi) \mid S$ *satisfies* $f\}$.

Proof. For the $\supseteq$ direction, let $S \in \mathcal{AS}(\Pi)$ and S satisfy f. Then $\Pi^S = \Pi'^S$ (since $ic(f)$ is entirely removed from the Gelfond-Lifschitz reduct of Π' wrt. S). Therefore, by assumption, S is a subset-minimal set satisfying Π'^S and hence $S \in \mathcal{AS}(\Pi')$.

For the $\subseteq$ direction, let $S \in \mathcal{AS}(\Pi')$. If S would not satisfy f, the Gelfond-Lifschitz reduct Π'^S would contain the rule "$\leftarrow$" due to $ic(f)$, and therefore be unsatisfiable, resulting in $S \notin \mathcal{AS}(\Pi')$, contradicting our assumption. Hence S must satisfy f, resulting in $\Pi^S = \Pi'^S$ as above, therefore $S \in \mathcal{AS}(\Pi')$ implies $S \in \mathcal{AS}(\Pi)$. $\square$

Note that this theorem also entails $\mathcal{AS}(\Pi') \subsetneq \mathcal{AS}(\Pi)$ due to the definition of $\mathcal{F}(\Pi)$.

Lemma 1. *Given a logic program* Π, *applying a navigation step* $(\Pi \overset{f}{\Longrightarrow} \Pi')$ *will never cause the generation of an unsatisfiable logic program* Π'.

Proof. By definition, $f \in \mathcal{F}(\Pi)$ means that there is some $p(\bar{t}) \in \mathcal{BC}(\Pi) \setminus \mathcal{CC}(\Pi)$. From $p(\bar{t}) \in \mathcal{BC}(\Pi)$ immediately follows that there is some $S \in \mathcal{AS}(\Pi)$ with $p(\bar{t}) \in S$. On the other hand, from $p(\bar{t}) \notin \mathcal{CC}(\Pi)$ follows that there is some $S' \in \mathcal{AS}(\Pi)$ with $p(\bar{t}) \notin S$. Therefore, applying Theorem 1, either $S \in \mathcal{AS}(\Pi')$ (if f is inclusive) or $S' \in \mathcal{AS}(\Pi')$ (if f is exclusive). Hence, Π' is satisfiable in any case. $\square$

Figure 1 sketches a sequence of navigation steps, and depicts the correlation of the resulting programs, answer-sets and facets.

3.2   Free Navigation Mode

In the previous setting, the assumption was that only facets of the current program are available to be applied in the next step. This ensures a conflict free navigation eventually resulting in a single answer-set. This might be convenient in some situations, however, we intend to relax this stringent process and extend the faceted navigation approach and allow the application of arbitrary facets from the initial program in any step. This inherently leads to conflicts; i.e. would cause an unsatisfiable program if two or more facets in combination enforce solutions that do not exist.

Therefore, when applying a facet that would lead to an unsatisfiable program, we aim to pick facets applied in previous steps that necessarily need to be retracted, in order to apply the desired facet. We start by identifying all facets that have already been applied.

Definition 4 (Active Facets). *For a program Π^n, obtained after an application of n navigation steps, i.e. $\Pi^0 \overset{f_0}{\Longrightarrow} \dots \overset{f_{n-1}}{\Longrightarrow} \Pi^n$, we denote with $\mathcal{F}_a(\Pi^n)$ the set of facets active in Π^n, i.e. $\mathcal{F}_a(\Pi^n) = \{f_0, \dots, f_{n-1}\}$.*

Amongst these active facets, some might be incompatible with some facet f from the initial program. We now aim to identify those facets that need to be retracted in order to be able to apply $f-$ and call such a set *correction set*.

Definition 5 (Correction Set). *Let $f \in \mathcal{F}(\Pi^0)$ be the facet chosen to be applied next to a program Π^n, but $f \notin \mathcal{F}(\Pi^n)$. A set $K \subseteq \mathcal{F}_a(\Pi^n)$, is a correction set of Π^n w.r.t. f, if $\Pi^n \setminus ic(K) \cup \{ic(f)\}$ is satisfiable. We denote by $\mathcal{K}(\Pi^n)$ the set of all correction sets of Π^n w.r.t. f.*

Example 3. Continuing with $\Pi_2 \overset{a}{\Longrightarrow} \Pi_2' \overset{\bar{e}}{\Longrightarrow} \Pi_2''$ from Example 2, where $\mathcal{F}(\Pi_2) = \{a, b, e, d, c, \bar{a}, \bar{b}, \bar{e}, \bar{d}, \bar{c}\}$ and $\mathcal{F}_a(\Pi_2'') = \{a, \bar{e}\}$. For $b \in \mathcal{F}(\Pi_2)$ we therefore have the correction sets $\{a\}$ and $\{a, \bar{e}\}$ for Π_2''.

It is now of interest to highlight how correction sets can be computed. As it turns out, this can be done by a program obtained from the original one by adding some extra rules.

Definition 6. *Given a navigation path of length n, $\Pi^0 \overset{f_0}{\Longrightarrow} \dots \overset{f_{n-1}}{\Longrightarrow} \Pi^n$, a facet $f \in \mathcal{F}(\Pi^0) \setminus \mathcal{F}(\Pi^n)$. Then the program $\Pi^{\mathcal{K}}$ is defined as:*

$$\Pi^{\mathcal{K}} := \Pi^0 \cup \{ic(f)\} \cup \{remove(i) \leftarrow neg(f_i) \mid f_i \in \mathcal{F}_a(\Pi^n) \text{ for all } 0 \le i < n\}$$

where "remove" is a new predicate name.

Lemma 2. *For each $S \in \mathcal{AS}(\Pi^{\mathcal{K}})$ there exists a correction set K such that*

$$K = \{f_i \in \mathcal{F}_a(\Pi^n) \mid remove(i) \in S, 0 \le i < n\}.$$

Proof. Let $S \in \mathcal{AS}(\Pi^{\mathcal{K}})$. First observe, that S certainly contains at least one (ground) atom $remove(i)$. Since $\mathcal{F}_a(\Pi^n) \neq \emptyset$, we construct a non-empty set E, s.t. for all $0 \leq i < n$

$$E := \{f_i \in \mathcal{F}_a(\Pi^n) \mid f_i \notin S, remove(i) \in S\} \cup$$
$$\{\bar{f}_i \in \mathcal{F}_a(\Pi^n) \mid f_i \in S, remove(i) \in S\},$$

and find $E \subseteq \mathcal{F}_a(\Pi^n)$. It remains to show that, $\Pi^\star := (\Pi^n \setminus ic(E) \cup \{ic(f)\})$ is satisfiable. Because of the definition of E and $\Pi^{\mathcal{K}}$, every $f_i \in E$ corresponds to some $remove(i)$ in some $S \in \mathcal{AS}(\Pi^{\mathcal{K}})$ where for every S we have $f \in S$. Which means that for every $f_i \in E$, the body of the corresponding rule in $\Pi^{\mathcal{K}}$, namely $remove(i) \leftarrow neg(f_i)$, must evaluate to true, hence f_i (whether inclusive or exclusive) to false. This is equivalent to the removal of $ic(f_i)$ from Π^n for all $f_i \in E$. Knowing that $\Pi^{\mathcal{K}}$ is satisfiable, moreover $\Pi^0 \cup \{ic(f)\}$ is satisfiable, then $\Pi^\star$ must be satisfiable as well. □

Lemma 3. *Given a navigation path* $\Pi^0 \overset{f_0}{\Longrightarrow} \ldots \overset{f_{n-1}}{\Longrightarrow} \Pi^n$*, a facet* $f \in \mathcal{F}(\Pi^0)$*, but* $f \notin \mathcal{F}(\Pi^n)$*, and the program* $\Pi^{\mathcal{K}}$*. Then for every correction set* $K \in \mathcal{K}(\Pi^n)$ *w.r.t.* f*, there exists an answer-set* $S \in \mathcal{AS}(\Pi^{\mathcal{K}})$ *induced by* K*.*

Proof. For arbitrary $K \in \mathcal{K}(\Pi^n)$, let $\bar{K} := \mathcal{F}_a(\Pi^n) \setminus K$ be of those facets that can safely remain in Π^n; i.e. $\Pi' = \Pi^0 \cup \{ic(f)\} \cup ic(\bar{K})$ is satisfiable. Consequently, the program

$$\Pi'' := \Pi' \cup \{remove(i) \leftarrow neg(f_i) \mid f_i \in K\}$$

is also satisfiable, thus let $S \in \mathcal{AS}(\Pi'')$. In particular, $\{remove(i) \mid f_i \in K\} \subset S$. Notice that Π'' is similar to $\Pi^{\mathcal{K}}$, except that $\Pi^{\mathcal{K}}$ does not contain the integrity constraints $ic(\bar{K})$, but instead the corresponding rules with a "$remove(i)$" atom in the head. Due to the construction of Π'' and the restrictions imposed by the integrity constraints $ic(\bar{K})$, we find that $\mathcal{AS}(\Pi'') \subseteq \mathcal{AS}(\Pi^{\mathcal{K}})$ and thus $S \in \mathcal{AS}(\Pi^{\mathcal{K}})$. □

3.3   Preferred Correction Sets

Inherently, there are potentially many correction sets, though it is natural to prefer correction sets for which most of the active facets can be retained; in other words, we would like to obtain correction sets that contain only facets that necessarily need to be retracted. We therefore introduce two preference notions.

Definition 7 (Minimal Correction Set). *A correction set K for some program Π w.r.t. to some facet f is minimal, if there exist no other correction set K', s.t. $K' \subset K$. Then $\mathcal{K}_{\subset}(\Pi) = \{K \mid K \text{ is minimal}\}$, is the set of all minimal correction sets for some program Π w.r.t. to some facet f.*

Amongst all minimal correction sets, which might vary in size, we now further restrict the preference to those that are also cardinality minimal.

Definition 8 (Small Correction Set). *A correction set K for some program Π w.r.t. to some facet f is small, if there exist no other correction set K', s.t. $|K'| < |K|$. Then $\mathcal{K}_{|<|}(\Pi) = \{K \mid K \text{ is small}\}$, is the set of the smallest correction sets for some program Π w.r.t. to some facet f.*

Amongst the correction sets from Example 3, only $\{a\}$ is minimal as well as the smallest. In order to find all correction sets for some program Π^n w.r.t. some facet $f \in \mathcal{F}(\Pi^0) \setminus \mathcal{F}(\Pi^n)$, the program $\Pi^{\mathcal{K}}$ needs to be constructed, from which then the correction sets are extracted from the answer-sets. In general, $|\mathcal{AS}(\Pi^{\mathcal{K}})|$ is quite large which hinders the computation of all correction sets; and is another practical reason for preferences over correction sets. However, since finding minimal correction sets is also computationally expensive, we propose an incremental computation of $\mathcal{K}_{\subseteq}(\Pi^n)$, starting from $\mathcal{K}_{|<|}(\Pi^n)$. The advantage that small correction sets have over the minimal ones is that once we find the size of a small correction set we do not need to investigate further. This does not apply for the minimal correction sets which they might differ in size. In order to have a feasible way of computing $\mathcal{K}_{\subseteq}(\Pi^n)$, we can not simply use $\Pi^{\mathcal{K}}$ as defined earlier (without modification), to generate all correction sets and then filter out the minimal ones, because we would run into problems when it comes to $\Pi^{\mathcal{K}}$s with a large number of answer-sets. Therefore, it is shown next how to generate $\mathcal{K}_{|<|}(\Pi^n)$, from which $\mathcal{K}_{\subseteq}(\Pi^n)$ can be computed.

Small Correction Sets. Given Π^0 and Π^n where $\Pi^0 \overset{f_0}{\Longrightarrow} \dots \overset{f_{n-1}}{\Longrightarrow} \Pi^n$ and a facet $f \in \mathcal{F}(\Pi^0) \setminus \mathcal{F}(\Pi^n)$; $\mathcal{K}_{|<|}(\Pi^n)$ w.r.t. f can be computed via the program $\Pi^{\mathcal{K}}$ as mentioned earlier, then extending it with the following rule, $\varrho_i = \leftarrow not\#count\{Y : remove(Y)\}i$, where $0 < i \leq n$. Basically, ϱ_i enforce to have at most i *remove* atoms present in an answer-set. Since $f \in \big(\mathcal{F}(\Pi^0) \setminus \mathcal{F}(\Pi^n)\big)$, it is guaranteed that there exists no answer-set $S \in \mathcal{AS}(\Pi^{\mathcal{K}})$ where S does not contain any atom with *"remove"* as predicate name, and thus it can not be the case that $i = 0$. Therefore, the solver would be called at most (worst case) n times and the answer-sets of the first satisfiable $\Pi^{\mathcal{K}}$ will contain the answer-sets that provide all small correction sets of Π^n w.r.t. f. The refinement of this rule plus the creation of $\Pi^{\mathcal{K}}$ is shown in the first algorithm in the next section.

Minimal Correction Sets. Based on $\mathcal{K}_{|<|}(\Pi^n)$ w.r.t. some f, $\mathcal{K}_{\subseteq}(\Pi^n)$ w.r.t. f can be computed. But first, we need to introduce a variation of the function $ic(\mathcal{F})$, namely $cic(\mathfrak{F})$, where $\mathfrak{F}$ is a set of sets of facets, defined as:

$$cic(\mathfrak{F}) = \bigcup_{\mathcal{F} \in \mathfrak{F}} \{\leftarrow neg(f_0), \dots, neg(f_n) \mid \mathcal{F} = \{f_0, \dots, f_n\}\}.$$

Initially, we describe the computation of $\mathcal{K}_{\subseteq}(\Pi^n)$ informally. Let $|K| = d$ where $K \in \mathcal{K}_{|<|}(\Pi^n)$ w.r.t. some $f \in \mathcal{F}(\Pi^0)$ but $f \notin \mathcal{F}(\Pi^n)$. For every small K, we add an integrity constraint of the form $"cic(K)"$ to $\Pi^{\mathcal{K}}$ (thus obtaining $\Pi^{\mathcal{K}'}$), then for all $S \in \mathcal{AS}(\Pi^{\mathcal{K}})$ that lead to the generation of some small correction set

$K \in \mathcal{K}_{|<|}(\Pi^n)$, we have $S \notin \mathcal{AS}(\Pi^{\mathcal{K}'})$. If $\mathcal{AS}(\Pi^{\mathcal{K}'}) \neq \emptyset$, then there must exist some answer-set $S' \in \mathcal{AS}(\Pi^{\mathcal{K}'})$ s.t. $K' = \{f_i \in \mathcal{F}_a(\Pi^n) \mid remove(i) \in S', 0 \leq i < n\}$. For the small correction sets K' we know that $K' \not\subseteq K$ for any $K \in \mathcal{K}_{|<|}(\Pi^n)$ and since $\mathcal{AS}(\Pi^{\mathcal{K}'}) \subset \mathcal{AS}(\Pi^{\mathcal{K}})$ – follows from Theorem 1 – we conclude that $K' \in \mathcal{K}_{\subseteq}(\Pi^n)$. In the following lemma, we adjust the notation of a correction set of a program Π^n w.r.t. some f by adding a superscript, namely K^{d+j}, where $d + j$ is the size of K, d is the size of the small correction sets and $0 \leq j < n$.

Lemma 4. *Let d be the size of a small correction set of some Π^n w.r.t. some f; let K^{d+j} be a correction set of Π^n w.r.t. the same f and obtained from some $S \in \mathcal{AS}(\Pi^{\mathcal{K}})$ such that $K^{d+j} \in \mathcal{K}_{\subseteq}(\Pi^n)$. We define $\Pi^{\mathcal{K}'} = \bigcup\limits_{0 \leq l < d+j} cic(\mathcal{K}_{\subseteq}^l(\Pi^n)) \cup \Pi^{\mathcal{K}} \cup \{\varrho_{d+j}\}$; if $\mathcal{AS}(\Pi^{\mathcal{K}'}) \neq \emptyset$, then the following holds: For every $K^{d+j} \in \mathcal{K}_{\subseteq}(\Pi^n)$, there must exist some $S' \in \mathcal{AS}(\Pi^{\mathcal{K}'})$ that induces some K' s.t. $K' = K^{d+j}$.*

Proof. By the definition of $\Pi^{\mathcal{K}'}$, we can conclude that for every $S' \in \mathcal{AS}(\Pi^{\mathcal{K}'})$ and every set of "$remove(\_)$" atoms that correspond to some K^l we have that

$$\{remove(i) \mid f_i \in K^l\} \not\subseteq S'$$

We also know that $\mathcal{AS}(\Pi^{\mathcal{K}'}) \subset \mathcal{AS}(\Pi^{\mathcal{K}})$ – which follows from Theorem 1 but we do not prove it – then for all $S' \in \mathcal{AS}(\Pi^{\mathcal{K}'})$ we have $S' \in \mathcal{AS}(\Pi^{\mathcal{K}})$ and for every K' obtained from some S' we have $S' = S \in \mathcal{AS}(\Pi^{\mathcal{K}})$ and $|K'| = d+j$ (Because of the rule ϱ_{d+j}). Which means that $K' = K^{d+j}$. $\square$

Therefore, in order to compute the set $\mathcal{K}_{\subseteq}(\Pi^n)$, we first compute $\mathcal{K}_{|<|}(\Pi^n)$, create the program $\Pi^{\mathcal{K}'} = cic(\mathcal{K}_{|<|}(\Pi^n)) \cup \Pi^{\mathcal{K}}$. If $\mathcal{AS}(\Pi^{\mathcal{K}'}) \neq \emptyset$, then we update $\Pi^{\mathcal{K}'}$ by adding the rule ϱ_i that enforces a restriction on the size of the correction sets obtained from $S' \in \mathcal{AS}(\Pi^{\mathcal{K}'})$, i.e. $\Pi^{\mathcal{K}'} = \Pi^{\mathcal{K}'} \cup \{\varrho_{d+j}\}$ where $j = 1$. If the updated $\Pi^{\mathcal{K}'}$ is satisfiable, then we can extract all minimal correction sets of Π^n with the size $d + 1$. If it is not the case, we increase the value of j by one, and we keep on increasing the value of j until we reach the first satisfiable version of the updated $\Pi^{\mathcal{K}'}$. Since the initial condition is $\mathcal{AS}(\Pi^{\mathcal{K}'}) \neq \emptyset$ ($\Pi^{\mathcal{K}'}$ before adding ϱ_i), then we know that there must exist a value j where $\Pi^{\mathcal{K}'} \cup \{\varrho_{d+j}\}$ is actually satisfiable. We keep on repeating the whole process until we reach a program $\Pi^{\mathcal{K}^*}$ s.t. $\mathcal{AS}(\Pi^{\mathcal{K}^*}) = \emptyset$, hence computing $\mathcal{K}_{\subseteq}(\Pi^n)$. In the worst case scenario, the solver would be called less than $2 \times n$ times. The following example depict a case where the *free navigation* mode is applied.

Example 4. Let Π be a logic program defined as follows.

$$\{a; b; c; d\} \qquad\qquad e \leftarrow b$$
$$\leftarrow e, d, a \qquad\qquad e \leftarrow c$$

Since $\mathcal{F}(\Pi) = \{a, b, c, d, \bar{a}, \bar{b}, \bar{c}, \bar{d}\}$, we apply $\Pi \stackrel{a}{\Longrightarrow} \Pi^1$. Thus $\Pi^1 = \Pi \cup \{ic(a)\}$, and we obtain $\mathcal{F}(\Pi^1) = \{b, c, d, \bar{b}, \bar{c}, \bar{d}\}$. Applying $\Pi^1 \stackrel{b}{\Longrightarrow} \Pi^2$ yields

$\Pi^2 = \Pi^1 \cup \{ic(b)\}$. With $\mathcal{F}(\Pi^2) = \{c, d, \bar{c}, \bar{d}\}$, we apply $\Pi^2 \overset{c}{\Longrightarrow} \Pi^3$, and obtain $\Pi^3 = \Pi^2 \cup \{ic(c)\}$. At this stage of the faceted navigation, $\mathcal{F}(\Pi^3) = \emptyset$; for $d \in \mathcal{F}(\Pi)$, which is an inactive facet, we have $d \notin \mathcal{F}(\Pi^3)$ and therefore $\Pi^3 \overset{d}{\Longrightarrow} \Pi^4$ can not be applied. We compute $\mathcal{K}_\subseteq(\Pi^3)$ w.r.t. d as follows.

1. Generate $\Pi^\mathcal{K} = \Pi \cup \overbrace{\{r(1) \leftarrow not\, a,\ r(2) \leftarrow not\, b,\ r(3) \leftarrow not\, c\}}^{\mathcal{R}} \cup \{ic(d)\}$.
2. Extend $\Pi^\mathcal{K}$ with ϱ_1, i.e. $\Pi^\mathcal{K} = \Pi^\mathcal{K} \cup \{ \leftarrow not\,\#count\,\{Y : r(Y)\}\,1\}$.
3. $\mathcal{AS}(\Pi^\mathcal{K}) = \{\{b, c, d, e, r(1)\}\}$; moreover $\mathcal{K}_{|<|}(\Pi^3) = \{\{a\}\}$.
4. Compute $\Pi^{\mathcal{K}'} = \Pi \cup \mathcal{R} \cup \{ic(d)\} \cup cic(\{\{a\}\})$.
5. Since $\mathcal{AS}(\Pi^{\mathcal{K}'}) \neq \emptyset$, there must exist some $S' \in \mathcal{AS}(\Pi^{\mathcal{K}'})$ that leads to some correction sets of Π^3 w.r.t. d.
6. Extend $\Pi^{\mathcal{K}'}$ with ϱ_2, i.e. $\Pi^{\mathcal{K}'} = \Pi^{\mathcal{K}'} \cup \{ \leftarrow not\,\#count\,\{Y : r(Y)\}\,2\}$.
7. $\mathcal{AS}(\Pi^{\mathcal{K}'}) = \{\{a, d, r(2), r(3)\}\}$; moreover $\mathcal{K}_\subseteq(\Pi^3) = \mathcal{K}_{|<|}(\Pi^3) \cup \{\{b, c\}\}$.
8. At this stage, we can terminate the search for more minimal correction sets of Π^n w.r.t. d because $\Pi^{\mathcal{K}''} = \Pi \cup \mathcal{R} \cup \{ic(d)\} \cup cic(\{\{a\}\}) \cup cic(\{\{b, c\}\})$ is unsatisfiable; which means all minimal correction sets have been computed.

4   Implementation and Evaluation

The following algorithm describes the computation of the set of all minimal correction sets of some program Π^n where $\Pi^0 \overset{f_0}{\Longrightarrow} \ldots \overset{f_{n-1}}{\Longrightarrow} \Pi^n$.

Algorithm 1. *ASP-Based Minimal Correction Sets Generator*

Data: $\mathcal{F}_a(\Pi^n)$, f, Π^0

$Seq := list\big(\mathcal{F}_a(\Pi^n)\big); \mathcal{K}_\subseteq(\Pi^n) := \emptyset; j := 1;$
$\Pi^\mathcal{K} := \Pi^0 + ic(f);$
$counter := \text{":- } not\,\#count\,\{Y : remove(Y)\}\text{"} + str(j) + \text{"."};$

for $\big(i\ in\ 0 \ldots n\big)$ **do**
$\quad \mid \quad \Pi^\mathcal{K} += \text{"}remove(\text{"} + str(i) + \text{")"} + ic(Seq[i]);$
$\Pi^\mathcal{K} += counter;$

while $(j \leq n)$ **do**
$\quad \mid \quad Corrections = solve(\Pi^\mathcal{K});$
$\quad \mid \quad \mathcal{K}_\subseteq(\Pi^n).addAll(Corrections);$
$\quad \mid \quad j{+}{+}\ ;$
$\quad \mid \quad$ **if** $(Corrections \neq \emptyset)$ **then**
$\quad \mid \quad \mid \quad \Pi^\mathcal{K} += cic(Corrections);$
$\quad \mid \quad \mid \quad updatePi(counter, n);$ // replace in counter: j -> n
$\quad \mid \quad \mid \quad$ **if** $(!sat(\Pi^\mathcal{K}))$ **then**
$\quad \mid \quad \mid \quad \mid \quad break;$
$\quad \mid \quad updatePi(counter, j);$
return $\mathcal{K}_\subseteq(\Pi^n)$

As mentioned in the previous section, the size of the correction sets varies, and usually it is not clear what would the effect of applying a correction set be (In particular, what implicit consequential facets would be lost when a certain correction set is applied); therefore, our framework provides an additional functionality that computes the consequences of removing a certain set of facets $F \subseteq \mathcal{F}_a(\Pi^n)$ from Π^n. This computation is described in the following algorithm.

Algorithm 2. *Facets Removal Consequences*

Data: Π^n, F
$Constraints = \emptyset$;
for f *in* F **do**
   | $Constraints.add\big(ic(f)\big)$;
$\Pi^{tmp} = \Pi^n \setminus Constraints$;
return $\mathcal{CC}(\Pi^n) \setminus \big(\mathcal{CC}(\Pi^{tmp}) \cup F\big)$

Based on what has been introduced in this paper, we implemented a tool called INCA (Interactive General Configuration using Facets) that takes a logic program as an input and interactively applies the faceted navigation technique in both its *restricted* and *free* modes. INCA is programmed in Python 2.7 and uses Clingo 5.2, as the backbone reasoner and it is publicly available on Github[1]. It must be pointed out that the brave and cautious consequences of the input program are acquired via one of the built-in features of Clingo, which computes these consequences in an efficient reliable manner.

As already indicated in the introduction, the number of all solutions for the n-queens problem with $n > 27$ is still unknown [16]; therefore in the following table we display some performance results of INCA where different instances of the n-queens problem are plugged-in as an input (Tables 1 and 2).

Table 1. INCA performance for 8/30 – Queens.

	8-queens	30-queens
$\mathcal{F}(\Pi^0)$	0.011 s	1.054 s
$\Pi^0 \xrightarrow{f_0} \Pi^1$	0.016 s	6.935 s
$\mathcal{K}_{\subseteq}(\Pi^n)$	$(n = 4)$ 1 set in 0.028 s	$(n = 17)$ 1 set in 0.091 s
	$(n = 4)$ 3 sets in 0.017 s	$(n = 17)$ 16 sets in 0.211 s
	$(n = 4)$ 4 sets in 0.021 s	$(n = 17)$ 18 sets in 0.185 s

The first row shows the time spent on calculating all facets of the program, the second indicates the time needed to perform the first navigation step, whereas every entry in the third row displays the total number of correction sets of some program Π^n w.r.t different facets f (mostly the exclusive version of some consequential facets) where $f \in \mathcal{F}(\Pi^0)$ and $f \notin \mathcal{F}(\Pi^n)$. Another problem, where the

---

[1] https://github.com/lukeswissman/inca.

Table 2. INCA performance for 40/50 – Queens.

	40-queens	50-queens
$\mathcal{F}(\Pi^0)$	2.651 s	5.229 s
$\Pi^0 \overset{f_0}{\Longrightarrow} \Pi^1$	35.462 s	2:13.356 min
$\mathcal{K}_\subseteq(\Pi^n)$	$(n = 26)$ 145 sets in 1.188 s	$(n = 33)$ 60 sets in 1.760 s
	$(n = 26)$ 214 sets in 1.510 s	$(n = 33)$ 92 sets in 2.121 s
	$(n = 26)$ 284 sets in 2.040 s	$(n = 33)$ 114 sets in 3.695 s

calculation of all possible answer-sets is computationally expensive, is Sudoku. INCA takes approximately 0.186 s to compute all facets of an empty 9×9 Sudoku. The time needed to apply the first navigation step is approximately 2.930 s. The following shows the time spent to calculate different instances of the set $\mathcal{K}_\subseteq(\Pi^{40})$ with distinctive sizes depending on different facets f where $f \in \mathcal{F}(\Pi^0)$ and $f \notin \mathcal{F}(\Pi^{40})$ (Table 3).

Table 3. Computation of all minimal correction sets of 9×9 Sudoku for different facets.

$|\mathcal{K}_\subseteq(\Pi^{40})| = 497$	$|\mathcal{K}_\subseteq(\Pi^{40})| = 713$	$|\mathcal{K}_\subseteq(\Pi^{40})| = 2499$	$|\mathcal{K}_\subseteq(\Pi^{40})| = 4013$
3.559 s	4.650 s	47.122 s	2:10.874 min

5   Conclusion

We provide a general formal way to overcome the situation of answer-set programs with an unmanageable amount of answer-sets, where users might either be incapable of comprehending the space of answer-sets as a whole, or being able to identify a specific answer-set according to their needs. Our approach is therefore based on faceted navigation, wherein a facet can be seen as a partial solution that, if activated, is enforced to be present in any answer-set. This can be realized as stringent sequential process succeeding in a single answer-set, but also as navigation mode allowing unrestricted application of facets, potentially causing conflicts; i.e. *conflicting facets*. We provide a pure answer-set programming encoding to resolve conflicts, which besides giving a certain degree of freedom in navigation also contributes to the overall experience of answer-set exploration.

Regarding future work, we would like to extend the approach to support aggregate facets supporting to restrict the remaining answer-sets in terms of some numerical value. The same idea can be applied to preferences, which could be enriched with a cost value, depending on the underlying application scenario. It also remains imperative to explore the possibilities of enriching the user interface, e.g. by an aggregated presentation of atoms; unary ground atoms can be represented as (drop-down) lists. We see huge potential to explore answer-sets visually, where methods for visualizing large data-sets, established by other disciplines, could be reused. On the other hand our implementation can be used as backend to realize domain specific user interfaces. For example, product configurators, where users interactively can configure parts and properties of some product, being assisted in case of conflicting selections.

References

1. Arenas, M., Bertossi, L.E., Chomicki, J.: Specifying and querying database repairs using logic programs with exceptions. In: Larsen, H.L., Andreasen, T., Christiansen, H., Kacprzyk, J., Zadrozny, S. (eds.) FQAS 2000. Advances in Soft Computing, vol. 7, pp. 27–41. Physica, Heidelberg (2000). https://doi.org/10.1007/978-3-7908-1834-5_3
2. Brewka, G., Eiter, T., Truszczyński, M.: Answer set programming at a glance. Commun. ACM **54**(12), 92–103 (2011)
3. Delgrande, J.P., Faber, W. (eds.): LPNMR 2011. LNCS (LNAI), vol. 6645. Springer, Heidelberg (2011). https://doi.org/10.1007/978-3-642-20895-9
4. Eiter, T., Ianni, G., Krennwallner, T.: Answer set programming: a primer. In: Tessaris, S., et al. (eds.) Reasoning Web 2009. LNCS, vol. 5689, pp. 40–110. Springer, Heidelberg (2009). https://doi.org/10.1007/978-3-642-03754-2_2
5. Eiter, T., Leone, N., Mateis, C., Pfeifer, G., Scarcello, F.: The KR system dlv: progress report, comparisons and benchmarks. In: Cohn, A.G., Schubert, L.K., Shapiro, S.C. (eds.) Proceedings of the Sixth International Conference on Principles of Knowledge Representation and Reasoning (KR 1998), Trento, Italy, 2–5 June 1998, pp. 406–417. Morgan Kaufmann (1998)
6. Febbraro, O., Reale, K., Ricca, F.: ASPIDE: integrated development environment for answer set programming. In: Delgrande and Faber [3], pp. 317–330
7. Gebser, M., Kaminski, R., Kaufmann, B., Schaub, T.: Answer Set Solving in Practice. Synthesis Lectures on Artificial Intelligence and Machine Learning, vol. 6, pp. 1–238. Morgan and Claypool Publishers (2012)
8. Gebser, M., Kaminski, R., Kaufmann, B., Schaub, T.: Clingo = ASP + control: Preliminary report. CoRR abs/1405.3694 (2014)
9. Gebser, M., Kaminski, R., König, A., Schaub, T.: Advances in gringo series 3. In: Delgrande and Faber [3], pp. 345–351
10. Gelfond, M., Lifschitz, V.: Classical negation in logic programs and disjunctive databases. New Gener. Comput. **9**(3/4), 365–386 (1991)
11. Gertz, M.: Diagnosis and repair of constraint violations in database systems. Datenbank Rundbrief **19**, 96 (1997)
12. Kloimüllner, C., Oetsch, J., Pührer, J., Tompits, H.: **Kara**: a system for visualising and visual editing of interpretations for answer-set programs. In: Tompits, H., et al. (eds.) INAP/WLP -2011. LNCS (LNAI), vol. 7773, pp. 325–344. Springer, Heidelberg (2013). https://doi.org/10.1007/978-3-642-41524-1_20

13. Lifschitz, V.: What is answer set programming? In: Fox, D., Gomes, C.P. (eds.) Proceedings of the Twenty-Third AAAI Conference on Artificial Intelligence, AAAI 2008, 13–17 July 2008, pp. 1594–1597. AAAI Press (2008)
14. Niemelä, I.: Logic programs with stable model semantics as a constraint programming paradigm. Ann. Math. Artif. Intell. **25**(3–4), 241–273 (1999)
15. Oetsch, J., Pührer, J., Tompits, H.: Stepwise debugging of answer-set programs. TPLP **18**(1), 30–80 (2018)
16. Preußer, T.B., Engelhardt, M.R.: Putting queens in carry chains, No27. Signal Process. Syst. **88**(2), 185–201 (2017)

Clinical Decision Support Based on OWL Queries in a Knowledge-as-a-Service Architecture

Renan Gomes Barreto$^{(\boxtimes)}$, Lucas Oliveira Costa Aversari ,
Cecília Neta Alves Pegado Gomes , and Natasha Correia Queiroz Lino

Federal University of Paraíba, João Pessoa, Paraíba, Brazil
renangbarreto@ppgi.ci.ufpb.br, lucas.aversari@lavid.ufpb.br,
netapegado@gmail.com, natasha@ci.ufpb.br

Abstract. Facing the need to improve access to knowledge and the establishment of means for sharing and organizing data in the health domain, this research describes an architecture based on the paradigm of Knowledge-as-a-Service (KaaS) for knowledge sharing in the health domain, and, through the use of OWL queries, it's demonstrated how such architecture can be used for clinical decision support, together with its flow of execution. Additionally, it is shown a case study of the instantiation of the purposed architecture in the field of nephrology. The development of this research contributed to the creation of a new architecture, called H-KaaS, which established itself as a platform capable of managing multiple data sources and knowledge models, centralizing access to ontologies and other means of knowledge representation through an API that can be instantiated to different purposes, such as clinical decision support and education.

Keywords: Knowledge-as-a-Service · Ontology · Health informatics
Knowledge representation

1 Introduction

Computers have significantly changed the way humans do things, including health data processing, storage, and retrieval. Health Informatics or Medical Informatics is the application of information technology to health professionals with the objective of creating tools and procedures that help them in the diagnosis and treatment of patients with more precision and efficiency [15].

One of the objectives of Health Informatics is to assist in Computer-Based Clinical Decision Support (CDS), which can be defined as the use of the computer to bring relevant knowledge to support health and well-being of the patient [12].

This process can be executed automatically by using decision support systems with knowledge representation based on ontologies, for instance. In this type

© Springer Nature Switzerland AG 2018
C. Benzmüller et al. (Eds.): RuleML+RR 2018, LNCS 11092, pp. 226–238, 2018.
https://doi.org/10.1007/978-3-319-99906-7_15

of application, the ontologies have the objective of allowing an automatic and effective search of knowledge through guides of clinical practices [21].

Clinical Decision Support Systems developed using a set of guidelines for clinical practices as a knowledge base, can use these guides to make inferences based on validated decisions, actions and clinical recommendations, standardize healthcare delivery, and identify which patient data is really necessary and relevant [7,12].

With the advance of processing power and speed of data collection on the internet, many organizations focus on the development of tools, modeling techniques and the creation of structures dedicated to knowledge sharing. Knowledge representation, a subarea of Artificial Intelligence, aims to find ways to automatically represent, store and manipulate knowledge using reasoning algorithms [8].

For this reason, the amount of data collected in the health domain increases periodically, resulting in the emergence of diagnostic methods, chemical principles, and advances in molecular biology and genetics, among other medical advances [28]. Due to the need to improve access to knowledge and the creation of means of sharing and organizing data in the health domain, Health Informatics has been trying to find solutions to solve problems common to professionals and experts in the domain [9].

Service Oriented Architectures (SOA) can be used by developers to troubleshoot shared systems common problems, such as application integration, transaction management, security policy implementation, and compatibility with legacy systems [1].

In this context, the Knowledge-as-a-Service (KaaS) paradigm aims to provide centralized knowledge that is normally extracted from various data sources and can be maintained by different organizations. In it, a knowledge server responds to requests made by one or more knowledge consumers [29].

In this article, we propose an architecture based on the KaaS paradigm for knowledge sharing, and through the use of OWL queries, for instance, we demonstrate how such architecture can be used for clinical decision support, together with its flow of execution. Additionally, it is shown a case study of the instantiation of the purposed architecture in the field of nephrology.

The remaining of this paper is divided into five sections with the following topics: Sect. 2 presents concepts related to Knowledge Representation and Reasoning, Service Oriented Architectures, Health Informatics, Clinical Decision Support and Chronic Kidney Disease, which will be the object of the case study; Sect. 3 presents the proposed KaaS architecture for the health domain; Sect. 4 shows a case study of clinical decision support via OWL queries, in the field of nephrology; Sect. 5 lists some related work on the paradigm of Knowledge-as-a-Service and similar architectures, followed by Sect. 6, which presents the conclusions.

2   Background

2.1   Knowledge Representation, Ontologies, and Reasoning

Knowledge Representation is a subarea of Artificial Intelligence (AI) that is concerned with the way that knowledge can be represented symbolically and manipulated automatically by reasoning algorithms [8]. Given a structure of knowledge representation and a process of reasoning, it is possible to draw conclusions from previously modeled knowledge. These conclusions can be used to assist in decision making [17].

The term ontology, when used in the area of computer science, in the context of knowledge representation systems, refers to a general structure of concepts represented by a logical vocabulary [23]. To infer in ontologies, we need an inference mechanism, such as reasoning algorithms. These algorithms allow the comparison of the syntax, possibly normalized structure, and concepts expressed in the ontology [3].

HermiT is a reasoner based on Description Logic (DL) which aims to be efficient and implement a series of improvements that allow it to work with larger and more complex ontologies [25]. In addition, HermiT uses the OWL API, which provides support for extraction, validation, and visualization of ontology file syntax definitions in RDF or Web Ontology Language (OWL) format [14].

2.2   Service Oriented Architectures

Service-Oriented Architectures (SOA) arose from the need for business integration and automation over the internet [22]. In SOA, resources are packaged as well-defined services that produce a standardized output independently of the state or context of other parts of the application [11], providing several benefits to both service providers and their users [2], such as cost reduction, elasticity, automatic updates, easy implementation, and a new way of selling functionality to customers that competes with traditional business models [6].

In the context of knowledge sharing and distribution, the SOA advanced Knowledge-as-a-Service (KaaS) paradigm aims to centrally provide knowledge that is normally extracted from various data sources and can be maintained by different organizations. In it, a knowledge server responds to requests made by one or more knowledge consumers [29].

According to [29], in an implementation of a KaaS architecture, it is possible to find three main components: Data Owners, which are responsible for collecting data from their daily transactions and for filtering and protecting the collected information; Knowledge Service Provider, which aims to centralize and provide knowledge through its knowledge server, where data is extracted using an extractor algorithm; and Knowledge Consumers, which are applications that use the provided knowledge in their decision-making process, communicating with the server by using a previously established protocol.

2.3   Health Informatics

According to [16], Health Informatics can be defined as the field of science that deals with formal resources, equipment, and methods to optimize storage, reading and management of medical information in problem-solving and decision making.

With the evolution of technology and due to the difficulty of the management of information processing in the medical field, the Health Informatics area has tried to develop tools and algorithms with the objective of solving problems common to health professionals [9]. Thus, Health Informatics aims to improve the quality of health services, reducing costs and allowing the exchange of medical information [16].

2.4   Clinical Decision Support

According to [26], Clinical Decision Support systems have potential to reduce the number of medical errors and improve the quality and efficiency of the clinical treatment offered. In order to substantially improve the quality of service provided, it is necessary to aggregate acquired medical knowledge based on practice and medical literature into a common knowledge base, easily computable and adaptable. In this context, [12] stresses the importance of standardization of healthcare delivery and the correct identification of which patient data is really necessary and relevant.

2.5   Nephrology and Chronic Kidney Disease

Nephrology is an area of medicine that has as its objective the diagnosis and clinical treatment of diseases of the urinary system, mainly related to the kidney [24].

Chronic Kidney Disease (CKD) is defined as damage to the renal parenchyma (with normal renal function) and/or renal function impairment present for a period of three months or more. In its last stage, the kidneys are no longer able to maintain the normality of the patient's internal environment. Thus, early diagnosis and disease prevention have become increasingly important in order to take preventive measures that may delay or halt the progression of CKD [5].

3   H-KaaS: A Knowledge-as-a-Service Architecture for e-Health

Based on the study and analyses of the architecture proposed by [29] for the Knowledge-as-a-Service paradigm, it was investigated in this work a generic KaaS architecture aimed at the Health domain. For that, a similar, but extended and detailed platform, called H-KaaS, was designed.

H-KaaS aims to centralize access to knowledge generated from several distinct data sources, allowing efficient knowledge sharing. An overview of the H-KaaS architecture can be seen in Fig. 1.

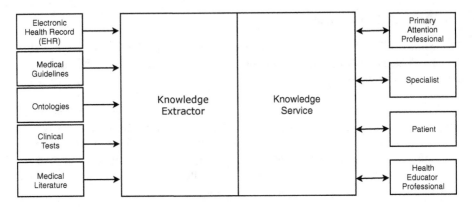

Fig. 1. An overview of the H-KaaS conceptual architecture based on the paradigm of Knowledge-as-a-Service adapted to the health domain (Source: Authors)

In the medical field, data sources could be considered, for instance: results of clinical tests, domain ontologies, books, periodicals, guidelines for diseases treatment, among others. Each data source has its own characteristics and must be treated independently in order to facilitate the inclusion and modification of new extraction rules.

For consumer applications, it is possible to create various solutions for each interested part that plays a role in the domain. For example, applications for clinical decision-making processes can be created to improve the service provided by specialists and primary care professionals.

The architecture H-KaaS has been divided into modules in order to be easier to maintain, understand and implement. The main modules that compose the architecture are the (1) knowledge service provider, (2) knowledge consumer, (3) communication API and (4) data sources: EHR, Medical Guidelines, Ontologies, Clinical Tests, and Medical Literature. In the next topics, it will be explained in details.

The knowledge service provider module aims to access and process data from the data source, manage knowledge models and serve queries made by knowledge consumers [29]. In the H-KaaS context, the knowledge service provider consists of two main parts: the knowledge extractor, responsible for inferences in the ontology, and the server-side implementation of the communication API, responsible for producing standardized responses that can be easily understood by consumer applications.

Applications which use the communication API to make queries to the central knowledge base are called knowledge consumers. Possible consumer applications in the Health domain are clinical decision support websites, mobile applications or embedded systems, electronic medical records, educational systems, among others.

The communication between the knowledge service provider and the consumer applications is made through the Application Programming Interface

(API), the H-KaaS API. According to [20], an API is a service, based on well-defined programming interfaces, which enables communication between applications. In other words, an API can be considered a medium in which communication between two computer programs is allowed.

The H-KaaS provides the possibility of multiple independent data sources, including ontologies, allowing greater flexibility in obtaining information and/or knowledge provided by external services. The data access system can vary according to its source and, therefore, the knowledge extractor is responsible for implementing the necessary means to read and extract the relevant information. Access to data can take place in two ways: local, in which data is organized in the same file system where the service is running; and remote, in which data is transferred from remote sources, occasionally unavailable.

3.1 OntoDecideDRC

The OntoDecideDRC [27] is a domain ontology that aims to provide clinical decision support to nephrology specialists and those working in primary health care. The ontology classes and properties provided the Clinical Decision Support related to the diagnosis, staging, and referral of patients with CKD.

OntoDecideDRC is composed of 184 classes and has object, data, and annotation properties. According to Protégé tool metrics, OntoDecideDRC has the number of 1240 axioms, counting with 479 logical axioms. With respect to the expressiveness of its description logic, Protégé has classified the ontology as "SHIF (D)" because it has an intersection of concepts, universal constraints, disjoint classes, complex concepts of negation, inverse properties, functional properties, data properties, among other features. OntoDecideDRC is composed of 13 main classes, where eleven of these classes have several subclasses.

OntoDecideDRC also provides information about basic clinical management techniques that should be performed by healthcare professionals in the management of CKD in patients, care related to the use of certain drugs in patients with CKD, and the list of vaccines that patients should have taken, according to their age group.

4 Case Study: Providing Clinical Decision Support to CKD

The objective of this case study is to adapt an existing prototype in the Health domain for an implementation of the proposed architecture. Two prototypes, EducaDRC [10] and OntoDecideDRC [27], were studied in order to choose one to be adapted to the new architecture, and both works have, as knowledge representation system, unique ontologies, created with the help of specialists in the nephrology field.

The main difference in the approaches is that EducaDRC, as a semantic repository, needs an additional database for storing triples and metadata, used to describe external resources. Therefore, due to database independence, the OntoDecideDRC was chosen as the ontology and base prototype to be adapted to the H-KaaS architecture.

The knowledge service provider was implemented in the PHP language and, in addition to containing the commands required for the extraction and inference of knowledge, also implements the commands described in the API specification.

For the adaptation of the ontology present in the OntoDecideDRC to the knowledge extractor module, it was necessary to write a command line application, able to execute the reasoner HermiT [25] and infer in an OWL-type ontology, using queries based on Description Logic. This application was implemented in the Java programming language and is part of the knowledge extractor module.

In the knowledge extractor, some auxiliary functions were also created to execute ontology queries. One of these is the implementation of the Glomerular Filtration Rate (GFR) calculation. This calculation uses the simplified Modification of Diet in Renal Disease (MDRD) formula specified by [19] and, through patient information, a numeric value is reached that will be used during inferences in the knowledge model.

The knowledge consumer module, a website called NefroService, had the objective to test the API and implement the service graphical interface of the chosen prototype. The programming language used for the implementation of NefroService was PHP and, in conjunction with the Wordpress framework, made possible the implementation of several pages for login, registration, password recovery, services list, method execution, contact, among others.

When adapting OntoDecideDRC, it was realized that the source code of its graphical interface was not available and, therefore, it was necessary to create a new form for data entry based on the original specification of the prototype. The data provided served as the basis for the staging method of the OntoDecideDRC service on the NefroService. All form fields have been rewritten and organized in a similar way to their original version but allowing the data to be serialized via the API communication for further processing by the knowledge extractor.

When accessing the NefroService, the user faces a form for inserting its credentials. These credentials are the responsibility of the consumer application, which enables the creation of different levels of access to the application, as well as better control of how information is shared.

Each service has a dedicated page, which can assist the user in choosing an appropriate method. After choosing the method, the user will face the data entry form and a brief description of how to fill it. Figure 2 A shows the staging method form, similar to that implemented in the original prototype of the OntoDecideDRC platform.

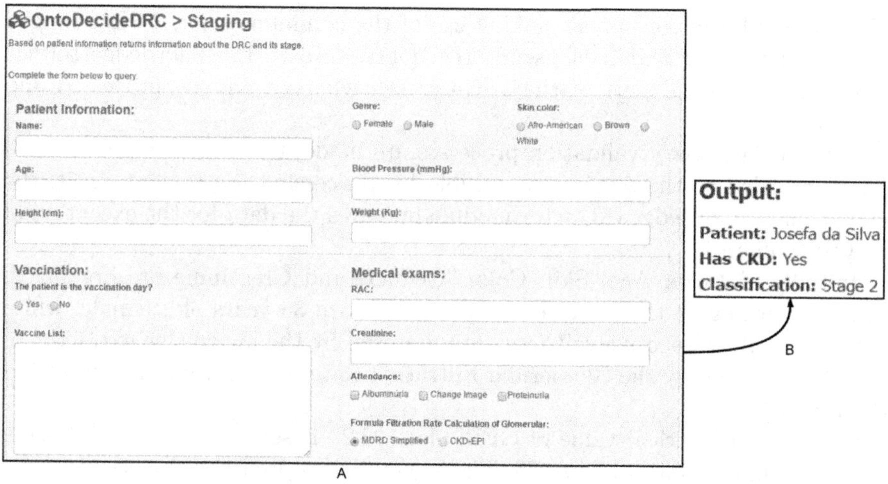

Fig. 2. CKD staging method form (A) and an example of its response (B)   (Source: Authors)

This form is generated dynamically, based on the rules and the data received from the communication API. When submitted, a request is sent to the API and, from it, the HTML code is created with the response that will be shown to the user (Fig. 2B). If during the processing of sending the request, an error occurs, an error message and a possible solution will be shown to the user.

The implementation of the knowledge consumer website enabled the platform user to perform queries using forms similar to those originally provided by the OntoDecideDRC platform, the prototype chosen to serve as a source of knowledge and basis for the creation of the graphical interface forms.

4.1   OWL Queries for Clinical Decision Support

In order to demonstrate how the OWL queries are executed within the architecture, the execution flow will be detailed given a clinical case as an example:

> A primary care medic receives a 35-year-old, female, white-skinned patient with a blood creatinine of 0.9 mg/dL and a change in imaging examination. The relationship between albumin and creatinine identified in this patient was of 35 mg/g [4].

The primary care professional fills the data in the graphical interface provided by the knowledge consumer application, which in case of the architecture in question, is a form exposed through a web page.

The knowledge consumer, making use of the communication API, arranged between the server and itself, sends the query data to the knowledge service provider, the central part of the architecture, where it will be processed and answered.

After all necessary validation processes are made, the data is validated and then forwarded to the service responsible for processing the request. In it, the implemented knowledge extractor module prepares the data for the execution of the OWL queries.

Initially, data on Age, Skin Color, Gender, and Creatinine are organized, which, according to the clinical case presented, are 35 years old, female, white and 0.9 mg/dL, respectively. These data are used by the knowledge extractor to calculate and classify the Glomerular Filtration Rate (GFR) using the Simplified MDRD formula.

Given the numerical value of GFR, class "T2" is selected, which represents the values in the range of 60 to 89. The same process occurs with respect to the examination of the relation between albumin and creatinine, which, according to the value provided, 35 mg/g, corresponds to class "A2".

According to the example, the knowledge extractor selects the classes identified as data-related: "Image Exam Alteration", "T2" and "A2", and develops an OWL query using the "Has" property, which will be executed through a reasoner to perform inference related to the diagnosis. This query, written in DL Query format, is presented as follows:

```
Has some (T2 and A2 and Image_Exam_Alteration)
```

The inference method returns the class "CKD" indicating that the patient has Chronic Kidney Disease.

In order to obtain the patient's risk degree, using the DRC class returned by the previous query, a new query is created which returns the class "Moderately Increased Risk".

```
((CKD) and (Has some (T2 and A2 and Image_Exam_Alteration)))
```

With regard to CKD staging, it is known that the stages are classified according to the "Glomerular Filtration Rate", so the reasoning logic only selects the "T2" class and develops the Query using the "Classified_by" property to perform the inference.

```
Classified_by some (T2)
```

The results of the query are serialized and sent in response to the knowledge service provider, which uses the communication API to notify the knowledge consumer application, i.e. the website, which will show to the user the result of the query.

A summary of the knowledge distribution process can be seen in Fig. 3.

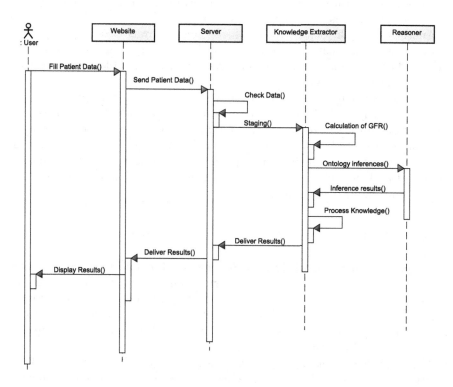

Fig. 3. An overview of the knowledge flow inside the proposed architecture (Source: Authors)

5   Related Work

In order to understand and compare similar researches, this section presents and analyses several proposals of architectures and frameworks applied to different domains.

It was proposed by [13] the Disaster-CDM, a KaaS framework, aiming to be able to store a large amount of disaster-related data from several sources, facilitating its search and indexing in addition to providing support and interoperability tools. Disaster-CDM has as its main form of data storage, the use of Relational Databases (RDB) and NoSQL databases. It communicates with consumer applications in three ways: ontologies, APIs, and services. These three forms of data access allow Disaster-CDM to respond to requests in an integrated manner without depending on how the data is saved internally.

In the Health domain, a relevant article by [30] describes a collaborative service-oriented architecture designed to facilitate sharing and cooperation between healthcare providers, while reducing costs for the patient. The architecture described has three main components: centralizer of medical collaborations; consumer applications and healthcare services providers.

Another research focused on the health domain was done by [18], which identifies the main characteristics of a collaborative medical services network and, in addition, explores ways in which KaaS could be used to create a private network of medical knowledge in China.

Thus, when analyzing the related work, we can see that service-based architectures can help in decision support in several domains. We can also see that most architectures use a textual format for data serialization and communication with consumers. On the other hand, we can see that the sources of knowledge vary according to the domain and availability of data holding services, showing the need to adapt each architecture to its domain, allowing a greater use and sharing of available domain knowledge.

6   Conclusion

In this paper, a new Knowledge-as-a-Service based architecture was presented in the health domain, with a detailed description of each of its modules together with its flow of execution. Additionally, was shown a case study of the instantiation of the purposed architecture in the field of nephrology, focusing on specific OWL queries to allow inferences in the modeled knowledge base and the creation of a clinical decision support mechanism.

The KaaS paradigm, although relatively new, is promising in terms of distribution and access to knowledge, being possible to use it better in domains where, although there is a large amount of data being collected daily, there are still no efficient ways to share knowledge satisfactorily.

In conclusion, the development of this research contributed to the emergence of a new architecture, called H-KaaS, which established itself as a platform capable of managing multiple data sources and knowledge models, centralizing access to ontologies and other means of knowledge representation through an API that can be instantiated to different purposes.

References

1. Alonso, G., Casati, F., Kuno, H., Machiraju, V.: Web services: concepts, architectures and applications. In: Web Services, pp. 123–149. Springer (2004). https://doi.org/10.1007/978-3-662-10876-5_5
2. Armbrust, M., Fox, A., Griffith, R., Joseph, A.D., Katz, R., Konwinski, A., Lee, G., Patterson, D., Rabkin, A., Stoica, I.: A view of cloud computing. Commun. ACM 53(4), 50–58 (2010)
3. Baader, F.: The Description Logic Handbook: Theory, Implementation and Applications. Cambridge University Press, New York (2003)
4. Barros, E., Gonçalves, L.F.: Nefrologia: Série No Consultório. Artmed Editora (2009)

5. Bastos, M.G., Kirsztajn, G.M.: Doença renal crônica: importância do diagnóstico precoce, encaminhamento imediato e abordagem interdisciplinar estruturada para melhora do desfecho em pacientes ainda não submetidos à diálise. Jornal Brasileiro de Nefrologia **33**(1), 93–108 (2011)
6. Benlian, A., Koufaris, M., Hess, T.: Service quality in software-as-a-service: developing the SaaS-qual measure and examining its role in usage continuance. J. Manag. Inf. Syst. **28**(3), 85–126 (2012). https://doi.org/10.2753/MIS0742-1222280303
7. Berner, E.S.: Clinical Decision Support Systems, vol. 233. Springer, New York (2007)
8. Brachman, R., Levesque, H.: Knowledge Representation and Reasoning - Book. New York **1**, p. 381 (2004). https://doi.org/10.1146/annurev.cs.01.060186.001351, http://www.amazon.com/dp/1558609326
9. Campos, S.: Sistema para raciocínio semântico no domínio dos hospitais de joão pessoa. Universidade Federal da Paraíba (2013)
10. Campos, S.P.R.: EducaDRC: Referatório Semântico de Objetos de Aprendizagem sobre Doença Renal Crônica destinado para Profissionais de Atenção Primária à Saúde. Master's thesis, Universidade Federal da Paraíba (2016)
11. Fremantle, P., Weerawarana, S., Khalaf, R.: Enterprise services. Commun. ACM **45**(10), 77–82 (2002)
12. Greenes, R.A.: Clinical Decision Support: The Road Ahead. Elsevier, Boston (2011)
13. Grolinger, K., Capretz, M.A.M., Mezghani, E., Exposito, E.: Knowledge as a service framework for disaster data management. In: Proceedings of the Workshop on Enabling Technologies: Infrastructure for Collaborative Enterprises, WETICE, pp. 313–318 (2013). https://doi.org/10.1109/WETICE.2013.48
14. Horridge, M., Bechhofer, S.: The OWL API: a Java API for OWL ontologies. Semant. Web **2**(1), 11–21 (2011). https://doi.org/10.3233/SW-2011-0025
15. Hovenga, E.J.: Health informatics: an overview, vol. 151. Ios Press, Boca Raton (2010)
16. Hoyt, R.E., Sutton, M., Yoshihashi, A.: Medical Informatics: Practical Guide for the Healthcare Professional 2008. Lulu.com (2008)
17. Ladeira, M.: Representação de Conhecimento e Redes de Decisão. Ph.D. thesis, Universidade Federal do Rio Grande do Sul (1997)
18. Lai, I.K., Tam, S.K., Chan, M.F.: Knowledge cloud system for network collaboration: a case study in medical service industry in China. Expert Syst. Appl. **39**(15), 12205–12212 (2012)
19. Levey, A.: A simplified equation to predict glomerular filtration rate from serum creatinine. J. Am. Soc. Nephrol. **11**, A0828 (2000)
20. Masse, M.: REST API Design Rulebook. O'Reilly Media Inc., Sebastopol (2011)
21. Mota, M.R.d.A.: Mapeamento sistemático sobre o uso de ontologias em informática médica. Master's thesis, Universidade Federal da Paraíba (2013)
22. Papazoglou, M.P.: Service-oriented computing: concepts, characteristics and directions. In: Proceedings of the Fourth International Conference on Web Information Systems Engineering. WISE 2003, pp. 3–12. IEEE (2003)
23. Russell, S., Norvig, P., Intelligence, A.: Artificial intelligence: a modern approach. In: Artificial Intelligence, vol. 25, p. 27. Prentice-Hall, Egnlewood Cliffs (1995)
24. SBN, S.B.d.N.: O que é nefrologia? (2016). http://sbn.org.br/publico/institucional/o-que-e-nefrologia/. Accessed 25 Nov 2016
25. Shearer, R., Motik, B., Horrocks, I.: Hermit: A highly-efficient owl reasoner. In: OWLED, vol. 432, p. 91 (2008)

26. Sim, I., Gorman, P., Greenes, R.A., Haynes, R.B., Kaplan, B., Lehmann, H., Tang, P.C.: Clinical decision support systems for the practice of evidence-based medicine. J. Am. Med. Inf. Assoc. 8(6), 527–534 (2001)
27. Tavares, E.A., Pegado, C.N.A., Lino, N.C.Q.: Suporte à decisão clínica no domínio da doença renal crônica. J. Health Inf. 8, 839–847 (2016)
28. Wechsler, R., Anção, M.S., Campos, C.J.R.D., Sigulem, D.: A informática no consultório médico. J. Pediatr. (Rio J) 79(1), 3–12 (2003)
29. Xu, S., Zhang, W.: Knowledge as a service and knowledge breaching. In: Proceedings - 2005 IEEE International Conference onServices Computing, SCC 2005 I, pp. 87–94 (2005). https://doi.org/10.1109/SCC.2005.60
30. Yoo, J.J.-W., Gnanasekaran, K., Cheng, C.-Y.: A collaborative healthcare service framework and performance evaluation. Am. J. Ind. Bus. Manag. 4(6), 274 (2014)

An Optimized KE-Tableau-Based System for Reasoning in the Description Logic $\mathcal{DL}_\mathbf{D}^{4,\times}$

Domenico Cantone, Marianna Nicolosi-Asmundo,
and Daniele Francesco Santamaria$^{(\boxtimes)}$

Department of Mathematics and Computer Science,
University of Catania, Catania, Italy
{cantone,nicolosi,santamaria}@dmi.unict.it

Abstract. We present a KE-tableau-based procedure for the main TBox and ABox reasoning tasks for the description logic $\mathcal{DL}\langle\mathsf{4LQS}^{\mathsf{R},\times}\rangle(\mathbf{D})$, in short $\mathcal{DL}_\mathbf{D}^{4,\times}$. The logic $\mathcal{DL}_\mathbf{D}^{4,\times}$, representable in the decidable multi-sorted quantified set-theoretic fragment $\mathsf{4LQS}^\mathsf{R}$, combines the high scalability and efficiency of rule languages such as the Semantic Web Rule Language (SWRL) with the expressivity of description logics.

Our algorithm is based on a variant of the KE-tableau system for sets of universally quantified clauses, where the KE-elimination rule is generalized in such a way as to incorporate the γ-rule. The novel system, called KE$^\gamma$-tableau, turns out to improve both the system introduced in [3] and the standard first-order KE-tableaux [10]. Suitable benchmark test sets executed on C++ implementations of the three mentioned systems show that the performances of the KE$^\gamma$-tableau-based reasoner are often up to about 400% better than the ones of the other two systems. This a first step towards the construction of efficient reasoners for expressive OWL ontologies based on fragments of computable set theory.

1 Introduction

Recently, decidability results in Computable Set Theory have been used for knowledge representation and reasoning, in particular, in the context of description logics (DLs) and rule languages for the Semantic Web. These efforts are motivated by the fact that there exists a natural translation function between set-theoretic fragments and languages for the Semantic Web.

In particular, the decidable four-level stratified set-theoretic fragment $\mathsf{4LQS}^\mathsf{R}$, involving variables of four sorts, pair terms, and a restricted form of quantification over variables of the first three sorts (cf. [1]), has been used in [2] to represent the description logic $\mathcal{DL}\langle\mathsf{4LQS}^{\mathsf{R},\times}\rangle(\mathbf{D})$, in short $\mathcal{DL}_\mathbf{D}^{4,\times}$.

The description logic $\mathcal{DL}_\mathbf{D}^{4,\times}$ supports various constructs on concepts and roles, and it also admits data types, relevant in real word applications. In addition, it permits to express the Semantic Web Rule Language (SWRL), an extension of the Ontology Web Language (OWL). Decidability of the *Conjunctive Query Answering* (CQA) problem for $\mathcal{DL}_\mathbf{D}^{4,\times}$ has been proved in [2] via a

© Springer Nature Switzerland AG 2018
C. Benzmüller et al. (Eds.): RuleML+RR 2018, LNCS 11092, pp. 239–247, 2018.
https://doi.org/10.1007/978-3-319-99906-7_16

reduction to the CQA problem for $4\mathsf{LQS}^\mathsf{R}$, whose decidability easily follows from that of $4\mathsf{LQS}^\mathsf{R}$ (see [1]). In [2], the authors provided a terminating KE-tableau based procedure that, given a $\mathcal{DL}_\mathbf{D}^{4,\times}$-query Q and a $\mathcal{DL}_\mathbf{D}^{4,\times}$-knowledge base $\mathcal{KB}$ represented in set-theoretic terms, determines the answer set of Q with respect to $\mathcal{KB}$. Such an algorithm serves also as a decision procedure for the consistency problem for $\mathcal{DL}_\mathbf{D}^{4,\times}$-knowledge bases (KBs). We recall that KE-tableaux systems [10] construct tableaux whose distinct branches define mutually exclusive situations, thus preventing the proliferation of redundant branches, typical of semantic tableaux.

The results presented in [2] have been extended in [3] to the main ABox reasoning tasks for $\mathcal{DL}_\mathbf{D}^{4,\times}$, such as instance checking and concept retrieval, by defining the Higher-Order Conjunctive Query Answering (HOCQA) problem for $\mathcal{DL}_\mathbf{D}^{4,\times}$. Such problem, instantiable to the principal reasoning tasks for $\mathcal{DL}_\mathbf{D}^{4,\times}$-ABoxes, has been defined by introducing Higher Order (HO) $\mathcal{DL}_\mathbf{D}^{4,\times}$-conjunctive queries, admitting variables of three sorts: individual and data type variables, concept variables, and role variables. Decidability of the HOCQA problem for $\mathcal{DL}_\mathbf{D}^{4,\times}$ has been proved via a reduction to the HOCQA problem for the set-theoretic fragment $4\mathsf{LQS}^\mathsf{R}$.

In [4], an implementation of the KE-tableau procedure defined in [3] has been presented. Such prototype, written in C++, supports $\mathcal{DL}_\mathbf{D}^{4,\times}$-KBs serialized in OWL/XML. It has been implemented only for TBox-reasoning services, namely, for verifying the consistency of given ontologies. Purely universal quantifiers are eliminated by the reasoner during a preprocessing phase, in which each quantified formula is instantiated in a systematic way with the individuals of the KB. The resulting instances are then suitably handled by applying to them the KE-elimination and bivalence rules. In the light of the benchmarking of the prototype, it turned out that the preprocessing phase of the universally quantified formulae is more and more expensive as the size of the KB grows.

In this paper, the KE-tableau-based procedure defined in [3] is modified, by eliminating the preprocessing phase for universally quantified formulae and replacing the standard KE-elimination rule with a novel elimination rule, called E^γ-rule, that incorporates the standard rule for treating universally quantified formulae (γ-rule). The resulting system[1] turns out to be more efficient than the KE-system in [4] and the First-Order (FO) KE-system in [10], as shown by suitable benchmarking tests executed on C++ implementations of the three systems. The main reason for such a speed-up relies on the fact that the E^γ-rule does not need to store the instances of the quantified formulae on the KE-tableau.

2   Preliminaries

2.1   The Set-Theoretic Fragment

It is convenient to recall the main set-theoretic notions behind the description logic $\mathcal{DL}_\mathbf{D}^{4,\times}$ and its reasoning problems. For space reasons, we do not report the

---

[1] The source code is available at https://github.com/dfsantamaria/DL4xD-Reasoner.

syntax and semantics of the whole 4LQS^R: the interested reader can find it in [1], together with the decision procedure for its satisfiability problem. Thus, we just focus on the class of 4LQS^R-formulae actually involved in the set-theoretic representation of $\mathcal{DL}_D^{4,\times}$, namely, the propositional combinations of 4LQS^R-quantifier-free literals (atomic formulae and their negations) and of 4LQS^R purely universal formulae of the types displayed in Table 1. For the sake of conciseness, we refer to such class of 4LQS^R-formulae as 4LQS$^R_{\mathcal{DL}_D^{4,\times}}$.

We recall that the fragment 4LQS^R admits four collections, Var_i, of variables of sort $i = 0, 1, 2, 3$, which are denoted by $X^i, Y^i, Z^i, \ldots$ (in particular, variables of sort 0 are also denoted by $x, y, z, \ldots$). In addition to variables, also *pair terms* of the form $\langle x, y \rangle$, with $x, y \in \mathsf{Var}_0$, are allowed. Since the types of formulae illustrated in Table 1 do not involve variables of sort 2, notions and definitions concerning 4LQS$^R_{\mathcal{DL}_D^{4,\times}}$-formulae will refer to variables of sorts $0, 1$, and 3 only.

Table 1. Types of literals and quantified formulae admitted in 4LQS$^R_{\mathcal{DL}_D^{4,\times}}$.

Quantifier-free literals of level 0	Purely universal quantified formulae of level 1
$x = y$, $x \in X^1$, $\langle x, y \rangle \in X^3$ $\neg(x = y)$, $\neg(x \in X^1)$, $\neg(\langle x, y \rangle \in X^3)$	$(\forall z_1) \ldots (\forall z_n)\varphi_0$, where $z_1, \ldots, z_n \in \mathsf{Var}_0$ and φ_0 is any propositional combination of quantifier-free atomic formulae of level 0

The variables $z_1, \ldots, z_n$ are said to occur *quantified* in $(\forall z_1) \ldots (\forall z_n)\varphi_0$. A variable occurs *free* in a 4LQS$^R_{\mathcal{DL}_D^{4,\times}}$-formula φ if it does not occur quantified in any subformula of φ. For $i = 0, 1, 3$, we denote with $\mathsf{Var}_i(\varphi)$ the collections of variables of sort i occurring free in φ.

For space reasons, the notions of 4LQS$^R_{\mathcal{DL}_D^{4,\times}}$-*substitution* and of 4LQS$^R_{\mathcal{DL}_D^{4,\times}}$-*interpretation* are not included here, but they can be found in [5].

2.2 The Logic $\mathcal{DL}_D^{4,\times}$

In what follows, we present the syntax and semantics of the description logic $\mathcal{DL}_D^{4,\times}$.

Let $\mathbf{R_A}, \mathbf{R_D}, \mathbf{C}, \mathbf{I}$ be denumerable pairwise disjoint sets of abstract role names, concrete role names, concept names, and individual names, respectively.

The definition of data types relies on the notion of data type map, given according to [11] as follows. A *data type map* is a quadruple $\mathbf{D} = (N_D, N_C, N_F, \cdot^{\mathbf{D}})$, where N_D is a finite set of data types, N_C is a function assigning a set of constants $N_C(d)$ to each data type $d \in N_D$, N_F is a function assigning a set of facets $N_F(d)$ to each $d \in N_D$, and $\cdot^{\mathbf{D}}$ is a function assigning a data type interpretation $d^{\mathbf{D}}$ to each $d \in N_D$, a facet interpretation $f^{\mathbf{D}} \subseteq d^{\mathbf{D}}$ to each facet $f \in N_F(d)$, and a data value $e_d^{\mathbf{D}} \in d^{\mathbf{D}}$ to every constant $e_d \in N_C(d)$. We shall assume that the interpretations of the data types in N_D are nonempty pairwise disjoint sets.

(a) $\mathcal{DL}_{\mathbf{D}}^{4,\times}$-*data type*, (b) $\mathcal{DL}_{\mathbf{D}}^{4,\times}$-*concept*, (c) $\mathcal{DL}_{\mathbf{D}}^{4,\times}$-*abstract role*, and (d) $\mathcal{DL}_{\mathbf{D}}^{4,\times}$-*concrete role terms* are constructed according to the following syntax rules:

(a) $t_1, t_2 \longrightarrow dr \mid \neg t_1 \mid t_1 \sqcap t_2 \mid t_1 \sqcup t_2 \mid \{e_d\}$,
(b) $C_1, C_2 \longrightarrow A \mid \top \mid \bot \mid \neg C_1 \mid C_1 \sqcup C_2 \mid C_1 \sqcap C_2 \mid \{a\} \mid \exists R.Self \mid \exists R.\{a\} \mid \exists P.\{e_d\}$,
(c) $R_1, R_2 \longrightarrow S \mid U \mid R_1^{-1} \mid \neg R_1 \mid R_1 \sqcup R_2 \mid R_1 \sqcap R_2 \mid R_{C_1\mid} \mid R_{\mid C_1} \mid R_{C_1} \mid C_2 \mid$
$\quad id(C) \mid C_1 \times C_2$,
(d) $P_1, P_2 \longrightarrow T \mid \neg P_1 \mid P_1 \sqcup P_2 \mid P_1 \sqcap P_2 \mid P_{C_1\mid} \mid P_{\mid t_1} \mid P_{C_1\mid t_1}$,

where dr is a data range for $\mathbf{D}$, t_1, t_2 are data type terms, e_d is a constant in $N_C(d)$, a is an individual name, A is a concept name, C_1, C_2 are $\mathcal{DL}_{\mathbf{D}}^{4,\times}$-concept terms, S is an abstract role name, U is an abstract role name denoting the universal role, R, R_1, R_2 are $\mathcal{DL}_{\mathbf{D}}^{4,\times}$-abstract role terms, T is a concrete role name, and P, P_1, P_2 are $\mathcal{DL}_{\mathbf{D}}^{4,\times}$-concrete role terms. We remark that data type terms are introduced in order to represent derived data types.

A $\mathcal{DL}_{\mathbf{D}}^{4,\times}$-KB is a triple $\mathcal{K} = (\mathcal{R}, \mathcal{T}, \mathcal{A})$ such that $\mathcal{R}$ is a $\mathcal{DL}_{\mathbf{D}}^{4,\times}$-*RBox*, $\mathcal{T}$ is a $\mathcal{DL}_{\mathbf{D}}^{4,\times}$-*TBox*, and $\mathcal{A}$ is a $\mathcal{DL}_{\mathbf{D}}^{4,\times}$-*ABox*. For space constraints, the definitions of $\mathcal{DL}_{\mathbf{D}}^{4,\times}$-*RBox*, $\mathcal{DL}_{\mathbf{D}}^{4,\times}$-*TBox*, $\mathcal{DL}_{\mathbf{D}}^{4,\times}$-*ABox* and the semantics of $\mathcal{DL}_{\mathbf{D}}^{4,\times}$ are omitted here, but the interested reader can find them in [5].

Expressiveness of the Description Logic $\mathcal{DL}_{\mathbf{D}}^{4,\times}$. Despite the fact that the description logic $\mathcal{DL}_{\mathbf{D}}^{4,\times}$ is limited as far as the introduction of new individuals is concerned, it is more liberal than $\mathcal{SROIQ}(\mathbf{D})$ [7] in the construction of role inclusion axioms, since the roles involved are not restricted by any ordering relationship, the notion of simple role is not needed, and Boolean operations on roles and role constructs such as the product of concepts are admitted. Moreover, $\mathcal{DL}_{\mathbf{D}}^{4,\times}$ supports more OWL constructs than the DLs underpinning the profiles OWL QL, OWL RL, and OWL EL [8], such as disjoint union of concepts and union of data ranges. Furthermore, basic and derived data types can be used inside inclusion axioms involving concrete roles. In addition, concerning the expressiveness of rules, the set-theoretic fragment $4\mathsf{LQS}^R_{\mathcal{DL}_{\mathbf{D}}^{4,\times}}$ underpinning $\mathcal{DL}_{\mathbf{D}}^{4,\times}$ allows one to express the disjunctive Datalog fragment admitting negation, equality and constraints, subject to no safety condition, and supporting for data types.

Reasoning with the Description Logic $\mathcal{DL}_{\mathbf{D}}^{4,\times}$. Next, we introduce the reasoning services available for the description logic $\mathcal{DL}_{\mathbf{D}}^{4,\times}$, i.e., the type of inferences that can be drawn from what is explicitly asserted in a $\mathcal{DL}_{\mathbf{D}}^{4,\times}$-KB. Specifically, we focus on two families of reasoning tasks, concerning respectively TBoxes and ABoxes. Among the main TBox reasoning problems, such as *satisfiability of a concept*, *subsumption of concepts*, *equivalence of concepts*, and *disjunction of concepts*, the problem of deciding the consistency of a $\mathcal{DL}_{\mathbf{D}}^{4,\times}$-KB is the most representative one, as it includes the majority of them.[2] In [2],

---

[2] A separate analysis, to be addressed in a future work, is required by the classification problem of a TBox, consisting in the computation of ancestor and descendant concepts of a given concept in a TBox.

we proved the decidability of the consistency problem of a $\mathcal{DL}_{\mathbf{D}}^{4,\times}$-KB and of a relevant ABox reasoning task, namely the *Conjunctive Query Answering* (CQA) problem for $\mathcal{DL}_{\mathbf{D}}^{4,\times}$ consisting in computing the answer set of a $\mathcal{DL}_{\mathbf{D}}^{4,\times}$-conjunctive query with respect to a $\mathcal{DL}_{\mathbf{D}}^{4,\times}$-KB. In [3], we generalized the problem introducing the *Higher Order Conjunctive Query Answering* (HOCQA) problem for $\mathcal{DL}_{\mathbf{D}}^{4,\times}$. Such problem is characterized by *Higher Order* (HO) $\mathcal{DL}_{\mathbf{D}}^{4,\times}$-conjunctive queries admitting variables of three sorts: individual and data type variables, concept variables, and role variables (the interested reader can find in [3] the definitions of HO-conjunctive queries, HO-substitutions, and HOCQA problem).

As illustrated in [3], the HOCQA problem can be instantiated to significant ABox reasoning problems such as (A) *role filler retrieval*, the problem of retrieving all the fillers x such that the pair (a, x) is an instance of a role R; (B) *concept retrieval*, the problem of retrieving all concepts which an individual is an instance of; (C) *role instance retrieval*, the problem of retrieving all roles which a pair of individuals (a, b) is an instance of; and (D) *conjunctive query answering*, the problem of finding the answer set of a conjunctive query.

In [3], we solved the HOCQA problem just stated by reducing it to the analogous problem formulated in the context of the fragment $\mathsf{4LQS}^R_{\mathcal{DL}_{\mathbf{D}}^{4,\times}}$ (and in turn of the decision procedure for $\mathsf{4LQS}^R$ presented in [1]).

The HOCQA problem in the $\mathsf{4LQS}^R_{\mathcal{DL}_{\mathbf{D}}^{4,\times}}$ context can be stated as follows. Let ϕ be a $\mathsf{4LQS}^R_{\mathcal{DL}_{\mathbf{D}}^{4,\times}}$-formula and ψ a conjunction of $\mathsf{4LQS}^R_{\mathcal{DL}_{\mathbf{D}}^{4,\times}}$-literals. The *HOCQA problem for* ψ *w.r.t.* ϕ consists in computing the HO *answer set* of ψ w.r.t. ϕ, namely, the collection Σ' of all the substitutions σ' such that $\mathcal{M} \models \phi \wedge \psi\sigma'$, for some $\mathsf{4LQS}^R_{\mathcal{DL}_{\mathbf{D}}^{4,\times}}$-interpretation $\mathcal{M}$.

In view of the decidability of the satisfiability problem for $\mathsf{4LQS}^R$-formulae, the HOCQA problem for $\mathsf{4LQS}^R_{\mathcal{DL}_{\mathbf{D}}^{4,\times}}$-formulae is decidable as well. The reduction is carried out by means of a function θ that maps the $\mathcal{DL}_{\mathbf{D}}^{4,\times}$-KB $\mathcal{KB}$ in a $\mathsf{4LQS}^R_{\mathcal{DL}_{\mathbf{D}}^{4,\times}}$-formula $\phi_{\mathcal{KB}}$ in Conjunctive Normal Form (CNF) and the HO $\mathcal{DL}_{\mathbf{D}}^{4,\times}$-conjunctive query Q in the $\mathsf{4LQS}^R_{\mathcal{DL}_{\mathbf{D}}^{4,\times}}$-formula ψ_Q (see [2] for details). Specifically,

$$\phi_{\mathcal{KB}} := \bigwedge_{H \in \mathcal{KB}} \theta(H) \wedge \bigwedge_{i=1}^{12} \xi_i, \quad \text{and} \quad \psi_Q := \theta(Q).$$

Let Σ be the HO-answer set of Q w.r.t. $\mathcal{KB}$ (see [3] for the definition of HO-answer set) and Σ' the HO-answer set of ψ_Q w.r.t. $\phi_{\mathcal{KB}}$. Then Σ consists of all substitutions σ (involving exactly the variables occurring in Q) such that $\theta(\sigma) \in \Sigma'$. By Lemma 1 in [3], Σ' can be effectively computed and thus Σ can be effectively computed as well.

3   A KE-Tableau Based Algorithm for Reasoning in $\mathcal{DL}_{\mathbf{D}}^{4,\times}$

In what follows, we briefly discuss the procedures *Consistency*-$\mathcal{DL}_{\mathbf{D}}^{4,\times}$ and *HOCQA*$^\gamma$-$\mathcal{DL}_{\mathbf{D}}^{4,\times}$. The procedure *Consistency*-$\mathcal{DL}_{\mathbf{D}}^{4,\times}$ checks the consistency of its input $4\mathsf{LQS}^R_{\mathcal{DL}^{4,\times}_D}$-formula $\phi_{\mathcal{KB}}$, representing a $\mathcal{DL}^{4,\times}_D$-KB. When $\phi_{\mathcal{KB}}$ is consistent, it builds a KE-tableau $\mathcal{T}_{\mathcal{KB}}$ whose distinct open and complete branches induce the models of $\phi_{\mathcal{KB}}$. Then the procedure $HOCQA^\gamma\text{-}\mathcal{DL}^{4,\times}_D$ computes the HO-answer set of a given $4\mathsf{LQS}^R_{\mathcal{DL}^{4,\times}_D}$-formula ψ_Q (representing a $\mathcal{DL}^{4,\times}_D$-HO conjunctive query Q) w.r.t. $\phi_{\mathcal{KB}}$, by means of a forest of decision trees based on the branches of the KE-tableau $\mathcal{T}_{\mathcal{KB}}$ computed by the procedure $Consistency\text{-}\mathcal{DL}^{4,\times}_D$ with input $\phi_{\mathcal{KB}}$.

We now shortly introduce a variant of KE-tableau called KE$^\gamma$-tableau.[3] Let $\Phi := \{C_1, \ldots, C_p\}$, where each C_i is either a $4\mathsf{LQS}^R_{\mathcal{DL}^{4,\times}_D}$-literal of the types illustrated in Table 1 or a $4\mathsf{LQS}^R_{\mathcal{DL}^{4,\times}_D}$-purely universal quantified formula of the form $(\forall x_1)\ldots(\forall x_m)(\beta_1 \vee \ldots \vee \beta_n)$, with $\beta_1, \ldots, \beta_n$ $4\mathsf{LQS}^R_{\mathcal{DL}^{4,\times}_D}$-literals. $\mathcal{T}$ is a KE$^\gamma$-*tableau* for Φ if there exists a finite sequence $\mathcal{T}_1, \ldots, \mathcal{T}_t$ such that (i) $\mathcal{T}_1$ is the one-branch tree consisting of the sequence $C_1, \ldots, C_p$, (ii) $\mathcal{T}_{i+1}$ is obtained from $\mathcal{T}_i$, for each $i < t$, either by an application of one of the rules (E$^\gamma$-rule or PB-rule) in Fig. 1 or by applying a substitution σ to a branch ϑ of $\mathcal{T}_i$ (in particular, the substitution σ is applied to each formula X of ϑ; the resulting branch will be denoted with $\vartheta\sigma$), and (iii) $\mathcal{T}_t = \mathcal{T}$. In the definition of the E$^\gamma$-rule reported in Fig. 1 we have: (a) $\tau := \{x_1/x_{o_1}\ldots x_m/x_{o_m}\}$ is a substitution such that $x_1, \ldots, x_m$ are the quantified variables in ψ and $x_{o_1}, \ldots, x_{o_m} \in \mathsf{Var}_0(\Phi)$; (b) $\mathcal{S}^{\overline{\beta}_i\tau} := \{\overline{\beta}_1\tau, \ldots, \overline{\beta}_n\tau\} \setminus \{\overline{\beta}_i\tau\}$ is a set containing the complements of all the disjuncts $\beta_1, \ldots, \beta_n$ to which the substitution τ is applied, with the exception of the disjunct β_i.

$$\frac{\psi \qquad \mathcal{S}^{\overline{\beta}_i\tau}}{\beta_i\tau} \text{ E}^\gamma\text{-rule} \qquad\qquad \frac{}{A \mid \overline{A}} \text{ PB-rule}$$

where
$\psi = (\forall x_1)\ldots(\forall x_m)(\beta_1 \vee \ldots \vee \beta_n)$,
$\tau := \{x_1/x_{o_1}\ldots x_m/x_{o_m}\}$,
and $\mathcal{S}^{\overline{\beta}_i\tau} := \{\overline{\beta}_1\tau, \ldots, \overline{\beta}_n\tau\} \setminus \{\overline{\beta}_i\tau\}$,
for $i = 1, \ldots, n$

where A is a literal

Fig. 1. Expansion rules for the KE$^\gamma$-tableau.

Let $\mathcal{T}$ be a KE$^\gamma$-tableau. A formula $\psi = (\forall x_1)\ldots(\forall x_m)(\beta_1 \vee \ldots \vee \beta_n)$ is *fulfilled* in a branch ϑ, if ϑ contains $\beta_i\tau$ for some $i = 1, \ldots, n$ and for all τ having as domain the set $Q\mathsf{Var}_0(\psi) = \{x_1, \ldots, x_m\}$ of the quantified variables occurring in ψ and as range the set $\mathsf{Var}_0(\vartheta)$ of the variables of sort 0 occurring free in ϑ. Notice that since the procedure $Consistency\text{-}\mathcal{DL}^{4,\times}_D$ does not introduce any new variable, $\mathsf{Var}_0(\vartheta)$ coincides with $\mathsf{Var}_0(\phi_{\mathcal{KB}})$, for every branch ϑ. A branch ϑ is *fulfilled* if every formula $\psi = (\forall x_1)\ldots(\forall x_m)(\beta_1 \vee \ldots \vee \beta_n)$ occurring in ϑ is fulfilled. A KE$^\gamma$-tableau is *fulfilled* when all its branches are fulfilled. A branch

---

[3] KE-tableaux are a refutation system inspired to Smullyan's semantic tableaux [13] (see [10] for details).

ϑ of $\mathcal{T}$ is *closed* if either it contains both A and $\neg A$, for some formula A, or a literal of type $\neg(x = x)$; otherwise, it is *open*. A KE^γ-tableau is *closed* when all its branches are closed. A branch ϑ is *complete* if either it is closed or it is open, fulfilled, and it does not contain any literal of type $x = y$, with x and y distinct variables. A KE^γ-tableau is *complete* (resp., *fulfilled*) if all its branches are complete (resp., fulfilled or closed). The notions of branch and KE^γ-tableau *satisfiability* are the standard ones.

The procedure *Consistency-$\mathcal{DL}_\mathbf{D}^{4,\times}$* takes care of the literals of type $x = y$ occurring in the branches of $\mathcal{T}_{\mathcal{KB}}$ by constructing, for each open and fulfilled branch ϑ of $\mathcal{T}_{\mathcal{KB}}$, a substitution σ_ϑ such that $\vartheta\sigma_\vartheta$ does not contain literals of type $x = y$ with distinct x, y. Then, for every open and complete branch $\vartheta' := \vartheta\sigma_\vartheta$ of $\mathcal{T}_{\mathcal{KB}}$, the procedure *HOCQA$^\gamma$-$\mathcal{DL}_\mathbf{D}^{4,\times}$* constructs a decision tree $\mathcal{D}_{\vartheta'}$ whose maximal branches induce substitutions σ' such that $\sigma_\vartheta\sigma'$ belongs to the HO-answer set of ψ_Q with respect to $\phi_{\mathcal{KB}}$ (the definition of $\mathcal{D}_{\vartheta'}$ can be found in [5]).[4]

We recall that the HOCQA problem can be solved in exponential-time when the $\mathcal{DL}_\mathbf{D}^{4,\times}$-KBs do not contain qualified cardinality restrictions and role chain axioms, otherwise it can be solved in double-exponential time (see [5] for details).

Remarks on Different Versions of the Algorithm. The C++ implementation of the algorithm presented in this paper, called KE^γ-system, is more efficient than the prototype KE-system proposed in [4]. The main motivation behind this performance improvement relies on the introduction of the E^γ-rule (see Fig. 1) that acts on the $4LQS_{\mathcal{DL}_\mathbf{D}^{4,\times}}^R$-purely universal quantified formulae in the KB by systematically instantiating them and applying the standard E-rule (elimination rule) on-the-fly. The E^γ-rule replaces the preliminary phase of systematic expansion of the $4LQS_{\mathcal{DL}_\mathbf{D}^{4,\times}}^R$-purely universal quantified formulae in the KB and the subsequent application of the E-rule implemented by the KE-system presented in [3]. In addition, the KE^γ-system turns out be also more efficient than the implementation FO KE-system of the FO KE-tableau in [10], that applies the standard γ- and E-rules. Incidentally, it turns out that the KE-system and the FO KE-system have similar performances. As shown in [5, Fig. 3], the KE^γ-system has a better performance, up to about 400%, than the other two, even if in some cases (lowest part of the plot) the performances of the three systems are comparable. Thus the KE^γ-system is always convenient, also because the collection of the expansions of $\mathcal{DL}_\mathbf{D}^{4,\times}$-purely universal quantified formulae of level 1 (exponential in the size of the KB) is not stored in memory.

The benchmarking process is based on a huge amount of KBs of different sizes and kinds, constructed *ad hoc* just for the purpose of comparing the three mentioned systems, and on some real-world ontologies developed by the authors.

---

[4] The procedures *Consistency-$\mathcal{DL}_\mathbf{D}^{4,\times}$* and *HOCQA$^\gamma$-$\mathcal{DL}_\mathbf{D}^{4,\times}$* can be found in [5] together with their correctness, completeness, and termination proofs.

4   Conclusions and Future Work

We presented an improvement, called KE$^\gamma$-tableau, of the KE-tableau in [3] for the most widespread reasoning tasks for $\mathcal{DL}_\mathbf{D}^{4,\times}$-TBoxes and $\mathcal{DL}_\mathbf{D}^{4,\times}$–ABoxes. These reasoning problems are addressed by translating $\mathcal{DL}_\mathbf{D}^{4,\times}$-KBs and queries in terms of formulae of the set-theoretic language 4LQS$_{\mathcal{DL}_\mathbf{D}^{4,\times}}^R$. The procedure introduced in this paper generalizes the KE-elimination rule in such way as to incorporate the γ-rule, namely, the expansion rule for handling universally quantified formulae. The KE$^\gamma$-tableau procedure has remarkable aftermath, since its implementation is markedly more efficient in terms of space and execution time than the KE-system [4] and the implementation FO KE-system of the FO KE-tableau [10], as observed in our experimental tests.

In order to be able to reason with description logics admitting full existential and universal quantification, we plan to extend the set-theoretic fragment underpinning our reasoner with a restricted version of the operator of relational composition. Results and notions presented in [9] will be of inspiration for such a task. We also intend to improve our reasoner so as to deal with the reasoning problem of ontology classification. We shall compare the resulting reasoner with existing well-known reasoners such as Hermit [6] and Pellet [12], providing also some benchmarking. In addition, we plan to allow data type reasoning by either integrating existing solvers for the Satisfiability Modulo Theories (SMT) problem or by designing *ad hoc* new solvers. Finally, as each branch of a KE$^\gamma$-tableau can be independently computed by a single processing unit, we intend to implement a parallel version of the software by using the Nvidia CUDA framework.

References

1. Cantone, D., Nicolosi-Asmundo, M.: On the satisfiability problem for a 4-level quantified syllogistic and some applications to modal logic. Fundamenta Informaticae **124**(4), 427–448 (2013)
2. Cantone, D., Nicolosi-Asmundo, M., Santamaria, D.F.: Conjunctive query answering via a fragment of set theory. In: Proceedings of ICTCS 2016, Lecce, 7–9 September, vol. 1720, pp. 23–35. CEUR-WS (2016)
3. Cantone, D., Nicolosi-Asmundo, M., Santamaria, D.F.: A set-theoretic approach to abox reasoning services. In: Costantini, S., Franconi, E., Van Woensel, W., Kontchakov, R., Sadri, F., Roman, D. (eds.) RuleML+RR 2017. LNCS, vol. 10364, pp. 87–102. Springer, Cham (2017). https://doi.org/10.1007/978-3-319-61252-2_7
4. Cantone, D., Nicolosi-Asmundo, M., Santamaria, D.F.: A C++ reasoner for the description logic $\mathcal{DL}_\mathbf{D}^{4,\times}$. In: Proceedings of CILC 2017, Naples, Italy, 26–29 September 2017, vol. 1949, pp. 276–280. CEUR WS (2017). ISSN 1613-0073
5. Cantone, D., Nicolosi-Asmundo, M., Santamaria, D.F.: An optimized KE-tableau-based system for reasoning in the description logic $\mathcal{DL}_\mathbf{D}^{4,\times}$. CoRR, 1804.11222 (2018). Extended version
6. Glimm, B., Horrocks, I., Motik, B., Stoilos, G., Wang, Z.: HermiT: an OWL 2 reasoner. J. Autom. Reason. **53**(3), 245–269 (2014)

7. Horrocks, I., Kutz, O., Sattler, U.: The even more irresistible SROIQ. In: Doherty, P., Mylopoulos, J., Welty, C.A. (eds.) Proceedings of 10th International Conference on Principle of Knowledge Representation and Reasoning, pp. 57–67. AAAI Press (2006)

8. Krötzsch, M.: OWL 2 profiles: an introduction to lightweight ontology languages. In: Eiter, T., Krennwallner, T. (eds.) Reasoning Web 2012. LNCS, vol. 7487, pp. 112–183. Springer, Heidelberg (2012). https://doi.org/10.1007/978-3-642-33158-9_4

9. Cristiá, M., Rossi, G.: A decision procedure for restricted intensional sets. In: de Moura, L. (ed.) CADE 2017. LNCS, vol. 10395, pp. 185–201. Springer, Cham (2017). https://doi.org/10.1007/978-3-319-63046-5_12

10. Mondadori, M., D'Agostino, M.: The taming of the cut. Classical refutations with analytic cut. J. Logic Comput. 4, 285–319 (1994)

11. Motik, B., Horrocks, I.: OWL datatypes: design and implementation. In: Sheth, A., et al. (eds.) ISWC 2008. LNCS, vol. 5318, pp. 307–322. Springer, Heidelberg (2008). https://doi.org/10.1007/978-3-540-88564-1_20

12. Sirin, E., Parsia, B., Grau, B.C., Kalyanpur, A., Katz, Y.: Pellet: a practical OWL-DL reasoner. J. Web Semant. 5(2), 51–53 (2007)

13. Smullyan, R.M.: First-order Logic. Dover Books on Advanced Mathematics. Dover, New York (1995)

A Case-Based Inquiry into the Decision Model and Notation (DMN) and the Knowledge Base (KB) Paradigm

Marjolein Deryck[1(✉)], Faruk Hasić[2], Jan Vanthienen[2], and Joost Vennekens[1]

[1] Department of Computer Science, KU Leuven, Campus De Nayer,
Sint-Katelijne-Waver, Belgium
{marjolein.deryck,joost.vennekens}@kuleuven.be
[2] Department of Decision Sciences and Information Management,
KU Leuven, Leuven, Belgium
{faruk.hasic,jan.vanthienen}@kuleuven.be

Abstract. Modelling decisions in organisations is a challenging task. Deciding which modelling language to use for the problem at hand is a fundamental question. We investigate the Decision Model and Notation (DMN) standard and the IDP knowledge base system (KBS) in their effectiveness to model and solve specific real-life case problems. This paper presents two cases that are solved with DMN and IDP: (1) Income taxation for foreign artists temporarily working in Belgium; and (2) Registration duties when purchasing real-estate in Belgium. DMN is used as a front-end method, assisting the business analyst in the analysis and modelling of the business domain and communication with the domain expert. It is complemented with the representation of the logic in IDP as back-end system, which allows more forms of inference.

Keywords: Decision modelling · Decision Model and Notation
DMN · Knowledge base paradigm · IDP

1 Introduction

Today companies face a high level of complexity: omnichannel distribution, geographical dispersion, customised product offers, customer's pressure for short delivery cycles, etc. Moreover, regulations on topics like reporting (e.g., Sarbanes-Oxley Act), consumer data processing (e.g., EU General Data Protection Regulation), product quality (e.g., EU General Product Safety Directive) are becoming ever more stringent [1–3]. To top it all off, these challenges are in themselves subject to rapid change. In light of this complex, changing and highly demanding environment, coherent, traceable and adaptable operational decisions are a must. Consequently, automated correctness and consistency checking should be common practice [4]. In practice, however, the bulk of business knowledge exists only in informal policies, operating procedures, the source code of legacy systems,

© Springer Nature Switzerland AG 2018
C. Benzmüller et al. (Eds.): RuleML+RR 2018, LNCS 11092, pp. 248–263, 2018.
https://doi.org/10.1007/978-3-319-99906-7_17

system parameters or even in experts' heads [4,5]. In other words, a separate database of business rules that can be maintained and managed as a whole, is rare. This is surprising, as there exists a large variety of business rule methods and tools. Perhaps a lack of insight in the applicability and pros and cons of these methods can explain this enigma. Or perhaps the ideal method, that combines user-friendliness with versatile use is lacking up to now. In this paper we investigate the combination of two decision logic methods: Decision Modelling (DM) that excels in user friendliness, and the Knowledge Base Paradigm (KBP) that excels in versatility. In two case studies we apply both methods and evaluate their respective contributions. Both methods describe the problem domain, each in their own way, without imposing a particular execution strategy on this knowledge. By separating the business knowledge from the execution procedure they produce models that are more easily readable and adjustable, which improves the agility of the business logic.

For decision modelling we use Decision Model and Notation (DMN), a standard published by the Object Management Group (OMG) [6]. Because of the intuitive graphical notation, decisions in DMN format can easily be read and validated by business users. The KBP-system IDP uses a derivative of First Order Logic (FO(.)) to formalise knowledge of the problem domain. Afterwards different algorithms use this information to find suitable solutions for the user. As such the use of the KBP offers a company the possibility to use the information in ways that were perhaps not envisaged beforehand [7].

This paper is structured as follows. In Sect. 2, relevant work on decision modelling and knowledge representation is discussed. Section 3 presents two real-life cases that are solved with DMN and IDP, while Sect. 4 outlines advantages and disadvantages of each approach and provides a broader discussion on the comparison between the two paradigms, i.e. the decision modelling paradigm and the knowledge base paradigm. Finally, Sect. 5 provides conclusions and directions for future research.

2 Decision Modelling and the Knowledge Base Paradigm

For our case studies we selected DMN and KBP as methods to model the decision logic. Both methods are declarative in nature, meaning that only what needs to be achieved is formalised, but not how this should be done.

2.1 Decision Modelling

An increased interest in modelling decision is present in scientific work in the field of process management, as illustrated by the body of recent literature on Decision Model and Notation (DMN) [6,8–11]. DMN is a declarative decision language and it does not provide a decision resolution mechanism, which is left to the invoking context. The same holds for the processing and storage of outputs and intermediate results. With this recently introduced OMG standard for modelling decisions, it has become possible to extract decisions from processes and to model them separately according to the *Separation of Concerns* paradigm, hence enhancing the understandability, scalability, and maintainability of processes, as well as that of the underlying decisions [12–15]. DMN consists of two levels. First, the decision requirement level takes the form of a Decision Requirement Diagram (DRD) that depicts decisions and subdecisions, business knowledge models, input data, and knowledge sources. It is used to portray the requirements of decisions and the dependencies between the different constructs in the decision model. Second, the decision logic level is used to specify the underlying decision logic. It is usually represented in the form of decision tables. The standard also provides a formal expression language FEEL (Friendly Enough Expression Language) that allows the execution of decision tables on a decision engine, as well as boxed expressions and a metamodel and schema. Decision tables are considered the core concept of DMN, and they contain the necessary information to automate decision-making. The DRD is mainly used to get a high-level understanding of the structure of the problem domain, but does not contain additional information.

Literature has focused mainly on the integration of decision and process models, as well as on decision services based on DMN [8,14,16,17]. Little attention is given to the interaction of DMN with other paradigms, e.g. the knowledge base paradigm [9]. This paper aims at closing that gap in the following sections.

2.2 Knowledge Representation and Reasoning

The field of Knowledge Representation and Reasoning offers many different approaches and systems. In this paper, we have chosen to make use of the IDP system, a state-of-the-art implementation of the Knowledge Base Paradigm [7,18]. IDP allows domain knowledge to be expressed in the FO(.) language, a rich, typed extension of classical logic. It then allows a variety of different inference tasks to be applied to such a knowledge base. Probably the most used inference task is that of *model expansion*: given an interpretation I for part of the vocabulary of a given theory T, the IDP system is asked to compute a interpretation J for the remaining part of the vocabulary such that the two interpretations together satisfy the theory, i.e., $I \cup J \models T$.

For instance, in order to compute a coloring of a graph, we might consider the typed vocabulary consisting of types *Node* and *Color*, the relation *Edge(Node, Node)* and the function *Color* : *Node* → *Color*. We can then express the required domain knowledge by the theory T that consists of the following formula, stating that two connected nodes must have a different color:

$$\forall x\, y : Edge(x,y) \Rightarrow Color(x) \neq Color(y).$$

We can then provide the IDP system with an interpretation I for the types $Node$ and $Color$, and the predicate $Edge$, e.g.:

$$Node^I = \{A, B, C\}$$
$$Color^I = \{R, G, B\}$$
$$Edge^I = \{(A, B), (B, C), (A, C)\}$$

and ask it to compute an interpretation J for the function $Color$ such that $I \cup J \models T$. Alternatively, we may also provide an interpretation for the function $Color$ and ask IDP to compute a corresponding interpretation for the relation $Edge$; in other words, the same IDP theory can be used for different input/output behaviors. The IDP systems contains a number of different algorithms and techniques from domains such as Answer Set Programming, Constraint Programming and Logic Programming that allow it to efficiently implement this flexible behavior.

In addition to model expansion, IDP also allows other inference tasks to be solved for a given theory. For instance, it also supports the task of *optimising* the value of a given term. If we consider the term $\#\{x : Color(x) = R\}$, which represents the cardinality of the set of nodes that are red, we can ask IDP to compute not just any model expansion of the theory T and a particular input interpretation I, but the model expansion J for which the interpretation t^J of this term t is minimal. In this way, we compute the graph coloring in which as few nodes as possible are colored red.

As a final example, we mention the inference task of *propagation*: given an input interpretation I and a theory T, compute all of the consequences of I according to T, formally defined as the set of all atomic properties that are either true in all model expansions of T in I, or false in all of them. Informally this means that, given an input interpretation I, forced and forbidden values are derived and uncertain values are reported.

3   Case Studies

In this section we provide two case studies that have been tackled by both decision modelling and knowledge representation. The first case deals with income tax policies for visiting artists in Belgium and is implemented in the Avola decision management tool. The second case concerns registration duties when buying property in Belgium. It is implemented in the open source tool OpenRules. This tool is Excel-based, which is an advantage for the notary who is already familiar with the spreadsheet program. For both cases, the advantages and disadvantages of each solution are elaborated upon.

3.1   Income Tax Management

Background. Like researchers, artists often travel to other countries to present their work. They are remunerated in the country where they perform, which raises questions regarding income taxation. The legislation on income tax for these specific situations is quite complex, and so are the double taxation agreements between different countries, as they all tend to differ from each other quite significantly. Hence, there is a need for transparency, not only for the artists who need to know how much they can earn, where to file for taxes and under which tariffs, but also for arts and culture institutions inviting foreign artists to their country, production studios invoking the help of foreign artists in their productions, and even government employees charged with tax collection. A decision model can be offered as a service to all parties involved in the tax management problem: government agencies, artists subject to taxation, production studios, and arts and culture institutions and federations. This case was put forward by oKo, a Belgian industry federation for the arts, and was carried out in collaboration with Avola, a decision management tool vendor. The problem was modelled in the Avola tool and implemented as a web service.

Decision Modelling. The resulting DMN model distinguishes eight core decisions needed for the implementation of the tax regulations. A simple decision requirements model can be found in Fig. 1. `Income Tax` is the top-level decision and it provides the category of income tax that the travelling artist belongs to, e.g. fully taxable, not taxable, partially taxable, or specific tax rates. `Subsidised Exemption` determines whether the artist can enjoy tax exemptions based on subsidies allocated to the artist's organisation by the government. `Individual Exemption` investigates whether the artist can enjoy tax exemptions based on his personal situation, e.g. depending on the number of full time equivalent days that he worked in the country of the performance. `Organisational Exemption` determines whether the artist can enjoy tax exemptions based on potential special treatments and agreements that the artist's working organisation enjoys from the government of the country of performance. `Fiscal Articles` figures out which fiscal articles are applicable to the artist. `Double Tax Agreement` indicates the logic and the rates of the double tax agreement between the originating country and the country of performance. `Initiation of Double Tax Agreement` gives the date of validity of the double tax agreement between the originating country and the country of performance. Finally, `Application Area` evaluates whether the time the artist worked in the country he visited falls under a period of double tax agreements between the artist's country of origin and the country of performance.

Followed Approach. The information relevant for the tax decision is available in the form of law texts and procedures. Hence we primarily need to construct decision tables from the textual descriptions. The decision tables can then be checked for completeness, correctness and possible contradictions. After this post processing step, the decision tables can be simplified and represented in an unambiguous manner.

However, the legal texts were not sufficient to model the tax management problem, as they are at times rather complex to understand without the necessary legal training. The modellers have an information systems background

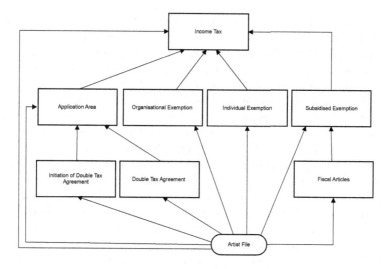

Fig. 1. Tax management decision model.

and not a legal one. Therefore, the models obtained from the texts were built in close interaction with domain experts. In a dialogue mode, the modeller and the experts gradually discover relevant criteria and outcomes and refine the tables until a full description of the decision logic is obtained. For this tax management problem, we had multiple iterative meetings to validate, amend, clarify, and improve the decision logic obtained in the modelling cycles from the law texts. The knowledge authorities that were consulted are legal experts attached to either a Belgian industry federation for performing artists or the ministry of culture and media. The experts in both industry and government provided valuable input towards understanding all legal requirements specified in laws, tax agreements, and government policies. This ensured the correct translation of legal requirements into decision rules.

Hence, this decision elicitation process happened in an iterative manner in the following steps:

1. Obtain conditions, condition intervals and outcomes of the law texts.
2. Formalise the conditions and outcomes into decision rules.
3. Aggregate the specified rules into decision tables.
4. Check for completeness, correctness and contradictions.
5. Simplify the decision table and display it.
6. Present the decision tables to the domain expert for validation.
7. If needed, go back to the previous steps until a full description of the decision logic is obtained that is validated by the domain experts.

Especially Step 6 is an important step to ensure correct interpretation of law texts, i.e., using decision tables as a communication tool for logic discussion and validation with domain experts. This is due to the fact that decision tables are relatively easy to read and to understand, even for non-expert decision modellers.

Evaluation. Based on the decision model, the Avola decision management tool allowed us to easily deploy a decision web service that returns the decision outcome of the top-level decision *Income Tax* given a number of input data entries provided by the user of the service. This service can be used by artists to query in which income tax category they belong, by industry organisations and production houses that wish to employ foreign performing artists, as well as by government employees for decision support in tax collection. That way, tax rule compliance becomes transparent to all parties and ambiguities are avoided. We briefly sum up the data input fields needed for the service invocation: the country in which the artist is performing (currently only implemented for Belgium), the origin country of the performing artist, type of legal personality of the organisation or artist, the origin country of the performing organisation, income earned by the artist in the visiting country in the past year, whether all performing artists of the performance share the same origin country within the organisation, date of performance, whether the artist resided for more than 183 days over the past year in the country that he is visiting, the country of fiscal domicile of the artist, and the percentage of government subsidies allocated to the performance. Based on these ten input values, the web service invokes its underlying decision model and returns the tax policy category.

In analogy with the model constructed for Belgium, the service can be expanded for other countries of the European Union and offered in different languages. Currently, oKo is looking to share this model with the European industry federation which will then disseminate the approach to all national and regional industry federations in order to achieve unanimity in tax transparency across the European Union.

Knowledge Representation. Once the DMN tables were completed, they were used as starting point for the development of the knowledge base in IDP. The lessons learned from this case are overlapping with the lessons learned from the next case, and will be presented there.

3.2 Registration Duties

Background. When purchasing real-estate in Belgium, registration duties must be paid. Duties differ between regions and may deviate depending on characteristics of the buyer, the property, the seller and the location of the real-estate. The decision model of the applicable law needs to translate all legal requirements in a user-friendly, comprehensible overview. As some of the exemptions are not cumulative, the implementation should allow for the optimisation of the amount to be paid. It should also avoid asking the user for information that is difficult to retrieve, if it is already clear from the available information that an exemption cannot be granted. Therefore the system should allow flexible and minimal information input. The request for this application originated from a notary's office, with the explicit demand to focus on exceptional cases and on reasoning with partial information.

Decision Modelling. The calculation of registration fees depends on multiple sub-decisions: the value of the property taking into account possible discounts, called *abattement*, the applicable tax rate, and portability of earlier paid registration duties. The use of the DRD to have a visual overview of the different sub-decisions and their dependencies is a convenient starting point to understand the problem at hand, and to structure the development of both the decision tables and the IDP model.

Followed Approach. OpenRules was used as decision engine as it is available for free and has a low entry effort because it is based on Microsoft Excel files. Although the development of a DRD is recommended as a first step, the program itself does not contain DRD-drawing functionalities. The DRD can be included in the executable file as documentation, but this is optional as the DRD does not impact execution. For this case, multiple overview models with different levels of granularity were developed. At first a rather high-level DRD (upper right panel of Fig. 2) was developed.

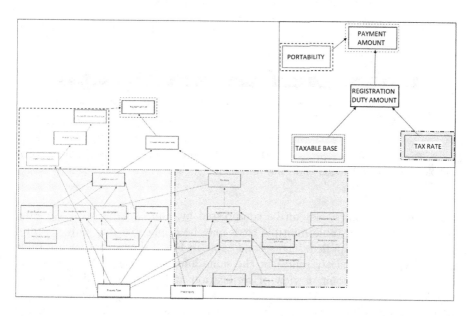

Fig. 2. DRD registration duties with abstract (top right) and expanded (bottom left) view.

The advantage of this figure is its simplicity: for readers it is easy to understand which elements impact the the registration duties. However, the abstraction level is too high to use it as a practical input for the decision tables. Therefore a second DRD with all decision nodes was developed (see left panel of Fig. 2). Although this one is complete, it loses the advantage of comprehensibility of the high level model. Of course both DRDs are interrelated in the sense that the elaborate DRD detailed the decisions that were captured in one decision node in the high level DRD. It is an intuitive extension of the DMN standard to expand the abstract top right DRD in the bottom left finer-grained DRD.

Next, the decision tables were constructed. Each row describes a combination of conditions, i.e., one condition per column (*if* or *condition* column) that all need to be applicable, and leads to one or multiple output columns (*then* or *conclusion* columns). It is considered a good design principle to represent all possible combinations and to ensure mutual exclusivity of all rows, which results in single hit tables with the *Unique* hit policy [19]. The relevant legislation identifies several discounts which are each applicable in a specific situation that is characterised by a conjunction of multiple conditions. In this case, tables with the *Unique* hit policy become long and triangularly filled, as shown by the upper table in Fig. 3. An empty cell in such a table means that any value can be chosen.

DecisionTable RenovationAbattement				
If	If	If	If	Then
DestinyPurchase	RegistrationDateNeglectedHouse	Domicile	DwellingNaturalPerson	RenovationAbattement
no habitation				
social habitation				0
habitation	> PurchaseDate - 40000			
	<= PurchaseDate - 40000	N		
		Y	N	
			Y	30000

DecisionTable RenovationAbattement				
If	If	If	If	Then
DestinyPurchase	RegistrationDateNeglectedHouse	Domicile	DwellingNaturalPerson	RenovationAbattement
habitation	<= PurchaseDate - 40000	Y	Y	30000
				0

Fig. 3. Decision Tables representing the same logic to grant a renovation abattement modelled with resp. Unique and First hit policy.

Alternatively this table can be compressed by using a table with the *First* hit policy. In such a table multiple rows may be applicable, but only the first of these is actually applied. The second table in Fig. 3 shows that such a table can be used to compactly represent the same information as in the first table. However, from the point of view of verification and validation this solution is considered bad practice. At one hand the use of *First* hit policy means that the order of the rows in the table affects its correctness. At the other hand the use of a blank row always leads to a complete table, but prevents the detection of missing combinations in the other rules of the table. The explicit assignment of hit policies is not possible in OpenRules, but the execution of single hit tables finishes after a hit is found, i.e. de facto first hit policy.

Evaluation. The *First* hit policy can be used to create concise and easily readable tables. Users should be aware that DMN offers more possible hit policies, and that the use of *First* hit policy is debatable, as this complicates the (visual) consistency and completeness checking of tables [19]. Moreover, it goes against the declarative assertion of DMN, because it means that the order in which conditions are checked is relevant [20].

OpenRules evaluates tables in a context-dependent way. For instance, to determine if a buyer can register for *modest housing*, a certain condition must be checked for all previously acquired properties of the buyers. This is modelled with an iterate table. For each property some information is introduced, e.g., if it is a plot or a house, and the value assigned to the real-estate, called *cadastral income*. This information is also needed for the actual purchase itself. The same variable name can be used in both situations and the meaning is derived from the context. It is not possible to refer specifically to the *cadastral income* of a particular property.

OpenRules executes the specified rules in a predefined order. When information is missing, the output value will be put at −1. Rules that can be executed with the available information will be executed, which may lead to a solution that simply ignores unknown facts. Although this way of working might be desirable in some situations, it does not comply with the way the notary wants to use partial information. He prefers to use available information to narrow down the complete domain of possible solutions, keeping visible other options on which no information is currently available.

The decision tables were instrumental to make sure the complex juridical jargon was understood correctly, as the tables are easily readable by domain experts. From the modeller's point of view it was easy to start creating the application, as it is straightforward for (business) people familiar with Excel. The possibility to reuse the outcome from one table in others is essential for this. The requirement to formalise all variables in a glossary helps to keep overview.

The data modelled in OpenRules can be used to find a solution based on the available inputs. A distinction is made between input variables, internal variables (i.e. intermediate results), and output variables. The value of an internal variable cannot be forced manually. Instead, values provided for internal or output variables will be checked against the calculated outcome, and deviations will be reported as an error. The format allows manual checks for correctness and completeness and proves to be useful in the process of knowledge elicitation. DMN tables in theory allow for reverse reasoning from output to input variables, but this functionality is not supported by OpenRules. The optimisation of registration rights is done by introducing different variables for the different options and comparing them in a later stage, as demonstrated in Fig. 4.

Knowledge Representation. As the functions of reasoning with partial information and optimisation of registration rights that are important for the notary's office are not performed satisfactorily by OpenRules, we also tried to use the IDP-system.

DecisionTable RegistrationDutiesAbattement
Action
RegistrationDutiesAbattement
(PurchasePrice - Abattement - AdditionalAbattement - RenovationAbattement) * TaxRate/100

DecisionTable RegistrationDutiesPortability
Action
RegistrationDutiesPortability
((PurchasePrice - RenovationAbattement) * TaxRate/100) - TotalPortability

DecisionTable Advice	
Condition	Message
RegistrationDutiesAbattement	**Explanation**
>	Use Portability
< RegistrationDutiesPortability	Use Abattement
=	Use Portability or Abattement

Fig. 4. Optimisation in OpenRules.

Followed Approach. The DMN tables were transferred to IDP-definitions one by one. Here the definition of default values was used frequently. For instance, the table in Fig. 3 was formulated as:

{ RenovationAbattement = -30000 ← DestinyPurchase = habitation &
　　　　　　　　　　　　RegistrationDateNeglectedHouse ≥ PurchaseDate - 40000 &
　　　　　　　　　　　　Domicile &
　　　　　　　　　　　　DwellingNaturalPerson.
RenovationAbattement = 0 ← RenovationAbattement ≠ -30000. }

This results in a correct and concise representation. With *model expansion* all models that comply with the given information can be obtained. To handle the requirements of reasoning with incomplete information, we used the approach from [9]. The inference task *propagation* is used to derive all consequences of the information that is already available. Based on this, the GUI shown in Fig. 5 is updated: mandatory values are highlighted in green and impossible values in red. As long as no colour is assigned, information relevant for this decision is missing. The translation of variable types from OpenRules to IDP can happen in multiple ways. Consider for instance the *cadastral income* of a specific property: It was captured as the variable Ki in OpenRules, and depending on the context this pointed to the Ki of the current purchase, or the Ki of previously acquired real estate. In IDP this can be solved by creating a function that maps all properties to their *cadastral income*, as shown in the right panel of Fig. 5. This option seems logically consistent, but it could lead to the use of (less preferred) partial functions for attributes of the property that are relevant for the current purchase but not for the other real estate. A way to circumvent this, is to create a function specifically for previously acquired real estate, and to create an additional constant to reflect the *cadastral income* of the current purchase, as shown in the left panel of Fig. 5. It has an additional advantage of a clearer distinction between data from both types of purchases. The effect of this choice on the GUI is shown in the screenshots below.

Another form inference that was used is the *optimisation* of selected terms. In many cases buyers want to minimise current total registration duty payment. This can be done by minimising following term:

$termRegistrationPayment : V\{(BaseAmount * TaxRate) - TotalPortability\}$

It is possible to create other terms to optimise other criteria.

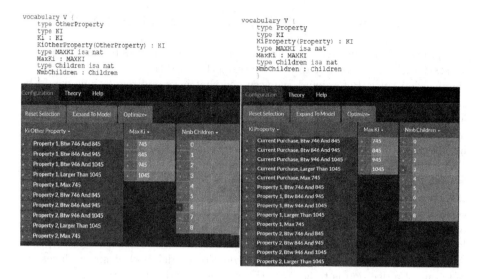

Fig. 5. Translation of variables and impact on interface.

Evaluation. The fact that the analysis of the problem domain was already done with the DMN-tables allowed the modeller to focus exclusively on the formulation in the FO(.) language. Therefore the development of the IDP model was relatively easy. The GUI is derived automatically from the IDP model and requires no extra work. The interface in which the propagation of available information is visible, is perceived as very user friendly. The notary sees at a glance which information needs to be requested from the buyer, and which information is superfluous. Therefore the application provides useful support during client meetings. Further improvements in usability can be obtained by further exploring the possibilities of separated vocabularies. For the discounts for modest housing, *abattement* and portability certain settlement restrictions are in place. These restrictions differ slightly for the different discounts. As a result three variables with almost the same name are created. By working with different vocabularies groups of related variables can be grouped together, making it easier to visually relate the correct settlement variable with the intended concept.

Inherent to the concept of a KBS is the absence of a distinction between input and output variables. Besides the different inference possibilities this also means in this case that variables referred to as *internal* by OpenRules can be selected manually. An example is the definition of a professional seller. If this is a large organisation or a frequent client of the notary, the notary probably knows it is a professional seller without checking the different conditions. However, for a new professional buyer/seller the determination of the legal statute should happen by defining the prerequisite conditions. IDP allows the notary to choose if he wants to manually select the value *Professional Buyer*, or if he wants to check the preconditions.

4   Insights on the Modelling and Usage of DMN and IDP

By applying DMN and KRR in these two cases, some insights became apparent. To start with, it turned out to be less straightforward than expected to describe the decision rules. Beforehand, we assumed that laws and regulations would be easy to formalise as they state clear rules. In practice, however, laws are often formulated cryptically and vaguely, which make them hard to understand for unversed readers and open to interpretation. Law rulings may give or change such interpretations, which makes legislation a living matter rather than a fixed fact. Changes and exceptions occur most often at a detailed level. Another difficulty is that rules that apply to a subject are often impacted by rules that apply to the group of which the subject is part, e.g., an artist's taxation depends on the company. This phenomenon occurs in both cases studies. The general structure of the decision tree is not immediately impacted, but at the most fine-grained level the number of columns in decision tables tends to expand for each exception. As living matter, the exceptions are hardest to model, and at some places the outcome of a decision is to check with an expert. Sadly, the largest added value of an automated system would be to give a certain decision for these difficult cases. The conclusion from the case studies suggests that rule-based systems for legislation should either be conceived as decision support systems, or that experts themselves should continue to model their knowledge for the very exceptional cases. It also suggests that the quality and consistency of law texts could benefit from the use of decision tables in their creation process.

Another concern from a modelling point of view is the use of the DRDs in DMN. Currently the modeller has the choice between a high level DRD that shows the large structure of the problem domain at a glance, and a detailed DRD that can be used as the basis for the decision tables. Although a mapping between these two levels is possible, it would be a natural extension of DMN to have a separate notation for high level decision nodes that can be expanded into lower level decisions, analogous to the formulation of sub-processes in BPMN [21].

IDP and DMN prove to be rather compatible as DMN decision tables can be used as a starting point for the creation of IDP rules. We consider this good practice as DMN tables allow for the verification and validation of decision rules, e.g., identifying missing or overlapping rules [22,23]. IDP, however, does not provide such verification and validation mechanisms. Rather, in IDP errors need to be discovered by checking the different solutions. Another incentive to start from DMN when building IDP rules is that DMN, unlike IDP, boasts a visual notation that is understandable to the domain experts. As such, DMN decision tables can be used as a means of communication between the modeller and the domain experts for the purpose of decision rule checking and validation as often proved necessary in our two case studies.

When it comes to the use of DMN and IDP, both are declarative, which means that they are not reserved for a specific inference form. However, DMN tool developers usually stick to simple forward chaining approaches with complete and correct input data, thus only answering a single question: given the input data, what is the outcome of the top-level decision? The DMN standard [6] allows for the use of different inference strategies, with missing data or top-down approaches such as backward chaining. Until now, the implementation of such inference strategies is largely lacking. In IDP, on the other hand, more algorithms have been developed to allow different forms of inference and answer different kind of questions based on the same model.

5 Conclusion and Future Work

In this paper, we have assessed the use of the Decision Model and Notation (DMN) and the Knowledge Base (KB) paradigm in the form of IDP through two case studies. Takeaways on the modelling and the use of both DMN and IDP were inferred from the case studies: (1) Income taxation for foreign artists temporarily working in Belgium; and (2) Registration duties when purchasing real-estate in Belgium. Based on these case studies, the advantages, disadvantages, as well as synergies of DMN and IDP were discussed. The analysis shows that both DMN and IDP are very suitable when it comes to solving decision-dependent problems and that DMN and IDP are often similar and compatible with each other. However, some dissimilarities were identified as well, as DMN and IDP are not always usable for the same kind of problem solving.

In future work, we will analyse to which extent the existing DMN tools adhere to the DMN standard by assessing their level of support of DMN features and concepts relating to the decision requirements diagram, decision logic specifications and the (S)FEEL expression language. Additionally, we will look into the automatised transformation of DMN decision tables into IDP rules. Finally, we will focus on the complexity of DMN decision models in relation to their granularity, i.e. a trade off between large DRD models accompanied by smaller decision tables versus simpler DRD models with larger and more complex decision tables at their core.

Acknowledgements. We would like to thank Avola for giving us access to their decision management tool and the following case study participants for their assistance with the analysis, interpretation and completion of the case studies: the Belgian industry federation for the arts (oKo), Kunstenloket, and notary Van Pelt.

References

1. Trunomi: GDPR Portal. https://www.eugdpr.org/
2. 107th Congress: Public law 107–204. https://www.gpo.gov/fdsys/pkg/PLAW-107publ204/html/PLAW-107publ204.htm
3. European Commission: General Product Safety Directive. https://ec.europa.eu/info/general-product-safety-directive_en
4. Mitra, S., Chittimalli, P.K.: A systematic review of methods for consistency checking in SBVR-based business rules. In: CEUR Workshop Proceedings, vol. 1819. CEUR-WS.org (2017)
5. Nelson, M.L., Peterson, J., Rariden, R.L., Sen, R.: Transitioning to a business rule management service model: case studies from the property and casualty insurance industry. Inf. Manag. **47**(1), 30–41 (2010)

6. OMG: Decision Model and Notation 1.1 (2016)
7. Denecker, M., Vennekens, J.: Building a knowledge base system for an integration of logic programming and classical logic. In: Garcia de la Banda, M., Pontelli, E. (eds.) ICLP 2008. LNCS, vol. 5366, pp. 71–76. Springer, Heidelberg (2008). https://doi.org/10.1007/978-3-540-89982-2_12
8. Hasić, F., Devadder, L., Dochez, M., Hanot, J., De Smedt, J., Vanthienen, J.: Challenges in refactoring processes to include decision modelling. In: Teniente, E., Weidlich, M. (eds.) BPM 2017. LNBIP, vol. 308, pp. 529–541. Springer, Cham (2018). https://doi.org/10.1007/978-3-319-74030-0_42
9. Dasseville, I., Janssens, L., Janssens, G., Vanthienen, J., Denecker, M.: Combining DMN and the knowledge base paradigm for flexible decision enactment. In: RuleML 2016 Supplementary Proceedings (2016)
10. De Smedt, J., Hasić, F., vanden Broucke, S.K.L.M., Vanthienen, J.: Towards a holistic discovery of decisions in process-aware information systems. In: Carmona, J., Engels, G., Kumar, A. (eds.) BPM 2017. LNCS, vol. 10445, pp. 183–199. Springer, Cham (2017). https://doi.org/10.1007/978-3-319-65000-5_11
11. Horita, F.E., de Albuquerque, J.P., Marchezini, V., Mendiondo, E.M.: Bridging the gap between decision-making and emerging big data sources: an application of a model-based framework to disaster management in brazil. Decis. Support Syst. **97**, 12–22 (2017)
12. Biard, T., Le Mauff, A., Bigand, M., Bourey, J.-P.: Separation of decision modeling from business process modeling using new decision model and notation (DMN) for automating operational decision-making. In: Camarinha-Matos, L.M., Bénaben, F., Picard, W. (eds.) PRO-VE 2015. IAICT, vol. 463, pp. 489–496. Springer, Cham (2015). https://doi.org/10.1007/978-3-319-24141-8_45
13. Hu, J., Aghakhani, G., Hasić, F., Serral, E.: An evaluation framework for design-time context-adaptation of process modelling languages. In: Poels, G., Gailly, F., Serral Asensio, E., Snoeck, M. (eds.) PoEM 2017. LNBIP, vol. 305, pp. 112–125. Springer, Cham (2017). https://doi.org/10.1007/978-3-319-70241-4_8
14. Hasić, F., De Smedt, J., Vanthienen, J.: Augmenting processes with decision intelligence: principles for integrated modelling. Decis. Support Syst. **107**, 1–12 (2018)
15. Hasić, F., De Smedt, J., Vanthienen, J.: An illustration of five principles for integrated Process and Decision Modelling (5PDM). Technical report, KU Leuven (2017)
16. Boumahdi, F., Chalal, R., Guendouz, A., Gasmia, K.: Soa^{+d}: a new way to design the decision in soa-based on the new standard decision model and notation (DMN). Serv. Oriented Comput. Appl. **10**(1), 35–53 (2016)
17. Hasić, F., De Smedt, J., Vanthienen, J.: A service-oriented architecture design of decision-aware information systems: decision as a service. In: Panetto, H. (ed.) OTM 2017. LNCS, vol. 10573, pp. 353–361. Springer, Cham (2017). https://doi.org/10.1007/978-3-319-69462-7_23
18. de Cat, B., Bogaerts, B., Bruynooghe, M., Denecker, M.: Predicate logic as a modelling language: the IDP system. CoRR abs/1401.6312 (2014)
19. Vanthienen, J., Dries, E.: Developments in decision tables: evolution, applications and a proposed standard. DTEW Research report 9227, pp. 1–40 (1992)
20. Silver, B.: DMN Method and Style. Cody-Cassidy Press, Aptos, p. 305 (2016)

21. OMG: Business process model and notation (BPMN) 2.0 (2011)
22. Vanthienen, J., Dries, E.: Illustration of a decision table tool for specifying and implementing knowledge based systems. Int. J. Artif. Intell. Tools **3**(2), 267–288 (1994)
23. Calvanese, D., Dumas, M., Laurson, Ü., Maggi, F.M., Montali, M., Teinemaa, I.: Semantics, analysis and simplification of DMN decision tables. Inf. Syst. (2018)

Rule-Based Drawing, Analysis and Generation of Graphs Applied to Mason's Mark Design

Thom Frühwirth[✉]

Ulm University, Ulm, Germany
thom.fruehwirth@uni-ulm.de
http://www.informatik.uni-ulm.de/pm/fileadmin/pm/home/fruehwirth/

Abstract. We are developing a rule-based implementation of a tool to analyse and generate graphs. It is used in the domain of mason's marks. For thousands of years, stonemasons have been inscribing these symbolic signs on dressed stone. Geometrically, mason's marks are line drawings. They consist of a pattern of straight lines, sometimes circles and arcs. We represent mason's marks by connected planar graphs.

Our prototype tool for analysis and generation of graphs is written in the rule-based declarative language Constraint Handling Rules. It features

- a vertex-centric logical graph representation as constraints,
- derivation of properties and statistics from graphs,
- recognition of (sub)graphs and patterns in a graph,
- automatic generation of graphs from given constrained subgraphs,
- drawing graphs by visualization using scalable vector graphics.

In particular, we started to use the tool to classify and to invent mason's marks. In principle, our tool can be applied to any problem domain that admits a modeling as graphs. The drawing and generation module of our tool is available online at (http://chr.informatik.uni-ulm.de/mason).

1 Introduction

Mason's marks are symbols often found on dressed stone in historic buildings. These signs go back about 4500 years, to the tombs of the advanced ancient civilization of Egypt. In Europe, they were common from the 12th century on [Fri32, Dav54]. There, one can mainly find mason's marks from the medieval ages, mostly in churches, cathedrals and monasteries. In one such building, there may be a thousand mason's marks of hundred different designs. Over time, mason's marks got smaller and more complex.

These mason's marks were inscribed on the stones by stonemasons during construction of a building to identify their work, presumably for quality control and probably to receive payment. This was important for masons who were free of servitude and therefore allowed to travel the country for work (see [Fol10]

© Springer Nature Switzerland AG 2018
C. Benzmüller et al. (Eds.): RuleML+RR 2018, LNCS 11092, pp. 264–273, 2018.
https://doi.org/10.1007/978-3-319-99906-7_18

for popular fiction on the subject). Only stonemason masters were allowed to inscribe their mark in a blazon. Their mason's marks are also found on medieval documents and masons tombstones. The master would give a personal mason's mark to his apprentices, provided they had enough skill to construct and interpret the mason's mark symbol. A challenging design and interpretation would make it harder to appropriate or misuse a mason's mark. Stonemason's marks are an important source of information for art and architecture historians and archaeologists, in particular to reconstruct the construction process of buildings.

Mason's marks tend to be simple geometric symbols, usually constructed using rulers and compasses and precisely cut with a chisel. In this way, a distinctive sign consisting of straight lines and curves could be produced with little effort. The geometric construction of mason's marks implies that they exhibit a structural regularity. This was first discussed and formalized by von Ržiha [Rži81]. He claimed that mason's marks are small subfigures of regular grids, which consist either of squares or equilateral triangles together with circles inscribed in each other. His theory is obsolete, because there is no historical evidence that grids were explicitly used and because not all marks fit these grid patterns. It is, however, clear that the construction of the mason's marks with compasses and rulers lends itself to the prevalence of certain angles (multiples of 30 and 45°) between lines and certain multiples of line lengths $(1, \sqrt{2}, \sqrt{3}, 2, \sqrt{5} \ldots)$ due to the use of diagonals in squares and altitudes in triangles.

We are developing a graph tool and apply it to draw, analyse, and generate mason's mark designs [Frü18a,Frü18c]. In this paper, we shortly present the representation of straight-line graphs, how, for analysis we produce statistics about graph properties, and how we recognize subgraphs using pattern matching rules. Then, we introduce our node-centric representation of line graphs and describe how to exhaustively or randomly generate graphs from given small constrained subgraphs. We conclude by discussing related and future work.

2   Tool Description

Our prototype graph analysis and generation tool is currently implemented using Constraint Handling Rules (CHR) in SWI Prolog [WDKTF14]. We assume some basic familiarity with Prolog and CHR [Frü09,Frü15,Frü18b,FR18].

In these declarative, logic-based programming languages, the notion of logical variable is essential. It behaves like a variable in a mathematical equation: when introduced, it is unbound. During computation, it may be bound to a value. From then on, it is indistinguishable from that value and the value cannot be changed, the variable cannot be overwritten.

In CHR, Constraints are relations, predicates of first order logic. Constraints are rewritten by CHR rules, consisting of a left-hand-side pattern, a guard, and a right-hand-side such as `LeftSide <=> Guard | RightSide`. When the constraint pattern on the left-hand-side matches some of the current constraints and the guard test (precondition) succeeds under this matching, the right-hand side of the rule is executed. Depending on the rule type, matched constraints

may be removed or kept. (The different rule types will be introduced as they
are used in the program code.) The right-hand side of a rule will compute and
add new constraints or do nothing (which is denoted by true). Starting from
an initial state containing constraints, rules are applied eagerly to exhaustion,
in textual order, until a final state of constraints is reached.

2.1   Representation of Mason Marks as Graphs

We represent mason's marks by connected *planar straight-line graphs*, a drawing
of planar graphs in the plane such that its edges are straight line segments
[Tam13]. (We will support arcs in the near future.) A line (segment) has two
nodes, or two endpoints, given by Cartesian coordinates. Each point is defined by
a pair of numbers written X-Y. For convenience of manipulation, we redundantly
represent lines at the same time by polar coordinates, which consist of a reference
point (pole), which is the first endpoint of the line, a line length (radius) and an
angle (azimuth) in degrees. This leads to the line constraint l:

```
l(EndPoint1, EndPoint2, LineLength, Angle)
```

With polar coordinations, translation, rotation and scaling of lines is straightforward. With Cartesian coordinates, visualization by translation into scalable
vector graphics (svg) is easy. Only when the lines are drawn, missing point coordinates are computed:

```
l(X1-Y1,P2,L,A) ==> numbers(X1,Y1,L,A) |
        X2 is X1+L*U*cos(A*pi/180), Y2 is Y1+L*U*sin(A*pi/180),
        P2=(X2-Y2).
% analogously for point P1 when P2 is known
```

Note that variable names start with upper case letters in Prolog and CHR.
This CHR *propagation rule* of the form LeftSide ==> Guard | RightSide can
be read as follows: If a line matching the left-hand side l(X1-Y1,P2,L,A) is found
where X1,X2,L,A are numbers (instead of yet unbound variables), then execute
the right-hand side of the rule: compute X2 and Y2 using Prolog's is built-in
and equate (unify) the endpoint P2 with the coordinate X2-Y2 using Prolog's
= built-in. If P2 was a free (unbound) variable, it will be bound, otherwise an
equality check will be performed (without removing the LeftSide, i.e., the line
constraint).

2.2   Analysis of Graphs

From a given graph, i.e., its line constraints, we can generate information using
propagation rules. For example, one can compute counts for the occurrences
of each value in the components of a line (points, lengths, angles) to collect
statistical information about the graph. Note that the number of occurrences of
a node corresponds to the degree of that node.

The constraint a(Type, Count, Value) can be considered as an array entry that contains for each Value of a certain Type its Count of occurrences. Below, the first rule adds such entries for the same Type, Value pair. The second rule computes relevant information from a single line.

```
% add counts for two entries of the same T(ype), V(alue) pair
a(T,N1,V), a(T,N2,V) <=> N is N1+N2, a(T,N,V).
```

```
% compute statistical information about lines of a graph
% Types: l(ine)c(ount), n(ode), l(ine )l(ength), a(ngle)
l(P1,P2,L,A) ==> a(lc,1,1),a(n,1,P1),a(n,1,P2),a(ll,1,L),a(a,1,A).
```

The first rule is a CHR *simplification rule* without a guard. It replaces the left-hand side by the right-hand side, i.e., two (different) matching a constraints by a new one containing the sum. We can compute relative angles and line length proportions between lines as follows.

```
% angles between lines that share a node, e.g. first node
l(P1,P2,L1,A1), l(P1,P4,L2,A2) ==> A is abs(A1-A2), a(al,1,A).
```

```
% proportions between lines lengths of any two lines in a graph
l(P1,P2,L1,A1), l(P3,P4,L2,A2) ==> R is L1/L2, a(pl,1,R).
```

2.3   Pattern Matching of Graphs

We want to find patterns and recognize subgraphs in a graph. For recognition, we assume that all lines have angles between 0 and 180°. (Lines with an angle between 180 and 360° can be inverted.) Note that size and orientation of graphs can differ. To account for scaling and rotation, we introduce two Prolog predicates that we will use in the guard of rules.

The Prolog predicate scaled(Ls,Ps,R) accounts for scaling. It checks that the ratio between the next element from the list Ls and the next element from the list Ps is always the ratio R. The intended use is that Ls is a list of actual line lengths while Ps is a list of required proportions between these line lengths. Analogously, the Prolog predicate rotated(Ls,Ps,A) accounts for rotation.

```
scaled([],[],R).
scaled([L|Ls],[P|Ps],R):- R is L/P, scaled(Ls,Ps,R).
```

```
rotated([],[],A).
rotated([L|Ls],[P|Ps],A):- A is (L-P) mod 360, rotated(Ls,Ps,A).
```

The above code can be modified to account for imprecisions in the measurements of lengths and angles by using rounding or interval arithmetics.

Below are two examples of graph mining: how to recognize parallel lines and the subgraph depicted in Fig. 1. We use recognized(What,NodeList) to record in a constraint what has been recognized for which nodes.

```
% two parallel lines have the same angle
l(A,B,L1,A), l(C,D,L2,A) ==> recognized(parallel,[A,B,C,D]).
```

```
% recognize subgraph comprised of four lines given in Figure 1
l(A,B,L1,A1), l(B,C,L2,A2), l(E,C,L3,A3), l(C,D,L4,A4) ==>
                 rotated([A1,A2,A3,A4],[90,0,90,90]),
                 scaled([L1,L2,L3,L4],[1,1,1,1]) |
                      recognized(y_sign,[A,B,C,D,E]).
```

Fig. 1. Graph of Y-Sign

Fig. 2. Graph [2,90,1,90,2]

Fig. 3.   Graph [2,90,1-I,90,2], [3,45,3-I,45,3]

Fig. 4.   Graph [2-I,90,1,90,2], [3,45,3-I,45,3]

2.4   Node-Centric Representation of Graphs Using Shared Lines

Through exhaustive initial experiments, we found that for the encoding and generation of mason's marks a *node-centric* (vertex-centric) representation of their underlying connected planar straight-line graph is helpful. The constraint for a node is defined as follows:

```
node(NodePoint, NodeList)
NodePoint ::= Number-Number
NodeList  ::= [LineLength] ; [LineLength,Angle|NodeList]
```

Each node is at the center of several lines leaving it. We record the length of these lines and the angle between neighboring lines (going clockwise). (The last angle can be omitted, because all angles have to sum up to the 360° of the full circle.) NodeList is a list with elements that are alternating between line lengths and angles, starting and ending in a line length. We may omit the NodePoint and just use node(NodeList). For example in node([2,90,1,90,2]), the line lengths are 2, 1, 2 and the angles between the lines are 90, 90. This constraint represents a turnstile symbol ⊢, see Fig. 2.

Note that each such node forms a small subgraph by itself.

In order to describe larger connected graphs, the node data structure representation is extended to allow identifiers for lines. These identifiers are optionally attached to the line-lengths. If such an identifier is shared between two lines in different nodes it means that these lines are the same, with the two nodes as endpoints. Such annotated lines we call *shared lines*. One needs a matching pair of them to form a valid line.

When the nodes are translated into line constraints, the subgraphs of the two nodes connected by this common line are scaled and rotated such that the shared lines become identical. This is discussed in the next Section.

2.5 Merging Shared Lines

Two shared lines with identical identifiers react with each other by the following rule. Scaling and rotation is applied to the complete subgraph in which the second shared line occurs using the constraint `update(Node,Scaling,Rotation)`. Finally, the nodes of the two shared lines are identified and a new proper full line without identifier replaces the two merged shared lines. (At this point, the node points are still unbound variables, their coordinates have no values yet.)

```
% find two shared lines whose identifier is the same
% to connect their subgraphs
l(N1,N2,M1-I1,A1), l(N3,N4,M2-I2,A2) <=> I1==I2 | % share line id
    alldiff(N1,N2,N3,N4),       % all nodes must be different
    M is M1/M2, A is A1+180-A2, % compute scaling and rotation
    update(N3,M,A), % scale and rotate N3 graph to fit N1 graph
    N1=N4, N2=N3,   % equate nodes of now identical shared lines
    l(N1,N2,M1,A1). % merged line replaces the two shared lines
```

The rule for updating a line by constraint `update(Node,Scaling,Rotation)` using scaling and rotation and for updating all lines connected to that line is shown below. It has to avoid repeated updates of the same line. Therefore the update removes the line and produces an intermediate representation of the line using constraint `lu` (line updated).

```
% update line with node N1 by scaling and rotation
update(N1,M,A) \ l(N1,N2,M1,A1) <=>  numbers(M1,A1) |
    M2 is M1*M, A2 is A+A1,
    lu(N1,N2,M2,A2),  % intermediate updated line
    update(N2,M,A).   % propagate update to node N2
% analogously for line with node N2 to update
```

This CHR *simpagation rule* keeps the `update` constraint, but removes the line constraint `l`. So in this rule, a single `update` constraint can update all lines that have `N1` as first node. A line `l` is replaced by the updated line constraint `lu` and the update is also applied to lines containing the other node `N2`. This produces a chain of updates for the subgraph that is reachable from node `N1`. In effect, the complete subgraph is scaled and rotated. Only when all updates are done, all the intermediate `lu` lines are replaced by original `l` lines with the help of some additional rules.

For example, `node([2,90,1-I,90,2]),node([3,45,3-I,45,3])` depicts the graph given in Fig. 3, where the common identifier I denotes the shared line. In effect, the subgraph `node([3,45,3-I,45,3])` is rotated and scaled (becoming `node([1,45,1-I,45,1])`) in order to meet the shared line in `node([2,90,1-I, 90,2])` with the same length and orientation. Contrast this with the situation in Fig. 4, where the shared line of the first node has changed (but not the second). The two subgraphs are now connected by different shared lines.

2.6 Exhaustive Generation of Arbitrary Graphs

We can exhaustively generate graphs from a given node-centric representation containing shared lines with free unbound logical variables as identifiers. Different resulting graphs are possible, depending on which shared lines are identified by binding (aliasing) their variable identifiers. Not all such matchings lead to a valid graph, because the resulting graph may not be geometrically possible or a shared line may be left unmatched.

In our implementation, the given graph in node-centric representation is translated into a conjunction of lines, where some of them are shared lines containing identifiers. First, all identifiers of shared lines are collected into a list. The identifiers can be unbound variables, in that case identifiers can be bound to each other, making them equivalent. Then a recursion on this list using the constraint `pairlines` equates the next identifier in the list with one of the remaining identifiers using the Prolog built-in `select(Element,List,RestList)` that non-deterministically removes an element from a list. On backtracking, all choices will be tried. Recursion continues with the remaining list `L1`.

```
% combine pairs of shared lines by equating their identifiers
pairlines([]) <=> true.
pairlines([I1|L]) <=> select(I2,L,L1), I1=I2, pairlines(L1).
```

2.7 Random Generation of Graphs for Mason Marks

We have encoded a number of mason's marks from [Rži81] in our node-centric representation, in particular for the Ulm Minster (see Fig. 5). Most of these marks can be described using just 4 to 5 `node` constraints containing 3 to 4 lines. In each mason's mark there is typically a node that is connected to most nodes and that is located near the geometric center of the mason's mark. Such a node is heuristically chosen as the *primary node* of the mason's mark graph. We collected all `node` constraints for primary nodes and for all other nodes from our encoding of existing mason's marks.

For random generation of similarly shaped mason's mark graphs, first we choose one primary node and two other nodes randomly, and then check if their angles are either multiples of 30 or 45°. If so, we choose a fourth node from the remaining other nodes (ignoring duplicates). The resulting graph may not be valid due to unmatched shared lines. We then use Prolog's backtracking to try all possible fourth nodes. In this way, zero, one or more valid mason's marks are randomly produced from the given subgraph nodes. Figure 6 shows some examples of mason's marks generated in this way. More examples can be found in the upcoming book [Frü18c].

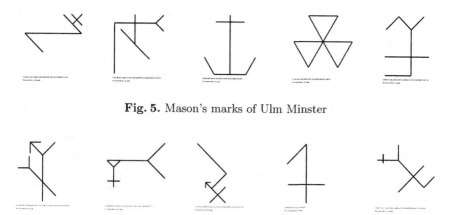

Fig. 5. Mason's marks of Ulm Minster

Fig. 6. Randomly generated Mason's Marks derived from Ulm Minster marks

3 Related Work

To the best of our knowledge, our work is the first that not only represents, but also analyses and generates mason's marks. Moreover, we proposed and use a novel node-centric graph representation.

The only related work we could find is [KMMS02]. Given a prototype graph of a mason's mark and the skeleton graph of an input image, the recognition of this image is considered as search of matchings paths in the skeleton graph with a minimal number of mismatchings. It is not clear from the description of the algorithm how it accounts for scaling and rotation. In contrast, our recognition rules match line edges directly, independent of scale and rotation. Efficiency of matching relies on optimizations of the CHR compiler such as indexing. Imprecision could be taken into account and controlled by rounding the numerical values of coordinates, lengths, and angles or by using interval arithmetics.

In the work [Dür96], structural character descriptions for East Asian ideograms (Kanji font characters) are analyzed and generated. Sketches of characters are produced from a symbolic coordinate-free description, which is a system of constraints. The authors developed a special finite domain constraint solving algorithm tailored to the problem in CHR. This approach proved to be more efficient and versatile than using existing built-in solvers. Kanji characters are decomposed into subfigures and those are described by strokes (lines), called bars. The representation of bars is similar to our node-centric representation. However, their work employs only the four main directions and lengths are always implicit, while we allow for arbitrary angles and arbitrary explicit lengths.

4   Conclusions and Future Work

We presented our prototype tool to analyse, generate and draw straight-line graphs based on a novel node-centric representation of graphs using constraints. We have applied the tool to the domain of stonemason's marks, see the book [Frü18c]. The drawing and generation module of the tool is online at http://chr. informatik.uni-ulm.de/mason. For a more complete coverage of mason's marks, we need to add the representation of arcs and other curves. We currently work on representing the mason's marks found on buildings in the Alicante province in Spain, because these have not been encoded so far.

This tool shows the power of declarative modeling, handling, analysis, and generation of pictorial information using a logic-based programming language that results in compact and concise code. We are currently working with masons and art historians to explore the potential of our generation and analysis approach for mason's marks. We also plan to explore the graphical representation of constraint networks, in particular in the domain of temporal and spatial reasoning [Frü94,FB98]. In principle, our tool can be applied to any problem domain that admits a modeling as graphs.

Acknowledgements. We thank Daniel Gall for providing the web interface for our tool. We thank the anonymous reviewers for their helpful suggestions on how to improve the paper, including detailed corrections of typos and commas.

References

[Dav54] Davis, R.H.C.: A catalogue of masons' marks as an aid to architectural history. J. Br. Archaeol. Assoc. **17**(1), 43–76 (1954)

[Dür96] Dürst, M.J.: Prolog for structured character description and font design. J. Logic Program. **26**(2), 133–146 (1996)

[FB98] Frühwirth, T., Brisset, P.: Optimal placement of base stations in wireless indoor telecommunication. In: Maher, M., Puget, J.-F. (eds.) CP 1998. LNCS, vol. 1520, pp. 476–480. Springer, Heidelberg (1998). https://doi. org/10.1007/3-540-49481-2_47

[Fol10] Follett, K.: The Pillars of the Earth. Penguin (2010)

[FR18] Frühwirth, T., Raiser, F.: Constraint handling rules-compilation, execution, and analysis: Large Print Edition. BoD (2018)

[Fri32] Friedrich, K.: Die Steinbearbeitung in ihrer Entwicklung vom 11. bis zum 18. Jahrhundert. Filser, 1932. Reprint Aegis Ulm (1988)

[Frü94] Frühwirth, T.: Temporal reasoning with constraint handling rules. Technical Report ECRC-94-5, European Computer-Industry Research Centre, Munchen, Germany (1994)

[Frü09] Frühwirth, T.: Constraint Handling Rules. Cambridge University Press, Cambridge (2009)

[Frü15] Frühwirth, T.: Constraint handling rules - what else? In: Bassiliades, N., Gottlob, G., Sadri, F., Paschke, A., Roman, D. (eds.) RuleML 2015. LNCS, vol. 9202, pp. 13–34. Springer, Cham (2015). https://doi.org/ 10.1007/978-3-319-21542-6_2

[Frü18a] Frühwirth, T.: A rule-based tool for analysis and generation of graphs applied to Mason's Marks - extended abstract. In: Workshop on Logic and Practice of Programming (LPoP 2018), July 2018

[Frü18b] Frühwirth, T.: The CHR Web Site. Ulm University (2018). http://www.constraint-handling-rules.org

[Frü18c] Frühwirth, T.: The computer art of Mason's mark design. BOD (2018)

[KMMS02] Kiiko, V., Matsello, V., Masuch, H., Stanke, G.: Recognition of mason marks images, found on Citeseer (2002)

[Rži81] von Ržiha, F.: Studien über Steinmetz-Zeichen. Kaiserlich-Königliche Hof-und Staatsdruckerei, 1881. Reprint Bau-Verlag (1989)

[Tam13] Tamassia, R.: Handbook of Graph Drawing and Visualization. CRC Press, Boca Raton (2013)

[WDKTF14] Wielemaker, J., Koninck, L.D., Triska, M., Frühwirth, T.: SWI prolog reference manual 7.1. BOD (2014)

The MET: The Art of Flexible Reasoning with Modalities

Tobias Gleißner$^{(\boxtimes)}$ and Alexander Steen

Institute of Computer Science, Freie Universität Berlin, Berlin, Germany
{tobias.gleissner,a.steen}@fu-berlin.de

Abstract. Modal logics have numerous applications in computational linguistics, artificial intelligence, rule-based reasoning, and, in general, alethic, deontic and epistemic contexts. Higher-order quantified modal logics additionally incorporate the expressiveness of higher-order formalisms and thereby provide a quite general reasoning framework. By exploiting this expressiveness, the Modal Embedding Tool (MET) allows to automatically encode higher-order modal logic problems into equivalent problems of classical logic, enabling the use of a broad variety of established reasoning tools. In this system description, the functionality and usage of MET as well as a suitable input syntax for flexible reasoning with modalities are presented.

1 Introduction

Various powerful automated and interactive theorem proving systems (ATP and ITP, respectively) for first-order (FO) and higher-order (HO) logics have been developed over the past decades, including the first-order ATP E [1], the higher-order ATPs Satallax [2], LEO-II [3] and Leo-III [4], and the higher-order ITP Isabelle/HOL [5]. While many of these systems are meanwhile quite robust and mature, they often support reasoning in classical logics only. This is in contrast to the fact that non-classical logics have many topical applications in mathematics, computer science and beyond. In this work, we focus on the automation of quantified (multi-)modal logics [6] which can be fruitfully applied in the context of artificial intelligence, computational linguistics and rule-based reasoning. They also play an important role in various areas of philosophy, including ontology, (computer-)ethics, philosophy of mind and philosophy of science. Many challenging applications, however, as recently explored in metaphysics [7–9], require quantified and in particular higher-order quantified modal logics (HOMLs). But even for first-order non-classical logics only a small number of implemented systems is available to date, and the situation is even worse for higher-order quantified logics. In particular, the development of ATPs for HOMLs is still in its infancy, hence impeding more complex computer-assisted studies of relevant topics.

To overcome this situation, in this work we present the **M**odal **E**mbedding **T**ool (MET for short) that bridges the above gap by enabling the employment

---

Alexander Steen is partially supported by the Volkswagenstiftung (project CRAP).

C. Benzmüller et al. (Eds.): RuleML+RR 2018, LNCS 11092, pp. 274–284, 2018.
https://doi.org/10.1007/978-3-319-99906-7_19

of classical higher-order reasoning systems, including powerful HO ATPs, for reasoning in a broad variety of quantified modal logics. Recall that for quantified modal logics there exist multiple different notions of semantics, most of which usually used in different application domains. The exact semantics of a given quantified modal logic can be regarded a product of multiple individual semantical parameters, including:

(i) Modal axiomatization: *What properties hold for each modality?*
    The properties range from axiom scheme K alone to the strong assumptions of logic S5, and any intermediate system (cf. the modal logic cube [6]).
(ii) Quantification semantics: *What are the domains of quantified variables?*
    Usual choices include so-called cumulative, decreasing, constant and varying domain semantics.
(iii) Rigidity: *Is the meaning of a symbol the same in every possible world?*
    Possible choices include rigid and world-dependent constant symbols.

Also, there exist different choices for logical consequence relations, including at least so-called local and global consequence [6]. When taking all possible parameter combinations into account this amounts to more than 120 different HOMLs.

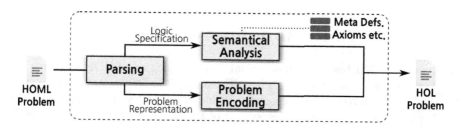

Fig. 1. Working principle of the MET: A modal logic problem statement is given to the system which it then transforms and augments with suitable technical definitions. The resulting problem is formulated in classical logic and only valid if the original problem was valid.

MET implements a shallow semantical embedding approach [10] in which formulas of modal logic are identified with specific terms of classical higher-order logic such that a notion of modal validity can be defined within HOL that coincides with the desired modal logic semantics. More concretely, a modal logic formulated in a suitable machine-readable syntax (cf. Figs. 2 and 3) is translated by MET to a problem statement in the de-facto standard TPTP THF syntax [11,12] for HO ATP systems. The transformation process is thereby validity preserving and thus allows the use of common reasoning systems that do not support modal logic reasoning on their own. The process is visualized in Fig. 1. Although the here discussed approach involves an indirection over classical HOL, recent evaluations confirm that the reasoning effectivity of HO ATPs used in conjunction with MET are on a par with established modal logic reasoners [4].

Additionally, reasoning using MET is much more flexible than the employment of these special purpose systems as it allows a completely free choice of all relevant semantical parameters (supporting every existent normal modal logic) whereas native modal logic reasoners are limited to a small subset of modal logic systems and usually have fixed choices for quantification semantics, symbol rigidity and consequence. In fact, even more general modal logics are supported via a fine-grained control over the properties of individual quantification domains, modal operators, etc [13].

Whereas earlier work focused on the theoretical foundations [10], and the development of the automatic embedding procedure itself [13], in this paper, we present the prover-independent tool MET and its practical employment in relevant application scenarios.

Higher-Order Modal Logics. HOMLs as addressed here are extensions of HOL [14]. HOL provides λ-abstraction as an elegant means to denote unnamed functions, predicates and sets (by their characteristic functions). HOML, in turn, augments HOL with a set of modal operators $\Box^i$, $i \in I$, for some index set I, and is equipped with a suitable combination of HOL semantics and a Kripke-style modal semantics [13]. In our approach an adequate notion of Henkin semantics for both HOML and HOL is assumed [10,13].

2   A Syntax for HOML and Its Semantics

A standard ASCII-based machine-readable representation of HOL problems for ATP systems is given by the TPTP THF dialect [12]. This syntax is supported by most of the current HOL reasoners, including all HO systems mentioned in the beginning of Sect. 1. Since the syntax of HOML is a conservative extension of that of classical HOL, the THF representation language can as well easily be augmented by introducing the modal operators $box and $dia as new primitive connectives, representing the modal connectives $\Box$ and $\Diamond$, respectively (in a mono-modal settings). For multi-modal logics, there exist analogous operators that are additionally given an index as first argument and the formula as second argument. The remaining syntax coincides with standard THF and is described in the literature [12].

As sketched in Sect. 1, there is no single semantics of quantified modal logics. As a consequence, there is additional need for explicitly stating the semantical setting in which a problem is to be assessed by a reasoning system. This is realized in the here proposed syntax by including a meta-logical specification into the problem header. Such a specification statement is displayed in Fig. 2: In this logic specification, the identifiers $constants, $quantification and $consequence specify the exact semantical settings for the rigidity of constant symbols, the quantification semantics and the consequence relation, respectively. Finally, $modalities specifies the properties of the modal connectives by means of fixed modal logic system names or, alternatively, a list of individual modal axiom schemes. The valid parameter values are given in Table 1.

```
% Begin of logic specification
thf(⟨name₀⟩, logic, ($modal := [
        $constants := ⟨const_spec⟩, $quantification := ⟨domain_spec⟩,
        $consequence := ⟨conseq_spec⟩, $modalities := ⟨modal_spec⟩ ] )).
% End of logic specification, begin of problem statement
thf(⟨name₁⟩, ⟨role₁⟩, ⟨formula₁⟩).
...
thf(⟨nameₙ⟩, ⟨roleₙ⟩, ⟨formulaₙ⟩).
```

Fig. 2. Layout of a general modal logic problem. The first statement (ll. 2–4) specifies a concrete modal logic, the remaining statements (ll. 6–8) formulate the problem itself. The ⟨name$_i$⟩ serve as syntactic identifier for that statement, a ⟨role$_i$⟩ (usually set to axiom or conjecture) tells the reasoning system how to interpret the ⟨formula$_i$⟩ formulated in the presented augmented THF syntax. Lines starting with % are comments.

Table 1. Semantic specification parameters. The parameter placeholders, written in angles ⟨·⟩, refer to the values for the logic specification of Fig. 2. The names of the modal logic system parameters (such as $modal_system_K or $modal_system_S5) refer to the respective systems from the modal logic cube [6]. The individual modal axiom schemes names (such as $modal_axiom_T or $modal_axiom_5) are named similarly.

Parameter	Valid values
⟨const_spec⟩	$rigid, $flexible
⟨domain_spec⟩	$constant, $varying, $cumulative, $decreasing
⟨conseq_spec⟩	$local, $global
⟨modal_spec⟩	$modal_system_X for X in {K, KB, K4, K5, K45, KB5, D, DB, D4, D5, D45, T, B, S4, S5, S5U} *or* [$modal_axiom_X₁, $modal_axiom_X₂, ...] for X$_i$ in {T, B, D, 4, 5, CD, C4, C}

The remaining placeholders of Fig. 2, ⟨name⟩, ⟨role⟩ and ⟨formula⟩, are standard and given by the TPTP language definition [11] to which we refer to for brevity. The semantics specification format presented in this paper is work-in-progress and stems from an ongoing TPTP language extension proposal.[1]

3   Application Examples

In this section, the practical employment of MET for reasoning with relevant non-trivial problem statements is discussed. The first application example, a formulation of the wise men puzzle, incorporates the use of multiple inter-related modality operators and quantification beyond first-order. The second example

---

[1] See proposal "Logic Specification Format" of the TPTP platform for more details.

focuses on the use of logic specification statements within the problem and illustrates the flexibility of the here presented reasoning approach.

3.1 Case Study: The Wise Men Puzzle

A classical example dealing with knowledge between agents and implicit knowledge transfer is the wise men puzzle (also known in a variation as muddy forehead puzzle). Epistemic logic, the logic about knowledge, can be interpreted as a form of multi-modal logic, were the modality operators represent *knowing* and are indexed with an agent's identifier from an index set I (referring to the particular agent whose knowledge it addresses). As an example, the sentence "agent a knows ϕ", for an agent $a \in I$, can be stated as $\Box^a\phi$. While dealing with common knowledge scenarios, often an additional artificial agent (sometimes referred to as *fool*) is defined for allowing statements such as "everybody knows ϕ", represented by $\Box^{\text{fool}}\phi$.

```
1   thf(wise_men_puzzle_semantics, logic , ( $modal := [
2       $constants := $rigid, $quantification := $varying,
3       $consequence := $global, $modalities := $modal_system_S5] )).
4
5   % $i type models the agents's hats
6   thf(agent_a, type, (a: $i)).
7   thf(agent_b, type, (b: $i)).
8   thf(agent_c, type, (c: $i)).
9
10  % Property of an agent's hat: ws represents "having a white spot"
11  thf(white_spot, type, (ws: ($i>$o))).
12
13  % Common knowledge: At least one agent has a white spot
14  thf(axiom_1, axiom, ($box_int @ 0 @ ((ws @ a) | (ws @ b) | (ws @ c)))).
15
16  % If one agent has a white spot all other agents can see this
17  thf(axiom_2ab, axiom, ($box_int @ 0 @ ((ws @ a) => ($box_int @ 2 @ (ws @ a))))).
18  thf(axiom_2ac, axiom, ($box_int @ 0 @ ((ws @ a) => ($box_int @ 3 @ (ws @ a))))).
19  thf(axiom_2ba, axiom, ($box_int @ 0 @ ((ws @ b) => ($box_int @ 1 @ (ws @ b))))).
20  thf(axiom_2bc, axiom, ($box_int @ 0 @ ((ws @ b) => ($box_int @ 3 @ (ws @ b))))).
21  thf(axiom_2ca, axiom, ($box_int @ 0 @ ((ws @ c) => ($box_int @ 1 @ (ws @ c))))).
22  thf(axiom_2cb, axiom, ($box_int @ 0 @ ((ws @ c) => ($box_int @ 2 @ (ws @ c))))).
23
24  % If one agent has a black spot all other agents can see this
25  thf(axiom_3ab, axiom, ($box_int @ 0 @ ((~(ws @ a)) => ($box_int @ 2 @ (~(ws @ a)))))).
26  thf(axiom_3ac, axiom, ($box_int @ 0 @ ((~(ws @ a)) => ($box_int @ 3 @ (~(ws @ a)))))).
27  thf(axiom_3ba, axiom, ($box_int @ 0 @ ((~(ws @ b)) => ($box_int @ 1 @ (~(ws @ b)))))).
28  thf(axiom_3bc, axiom, ($box_int @ 0 @ ((~(ws @ b)) => ($box_int @ 3 @ (~(ws @ b)))))).
29  thf(axiom_3ca, axiom, ($box_int @ 0 @ ((~(ws @ c)) => ($box_int @ 1 @ (~(ws @ c)))))).
30  thf(axiom_3cb, axiom, ($box_int @ 0 @ ((~(ws @ c)) => ($box_int @ 2 @ (~(ws @ c)))))).
31
32  % Agents 1 and 2 do not know their hat color
33  thf(axiom_9, axiom, ($box_int @ 0 @ (~($box_int @ 1 @ (ws @ a))))).
34  thf(axiom_10, axiom, ($box_int @ 0 @ (~($box_int @ 2 @ (ws @ b))))).
35
36  % Agent 3 can deduce the color of his hat (white spot)
37  thf(con, conjecture, ($box_int @ 3 @ (ws @ c))).
```

Fig. 3. The wise men puzzle formulated in modal THF syntax. The term `$box_int @ i` represents a box operator $\Box^i$ for which the set of integers serves as index set I. In this example, the common knowledge agent (the *fool*) is given by index 0, the remaining three agents by indexes $1, 2$ and 3.

A formulation of the wise men puzzle is given in Fig. 3. In the logic specification, the modalities (including the common knowledge modality) are given an S5 axiomatization to capture the usual assumptions about knowledge. Additionally, a varying domain semantics is used for this experiment. The modal operators $\Box^a$ for some agent $a \neq$ fool $\in I$ are related to common knowledge $\Box^{\text{fool}}$ using so-called bridge-rules stating that everything that is common knowledge is also known by the individual agents (cf. ll. 16–30). The common knowledge fact that the first two agents do not know their hat color is given by two axioms (ll. 33–34) and finally the conjecture that the third agent now knows its hat color is given by the conjecture (l. 37). The wise men problem in the presented formulation can be solved using MET in conjunction with Leo-III as reasoner back end in under 5s, cf. Appendix A for a detailed display of the tools usage.

3.2 Case Study: Experiments with Semantical Variations

In this case study, we focus on the flexibility the logic specification within a problem provides for experiments in different semantical settings. Figure 4 displays an example modal logic formula that is an instance of a corollary of Becker's postulate [15]. It essentially expresses that everything that is possibly necessary it, in fact, necessary. Since this formula is obviously debatable, one might want to explicitly include or exclude this fact from a logical system. It is known from the literature, that Becker's postulate is indeed valid in S5 modal logics but not in any weaker logic systems. Even without this knowledge, the MET allows to experimentally reproduce these results with only simple modification of the logic specification statements. To that end, each semantical setting can be formulated as logic specification and then transformed by MET to HOL problems. These HOL problems are then in turn given to HO reasoning systems for verifying or refuting the conjecture.

```
thf(s5_spec, logic, ($modal := [
        $constants := $rigid, $quantification := $constant,
        $consequence := $global, $modalities := $modal_system_S5 ])).
thf(becker,conjecture,( ! [P:$i>$o,F:$i>$i, X:$i]: (? [G:$i>$i]:
        (($dia @ ($box @ (P @ (F @ X)))) => ($box @ (P @ (G @ X))))))).
```

Fig. 4. A corollary of Becker's postulate formulated in modal THF, representing the formula $\forall P_{\iota \to o} \forall F_{\iota \to \iota} \forall X_\iota \exists G_{\iota \to \iota}(\Diamond \Box P(F(X)) \Rightarrow \Box P(G(X)))$.

In the example of Becker's postulate, the higher-order ATP system Leo-III and the counter-model finder Nitpick [16] verify the above claim. The systems produce proofs resp. explicit, finite, counter-models of the validity the conjecture in each modal logic system. The results of these experiments are summarized in Table 2. It can be seen that, for every modal logic system, the combination of both reasoners successfully assess the conjecture and yield the expected results.

Each invocation of the reasoning systems (including the pre-processing by MET) takes less than 1 s. Note that both systems are in a sense complementary, i.e. theorem proving systems are usually stronger for proving the validity of a conjecture while counter-model finders focus on counter-satisfiability. Using both systems, positive and negative results can be established as desired.

The example of Becker's postulate is chosen for demonstrative purposes. Similarly interesting formulas for certain modal logics such as Barcan's formula (or its converse) can be analyzed analogously using MET [13]. In a more general setting, the semantical flexibility of the here presented approach allows for an empirical assessment of a formal system's adequateness for a specific application; and to explore further, possibly unintended, consequences of a given formulation.

Table 2. Evaluation results of the validity of Becker's postulate from Fig. 4. For each semantical setting, the factual validity of the postulate (Expected) and the actual results of Leo-III and Nitpick (Result) are presented. ✓ and × denote validity resp. invalidity of the postulate under the respective semantics as well as a system's according result. A timeout of a system (i.e. no feasible result) is denoted †. Quantification semantics are abbreviated co and va for constant and varying domains, respectively.

(a) Leo-III

Modal System	K		B		T		S4		S5	
Domains	co	va	co	va	co	va	co	va	co	va
Expected	×	×	×	×	×	×	×	×	✓	✓
Result	†	†	†	†	†	†	†	†	✓	✓

(b) Nitpick

Modal System	K		B		T		S4		S5	
Domains	co	va	co	va	co	va	co	va	co	va
Expected	×	×	×	×	×	×	×	×	✓	✓
Result	×	×	×	×	×	×	×	×	†	†

4   Summary and Further Work

In this work, a self-contained syntax for formulating higher-order modal logic problems was sketched that is used as input format to the Modal Embedding Tool. This stand-alone tool acts as external pre-processor for HO reasoning systems and emits for a given input problem statement an equivalent (wrt. validity) HOL problem formulated in standard THF syntax. MET is implemented in Java and freely available at GitHub under BSD-3 license.[2] The higher-order ATP system Leo-III additionally incorporates a version of MET for automatically embedding modal logic problems without any need for external pre-processing.

When used in conjunction with further powerful HO ATP systems, MET has many topical applications for reasoning in knowledge bases, legal reasoning, smart contracts and, more generally, in alethic, epistemic and deontic contexts. An adaption of MET for accepting RuleML input syntax [17], OWL [18] or further languages for rule-based reasoning is, thanks to the flexible underlying embedding approach, straight-forward and current work-in-progress [19]. The MET can also be extended to serve as a translation tool between these different representation formats.

---

[2] See github.com/leoprover/embed_modal for details and further instructions.

A   Installation and Usage of MET

Acquisition and Installation

MET is freely available on GitHub (https://github.com/leoprover/embed_ modal) under BSD-3 license. The most current release is always accessible under https://github.com/leoprover/embed_modal/releases/latest. To get it, simply download the source archive and extract it so some location.

```
> wget https://github.com/leoprover/embed_modal/archive/1.0.tar.gz
> tar -xvzf 1.0.tar.gz
```

After extraction, MET can be built using Make. Simply `cd` to the extracted directory s and run Make:

```
> cd embed_modal-1.0
> make
```

After building, there should be a directory `bin/`, relative from the current directory. This directory contains the binary `embedlogic` of MET. You will also find a JAR in the directory `embed/target/` which you can use as a library for your own projects.

MET can optionally be installed by invoking

```
> make install
```

which copies the binary to the directory `$HOME/.local/bin` and adds it to your `$PATH`.

Usage

To execute MET, simply run the `embedlogic` command (assuming you have installed MET) or run `bin/embedlogic`. For brevity, we assume that `embedlogic` is available.

For the example of Becker's postulate, running

```
> embedlogic -i becker.p -o becker_embedded.p
```

will generate a new file `becker_embedded.p` that contains the embedded THF problem that is semantically equivalent to the modal problem of `becker.p` as given in Fig. 4 (the file is also contained in the distribution of MET in `examples/`). Now, any TPTP THF-compliant ATP system can be used, e.g. Leo-III can be invoked on the result:

```
> leo3 becker_embedded.p
% Axioms used in derivation (1): mrel_meuclidean
[...]
% SZS status Theorem for becker.p : 3443 ms resp. 1260 ms w/o parsing
```

Becker's Postulate Embedded

The embedded file `becker_embedded.p` contains the following:

```
% declare type for possible worlds
thf(mworld_type,type,(
    mworld: $tType )).

% declare accessibility relations
thf(mrel_type,type,(
    mrel: mworld > mworld > $o )).

% define accessibility relation properties
thf(mreflexive_type,type,(
    mreflexive: ( mworld > mworld > $o ) > $o )).

thf(mreflexive_def,definition,
    ( mreflexive
    = ( ^ [R: mworld > mworld > $o] :
        ! [A: mworld] :
          ( R @ A @ A ) ) )).

thf(meuclidean_type,type,(
    meuclidean: ( mworld > mworld > $o ) > $o )).

thf(meuclidean_def,definition,
    ( meuclidean
    = ( ^ [R: mworld > mworld > $o] :
        ! [A: mworld,B: mworld,C: mworld] :
          ( ( ( R @ A @ B )
            & ( R @ A @ C ) )
          => ( R @ B @ C ) ) ) )).

% assign properties to accessibility relations
thf(mrel_mreflexive,axiom,(
    mreflexive @ mrel )).

thf(mrel_meuclidean,axiom,(
    meuclidean @ mrel )).

% define valid operator
thf(mvalid_type,type,(
    mvalid: ( mworld > $o ) > $o )).

thf(mvalid_def,definition,
    ( mvalid
    = ( ^ [S: mworld > $o] :
        ! [W: mworld] :
          ( S @ W ) ) )).

% define nullary, unary and binary connectives which are no quantifiers
thf(mimplies_type,type,(
    mimplies: ( mworld > $o ) > ( mworld > $o ) > mworld > $o )).

thf(mimplies,definition,
    ( mimplies
    = ( ^ [A: mworld > $o,B: mworld > $o,W: mworld] :
        ( ( A @ W )
        => ( B @ W ) ) ) )).

thf(mdia_type,type,(
    mdia: ( mworld > $o ) > mworld > $o )).

thf(mdia_def,definition,
    ( mdia
    = ( ^ [A: mworld > $o,W: mworld] :
        ? [V: mworld] :
          ( ( mrel @ W @ V )
          & ( A @ V ) ) ) )).

thf(mbox_type,type,(
    mbox: ( mworld > $o ) > mworld > $o )).

thf(mbox_def,definition,
    ( mbox
    = ( ^ [A: mworld > $o,W: mworld] :
        ! [V: mworld] :
          ( ( mrel @ W @ V )
          => ( A @ V ) ) ) )).

% define exists quantifiers
thf(mexists_const_type__o__d_i_t__d_i_c_,type,(
    mexists_const__o__d_i_t__d_i_c_: ( ( $i > $i ) > mworld > $o ) > mworld > $o )).

thf(mexists_const__o__d_i_t__d_i_c_,definition,
    ( mexists_const__o__d_i_t__d_i_c_
    = ( ^ [A: ( $i > $i ) > mworld > $o,W: mworld] :
        ? [X: $i > $i] :
          ( A @ X @ W ) ) )).
```

```
% define for all quantifiers
thf(mforall_const_type__o__d_i_t__o_mworld_t__d_o_c__c_,type,(
    mforall_const__o__d_i_t__o_mworld_t__d_o_c__c_: ( ( $i > mworld > $o ) > mworld > $o ) > mworld > $o )).

thf(mforall_const__o__d_i_t__o_mworld_t__d_o_c__c_,definition,
    ( mforall_const__o__d_i_t__o_mworld_t__d_o_c__c_
    = ( ^ [A: ( $i > mworld > $o ) > mworld > $o,W: mworld] :
        ! [X: $i > mworld > $o] :
          ( A @ X @ W ) ) )).

thf(mforall_const_type__o__d_i_c_,type,(
    mforall_const__o__d_i_c_: ( $i > mworld > $o ) > mworld > $o )).

thf(mforall_const__o__d_i_c_,definition,
    ( mforall_const__o__d_i_c_
    = ( ^ [A: $i > mworld > $o,W: mworld] :
        ! [X: $i] :
          ( A @ X @ W ) ) )).

thf(mforall_const_type__o__d_i_t__d_i_c_,type,(
    mforall_const__o__d_i_t__d_i_c_: ( ( $i > $i ) > mworld > $o ) > mworld > $o )).

thf(mforall_const__o__d_i_t__d_i_c_,definition,
    ( mforall_const__o__d_i_t__d_i_c_
    = ( ^ [A: ( $i > $i ) > mworld > $o,W: mworld] :
        ! [X: $i > $i] :
          ( A @ X @ W ) ) )).

% ------------------------------------------------------------------
% transformed problem
% ------------------------------------------------------------------

thf(1,conjecture,
    ( mvalid
    @ ( mforall_const__o__d_i_t__o_mworld_t__d_o_c__c_
      @ ^ [P: $i > mworld > $o] :
        ( mforall_const__o__d_i_t__d_i_c_
        @ ^ [F: $i > $i] :
          ( mforall_const__o__d_i_c_
          @ ^ [X: $i] :
            ( mexists_const__o__d_i_t__d_i_c_
            @ ^ [Q: $i > $i] :
              ( mimplies @ ( mdia @ ( mbox @ ( P @ ( F @ X ) ) ) ) @ ( mbox @ ( P @ ( Q @ X ) ) ) ) ) ) ) ) ) )).
```

References

1. Schulz, S.: E – a brainiac theorem prover. AI Commun. 15(2,3), 111–126 (2002)
2. Brown, C.E.: Satallax: An automatic higher-order prover. In: Gramlich, B., Miller, D., Sattler, U. (eds.) IJCAR 2012. LNCS (LNAI), vol. 7364, pp. 111–117. Springer, Heidelberg (2012). https://doi.org/10.1007/978-3-642-31365-3_11
3. Benzmüller, C., Sultana, N., Paulson, L.C., Theiß, F.: The higher-order prover LEO-II. J. Autom. Reason. 55(4), 389–404 (2015)
4. Steen, A., Benzmüller, C.: The higher-order prover Leo-III. In: Galmiche, D., Schulz, S., Sebastiani, R. (eds.) IJCAR 2018. LNAI, vol. 10900, pp. 108–116. Springer, Heidelberg (2018)
5. Nipkow, T., Paulson, L.C., Wenzel, M.: Isabelle/HOL: A Proof Assistant for Higher-Order Logic. Lecture Notes in Computer Science, vol. 2283. Springer, Heidelberg (2002). https://doi.org/10.1007/3-540-45949-9
6. Blackburn, P., van Benthem, J.F., Wolter, F.: Handbook of Modal Logic, vol. 3. Elsevier, Amsterdam (2006)
7. Benzmüller, C., Woltzenlogel Paleo, B.: The inconsistency in Gödel's ontological argument: a success story for AI in metaphysics. In: Kambhampati, S. (ed.) IJCAI 2016, vol. 1–3, pp. 936–942. AAAI Press (2016). (Acceptance rate ≤ 25%)
8. Benzmüller, C., Weber, L., Woltzenlogel Paleo, B.: Computer-assisted analysis of the Anderson-Hájek controversy. Logica Universalis 11(1), 139–151 (2017)
9. Fuenmayor, D., Benzmüller, C.: Types, Tableaus and Gödel's God in Isabelle/HOL. Archive of Formal Proofs (2017). This publication is machine verified with Isabelle/HOL, but only mildly human reviewed

10. Benzmüller, C., Paulson, L.: Quantified multimodal logics in simple type theory. Logica Universalis **7**(1), 7–20 (2013). (Special Issue on Multimodal Logics)
11. Sutcliffe, G.: The TPTP problem library and associated infrastructure. From CNF to TH0, TPTP v6.4.0. J. Autom. Reason. **59**(4), 483–502 (2017)
12. Sutcliffe, G., Benzmüller, C.: Automated reasoning in higher-order logic using the TPTP THF infrastructure. J. Formaliz. Reason. **3**(1), 1–27 (2010)
13. Gleißner, T., Steen, A., Benzmüller, C.: Theorem provers for every normal modal logic. In: Eiter, T., Sands, D. (eds.) LPAR-21. EPiC Series in Computing, Maun, Botswana, vol. 46, pp. 14–30. EasyChair (2017)
14. Andrews, P.: Church's type theory. In: Zalta, E.N. (ed.) The Stanford Encyclopedia of Philosophy. Stanford University, Metaphysics Research Lab (2014)
15. Becker, O.: Zur Logik der Modalitäten. Max Niemeyer Verlag (1930)
16. Blanchette, J.C., Nipkow, T.: Nitpick: A counterexample generator for higher-order logic based on a relational model finder. In: Kaufmann, M., Paulson, L.C. (eds.) ITP 2010. LNCS, vol. 6172, pp. 131–146. Springer, Heidelberg (2010). https://doi.org/10.1007/978-3-642-14052-5_11
17. Athan, T., Boley, H., Paschke, A.: Ruleml 1.02: Deliberation, reaction and consumer families. In: Bassiliades, N., et al. (eds.) Proceedings of the RuleML 2015 Challenge, the Special Track on Rule-based Recommender Systems for the Web of Data, the Special Industry Track and the RuleML 2015 Doctoral Consortium hosted by the 9th International Web Rule Symposium (RuleML 2015). CEUR Workshop Proceedings, vol. 1417. CEUR-WS.org (2015)
18. Cao, S.T., Nguyen, L.A., Szalas, A.: The web ontology rule language OWL 2 RL^{+} and its extensions. Trans. Comput. Collect. Intell. **13**, 152–175 (2014)
19. Boley, H., Benzmüller, C., Luan, M., Sha, Z.: Translating higher-order modal logic from RuleML to TPTP. In Giurca, A., et al. (eds.) Proceedings of the RuleML 2016 Challenge, the Special Industry Track and the RuleML 2016 Doctoral Consortium hosted by the 10th International Web Rule Symposium (RuleML 2016). CEUR Workshop Proceedings, vol. 1620. CEUR-WS.org (2016)

Nuance Reasoning Framework:
A Rule-Based System for Semantic Query Rewriting

Prateek Jain[1]([✉]), Peter Z. Yeh[1], William Jarrold[1], Ezra Story[1],
Julien Villemure[2], and David Martin[1]

[1] Nuance AI and Language Lab (NAIL), Nuance Communications Inc.,
Sunnyvale, CA 94085, USA
{prateek.jain,peterz.yeh,william.jarrold,ezra.story,
david.martin}@nuance.com
[2] Nuance Communications Deutschland GmbH, Jülicher Strasse 376,
52070 Aachen, Germany
julien.villemure@nuance.com

Abstract. We present the Nuance Reasoning Framework (NRF), a rule-based framework for semantic query rewriting and reasoning that is being utilized by Nuance Communications Inc. in speech-enabled conversational virtual assistant solutions for numerous automotive Original Equipment Manufacturer's (OEM). We focus on the semantic rewriting task performed by NRF, which bridges the conceptual mismatch between the natural language front-end of automotive virtual assistants and their back end databases, and personalizes the results to the driver. We also describe many of its powerful features such as rewriter arbitration, query mediation and more.

Keywords: Plug-n-play system · Semantic query rewriting
Virtual assistants

1 Introduction

At Nuance, we are building a generic framework called The Dragon Drive Framework (DDFW)[1] that can power a wide range of state of the art speech-enabled automotive virtual assistants. DDFW can be quickly configured to provide automotive OEM's with customized virtual assistants that can perform a variety of tasks such as shopping, dining, finding fuel and parking, etc.; and deliver accurate, personalized results to the driver for each task, resulting in a safer and more engaging user experience.

To accomplish these goals, DDFW must be able to bridge the gap between what the driver explicitly said, and how the back end databases might be organized. For example, the driver might ask for "safe parking nearby". However, the back end

---

[1] https://www.nuance.com/mobile/automotive/dragon-drive.html.

© Springer Nature Switzerland AG 2018
C. Benzmüller et al. (Eds.): RuleML+RR 2018, LNCS 11092, pp. 285–292, 2018.
https://doi.org/10.1007/978-3-319-99906-7_20

parking database might not have any information about safety, but knows about parking amenities such as gated, manned, etc. Rewriting the driver's request from "safe parking" to "parking that is gated or manned" will resolve the conceptual mismatch, leading to more accurate results.

Moreover, DDFW must also consider contextual information and the driver's preferences in order to personalize the results to the driver. Continuing with our previous example, if it's raining and the driver prefers covered parking when it's raining, then DDFW should further rewrite the request to "covered parking that is gated or manned" to further personalize the results and reduce cognitive load.

To enable these capabilities, one of the components in DDFW is the Nuance Reasoning Framework (NRF) [3]: an extensible reasoning framework that allows a variety of specialized semantic rewriters to be combined and used simultaneously (e.g. specialized domain rewriters or spatial rewriters). NRF performs the semantic rewriting by taking the Natural Language Understanding (NLU) output of a driver's request (represented as a SPARQL query) and producing a semantically enriched version of the SPARQL query that accounts for conceptual misalignments, contextual information, and driver preferences.[2]

NRF achieves these capabilities through the following design features:

1. **Plug-n-play Rewriters:** A extensible plug-n-play architecture that allows different semantic query rewriting technologies to be added via a common API. New rewriters need to implement the common interface, but the underlying semantic rewriting technology can be a black box.
2. **Arbitration Module:** An arbitration module that determines and selects the appropriate semantic rewriters to invoke based on each rewriters capability and the user's request, plus context. This module can be extended with custom arbitration strategies as needed.
3. **Mediation Module:** A mediation module that combines the conclusions of the invoked semantic rewriters into a consistent conclusion. Like the arbitration module, this module can also be extended with custom mediation strategies.

Underpinning these key features are several semantic technologies including SPARQL [4] as an interlingua to capture a user's request, RDF [1] to represent user preferences and context, etc.

The structure of the paper is as follows: In Sect. 2, we introduce our design goals and objectives. In Sect. 3, we give details about NRF's architecture, various components related to our framework and the plug-n-play approach. Finally we conclude with a summary and ideas for future work.

---

[2] NRF performs semantic query rewriting along with other reasoning tasks. In this paper, we focus on the semantic query rewriting task. The other reasoning tasks are outside the scope of this paper.

2 Design Goals and Objectives

Our motivation behind creating NRF is two fold:

- Semantically enrich the user's query to account for conceptual misalignments, contextual information, and driver preferences in order to provide tailored, accurate results.
- Provide a scalable and customizable solution which can be easily configured for different scenarios.

NRF achieves these goals with three key functionalities.

1. Allow simultaneous utilization of multiple rewriters with different domain expertise to enhance user queries to accommodate for different scenarios.
2. Identify the right subset of rewriters to use for each user queries (i.e., arbitration) to achieve scalability.
3. Create a uniform response by integrating the responses from the different semantic rewriters (i.e., mediation).

In addition to providing these functionalities, we also need to provide a flexible framework such that those tasked with creating new domains (or extending existing ones) can easily switch (a) one rewriter over another, (b) one arbitration strategy over another, and (c) one mediation strategy over another.

3 NRF Architecture

The architecture and data flow within NRF is illustrated in Fig. 1.

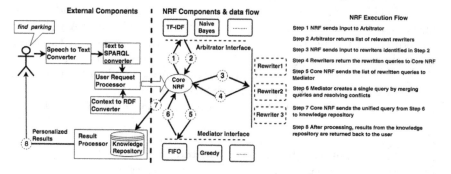

Fig. 1. Figure illustrating data flow within NRF. Components covered in this work are shown on the right hand side along with the steps which are executed.

The main components of NRF are as follows:

1. **Semantic Rewriters** - Semantic Rewriters are auxiliary components which can be easily plugged into NRF by altering an xml configuration file. Each rewriter functions independently of other rewriters and NRF. A rewriter's interaction with NRF is via a common interface which all rewriters obey. This mechanism ensures the internal implementation and processing of the rules are opaque to NRF and makes the plug-n-play architecture feasible.

2. **Arbitrators** - Depending on the problem, it is possible we might need to utilize multiple rewriters in parallel. As each components requires its own rule base and associated resources, it is vital that NRF minimizes the number of rewriter invocations. One way to achieve this is by utilizing an arbitration strategy which identifies the right set of rewriters to utilize for a given query. NRF utilizes an arbitration component to identify the most relevant set of rewriters for a given query. Similar to rewriters, an arbitrator interacts with NRF via a common interface which all arbitrators utilize. This makes it feasible to switch arbitration strategies without making any changes to the core NRF component.

3. **Mediators** - Create a uniform response by integrating the responses from the different rewriters.

4. **Core-NRF** - Core-NRF is the main driver program which parses resource and configuration files, instantiates various components, invokes the semantic rewriters, arbitrator, mediator and interacts with external components.

5. **Rules** - NRF utilizes rules to encode the information which is to be utilized by the different rewriters. The execution of NRF is independent from the rule syntax/format as, in principal, the rewriters interact with the rules. Hence, one can utilize any rule syntax as long as the rewriter is able to utilize them with an input SPARQL query and generate an output SPARQL query. For the rewriters which are bundled with NRF by default, a basic rule format is utilized. This rule format allows users to specify an antecedent and a consequent clause. In the antecedent clause, a user can provide a SPARQL query pattern which the rewriter matches the input query against. In the consequent the user can specify whether they want to assert or retract followed by the query pattern to be asserted or retracted. An example of such a rule is

```
?PARKING ns:type.object.type nuan:parking.generic.
nuan:ContextObj nuan:context.the_vehicle_type nuan:ElectricVehicle.
->
Assert:
OPTIONAL ?PARKING nuan:base.entity.amenities_are ?AMENITY.
FILTER (?AMENITY = nuan:amenity.ev_charging_station)
```

The rule above specifies that if the input SPARQL query has a pattern where the user is looking for a parking facility and contextual information about the vehicle indicates it is an Electric Vehicle, then the rewriter should assert two additional OPTIONAL components in the query. First: It should add a variable capturing the amenities related to parking in the OPTIONAL clause. Secondly, a FILTER clause is added within the OPTIONAL clause to bind the variable capturing amenities in the parking facility to an EV Charging Station.

By replacing **Assert** with **Retract**, the rewriters can be instructed to remove query patterns from the input SPARQL query.

3.1   Semantic Rewriters

As mentioned above, the purpose of the semantic rewriters is to enrich the input query by utilizing domain specific information encoded in the form of rules. For rewriters bundled with NRF, they execute the rules via the following three steps:

- **Step 1:** A rewriter tries to identify all the rules which match the input query's pattern. This is done by performing a match between the terms mentioned in the query with the terms mentioned in the antecedent of the rules associated with the rewriter. A successful match happens when the antecedent of the rule is a subset of the input query pattern. If the antecedent of the rule is not a subset of the query pattern, then the rule is not considered to be a match and will not be utilized for semantic query rewriting.
- **Step 2:** All the rules considered to be a match are then ranked in descending order of their priority. Priority for a rule is assigned by the rule writer signifying the relative importance of the rule with respect to the overall rule base used by the query rewriter.
- **Step 3:** Finally, the rewriter executes the rules one by one starting with the highest priority rule. The altered query created as a result of the output of the execution of the first rule is fed as input to the second rule and so on. The process continues until there are no more relevant rules remaining.
- **Step 4:** The altered query pattern is then returned back to the NRF. If no rules were fired, then the original unaltered query pattern is returned back to NRF.

To illustrate the process lets use an example from a query sent to a rewriter for the parking domain. The rewriter utilizes a rule stating:

If the user is looking for parking and driving an electric vehicle on low charge, then optionally require a parking option that has electric vehicle charging stations.

The rule encoded for use by NRF is shown below.

```
?PARKING ns:type.object.type nuan:parking.generic.
nuan:ContextObj nuan:context.the_vehicle_type nuan:ElectricVehicle.
   ->
Assert:
  OPTIONAL {?PARKING nuan:base.entity.amenities_are ?AMENITY.
  FILTER (?AMENITY = nuan:amenity.ev_charging_station)}
```

Lets assume that the rewriter receives the following query:

```
SELECT ?loc2 ?Name where {
?PARKING ns:type.object.type nuan:parking.generic.
?PARKING ns:type.object.name ?Name.
nuan:ContextObj nuan:context.the_vehicle_type nuan:ElectricVehicle.
}
```

In Step 1, the rewriter will match the two triples present in the query pattern `?loc2 ns:type.object.type nuan:parking.generic` and `nuan:ContextObj nuan:context.the_vehicle_type nuan:ElectricVehicle` with the constraints mentioned in the rule mentioned above as it consists of resources at subject and/or object position.

The second triple in the query `?loc2 ns:type.object.name ?Name.` is not utilized for the purpose of matching as it contains only variables at subject and object positions. As the antecedent of the rule is a subset of the input query pattern, this rule will be considered a match and will be utilized in the next step for rewriting the query pattern. As there is only one rule being utilized, the system will not perform the ranking step (Step 2) and directly move to Step 3.

In Step 3, the rewriter will enhance the query with the triples specified in the **Assert** component of the rule. The output of this step is:

```
SELECT ?PARKING ?Name where {
?PARKING ns:type.object.type nuan:parking.generic.
?PARKING ns:type.object.name ?Name.
nuan:ContextObj nuan:context.the_vehicle_type nuan:ElectricVehicle.
OPTIONAL {?PARKING nuan:base.entity.amenities_are ?AMENITY.
            FILTER (?AMENITY = nuan:amenity.ev_charging_station)}
}
```

Finally, the altered query is returned back to NRF which will then merge the queries returned back by the different rewriters into a single unified query to send to the content providers.

Some of the rewriters included with NRF are explained below:

1. **Parking Domain Rewriter** - This rewriter utilizes parking related rules. Example of such a rule is: If it is raining outside and the user searches for parking, then the system should insert an OPTIONAL clause to FILTER parking facilities which are covered or underground.
2. **Fuel Domain Rewriter** - This rewriter utilizes fuel related rules. Example of such a rule is: If the current range of the vehicle is less than 25 miles and user searches for gas stations, then the system should insert an OPTIONAL clause to FILTER gas stations which are less than 25 miles.

3.2   Arbitrators

NRF consists of a number of different semantic rewriters which utilize different domain specific rules. For example, a parking rewriter which utilizes parking domain rules and a personal preference rewriter which utilizes rules that capture user preferences such as preferred cuisines, brands, etc. While it is possible to utilize all the rewriters at the same time, NRF tries to minimize the overall processing time and resources by invoking only the rewriters relevant for a given query. To optimize for run time and resources, NRF utilizes an arbitrator to identify which rewriters are best suited for a given query.

An arbitrator performs a match between the input query and the rule base associated with the rewriters. The rewriters with the highest score (indicating their relevance), are then utilized to rewrite the query. NRF comes bundled with a number of different arbitrators that implement different strategies to identify the relevant set of rewriters such as a Broadcast Arbitration, Naive Bayes Arbitrator and a TF-IDF based rewriter.

NRF's architecture makes it possible to utilize any multi label classification algorithm as an arbitrator. Consequently, implementations made available with open source libraries such as WEKA [2] can be utilized as arbitrators provided the data is transformed into a format which the implementation utilizes.

3.3   Mediator

NRF includes a number of mediators which take as input the output of different rewriters and outputs a single query that can be executed against a knowledge repository to retrieve results. At its core, a mediator performs two tasks (1) Merging the query patterns from the output query of each rewriter, and (2) Resolving conflicts between the query patterns, should they arise (the resolution can be heuristically driven or logically driven).

NRF includes a number of pre-built mediators and a new mediation approach can be seamlessly plugged in by providing a suitable implementation and editing the NRF configuration file. Some of the pre-built mediation approaches included with NRF include (1) a greedy mediator which gives preference to higher ranked rewriter (2) fifo mediator which gives preference to responses from rewriters which return their result first.

4   Conclusion

In this paper, we presented the Nuance Reasoning Framework (NRF): an extensible reasoning framework that allows a variety of specialized semantic rewriters to be combined and used simultaneously. We presented the system architecture and its various components along with implementation details. NRF has been deployed as part of Nuance's Dragon Drive Framework, which powers speech-enabled conversational virtual assistant solutions for numerous automotive OEMs.

Acknowledgement. We would like to express our gratitude to Dr. Charles Ortiz, Director, Nuance Artificial Intelligence and Language Lab (NAIL Lab), Sunnyvale CA for supporting and encouraging our work. His comments were instrumental in setting the direction for the work and in refining the manuscript. Finally, we would also like to thank the reviewers for their insights.

References

1. Cyganiak, R., Wood, D., Lanthaler, M.: RDF 1.1 concepts and abstract syntax. W3C Recommendation, February 2014. https://www.w3.org/TR/2014/REC-rdf11-concepts-20140225/

2. Hall, M., Frank, E., Holmes, G., Pfahringer, B., Reutemann, P., Witten, I.H.: The weka data mining software: An update. SIGKDD Explor. Newsl. **11**(1), 10–18 (2009). http://doi.acm.org/10.1145/1656274.1656278
3. Jain, P., Yeh, P.Z., Story, E., Villemure, J., Martin, D.L., Jarrold, W.: Nuance reasoning framework. In: Nikitina, N., Song, D., Fokoue, A., Haase, P. (eds.) Proceedings of the ISWC 2017 Posters & Demonstrations and Industry Tracks Co-located with 16th International Semantic Web Conference (ISWC 2017), 23rd to 25th October 2017, Vienna, Austria, CEUR Workshop Proceedings, vol. 1963. CEUR-WS.org (2017). http://ceur-ws.org/Vol-1963/paper500.pdf
4. Prud'hommeaux, E., Seaborne, A.: SPARQL query language for RDF. W3C Recommendation, January 2008. http://www.w3.org/TR/rdf-sparql-query/

Learning Condition–Action Rules for Personalised Journey Recommendations

Matthew R. Karlsen and Sotiris Moschoyiannis[✉]

Department of Computer Science, University of Surrey, Guildford GU2 7XH, UK
{matthew.r.karlsen,s.moschoyiannis}@surrey.ac.uk

Abstract. We apply a learning classifier system, XCSI, to the task of providing personalised suggestions for passenger onward journeys. Learning classifier systems combine evolutionary computation with rule-based machine learning, altering a population of rules to achieve a goal through interaction with the environment. Here XCSI interacts with a simulated environment of passengers travelling around the London Underground network, subject to disruption. We show that XCSI successfully learns individual passenger preferences and can be used to suggest personalised adjustments to the onward journey in the event of disruption.

Keywords: Rule-based machine learning · XCSI
Passenger preferences

1 Introduction

Modern route recommendation systems suggest multiple routes, times and modes, with near instant results. However, unique passenger preferences are ignored. Here we use the Learning Classifier System [14] XCSI [17] (explained in Sect. 2) to learn individual transport mode preferences, given the current state of the transport network and other factors (e.g. weather). The idea is to provide advice as part of a "recommendation engine" that pro-actively suggests adjustments to a journey as data becomes available.

The remainder of this paper is structured as follows. XCSI and its application to making *personalised* recommendations is described in Sect. 2. Experiments, described in Sect. 3, are performed in relation to the above challenge. The results and accompanying discussion for these experiments is presented in Sect. 4. Related work is outlined in Sect. 5. The paper concludes in Sect. 6.

This research was partly funded by the Department for Transport, via Innovate UK and the *Accelerating Innovation in Rail* (AIR) Round 4 programme, under the *Onward Journey Planning Assistant (OJPA)* project.

© Springer Nature Switzerland AG 2018
C. Benzmüller et al. (Eds.): RuleML+RR 2018, LNCS 11092, pp. 293–301, 2018.
https://doi.org/10.1007/978-3-319-99906-7_21

2   Applying XCSI to Provision of Recommendations

The overall challenge is to provide a single integer recommendation (representing a mode or modes) for each unique situation (combination of passenger preferences, current context and environment state). The XCSI system used to achieve this is built in two steps. We first implement XCS [15, 16] according to the detailed algorithmic specification supplied by Butz and Wilson [2]. Following from this, the XCSI modification is implemented based on [17]. We use XCSI (with integer, rather than boolean variables) over XCS here because a number of factors relevant to onward journey recommendations have more than two possible states. Due to space limitations we refer to [8] for the full XCSI specification.

A learning classifier system possesses sensors, internal mechanisms of operation, and effectors. The system also possesses a 'feedback' mechanism to judge the impact of effector-implemented actions on the environment relative to the system's goals. The system adapts its internal structure over time to effectively model the environment with the aim of achieving these goals. The central system operation is the following: (1) detect the 'environment state' via the detectors, (2) convert this state in to an integer string (e.g. 42403015), (3) determine an integer-labelled action based on LCS internal structure, (4) implement the action in the environment, (5) obtain feedback via the feedback sensor, (6) use feedback to adapt internal structure to model the environment, (7) re-start at (1). In order to operate in the above manner XCSI is put together from a number of components, governed by a central algorithm (see [8] for more detail).

2.1   Detectors

The *situation* is comprised of environment factors, journey-specific factors the needs and preferences of the passenger. Here, our situation is comprised of a number of **environment factors** (Train QoS (quality of service) [0 or 5], Taxi QoS [0 or 5], Tube QoS [0 or 5], Boat QoS [0 or 5], Bus QoS [0 or 5]), **journey-specific factors** (delay on current route [0 or 5], delay on current mode [0 or 5], onward delay [0 or 5]), 4 relatively-invariant **passenger preferences** (value preference [0 to 5], speed preference [0 to 5], comfort preference [0 to 5], shelter preference [0 to 5]), and weather [0 to 5] (cf see Fig. 1).

By treating passenger preferences as external we treat the system as a kind of 'oracle'. An alternative would be to have one system per passenger and omit the passenger preference detectors. This would enable finer-tuned recommendations after many steps but would also mean slower learning (experience would not be shared between passengers) and greater resource costs. With the 'oracle' approach, the feedback acquired through use can be shared between passengers and *passengers still differ* due to their different ratings for each preference.

2.2   Population of Rules

The central component of the XCSI system is a population of IF <condition> THEN <action> rules of size N. Given the above inputs, we can construct a

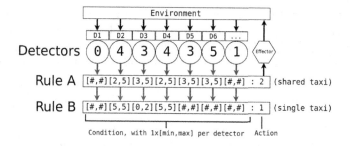

Fig. 1. The structure of the environment detectors and condition–action rules.

series of rules to relate given situations to particular transport 'actions' (travel options). For the current problem, XCSI takes as *input* a list of integers, where each integer corresponds to one of the above properties. The *output* at each step is a single integer representing the action that should be taken in the environment (or, in the present case the *recommended* travel mode), as shown in Fig. 1. The condition side of the rule represents the environment state that triggers the rule. The '#' symbols represent 'don't care', indicating that any detector integer value in this position is acceptable as part of a rule match. The right hand side of the rule is an action, represented as an integer.

2.3   Rule Matching

For a given integer string input some of the rules match whilst others do not, as shown in Fig. 1, where we have two rules, seven detectors, and an effector. Each detector takes a value in the range [0, 5]. Here the inputs read in are 0,4,3,4,3,5,1. Each of these detector values is compared with a related range within each rule. The [min,max] range indicates whether the particular rule matches the given input at that particular detector. All ranges must match the relevant detectors for the rule to match fully. As we can see in the example, rule 'A' matches but rule 'B' does not. Rule A corresponds to action 2 (recommend a shared taxi) and thus in this situation the recommended action supplied to the user (in the environment) is to book a shared taxi.[1]

2.4   Effector and Feedback Mechanism

In a real-world system the effector would display the suggested onward travel option via a passenger interface. In the experiments described herein, an integer is supplied to the simulation environment which determines whether the recommendation was correct or not. Possible onward journey modes that can be suggested to the passenger for short to medium distance journeys are numerous. Virtual 'journeys' are also possible [18]. Here we limit ourselves to no change (**0**),

---

[1] Note that in the simple example here we depict a match as immediately triggering the rule in question – the actual action selection is more complex.

single taxi (**1**), shared taxi (**2**), bus (**3**), boat or water bus (**4**), underground or tube (**5**), and regular train (**6**). For the simulation herein, the feedback mechanism provides a payoff of **1000** for a correct answer (i.e. the simulated passenger's preference is indeed for the suggested action) and **0** for an incorrect answer.

3   Experiments

The simulation involves 300 random passengers, *with individual preferences*, origin locations and destination locations. A number of planned journeys on the London Underground are generated, using passenger origins and destinations, exceeding the number of steps XCSI will run for. The shortest path for each journey is calculated using the A* implementation from GraphStream [5].

For each time step, 5% of links are randomly selected and marked as 'out-of-order'. If any of the links on the shortest path between the current node and the journey destination are out-of-order then the delay property is set to 5. If none are out of order it is set to 0. The value of the tube QoS detector is set to 0 if any links on the shortest path are out-of-order; otherwise it is set to 5.

The abstract 'start time' of each journey is randomly generated in the range [0, 99]. For each time step the weather property (0 to 5) is randomly generated. The availability of train, boat, bus and taxi is exogenous to the simulation and simply marked as either available (5) or unavailable (0). Once the journeys generation is complete their order is shuffled. The first journey with the minimum

Table 1. A sample of condition-action rules. From left to right, the conditions are the input factors described in Sect. 2.1. The suggested actions were described in Sect. 2.4.

Condition	:	Action
[0,0] [0,0] [0,0] [5,5] [5,5] [#,#] [#,#] [5,5] [0,1] [#,#] [2,5] [#,#] [#,#]	:	1
[0,0] [0,0] [0,0] [5,5] [5,5] [#,#] [#,#] [5,5] [0,1] [2,5] [#,#] [#,#] [#,#]	:	1
[0,0] [0,0] [0,0] [5,5] [5,5] [#,#] [#,#] [5,5] [2,3] [#,#] [4,5] [#,#] [#,#]	:	1
[0,0] [0,0] [0,0] [5,5] [5,5] [#,#] [#,#] [5,5] [2,3] [4,5] [#,#] [#,#] [#,#]	:	1
[0,0] [0,0] [0,0] [5,5] [5,5] [#,#] [#,#] [5,5] [0,1] [0,1] [2,3] [#,#] [#,#]	:	2
[0,0] [0,0] [0,0] [5,5] [5,5] [#,#] [#,#] [5,5] [0,1] [2,3] [0,1] [#,#] [#,#]	:	2
[0,0] [0,0] [0,0] [5,5] [5,5] [#,#] [#,#] [5,5] [0,1] [2,3] [2,3] [#,#] [#,#]	:	2
[0,0] [0,0] [0,0] [5,5] [5,5] [#,#] [#,#] [5,5] [2,3] [0,1] [2,3] [#,#] [#,#]	:	2
[0,0] [0,0] [0,0] [5,5] [5,5] [#,#] [#,#] [5,5] [2,3] [2,3] [2,3] [#,#] [#,#]	:	2
[0,0] [0,0] [0,0] [5,5] [5,5] [#,#] [#,#] [5,5] [4,5] [0,1] [2,3] [#,#] [#,#]	:	2
[0,0] [0,0] [0,0] [5,5] [5,5] [#,#] [#,#] [5,5] [4,5] [0,1] [4,5] [#,#] [#,#]	:	2
[0,0] [0,0] [0,0] [5,5] [5,5] [#,#] [#,#] [5,5] [4,5] [2,3] [2,3] [#,#] [#,#]	:	2
[0,0] [0,0] [0,0] [5,5] [5,5] [#,#] [#,#] [5,5] [4,5] [2,3] [4,5] [#,#] [#,#]	:	2
[0,0] [0,0] [0,0] [5,5] [5,5] [#,#] [#,#] [5,5] [0,1] [0,1] [0,1] [#,#] [#,#]	:	3
[0,0] [0,0] [0,0] [5,5] [5,5] [#,#] [#,#] [5,5] [2,3] [0,1] [0,1] [#,#] [#,#]	:	3
[0,0] [0,0] [0,0] [5,5] [5,5] [#,#] [#,#] [5,5] [2,3] [2,3] [0,1] [#,#] [#,#]	:	3
[0,0] [0,0] [0,0] [5,5] [5,5] [#,#] [#,#] [5,5] [4,5] [0,1] [0,1] [#,#] [#,#]	:	3

start time is then used to create the first state, the next journey with the same start time is used to create the second state, and so on. This process is then repeated with all the entries for all time steps, until all the states have been added to the final state sequence. It is this sequence that is used each time XCSI requests a state. The 'preference table' that relates consumer preferences to particular preferred actions is input as static. A sub-set is shown in Table 1.

3.1   Parameters

The original parameter settings from [2] are shown in the Default column while variations of these are shown in the Other Values column in Table 2.

Table 2. The parameter settings used.

Parameter	Default	Other values
N	15600	11700, 19500
θ_{del}	20	10, 30
δ	0.1	0.05, 0.2
γ	0.71	N/A
θ_{mna}	7	N/A
$P_{\#}$	0.55	0.35, 0.75
r_0	2	1, 3
p_I	10	N/A
ϵ_I	0	N/A
ϵ_0	0	5, 20
F_I	10	N/A
ϵ_0	10	N/A
θ_{sub}	20.0	10, 60
doActionSetSubsumption	true	false
doGaSubsumption	true	false
θ_{ga}	50	25, 150
χ	0.8	0.6, 1.0
μ	0.04	0.02, 0.08
m_0	1	2, 3
p_{explr}	0.5	0.25, 0.75
α	0.1	0.08, 0.12
ν	5.0	4.0, 6.0
β	0.15	0.1, 0.2
activateExploreAndExploitMode	true	false

3.2   Simulation Runs

For each combination of parameters in the table above (varying a single parameter away from default each time) we perform one 'experiment'. For each experiment we perform 32 repetitions, recording the minimum, maximum and average number of incorrect predictions across these repetitions.

For each experiment repetition we first set up the simulation environment. XSCI is then initialised with the required parameters. XCSI is then run for a number of steps as specified by the parameters (typically 50,000 steps). The evolved rules are then output. Next, p_{explr} is set to 0.0 and the feedback mechanism, action set updater and genetic algorithm are disabled (essentially all adaptation is disabled). XCSI then runs for a further 1000 steps and records the number of errors (incorrect suggestions) over these steps. The input from the training phase is *not* re-used in the test phase.

4   Results and Discussion

The results for the experiments are shown in Table 3.

The average error level for the 1000 test steps for the parameter settings used (with 50,000 'training' steps) is 3.1%. The number of errors falls as the number of training steps increases, from 6.1% errors with 25,000 steps to 2.0% per 75,000 steps. This is to be expected since logically the greater the number of learning iterations, the better the understanding of the passenger preferences (if the system is working as expected). Upon completion of these results an additional run was performed, combining the parameter setting shown in bold in Table 3. The results are minimum error 0.1%, average error 0.734%, and maximum error 2%.

5   Related Work

Present-day 'live' services such as Citymapper (citymapper.com) suggest routes, times and modes, but do not consider passenger preferences. Research in this direction is limited, with recent work proposing Bayesian networks [4], heuristics and traditional routing [1] and 'case-based reasoning' [6,9], which provide customised recommendations without actual specification of passenger preferences.

In previous work [8] we have applied the XCS variant [2] of LCS to study *controllability* [10] in Random Boolean Networks. The extension with integer-based conditions in XCSI is necessary to capture passenger preferences faithfully.

Specifically, XCSI is suited to the current problem for the following reasons: (1) the rules produced are human-readable making the gathered knowledge available for analysis, (2) they are on-line, hence can provide rapid responses manner (providing single input–output iterations) in contrast to batch-based approaches that require a number of training instances, (3) the system adapts to changes within the mapping of input states to preferred actions (i.e. the system can cope with concept drift), (4) the system is able to construct thousands of rules without direct human input which tend to be time consuming and prone to error.

Table 3. The results for the experiments, with 32 trials per experiment.

Parameter	Value	Min. error %	Avg. error %	Max. error %
Defaults	see above	0.8	3.1	7.1
trials	25000	3.1	6.1	10.0
trials	75000	0.5	2.0	6.6
N	11700	0.6	**2.8**	8.2
N	19500	1.3	3.0	5.9
activateExploreAndExploit	false	5.1	8.9	23.6
θ_{del}	10	1.2	**2.7**	5.2
θ_{del}	30	0.9	2.9	7.9
δ	0.05	0.9	**2.7**	6.0
δ	0.2	0.9	3.1	7.2
$P_{\#}$	0.35	0.4	**1.9**	4.2
$P_{\#}$	0.75	2.5	6.3	13.7
r_0	1	0.8	**2.7**	5.5
r_0	3	1.5	2.9	4.5
ϵ_0	5	0.8	**2.4**	5.1
ϵ_0	20	1.8	4.4	12.9
θ_{sub}	10	0.7	3.8	7.7
θ_{sub}	60	1.0	**2.7**	6.0
doActionSetSubsumption	false	0.0	**1.0**	2.0
doGaSubsumption	false	1.1	3.3	6.5
θ_{ga}	25	0.6	**1.9**	5.0
θ_{ga}	150	2.2	7.1	15.6
χ	0.6	1.1	3.4	6.4
χ	1	1.1	**2.7**	5.5
μ	0.02	1.8	5.5	11.3
μ	0.08	0.4	**2.1**	7.2
m_0	2	0.5	3.6	8.8
m_0	3	1.3	3.8	8.1
p_{explr}	0.25	0.9	3.8	8.1
p_{explr}	0.75	1.8	6.4	13.9
α	0.08	0.4	**2.7**	5.6
α	0.12	0.8	2.8	7.1
ν	4	0.8	3.0	7.6
ν	6	0.9	**2.6**	7.1
β	0.1	0.4	**1.8**	3.9
β	0.2	2.3	5.4	11.7

Pulugurta et al. [12] consider classifiers for predicting travel mode and find that the fuzzy logic model has superior performance over the multinomial logit model. Omrani [11] find that neural network-based approaches (multi layer perceptron and radial basis function networks) have higher performance than multinomial logistic regression and support vector machines. Sekhar et al. [13] find that the random forest classifier out-performs the multinomial logit model. Hagenauer et al. [7] compare seven classifiers applied to the task of predicting travel mode based on a number of inputs. They find that the Random Forest classifier produces the best performance of the seven. To the best of our knowledge XCSI has not been applied before to the provision of onward journey recommendations.

6 Concluding Remarks and Future Work

XCSI represents a comparatively novel approach to constructing an onward journey recommendation system. Our results in Sect. 4 indicate that an error rate of 3.1% is achievable with the default parameter settings. With adjusted parameter settings we find that the error rate is reduced yet further to just 0.734% on average. In this way, XCSI is demonstrably able to develop a relatively compact set of rules used to provide accurate recommendations to simulated travellers.

Directions for future work include more precise conditions for detectors with binary states, code optimisation, an XCSI extension to be used in a parallel by multiple passengers, an evaluation of the use of supervised learning rather than reinforcement learning, and implementation of multi-modal solutions.

Additionally we note that DMN (Decision Models and Notation)-based rules [3] may become prohibitively complex for a human to construct (with a large number of conditions or rules). It would be possible, particularly in conjunction with the messy encoding mentioned above, to evolve DMN rules using XCS. This approach could produce complex and adaptive rule sets without the need for human intervention in the system. Alternatively, the approach used to merge rules in [3] could well be used as a mechanism for rule set reduction in XCSI.

References

1. Bucher, D., Jonietz, D., Raubal, M.: A heuristic for multi-modal route planning. In: Gartner, G., Huang, H. (eds.) Progress in Location-Based Services 2016. LNGC, pp. 211–229. Springer, Cham (2017). https://doi.org/10.1007/978-3-319-47289-8_11
2. Butz, M.V., Wilson, S.W.: An algorithmic description of XCS. In: Luca Lanzi, P., Stolzmann, W., Wilson, S.W. (eds.) IWLCS 2000. LNCS (LNAI), vol. 1996, pp. 253–272. Springer, Heidelberg (2001). https://doi.org/10.1007/3-540-44640-0_15
3. Calvanese, D., Dumas, M., et al.: Semantics, analysis and simplification of DMN decision tables. Inf. Syst. (2018, in press)
4. Campigotto, P., Rudloff, C., Leodolter, M., Bauer, D.: Personalized and situation-aware multimodal route recommendations: the FAVOUR algorithm. IEEE Trans. Intell. Transp. Syst. 18(1), 92–102 (2017)

5. Dutot, A., Guinand, F., et al.: Graphstream: a tool for bridging the gap between complex systems and dynamic graphs. In: Emergent Properties in Natural and Artificial Complex Systems (2007)
6. Ginty, L.M., Smyth, B.: Collaborative case-based reasoning: applications in personalised route planning. In: Aha, D.W., Watson, I. (eds.) ICCBR 2001. LNCS (LNAI), vol. 2080, pp. 362–376. Springer, Heidelberg (2001). https://doi.org/10.1007/3-540-44593-5_26
7. Hagenauer, J., Helbich, M.: A comparative study of machine learning classifiers for modeling travel mode choice. Expert Syst. Appl. **78**, 273–282 (2017)
8. Karlsen, M.R., Moschoyiannis, S.: Evolution of control with learning classifier systems. J. Appl. Netw. Sci. (2018, in press)
9. McGinty, L., Smyth, B.: Personalised route planning: a case-based approach. In: Blanzieri, E., Portinale, L. (eds.) EWCBR 2000. LNCS, vol. 1898, pp. 431–443. Springer, Heidelberg (2000). https://doi.org/10.1007/3-540-44527-7_37
10. Moschoyiannis, S., Elia, N., Penn, A., et al.: A web-based tool for identifying strategic intervention points in complex systems. In: Proceedings of the Games for the Synthesis of Complex Systems. EPTCS, vol. 220, pp. 39–52 (2016)
11. Omrani, H.: Predicting travel mode of individuals by machine learning. Transp. Res. Procedia **10**, 840–849 (2015)
12. Pulugurta, S., Arun, A., Errampalli, M.: Use of artificial intelligence for mode choice analysis and comparison with traditional multinomial logit model. Procedia Soc. Behav. Sci. **104**, 583–592 (2013)
13. Sekhar, C.R., Madhu, E.: Mode choice analysis using random forrest decision trees. Transp. Res. Procedia **17**, 644–652 (2016)
14. Urbanowicz, R.J., Moore, J.H.: Learning classifier systems: a complete introduction, review, and roadmap. J. Artif. Evol. Appl. **2009**, 1 (2009)
15. Wilson, S.W.: Classifier fitness based on accuracy. Evol. Comput. **3**(2), 149–175 (1995)
16. Wilson, S.W.: Generalization in the XCS classifier system (1998)
17. Wilson, S.W.: Mining oblique data with XCS. In: Luca Lanzi, P., Stolzmann, W., Wilson, S.W. (eds.) IWLCS 2000. LNCS (LNAI), vol. 1996, pp. 158–174. Springer, Heidelberg (2001). https://doi.org/10.1007/3-540-44640-0_11
18. Wockatz, P., Schartau, P.: Traveller needs and UK capability study. Technical report, Transport Systems Catapult (2017)

A Rule-Based eCommerce Methodology for the IoT Using Trustworthy Intelligent Agents and Microservices

Kalliopi Kravari$^{(\boxtimes)}$ (iD) and Nick Bassiliades (iD)

Department of Informatics, Aristotle University of Thessaloniki,
54124 Thessaloniki, Greece
{kkravari,nbassili}@csd.auth.gr

Abstract. The impact of the Internet of Things will transform business and economy. This network of intercommunicating heterogeneous Things is expected to affect the commerce industry by driving innovation and new opportunities in the future. Yet, this open, distributed and heterogeneous environment raises challenges. Old eCommerce practices cannot be sufficiently applied while trustworthiness issues arise. This study proposes a rule-based eCommerce methodology that will allow Things to safely trade on the network. The proposed methodology represents Things as Intelligent Agents since they form an alternative to traditional interactions among people and objects while they are involved in a rich research effort regarding trust management. It also combines Intelligent Agents with the microservice architecture in order to deal with Things heterogeneity while it adopts the use of a social agent-based trust model. Well-known semantic technologies such as RuleML and defeasible logic is adopted in order to maximize interoperability. Furthermore, in order to deal with issues related to rule exchange with no common syntax, the methodology is integrated to a multi-agent knowledge-based framework. Finally, an eCommerce scenario is presented, illustrating the viability of the approach.

Keywords: Multi-agent systems · Defeasible reasoning · Trustworthiness

1 Introduction

The Internet of Things (IoT) seems to be an emerging IT technology. Its main innovation consists of creating a world where Things, devices, services or even humans, will be connected and able to make decisions and communicate [7]. An area that is expected to attract attention is eCommerce which has achieved a growth but due to IoT emergence, it faces new challenges. It must be clearly recognized that the application of IoT is still at an early stage while the relevant technology is not mature. Today, the IoT mostly sends data up towards the Cloud for processing. Many researchers believe that as both software and hardware continues to evolve, some of these processes may be bring back to the devices. Hence, in the IoT of tomorrow, value between devices and across industries could be uncovered using Intelligent Agents (IAs) that can add autonomy, context awareness, and intelligence [7]. Besides, current eCommerce evolved on the basis of the past retail sector, hence, product quality is difficult to

© Springer Nature Switzerland AG 2018
C. Benzmüller et al. (Eds.): RuleML+RR 2018, LNCS 11092, pp. 302–309, 2018.
https://doi.org/10.1007/978-3-319-99906-7_22

guarantee, the pay security, logistics and distribution systems need more automation. As more devices get connected and gain smart features, more data will be gathered, and consumer experience can be improved. Hence, although all these requirements exists in the IoT eCommerce, they have to be upgraded with intelligence, autonomy and semantic awareness (despite the need semantic languages are not used yet). With the penetration of IoT, a better management of inventory, easy loss tracking, increase in shopper intelligence and intelligent logistics systems with timeliness, convenience and safety properties should be developed. However, deployment of IoT to facilitate eCommerce applications raises important challenges such as information exchange and trust issues [3, 7]. In this context, we, as plenty others, propose a decentralized approach where devices combined with agents will become part of the Internet of Smart Things. Of course, there is much work to be done regarding decentralized Multiagent systems as a way to place decentralized intelligence in distributed computing.

The aim of this study is to propose a rule-based eCommerce methodology that will allow Things to locate proper partners, establish trust relationships and interact in the future IoT network. The proposed methodology adopts the use of IAs that are considered a technology that can deal with these challenges while there are involved in a rich research effort regarding trust management, even though it refers to Semantic Web [3]. The methodology integrates an IoT social agent-based reputation model in order to allow trust establishment in the environment. Furthermore, this study combines the agent technology with the microservice architecture, a promising modular approach [1]. A core concept of the methodology is the proper information exchange among Things in order to assure safe and robust transactions. Hence, the base of the methodology is a weakly-structured workflow with strong information technologies. Hence, well-known semantic technologies such as RuleML and defeasible logic is adopted, maximizing interoperability, reusability, automation and efficiency among Things. Additionally, the methodology is integrated to a multi-agent knowledge-based framework that supports rule exchange without the need of a common syntax.

2 Rule-Based eCommerce Methodology

All Things are represented as agents while microservice architecture is used for the implementation of services and devices [3]. Microservices have almost every known agent property while they allow control over even hardly reached devices. Here, we propose two types of microservices called DMicro, related to an IoT device, and SMicro, related to a service, represented as agents. Each IoT-oriented eCommerce website should have at least a SMicro agent that will act as proxy between the site and the Things. Hence, the proposed methodology involves three types of agents, modeling IoT Things, called T_{hv} (humans/virtual), T_{DMicro} (devices) and T_{SMicro} (services). Each agent's conceptual base follows this T_x tuple specification: A = {ID, T_x, LC, LP, B, S, ER, EV}(1), where ID is the agent's name, T_x is its type {$x \equiv T_{hv}|T_{SMicro}|T_{SMicro}$}, LC and LP are extendable lists of characteristics C and preferences P{LC_x^n & LP_x^n | $n \in [1, N]$, $x \equiv agent$}, B is agent's beliefs (facts) {$B = B_I \cup B_R$ | B_I by agent's interactions, B_R by reasoning processes}, S is its strategy rules, ER is the ratings derived by the agent's direct experience and EV contains its evaluation criteria. The LC list includes information such as the type of provided products/services. Preferences (LP) include information such as the desirable delivery time. For computational and priority purposes, each characteristic and preference is optionally assigned with a value of importance (weight) at the range [0, 1] $\left(W_c^n \; \& \; W_p^n \mid n \in [0.1], \right.$ $c \equiv characteristic, \; p \equiv preference)$, defining how much attention will be paid to it.

In this context, we propose a five stage weakly-structured workflow methodology for the IoT-oriented eCommerce, based on the philosophy that the procedure can be divided into groups of tasks forming special categories containing a number of steps. The proposed approach acknowledges five stages; 1. *Locate potential partners, 2. Establish trust, 3. Exchange request/data, 4. Negotiate terms, 5. Reach agreement.* Here, we focus mainly on the two first stages, namely locating partners and establish trust since they are critical for IoT success, yet, they are not sufficiently studied. In general, stages represent the main issues of the overall eCommerce process while steps represent individual actions that agents have to handle depending on their rule-based strategy. Thus, each specific stage requires a group of steps. Transitions between stages are sequential, but transitions between steps may be not. The involved agents have to proceed gradually from the first issue (locate partners) to the last while steps represent individual actions referring even to optional or repeatable actions.

In order to present the terms and defeasible rules of the approach in a compact way, we express them in the compact d-POSL syntax [4] of defeasible RuleML. Defeasible logic (DL) has the notion of rules that can be defeated. In DL strict rules (B:-A1, ..., An in d-POSL syntax) are rules in the classical sense. Defeasible rules (B: = A1, ..., An) can be defeated by contrary evidence. Defeaters (B: ∼A1, ..., An) are a special kind of rules, used to prevent conclusions and not to support them. DL does not support contradictory conclusions, instead seeks to resolve conflicts. In cases where no conclusion can be derived, a priority is expressed through a superiority relation among rules which defines where one rule override the conclusion of another.

Locating potential partners
The proposed approach offers two alternative options for locating partners, one of the major challenges for open distributed and large-scale systems. The first one is based on auction-inspired broadcasting with no rating requirements while the second is based on LOCATOR [5] which requires previously reported reputation ratings.

Broadcasting option: Whenever an agent (Tx) has no previous interaction history or it needs fast SMicro locating, it broadcasts a CFP reaching easily available agents. Agents that receive the CFP call either ignore it or reply with a propose message.

r_{i1}:   broadcastCFP(id→?id_x,   time→?t,   sender→?x,   receiver→?SMicro, typeRequest→?typeRequest, reasonImportance→?rim, specs→?specs) :- timeAvailablity(low),request(typeRequest→?typeRequest$_x$,specs→?specs$_x$,reasonImportance→? rim$_x$), reasonImportance_threshold(?rim), ?rim$_x$>?rim, ?typeRequest$_x$ = ?typeRequest.

A typical CFP message (r_{i1}) indicates that the sender asks the receiver (?SMicro) about a specific reason (typeRequest, e.g. rating request), stating how important is that request (reasonImportance at the range [0, 1]) and which are the specifications of the request (*specs, e.g.* service type). It will send the CFP if the time availability is low (there is such a fact to its beliefs: $B_R = \{timeAvailablity(low)\}$), the importance of the reason is greater than its threshold (*reasonImportance_threshold(?rim)*, $?rim_x > ?rim$) and it needs to fulfil such a type request (holds such goal: $G = \{fulfil(?typeRequest_x)\}$).

LOCATOR variation option: The second option is based on the philosophy of LOCATOR, a locating rating mechanism that uses features from both social graphs and peer-to-peer networks in order to incorporate potential social dimensions and relationships within the IoT. Here, we adopt the use of LOCATOR to locate potential SMicro partners. Our variation works as follow: A T_x agent interested in a T_{SMicro} agent, based on its preferences $\left(LP_{TR}^n\right)$ decides upon the characteristics $\left(LC_{TE}^n\right)$ it considers important. It assigns proper weights $\left(W_C^n\right)$ to them and searches its database for previously known agents that fulfil its requirements in order to ask them. Characteristics that weight more are more important in the sense that T_x believes that partners with these characteristics will be more reliable (social influence). In this context, T_x depending on its personal strategy ($S_X^n \in n\ [1,\ N]$, $x \equiv agent$) sends an offer request to known agents with one or two high-weighted characteristics. If the feedback is not satisfying, it sends requests to partners with lower-weighted characteristics.

After choosing local neighbors (direct request receivers), TR assigns a time thresholds (TTL) to its message and sends it to them. They, on their turn, either propose an offer or propagate it to their own local neighbors following the same procedure as long as they have time ($t < TTL$). In that case, these agents acting as subcontractors (RR) send the feedback offer to T_x as well as available ratings (see next subsection) for this partner. At the next step, T_x assigns a value V, an indication of relevance, to each received trusted path, calculated as follows: $V = (pl-0.25*hp)*C_{RR}$, $\sqrt{pl}<=5$ or $V = (pl-0.5*hp)*C_{RR}, \sqrt{pl}>=6$ (2), where pl stands for the length of the trusted path, hp stands for the number of network nodes while C_{RR} is the credit score of the local neighbor (RR agent) that returned that path. C_{RR} is based on RR agent's credits with a time stamp that fits in TR requested time period. Using this time period, TR has a clue about RR's latest behavior. The V value discards feedback, taking into account risk.

Establishing trust

Despite the chosen mechanism, as soon as, potential partners are located, T_x proceeds to the next stage, establishing a relationship with the most promising eCommerce partner (T_{SMicro} agent). We propose a reputation based approach. In general, reputation allows agents to build the degree to which an agent has confidence in another agent. Hence, reputation (trust) models help parties to decide who to trust, encouraging trustworthy behavior [3]. The core element here is the ratings, the evaluation reports of each transaction. According to our approach, a rating ($r \in ER_x$) is the fact: *rating (id→rating's_id, truster→truster's_name, trustee→trustee's_name, time→t EV_n^1 →value$_1$, EV_n^1→value$_2$, EV_n^1→value$_3$, EV_n^1→value$_4$, EV_n^1→value$_5$ EV_n^1→value$_6$, confidence→?conf*), where *confidence* is agent's certainty for that rating while we recommend six well-known evaluation criteria for EV_n^x values, namely *response time, validity, completeness, correctness, cooperation, confidence*.

The T_x agent combines (r_{i2} to r_{i4}) its own ratings (ER) with those received by recommenders (LOCATOR variation) to discard potential partners and next to estimate the reputation for the remaining in order to find the most well-reputed among them. These rules are defeasible and they all conclude conflicting positive literals for the same pair of agents (truster and trustee). That's why there is a superiority relationship between the rules.

r_{i2}: eligible_partner(rating→?id_x, cat→local, truster→?self, trustee→ ?x) := rating(id→?id_x, truster→?self, trustee→ ?x, confidence→?$conf_x$).

r_{i3}: eligible_ partner (rating→?id_x, cat→longerTie, truster→?a, trustee→ ?x) := confidence_threshold(?conf), rating(id→?id_x, truster→?a, trustee→ ?x, confidence→?$conf_x$), creditValue(?Vvalue), ?$conf_x$ >= ?conf.

r_{i4}: eligible_ partner (rating→?id_x, cat→longestTie, truster→?a, trustee→ ?x) := credit_threshold(?v), confidence_threshold(?conf), rating(id→?id_x, truster→?a, trustee→ ?x, confidence→?$conf_x$), creditValue(?Vvalue), ?$conf_x$ >= ?conf, ?Vvalue>=? v, where category (cat) local refers to previously known agent, longerTie indicates a less than (5) path length and longest ties a greater path length (>5) and $r_{i2} > r_{i3} > r_{i4}$.

Due to superiority relationship, rule r_{i2} indicates that personal opinion is important if there are ratings from itself (truster→?self,), otherwise logerTies opinion (r_{i3}) will be taken into account if it's confident (rating with confidence greater than T_x's ?conf threshold (confidence→?$conf_x$), ?$conf_x$ >=?conf) whereas longestTies opinion (r_{i4}) should be confident (?$conf_x$>= ?conf) and highly credit valued (creditValue(?Vvalue), ? Vvalue>=?v) based on T_x's threshold (?v) in order to be taken into account.

After this discarding process, the final reputation value (R_x, x≡entity) of a potential partner, at a specific time t, is based on the weighted (either personal W_{self} or recommended W_{RR}) sum of the relevant reports (normalized ratings in order to cross out extremely positive or extremely negative values) and is calculated as below. In the case that agent T_x had chosen the broadcasting method, it uses only the first part of the above formula with its personal ratings for the agents that replied to its request.

$$R(t) = \frac{W_{self}}{W_{self} + W_{RR}} * \frac{\sum\limits_{\forall t_{start} < t_i < t_{end}} \frac{w_n x \log\left(r^{ER^n}\right) * t_i}{\sum\limits_{n-1}^{N} w_n}}{\sum\limits_{\forall t_{start} < t_i < t_{end}} t_i} + \frac{W_{self}}{W_{self} + W_{RR}} * \frac{\sum\limits_{\forall t_{start} < t_i < t_{end}} \frac{w_n x \log\left(r^{ER^n}\right) * t_i}{\sum\limits_{n-1}^{N} w_n}}{\sum\limits_{\forall t_{start} < t_i < t_{end}} t_i}$$

(3)

Exchange data/request

Following this process, the T_x decides upon the preferred SMicro agent (highest R value) and sends to that agent an ACCEPT-PROPOSE message (r_{i5}) indicating that it is interest for this proposal (about→?proposeID) as long as there is a stored offer (propose fact) from that agent. The message includes a time threshold (tth→?t) for the interaction, greater than current time (?t>$t_{current}$) specifying time availability. The SMicro agent, on its behalf, checks the offered service/product availability (timeValid→?tv, specs→?$specs_j$) and replies either confirming or withdrawing its offer.

r_{i5}:   send_message(msg   →accept_proposal(about→?proposeID,   tth→?t),
sender→?self, receiver→?SMicro) := propose(id→?id$_x$, time → ?tt, sender→ ?SMi-
cro, receiver→ ?self, offer→ ?offer, timeValid→?tv, specs→?specs$_j$), ?t>t$_{current}$.

Negotiating terms
This stage is optional. If the T_x agent is interest in negotiating specifications (*specs*)
such as delivery time, it will continue by sending a negotiation request message to its
T_{SMicro} partner, which could accept or deny to negotiate depending on its strategy. The
agents may terminate the negotiation without agreement at any point. In case of
negotiation agreement, the message exchange sequence involves the following steps
(repeated as many times as necessary): *Step 1*: T_x (agent *i*) sends part of its belief
clauses ^iB_R to the T_{SMicro} agent (agent $_j$). *Step 2*: T_{SMicro} agent evaluates the clauses
$^jB_I (^jB_I \equiv {}^iB_R)$ using its own beliefs ^jB_R. *Step 3*: T_{SMicro} agent replies either with its
conclusions (part of its inferred clauses ^jB_R) or accepts the T_x demand (^iB_R clauses).

Reaching Agreement
Finally, the agents proceed with closing the eCommerce agreement. The T_{SMicro} prepares the eContract, including the terms (*terms→?terms*) and the time it will be valid
(*timeValid→?tv*, which should be greater than the signing time *?tv>t*), and sends a
signing request message (r_j) to the T_x agent specifying the offer (*about→?proposeID*),
the time (*time→?t*) and the terms (*terms→?terms*).

    r_j: send_message(msg →signing_request(about→?proposeID, time→?t, terms→?
terms), sender→?self, receiver→?x) := eContract(id→?id$_x$, time → ?t, provider→ ?
self, client→ ?x, terms→ ?terms, timeValid→?tv), ?tv>t.

3   Integration and Evaluation of the Methodology

The proposed methodology is integrated to EMERALD [6], a framework for inter-
operating knowledge-based intelligent agents. It provides, among others, a number of
reputation models and reasoning services, among which four that use defeasible reasoning. These services are wrapped by an agent interface, the Reasoner, allowing other
IAs to contact them via ACL messages. In essence, a Reasoner can launch an associated reasoning engine, in order to perform inference and provide results. The procedure is straightforward: each Reasoner stands by for new requests (*REQUEST*) and
when it receives a valid request, it launches the associated reasoning engine that
processes the input data (i.e. rule base) and returns the results (*INFORM*). As far as it
concerns the language integration of the methodology, we use RuleML (included in the
specifications of EMERALD) for our rules, representing and exchanging agent policies
and clauses. We use the RDF model for data and belief representation. This methodology allows each agent to exchange its argument base with any other agent, without
the need to conform to the same kind of rule paradigm or logic. Instead, via EMER-
ALD, IAs can utilize third-party reasoning services, that will infer knowledge from
agent rule bases and verify the results.

    As far as, it concerns evaluation we tried to simulate a realistic IoT environment,
hence, we used 20% of T_{hv} agents representing humans or virtual entities, 30% T_{SMicro}

agents representing web services and 50% of T_{DMicro} agents that represent devices. The aim of the experiments was to calculate the mean number of successful transactions (ending to an eContract agreement) when using the proposed methodology, compared to a random transaction approach (Fig. 1). The adopted testbed consists of provider and consumer agents and it can be embedded to any eCommerce case while each experiment is populated with a different number of providers and consumers. From experiment to experiment we increased the number of agents about 10% in order to evaluate how the methodology behaves in various populated networks. We run eleven experiments; the first was populated with 20 providers and 20 consumers whereas the last was populated with 100 agents, divided in providers and consumers. The testbed includes good (15%), ordinary (30%), bad (40%) and intermittent providers (15%), namely honest and malicious agents. Good, ordinary and bad providers have a mean level of performance, hence, their activity (actual performance) follows a normal distribution around this mean. Intermittent agents, on the other hand, cover all possible outcomes randomly. As a result, ratings (and reputation values) vary in the network.

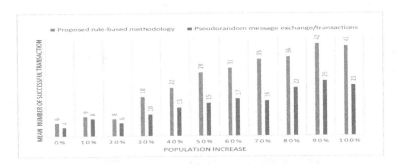

Fig. 1. Mean number of successful transactions.

4   Related Work

There are plenty approaches dealing with parts of the discussed topics, yet, there is still some lack to tightly related approaches combining a rule-based eCommerce perspective with microservices and agents for the IoT. In [8] a web service negotiation process is presented, focusing only on negotiation whereas our approach is more generic. The authors promote the reuse of the artefacts produced throughout the negotiation like our methodology which adopts the philosophy of clauses and policies reuse based on a rule-based mechanism. The authors support only web services opposed to our approach. As far as it concerns partner locating, Hang and Singh [2] also employ a graph-based approach but it focus only on measuring trust, with the aim to recommend a node in a social network using the trust network. The model uses the similarity between graphs to make recommendations. This approach similar to our LOCATOR variation attempts to take advantage of graphs in order to locate better partners, although this is just a part of our approach which takes into account more aspects in an attempt to sufficiently simulate eCommerce in the IoT.

5   Conclusion and Future Work

We presented a rule-based eCommerce methodology, forming a five-stage workflow, which allows Things to locate proper partners and establish trust relationships in the IoT network (there is no such support yet) via a social agent-based model for locating eCommerce partners and estimating their reputation. The study adopted agent technology, an increasing trend for IoT realization, combined the with the microservice architecture. A core concept of the methodology was the proper information exchange among heterogeneous Things, hence we proposed the use of semantic technologies such RuleML, although it is not yet adopted in IoT, in an attempt to support web evolution from Semantic Web to IoT and hopefully to the Internet of Agents. Finally, the methodology was integrated in EMERALD that provides appropriate Reasoners, supporting rule exchange with no common syntax. As for future directions, our intention is to enrich it with powerful mechanisms that will extract the relationships between potential partners as well as their past and future behavior. Hence, another direction is towards further improving it by adopting more technologies, such as ontologies, machine learning techniques and user identity recognition and management.

Acknowledgment. The Postdoctoral Research was implemented through an IKY scholarship funded by the "Strengthening Post-Academic Researchers /Researchers" Act from the resources of the OP "Human Resources Development, Education and Lifelong Learning" priority axis 6,8,9 and co-funded by The European Social Fund - the ESF and the Greek government.

References

1. Garriga, M.: Towards a taxonomy of microservices architectures. In: Cerone, A., Roveri, M. (eds.) SEFM 2017. LNCS, vol. 10729, pp. 203–218. Springer, Cham (2018). https://doi.org/10.1007/978-3-319-74781-1_15
2. Hang, C., Singh, M.P.: Trust-based recommendation based on graph similarity. In: AAMAS Workshop on Trust in Agent Societies (Trust), pp. 71–81 (2010)
3. Harwood, T., Garry, T.: Internet of Things: understanding trust in techno-service systems. J. Serv. Manage. **28**(3), 442–475 (2017)
4. Kontopoulos, E., Bassiliades, N., Antoniou, G.: Visualizing semantic web proofs of defeasible logic in the DR-DEVICE system. Knowl.-Based Syst. **24**(3), 406–419 (2011)
5. Kravari, K., Bassiliades, N.: Social principles in agent-based trust management for the Internet of Things. In: 14th Workshop on Agents for Complex Systems of 19th SYNASC (2017)
6. Kravari, K., Kontopoulos, E., Bassiliades, N.: EMERALD: a multi-agent system for knowledge-based reasoning interoperability in the semantic web. In: Konstantopoulos, S., Perantonis, S., Karkaletsis, V., Spyropoulos, C.D., Vouros, G. (eds.) SETN 2010. LNCS (LNAI), vol. 6040, pp. 173–182. Springer, Heidelberg (2010). https://doi.org/10.1007/978-3-642-12842-4_21
7. Lee, I., Lee, K.: The Internet of Things (IoT): applications, investments, and challenges for enterprises. Bus. Horiz. **58**(4), 431–440 (2015)
8. Silva, G.C., de Souza Gimenes, I.M., Fantinato, M., de Toledo, B.F.: Towards a process for negotiation of E-contracts involving web services. SBSI **2012**, 267–278 (2012)

Integrating Rule-Based AI Tools into Mainstream Game Development

Francesco Calimeri[iD], Stefano Germano[iD], Giovambattista Ianni[iD],
Francesco Pacenza[✉][iD], Simona Perri[iD], and Jessica Zangari[iD]

Department of Mathematics and Computer Science, University of Calabria,
Rende, Italy
{calimeri,germano,ianni,pacenza,perri,zangari}@mat.unical.it
https://www.mat.unical.it

Abstract. Rule-based declarative formalisms enjoy several advantages when compared with imperative solutions, especially when dealing with AI-based application development: solid theoretical bases, no need for algorithm design or coding, explicit and easily modifiable knowledge bases, executable declarative specifications, fast prototyping, quick error detection, modularity. For these reasons, ways for combining declarative paradigms, such as *Answer Set Programming* (ASP), with traditional ones have been significantly studied in the recent years; there are however relevant contexts, in which this road is unexplored, such as development of real-time games. In such a setting, the strict requirements on reaction times, the presence of computer-human interactivity and a generally increased impedance between the two development paradigms make the task nontrivial. In this work we illustrate how to embed rule-based reasoning modules into the well-known Unity game development engine. To this end, we present an extension of EMBASP, a framework to ease the integration of declarative formalisms with generic applications. We prove the viability of our approach by developing a proof-of-concept Unity game that makes use of ASP-based AI modules.

Keywords: *Answer Set Programming · Artificial Intelligence*
Game programming · Knowledge representation and reasoning
Logic programs · Rule-based systems · Unity

1 Context and Motivations

In the latest years, the steadily increasing availability of powerful and cheap hardware, experienced even in the mobile scenario, fostered an equally increasing deployment of applications that heavily rely on complex two- or three-dimensional graphics, requiring computational expensive renderings. Computer-Generated Imagery (CGI) applications, such as simulations or videogames, fall in this category. Furthermore, several facilities, tools and frameworks have been released with the aim of easing the development of such applications. This is especially true for the gaming context, where developers prefer to focus on the

© Springer Nature Switzerland AG 2018
C. Benzmüller et al. (Eds.): RuleML+RR 2018, LNCS 11092, pp. 310–317, 2018.
https://doi.org/10.1007/978-3-319-99906-7_23

design of the specific aspects of their products, such as storyline, graphic style, gameplay; hence, they look for facilitating development environments that relieve them from the burden of implementing technical features at lower abstraction levels. In this respect, Unity[1] is one of the most popular and widespread development environments in the game design field. In Unity, the development time of routine tasks is considerably shorter, and a vast range of ready-to-use solutions is available. Nevertheless, a major development task, which is nowadays scarcely automated, is the definition of some sort of AI needed, for instance, when implementing non-human players.

Interestingly, rule-based declarative formalisms can be of great help for the definition of such AIs: indeed, the declarative nature of rule-based knowledge bases allow to focus on specifying desiderata, thus getting rid of the burden of defining how to meet them; furthermore, knowledge is typically explicitly represented. Specifications written using declarative rules are definitely easier to be modified than implicit imperative solutions: one can start by quickly defining a first prototypical version and then iteratively rearrange it in increasingly sophisticated ways. On the other hand, when used in these contexts, declarative-based AI modules need to interact with other "non-declarative" components; i.e., one or more logic-based reasoning modules, handled by suitable declarative systems, must be integrated into larger, hybrid, architectures.

General ways for easing the embedding of declarative paradigms into imperative, and in particular object-oriented, programming approaches, have been significantly explored in the recent years, especially for *Answer Set Programming* [1,4,8], for which a number of solutions have been proposed [5-7,9-11].

Nonetheless, given the general impedance between the two different paradigm categories, there are a number of applicative contexts that still lack tools for the integration of rule-based formalisms, such as game development. Indeed, among the wide range of extensions offered to and by the Unity community, only few of them are aimed to provide *Artificial Intelligence* capabilities[2] and none of them enables developers to make use of a rule-based reasoning module.

In this work we present a novel solution for the integration of AI declarative modules within applications developed in Unity; our proposal is based on a proper extension EMBASP [6], an abstract framework. In the following, we first illustrate the requirements that must be met when integrating rule-based engines in the context of a game development engine following the Unity paradigm. A C# version of EMBASP, as it is the language adopted for the development in Unity, is shortly described; we then showcase a Unity-based game where the player is controlled by rule-based reasoning modules programmed in ASP.

---

[1] https://unity3d.com/unity.
[2] Among which:
https://assetstore.unity.com/packages/tools/ai/real-ai-112677,
https://assetstore.unity.com/packages/tools/ai/reaction-ai-66353.

2   EmbASP and *Answer Set Programming*

EMBASP[3] [6] is a framework for the integration of logic formalisms in external systems for generic applications; it consists of a general and abstract architecture, which can be instantiated in a programming language of choice, and easily allows for proper specializations to different platforms and knowledge-based solvers. The framework was originally mainly tailored on *Answer Set Programming* (ASP), but it has been generalized for enabling the embedding of further logic formalisms, far beyond those similar to ASP, such as PDDL. It has been implemented in Java and in Python, and permits the embedding of rule-based reasoning into desktop and mobile applications, making use of a wide range of solvers.

In our showcase application the rule-based specifications have been written in *Answer Set Programming* (ASP) [1,4,8]. ASP is a rule-based declarative formalism for knowledge representation and reasoning, developed in the field of logic programming and nonmonotonic reasoning. The language of ASP is based on rules, allowing (in general) for both disjunction in rule heads and nonmonotonic negation in the body. Also, optimization constructs such as weak constraints are allowed. Mainstream ASP engines accept declarative specifications expressed in the standardized input language ASP Core 2 [3].

3   Integrating Declarative Formalisms into Unity

Unity is a cross-platform game engine primarily used to develop video-games or simulations for more than 25 different platforms like mobile, computers and consoles. It supports 2D and 3D graphics, drag ad drop functionality and scripting using C# language.

Rapid development speed, a very active and powerful community, cross-platform integration and the availability of 3D models, ready to use scripts, shaders and other extensions, that can be easily added to a game, make Unity a user-friendly game engine easy to learn and use also for beginners; indeed, Unity is currently the leader of the global game development engine market, holding the 45% share, nearly three times the size of its nearest competitor.

Among the wide range of assets offered by the Unity community, only few of them are aimed to provide *Artificial Intelligence* capabilities (see footnote 2), and none of them enables developers to make use of a rule-based reasoning module. Making rule-based reasoning available in a game development engine such as Unity is attractive for several reasons:

1. fast prototyping and development of AI-based players, and of AI-based opponents; in particular:
   - rule-based specifications are more transparent and easier to be manually refined, compared to other approaches, such as machine learning;

---

[3] https://www.mat.unical.it/calimeri/projects/embasp.

- modifications are easier and faster, compared to tedious retraining stages; and,
- rule-based specifications make easier to keep AI modules independent from the overall hard-wired game logic.
2. possibility to introduce and control sophisticated planning strategies;
3. possibility to switch from one strategy to another by simply adding or changing rules.

Nevertheless, the development of an hybrid system that integrates an imperative graphic-tailored system like Unity with a knowledge- and rule-based evaluation system, needs to tackle and solve some impedance issues, some of which are discussed next.

- Modern development game engines require integration of external assets not only at runtime level, but also at design time. Thus, the integration of rule-based engines must be designed taking into account the possibility of invoking and solving declarative specifications also at design time.
- Design time in game development engines follows the properties paradigm. Properties combine traditional code with graphical design in a smooth and intuitive way. For instance, many game variables can be changed graphically and have immediate display on the design GUI: thus game blueprints can include and be affected by rule-based modules. As Unity strong relies on the notion of asset (i.e. a reusable component combining graphical elements and code), one might think of introducing rule-based, reusable AI controllers. This requires proper treatment, as designers expect consistent behaviors and visualizations, both at run-time and design-time.
- Imperative and external information flows need to be synchronized. Usually, imperative code is used to update the graphical interface, while declarative specifications are executed asynchronously. However, thread synchronization is one of the major weak points in most of the game engines, and, in particular, Unity APIs are not thread safe; hence, developers have to handle all the troubles coming when synchronizing information retrieved from the execution of an external module.
- Arithmetic calculations need to be treated uniformly. Logic-based formalism typically deal with small, discretized integer ranges, while graphical updates and physics simulation require floating point values. Thus, information about the state-of-world extracted from the graphic engine has to be properly matched when sent to and from rule-based reasoning engines.

As already stated before, in order to achieve our goal and develop a first working version of the hybrid system described above, we made usage of EMBASP. EMBASP eases and guide the generation of suitable libraries for the use of specific logic-based systems on particular platforms; resulting applications manage such systems as "black boxes". Given that the framework can be easily implemented in different object-oriented programming languages and its architecture can be specialized for different logic languages and solvers, we defined a C#

specialization of the framework, as C# is the main scripting language today adopted for the development in Unity.

In the following, we show how to employ the specialized C# libraries generated via EmbASP for making use of a rule-based reasoning module from within actual Unity applications.

4   Rule-Based Reasoning Modules into Unity at Work

In order to give an idea of how AI declarative modules can be integrated within applications developed in Unity via EmbASP, we developed a showcase application. We started from a public available open-source project[4], inspired from the original Pac-Man game, where human players control the Pac-Man moves, and designed a new version, where the Pac-Man plays autonomously according to moves suggested by an ASP module, instead.

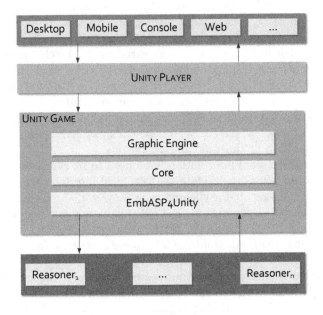

Fig. 1. General architecture of a Unity game relying on EmbASP

The layered architecture of the application is depicted in Fig. 1. The UNITY PLAYER component handles the Unity facilities specifically intended for helping developers in deploying an application on different platforms; it interacts with the UNITY GAME component, consisting in the actual implementation of the game, internally divided into three sub-modules: (*i*) the graphic engine, that takes care of the graphical rendering; (*ii*) the core module, managing the

---

[4] https://github.com/vilbeyli/Pacman.

logic of game; and (*iii*) the EMBASP4UNITY module, connecting with external reasoning engines. In order to perform AI tasks, the core sub-module interacts with the EMBASP specialization for Unity. In our case, such interaction is used to define Pac-Man moves; these are chosen according to an AI defined by means of ASP rules. More in detail, the core module identifies the current game state, models such information as an ASP rule-based knowledge base *KB*, and invokes an underlying ASP reasoner via the Unity specialization of EMBASP. In turn, the reasoner evaluates *KB* along with a ASP rule set *R* modelling the AI desired behavior; the reasoning engine outputs so-called *answer sets*, which encode suggested movements for the Pac-Man AI player, and these are returned to EMBASP, that forwards them back to the core module.

As anticipated in Sect. 3, the integration of rule-based modules into Unity requires to overcome some impedance issues; as for synchronization, we opted for calling external solvers via a synchronous call. Positions in the game map have been mapped to discrete cells, in contrast with the fact that sprites' positions in the game are modeled with the resolution of one pixel. Note that Unity continuously updates the game graphics with the aim of making the movements of involved characters smooth and more realistic, allowing to invoke custom code even on a per-pixel movement basis. By contrast, in a game like Pac-Man, in which reactivity is crucial, invoking solvers with a so high frequency is expensive and useless. This is why we opted for calling reasoning engines only when the currently chosen Pac-Man move has been completed, i.e., when the Pac-Man has been moved completely to the next discrete cell. Indeed, until a chosen Pac-Man move has not been graphically executed, the system would be invoked with the same input and it would return the same output, given that the Pac-Man position would be mapped to the same discrete cell.

The ASP program implementing the Pac-Man AI has been designed according the so-called "Guess/Check/Optimize" paradigm [2]: the *Guessing part* defines the search space (by means of disjunctive rules); the *Checking part* enforces solution admissibility (by means of integrity constraints); eventually, the *Optimizing part* specifies preference criteria (by means of weak constraints). For space reasons, we refrain from going into a complete description of the ASP logic program; also, we are not focusing on obtaining a state-of-the-art artificial Pac-Man player, but rather on proving the viability of our approach[5]. However, it is worth noting how the declarative approach allows to easily and quickly define an AI and facilitates changes in the strategy by simply modifying some rules. For instance, weak constraints in the optimizing part may guide the behaviour of the Pac-Man player by considering different factors, along with their importance. Hence, just by focusing on the optimizing part, by means of just a few changes we may significantly change the behaviour of the Pac-Man player, as shown next.

---

[5] All the development material, including logic programs, source code and a fully playable version of the game are available at https://github.com/DeMaCS-UNICAL/Pac-Man-Unity-EmbASP.

We briefly recall that each weak constraint has associated a pair consisting of a weight and a level; informally, an answer set pays, at each level, a penalty given by the sum of the weights. Moreover, higher levels have an higher priority [3]. The optimizing part guides the Pac-Man to:

1. eat Pac-Dots, if any:

```
:∼ nextCell(X,Y), empty(X,Y). [1@3]
```

The game grid is divided in cells identified by their (x, y) coordinates: the next Pac-Man position is given by $nextCell(X,Y)$, while $empty(X,Y)$ indicates that at coordinates (X, Y) there is an empty cell (i.e., there is no Pac-Dot nor Power-Pellet in it);

2. get away from the ghosts:

```
:∼ minDistanceNextGhost(D), D1=10-D, not powerup. [D1@4]
```

Let M be a candidate move, and D be the distance from the nearest ghost if M would be performed: M pays a penalty inversely proportional to D, unless Pac-Man has eaten a Power-Pellet;

3. chase the ghosts when a *power pellet* is eaten:

```
:∼ minDistanceNextGhost(D), powerup. [D@4]
```

In contrast to the previous constraint, if a Power-Pellet is eaten, candidate moves that make Pac-Man closer to the nearest ghost are given a lower penalty.

The points 2 and 3 are inherently more important than the first one: Pac-Man is primarily forced to consider the behaviour of the nearest ghost rather than to eat Pac-Dots. Notably, by just varying the associated levels the Pac-Man behaviour can be easily inverted.

5   Conclusions and Future Work

In this paper we presented our first working prototype, based on the EMBASP framework, which enables a game development environment to embed rule-based reasoning modules into their assets.

In future work we aim to tighten the integration of reasoning based modules in several respects: first, provide a standardized mapping strategy between game object properties and logical assertions; second, standardize how numerical values are treated along the flow between the core module and reasoning engines; third, provide the possibility of triggering events when external reasoners complete their tasks, thus providing an actual asynchronous event handling approach and, on the other hand, allow to encode events that trigger reasoning tasks on demand; last, but not least, we aim to introduce appropriate means to deal with real time requirements of typical of videogames, such as the introduction of time out killers, the configuration of default actions in case of time out, etc.

References

1. Brewka, G., Eiter, T., Truszczynski, M.: Answer set programming at a glance. Commun. ACM **54**(12), 92–103 (2011). http://doi.acm.org/10.1145/2043174.2043195
2. Buccafurri, F., Leone, N., Rullo, P.: Strong and weak constraints in disjunctive datalog. In: Dix, J., Furbach, U., Nerode, A. (eds.) LPNMR 1997. LNCS, vol. 1265, pp. 2–17. Springer, Heidelberg (1997). https://doi.org/10.1007/3-540-63255-7_2
3. Calimeri, F., et al.: Asp-core-2: Input language format (2012)
4. Calimeri, F., Gebser, M., Maratea, M., Ricca, F.: Design and results of the fifth answer set programming competition. Artif. Intell. **231**, 151–181 (2016). https://doi.org/10.1016/j.artint.2015.09.008
5. Febbraro, O., Leone, N., Grasso, G., Ricca, F.: JASP: A framework for integrating answer set programming with java. In: Brewka, G., Eiter, T., McIlraith, S.A. (eds.) Principles of Knowledge Representation and Reasoning: Proceedings of the Thirteenth International Conference, KR 2012, Rome, Italy, June 10–14, 2012. AAAI Press (2012). http://www.aaai.org/ocs/index.php/KR/KR12/paper/view/4520
6. Fuscà, D., Germano, S., Zangari, J., Anastasio, M., Calimeri, F., Perri, S.: A framework for easing the development of applications embedding answer set programming. In: Proceedings of the 18th International Symposium on Principles and Practice of Declarative Programming, Edinburgh, United Kingdom, pp. 38–49 (2016)
7. Gebser, M., Kaminski, R., Kaufmann, B., Schaub, T.: Clingo = ASP + control: Preliminary report. CoRR abs/1405.3694 (2014). http://arxiv.org/abs/1405.3694
8. Gelfond, M., Lifschitz, V.: Classical negation in logic programs and disjunctive databases. New Gener. Comput. **9**(3/4), 365–386 (1991). https://doi.org/10.1007/BF03037169
9. Ricca, F.: The DLV java wrapper. In: de Vos, M., Provetti, A. (eds.) Proceedings ASP03 - Answer Set Programming: Advances in Theory and Implementation, pp. 305–316. Messina, Italy, September 2003. http://CEUR-WS.org/Vol-78/
10. Schüller, P., Weinzierl, A.: Answer set application programming: a case study on tetris. In: Vos, M.D., Eiter, T., Lierler, Y., Toni, F. (eds.) Proceedings of the Technical Communications of the 31st International Conference on Logic Programming (ICLP 2015). CEUR Workshop Proceedings, Cork, Ireland, vol. 1433. CEUR-WS.org (2015), 31 August–4 September 2015. http://ceur-ws.org/Vol-1433/tc_17.pdf
11. Thimm, M.: Tweety: a comprehensive collection of java libraries for logical aspects of artificial intelligence and knowledge representation. In: Baral, C., Giacomo, G.D., Eiter, T. (eds.) Principles of Knowledge Representation and Reasoning: Proceedings of the Fourteenth International Conference, KR 2014, Vienna, Austria. AAAI Press, 20–24 July 2014. http://www.aaai.org/ocs/index.php/KR/KR14/paper/view/7811

Answer Set Programming Modulo 'Space-Time'

Carl Schultz[1]([✉]), Mehul Bhatt[2,3], Jakob Suchan[3],
and Przemysław Andrzej Wałęga[4,5]

[1] DIGIT, Aarhus University, Aarhus, Denmark
cschultz@eng.au.dk
[2] Örebro University, Örebro, Sweden
[3] University of Bremen, Bremen, Germany
[4] University of Oxford, Oxford, UK
[5] University of Warsaw, Warsaw, Poland

Abstract. We present ASP Modulo 'Space-Time', a declarative representational and computational framework to perform commonsense reasoning about regions with both spatial and temporal components. Supported are capabilities for mixed qualitative-quantitative reasoning, consistency checking, and inferring compositions of space-time relations; these capabilities combine and synergise for applications in a range of AI application areas where the processing and interpretation of spatiotemporal data is crucial. The framework and resulting system is the only general KR-based method for declaratively reasoning about the dynamics of 'space-time' regions as first-class objects.

1 Introduction

Answer Set Programming (ASP) has emerged as a robust declarative problem solving methodology with tremendous application potential [9,10,18]. Most recently, there has been heightened interest to extend ASP in order to handle specialised domains and application-specific knowledge representation and reasoning (KR) capabilities. For instance, ASP Modulo Theories (ASPMT) go beyond the propositional setting of standard answer set programs by the integration of ASP with Satisfiability Modulo Theories (SMT) thereby facilitating reasoning about continuous domains [2,9,13]; using this approach, integrating knowledge sources of *heterogeneous semantics* (e.g., infinite domains) becomes possible. Similarly, systems such as CLINGCON [8] combine ASP with specialised constraint solvers to support arithmetic constraints over integers. Other most recent extensions include the ASPMT founded *non-monotonic spatial reasoning* extensions in ASPMT(QS) [19] and ASP modulo *acyclicity* [5]. Indeed, being rooted in KR, in particular non-monotonic reasoning, ASP can theoretically characterise—and promises to serve in practice as—a modern foundational

---

Spatial Reasoning. www.spatial-reasoning.com.

C. Benzmüller et al. (Eds.): RuleML+RR 2018, LNCS 11092, pp. 318–326, 2018.
https://doi.org/10.1007/978-3-319-99906-7_24

language for several domain-specific AI formalisms, and offer a uniform computational platform for solving many of the classical AI problems involving planning, explanation, diagnosis, design, decision-making, control [6,18]. In this line of research, this paper presents ASP Modulo 'Space-Time', a specialised formalism and computational backbone enabling generalised commonsense reasoning about 'space-time objects' and their spatio-temporal dynamics [4] directly within the answer set programming paradigm.

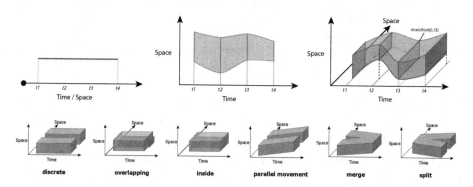

Fig. 1. Space-Time Histories in 1D and 2D; Spatio-temporal patterns and events, i.e., discrete, overlapping, inside, parallel movement, merge, and split.

Reasoning about 'Space-Time' (Motion). Imagine a moving object within 3D space. Here, the complete trajectory of motion of the moving object within a space-time localisation framework constitutes a 4D space-time history consisting of both spatial and temporal components – i.e., it is a region in *space-time* (Fig. 1). Regions in *space, time,* and *space-time* have been an object of study across a range of disciplines such as ontology, cognitive linguistics, conceptual modeling, KR (particularly qualitative spatial reasoning), and spatial cognition and computation. Spatial knowledge representation and reasoning can be classified into two groups: topological and positional calculi [1,14]. With topological calculi such as the Region Connection Calculus (RCC) [16], the primitive entities are spatially extended regions of space, and could be arbitrarily (but uniformly) dimensioned space-time histories. For the case of 'space-time' representations, the main focus in the state of the art has been on axiom systems (and the study of properties resulting therefrom) aimed at pure *qualitative reasoning*. In particular, axiomatic characterisations of mereotopologically founded theories with spatio-temporal regions as primitive entities are very well-studied [11,15]. Furthermore, the dominant method and focus within the field of spatial representation and reasoning—be it for topological or positional calculi—has been primarily on relational-algebraically founded semantics [14] in the absence of (or by discarding available) quantitative information. Pure qualitative spatial reasoning is very valuable, but it is often counterintuitive to not utilise or discard quantitative data if it is available (numerical information is typically available in domains involving sensing, interaction, interpretation, and control).

2   ASP Modulo 'Space-Time'

Spatial Domains. Spatial entities in our spatio-temporal domain ($\mathcal{ST}$) include *points* and *simple polygons*: a *2D point* is a pair of reals x, y; a *simple polygon* P is defined by a list of n vertices (points) $p_0, \ldots, p_{n-1}$ such that the boundary is non-self-intersecting, i.e., no two edges of the polygon intersect. We denote the number of vertices in P by $|P|$. A polygon is *ground* if all of its vertices are assigned real values. A translation vector t is a pair of reals (t_x, t_y). Given a point $p = (x, y)$ and a translation vector t let $p + t := (x + t_x, y + t_y)$. A *translation* is a ternary relation between two polygons P, Q and a translation vector t such that: $|P| = |Q| = n$ and $p_i = q_i + t$ where p_i is the ith vertex in P and q_i is the ith vertex in Q, for $0 \leq i < n$. A translation vector t is *ground* if t_x, t_y are assigned real values, otherwise it is *unground*.

Temporal domain $\mathcal{T}$. The temporal dimension is constituted by an infinite set of time points – each time point is a real number. The time-line is given by a linear ordering $<$ of time-points.

$\mathcal{ST}$ Histories. If we treat time as an additional dimension, then we can represent a moving two-dimensional spatial object s as a three-dimensional object in space-time. At each time point, the corresponding space-time region of s has a 2D spatial representation (a spatial *slice*). The space-time object is formed by taking all such slices over time. An $\mathcal{ST}$ *object* $o \in O$ is a variable associated with an ST domain D (e.g., the domain of 2D polygons over time). An *instance* of an object $i \in D$ is an element from the domain. Given $O = \{o_1, \ldots, o_n\}$, and domains $D_1, \ldots, D_n$ such that o_i is associated with domain D_i, then a *configuration* of objects ψ is a one-to-one mapping between object variables and instances from the domain, $\psi(o_i) \in D_i$. For example, a variable o_1 is associated with the domain D_1 of moving 2D points over time. An $\mathcal{ST}$ point moving in a straight line starting at spatial coordinates $(0, 0)$ at time 0 and arriving at 2D spatial coordinates $(10, 0)$ at time 1 is an instance of D_1. A configuration is defined that maps o_1 to a 3D line with end points $(0, 0, 0), (10, 0, 1)$, i.e., $\psi(o_1) = [(0, 0, 0), (10, 0, 1)]$.

$\mathcal{ST}$ Relations. Let $D_1, \ldots, D_n$ be spatio-temporal domains. A spatio-temporal relation r of arity n ($n > 0$) is defined as $r \subseteq D_1 \times \ldots \times D_n$. That is, each spatio-temporal relation is an equivalence class of instances of $\mathcal{ST}$ objects. Given a set of objects O, a relation r of arity n can be asserted as a constraint that must hold between objects $o_1, \ldots, o_n \in O$, denoted $r(o_1, \ldots, o_n)$. The constraint $r(o_1, \ldots, o_n)$ is satisfied by configuration ψ if $\big(\psi(o_1), \ldots, \psi(o_n)\big) \in r$. For example, if pp is a topological relation *proper part*, and $O = \{o_1, o_2\}$ is a set of moving polygon objects, then $pp(o_1, o_2)$ is the constraint that moving polygon o_1 is a proper part of o_2.

Table 1 presents definitions for $\mathcal{ST}$ relations that hold between s_1 and s_2, where t, t' range over a (dense) time interval with start and end time points t_0 and t_N in which s_1 and s_2 occur and $t \leq t'$. We define mereotopological relations using the Region Connection Calculus (RCC) [16]: all spatio-temporal RCC relations between $\mathcal{ST}$ regions are defined based on the RCC relations of

Table 1. Relations between $\mathcal{ST}$ regions s_1, s_2 over time interval $I = [t_0, t_N]$; $reverse(R)$ denotes relation R with reversed temporal ordering, $t' \leq t$; $p_i(t_j)$ is the centre point of s_i at t_j; Δ is the Euclidean distance between two points.

Relation	Definition	Relation	Definition
Topology		**Topology**	
disconnect (DC)	$\forall t\ dc(s_1(t), s_2(t))$	partial overlap (PO)	$\exists t\ po(s_1(t), s_2(t))$
discrete (DR)	$\forall t\ dr(s_1(t), s_2(t))$	external contact (EC)	$dr(s_1, s_2) \land \exists t\ ec(s_1(t), s_2(t))$
part of (P)	$\forall t\ p(s_1(t), s_2(t))$	proper part (PP)	$p(s_1, s_2) \land \exists t\ pp(s_1(t), s_2(t))$
nontangent proper part (NTPP)	$\forall t\ ntpp(s_1(t), s_2(t))$	tangent proper part (TPP)	$p(s_1, s_2) \land \exists t\ tpp(s_1(t), s_2(t))$
equal (EQ)	$\forall t\ eq(s_1(t), s_2(t))$	split	$p(s_1(t_0), s_2(t_0)) \land dc(s_1(t_N), s_2(t_N))$
contact (C)	$\exists t\ c(s_1(t), s_2(t))$	merge	$dc(s_1(t_0), s_2(t_0)) \land p(s_1(t_N), s_2(t_N))$
overlap (O)	$\exists t\ o(s_1(t), s_2(t))$		
Size		**Movement**	
fixed size	$\forall t \forall t' ($ $area(s(t)) = area(s(t')))$	move parallel	$moves(s_1) \land \forall t \forall t' ($ $p_2(t) - p_1(t) = (p_2(t') - p_1(t'))$
grows	$\neg fixed\_size(s) \land \forall t \forall t'$ $(area(s(t)) \leq area(s(t')))$	towards	$moves(s_1) \land$ $\neg moves\_parallel(s_1, s_2) \land \forall t \forall t'$ $\Delta(p_1(t), p_2(t)) \geq \Delta(p_1(t'), p_2(t'))$
shrinks	$reverse(grows(s_1, s_2))$	follows	$\forall t' \exists t\ duration(t, t') \leq \alpha \land$
Movement			$\Delta(p_1(t), p_2(t)) > \Delta(p_1(t'), p_2(t)) \land$
moves	$\exists t \exists t'\ p(t) \neq p(t')$		$\Delta(p_1(t), p_2(t)) < \Delta(p_1(t), p_2(t'))$
away	$reverse(towards(s_1, s_2))$		

their slices. An $\mathcal{ST}$ region s_1 *follows* $\mathcal{ST}$ region s_2 if, at each time step, s_1 moves towards a previous location of s_2, and s_2 moves away from a previous location of s_1.[1] We formalise the semantics of spatial reasoning by encoding qualitative spatial relations as systems of polynomial equations and inequalities. The task of determining whether a set of spatial relations is consistent is then equivalent to determining whether the set of polynomial constraints are satisfiable [3,19]. Integrating logic-based and arithmetic constraint solving has a long and rich history – see, e.g., [12].

2.1 Spatio-Temporal Consistency

Consider the topological *disconnected* relation. There is no polygon that is *disconnected* from itself, i.e., the relation is *irreflexive*. The following algebraic properties of $\mathcal{ST}$ relations are expressed as ASP rules and constraints: reflexivity, irreflexivity, symmetry, asymmetry, converse, implication, mutual (pair-wise) inconsistency, and transitive inconsistency. We have automatically derived these properties using our polynomial constraint solver *a priori* and generated the corresponding ASP rules. A violation of these properties corresponds to *3-path inconsistency* [14], i.e., there does not exist any combination of polygons that can violate these properties. In particular, a total of 1586 space-time constraints result.

---

[1] We introduce a user-specified maximum duration threshold α between these two time points to prevent unwanted scenarios being defined as *follows* events such as s_1 taking one step towards s_2 and then stopping while s_2 continues to move away from s_1.

Ground Polygons. We can determine whether a given $\mathcal{ST}$ relation r holds between two ground polygons P, Q by directly checking whether the corresponding polynomial constraints are satisfied, i.e. polynomial constraint variables are replaced by the real values assigned to the ground polygon vertices. This is accomplished during the *grounding* phase of ASP. For instance, two ground polygons are *disconnected* if the distance between them is greater than zero.

Unground Translation. Given ground polygons P_0, P_1, *unground* polygon P_0', and unground translation $t = (t_x, t_y)$, let P_0' be a t translation of P_0 such that r holds between P_0', P_1. The (exact) set of real value pairs that can be assigned to (t_x, t_y) such that P_0', P_1 satisfy r is precisely determined using the Minkowski sum method [20]; we refer to this set as the *solution set* of t for r. Given n ground polygons $P_1, \ldots, P_n$, and n relations $r_1, \ldots, r_n$ such that relation r_i is asserted to hold between polygon P_0, P_i, for $1 \le i \le n$, let M_i be the solution set of t for r_i. The conjunction of relations $r_1, \ldots, r_n$ is consistent if the *intersection* of solution sets $M_1, \ldots, M_n$ is non-empty. Computing and intersecting solution sets is accomplished during the *grounding* phase of ASP.

System Implementation. We have implemented our $\mathcal{ST}$ reasoning module in Clingo (v5.1.0) [7] based on an integration with specialised polynomial constraint solvers via numerical optimisation and Satisfiability Modulo Theories supporting real arithmetic. All models produced by our system are models in the usual ASP sense that are also *spatially consistent*. We install a *hook* in Clingo's answer set search for checking whether complete and partial assignments are spatially consistent using our spatial reasoning module $\mathcal{ST}$. If a spatial inconsistency is detected, the system *backtracks* the search (using Clingo's native backtracking mechanism) and creates a spatial conflict clause (nogood) using Clingo's learnt constraint mechanism. Thus, we leverage from all features provided by the standard Clingo solver with an extension to support spatio-temporal reasoning.

3   Reasoning with ASP Modulo Space-Time

Table 2 presents our system's predicate interface. Our system provides special predicates for (1) declaring spatial objects, and (2) relating objects spatio-temporally. Each $\mathcal{ST}$ object is represented with *st_object/3* relating the identifier of the $\mathcal{ST}$ entity, time point of this slice, and identifier of the associated geometric representation.

```
st_object(EntityId,at(Time),id(PolygonId)).
```

Polygons are represented using the *polygon/2* predicate that relates an identifier of the geometric representation with a list of x,y vertex coordinate pairs, e.g.:

```
polygon(id(pgBx2_0),(268,0,303,0,303,5)).
```

Table 2. $\mathcal{ST}$ entities and relation predicates.

Predicate	Description
$\mathcal{ST}$ Entities	
polygon(Pg, (X1, Y1, ..., Xn, Yn))	Polygon Pg has n ground vertices $(x_1, y_1), \ldots, (x_n, y_n)$
translation(Pg1, Pg2)	Polygon Pg2 is an unground translation of Pg1
st_object(E)	E is a spatio-temporal entity
st_object(E, at(Time), id(Pg))	2D polygon Pg is a spatial *slice* of spatio-temporal entity E at time point Time.
$\mathcal{ST}$ Relations	
spacetime(STAspect, E, time(T1,T2))	Derive unary ST relations for STAspect (topology, size, or movement) for entity E from time T1 to T2
spacetime(STAspect, E1, E2, time(T1,T2))	Derive binary ST relations for STAspect (topology, size, or movement) between entities E1,E2 from time T1 to T2
topology(Rel, E1, E2,time(T1,T2))	Topological relation Rel is asserted to hold between ST entities E1,E2 from time T1 to T2
size(Rel, E1, E2, time(T1,T2))	Size relation Rel is asserted to hold between ST entities E1,E2 from time T1 to T2
movement(Rel, E, time(T1,T2))	Unary movement relation Rel is asserted to hold for ST entity E from time T1 to T2
movement(Rel, E1, E2, time(T1,T2))	Binary movement relation Rel is asserted to hold between ST entities E1,E2 from time T1 to T2
spatial(witness, E, EWitness)	Ground entity EWitness is a consistent witness for unground entity E

Deriving $\mathcal{ST}$ Relations. The predicate *spacetime/3* is used to specify the entities between which $\mathcal{ST}$ relations should be derived:

```
% derive properites of entity e1 during time 25 to 75
spacetime(movement,e1, time(25,75)).
% derive relations between entities e5,e6 time 1 to 10
spacetime(movement,e5,e6, time(1,10)).
% derive relations between all entities for time 10 to 20
spacetime(movement,Entity1,Entity2,time(1,10)):-
    st_object(Entity1, _, _), st_object(Entity2, _, _).
```

Purely Qualitative Reasoning. If no geometric information for slices is given then our system satisfies 3-consistency, e.g., the following program includes transitively inconsistent spatio-temporal relations:

```
st_object(s1). st_object(s2). st_object(s3).
topology(ntpp,s1,s2). topology(pp,s2,s3). topology(dc,s1,s3).
UNSATISFIABLE
```

Mixed Qualitative-Numerical Reasoning. A new $\mathcal{ST}$ object can be specified that consists of *translated* slices of a given $\mathcal{ST}$ object. Our system determines whether translations exist that satisfy all given spatio-temporal constraints. Our system produces the solution set and a spatial witness that minimises the translation distance.

```
translation(st1, translated_st1).
topology(pp, translated_st1, st2).
spatial(witness, translated_st1, witness_st1).
```

▶ **Application Example: Motion planning.** We show how $\mathcal{ST}$ regions can be used for motion planning, e.g., in robotic manipulation tasks using abduction.

Example. *An agent (a robot with a manipulator) is at a desk in front of a laptop. A cup of coffee is positioned behind the laptop and the agent wants to get the cup of coffee without the risk of spilling the coffee on the laptop. The agent should not hit the computer while performing the task.*

This task requires abducing intermediate states that are consistent with the domain constraints. We model the laptop, hand, and cup from a top-down perspective as $\mathcal{ST}$ regions with polygonal slices, and give the initial shapes.

```
%% domain objects
desk_object(laptop). desk_object(hand). desk_object(cup).
```

The initial configuration is given for time 0:

```
%% polygonal shapes of objects
polygon(shape(laptop),  (0,0, ...)).
polygon(shape(hand),    (-105, 3, ...)).
polygon(shape(cup),     (205, 54, ...)).
%% initial position of objects at time 0
st_object(Object, at(0), id(shape(Object)))  :- desk_object(Object).
```

We model the scenario from time 0 to 2.

```
%% modelling two time steps
time(1..2).
%% it is possible that objects move at each time step
{moves(Object, at(T))} :- desk_object(Object), time(T).
%% objects that move are represented by an (unground) translation of their polygon
translation(shape(Object),translated_shape(Object, at(T))):-moves(Object, at(T)).
%% at the end of the time step we need a witness of moving objects
spatial(witness, translated_shape(Object, at(T)),
                 shape(Object, at(T))) :- moves(Object, at(T)).
%% slice of moving object at time T is a translated polygon
st_object(Object, at(T), id(translated_shape(Object, at(T)))) :-
        moves(Object, at(T)).
%% slice of stationary object at time T is polygon from last time step
st_object(Object, at(T), id(shape(Object, at(LastT)))) :-
        desk_object(Object), time(T), LastT = T - 1, not moves(Object, at(T)).
```

The goal is for the hand to make contact with the cup:

```
topology(c, hand, cup, time(1,2)).
```

We model default domain assumptions, e.g., the cup does not move by default. We express this by assigning costs to interpretations where objects move.

```
cost(0,Object) :- Object = (cup; laptop), time(T), -moves(Object, at(T)).
cost(1,Object) :- Object = (cup; laptop), time(T), moves(Object, at(T)).
#minimize{ C, X : cost(C,X)}.
```

The spatio-temporal constraints for planning the motion trajectory are that the hand and cup must remain disconnected from the laptop.

```
topology(dc, laptop, hand, time(0,2)). topology(dc, laptop, cup, time(0,2)).
```

Our system finds a consistent and optimal answer set where neither the laptop nor cup move in the period before the robot hand has made contact with the cup. Given the spatio-temporal constraints in this optimal answer set, our system then produces a consistent motion trajectory witness of the solution set (Fig. 2).

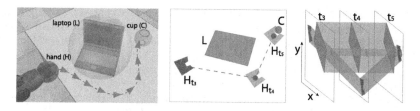

Fig. 2. Application in cognitive robotics – computing a motion trajectory.

4   Summary and Related Work

ASP Modulo extensions for handling specialised domains and abstraction mechanisms provides a powerful means for the utilising ASP as a foundational knowledge representation and reasoning (KR) method for a wide-range of application contexts. This approach is clearly demonstrated in work such as ASPMT [2,9,13], CLINGCON [8], and ASPMT(QS) [19]. Most closely related to our research is the ASPMT founded *non-monotonic spatial reasoning* system ASPMT($\mathcal{QS}$) [19]. Whereas ASPMT($\mathcal{QS}$) provides a valuable blueprint for the integration and formulation of geometric and spatial reasoning within answer set programming modulo theories, the developed system is a first-step and lacks support for a rich spatio-temporal ontology or an elaborate characterisation of complex 'space-time' objects as native (the focus there has been on enabling non-monotonicity with a basic spatial and temporal ontology). Furthermore **(1)** we generate *all* spatially consistent models compared to only one model in the standard ASPMT pipeline; **(2)** we compute optimal answer sets, e.g., add support preferences, which allows us to rank models, specify weak constraints; **(3)** we support quantification of space-time regions. The outlook of this work is geared towards enhancing the application of the developed specialised ASP Modulo Space-Time component specifically for non-monotonic spatio-temporal reasoning about large datasets in the domain of visual stimulus interpretation [18], as well as constraint-based motion control in the domain of home-based and industrial robotics [17].

Acknowledgements. This work was partially supported by the Germany Research Foundation (DFG) as part of the CRC EASE; and partially by the NCN grant 2016/23/N/HS1/02168.

References

1. Aiello, M., Pratt-Hartmann, I., van Benthem, J.: Handbook of Spatial Logics. Springer, Dordrecht (2007). https://doi.org/10.1007/978-1-4020-5587-4
2. Bartholomew, M., Lee, J.: System ASPMT2SMT: computing ASPMT theories by SMT solvers. In: Fermé, E., Leite, J. (eds.) JELIA 2014. LNCS (LNAI), vol. 8761, pp. 529–542. Springer, Cham (2014). https://doi.org/10.1007/978-3-319-11558-0_37

3. Bhatt, M., Lee, J.H., Schultz, C.: CLP(QS): a declarative spatial reasoning framework. In: Egenhofer, M., Giudice, N., Moratz, R., Worboys, M. (eds.) COSIT 2011. LNCS, vol. 6899, pp. 210–230. Springer, Heidelberg (2011). https://doi.org/10.1007/978-3-642-23196-4_12

4. Bhatt, M., Loke, S.: Modelling dynamic spatial systems in the situation calculus. Spat. Cogn. Comput. 8(1), 86–130 (2008)

5. Bomanson, J., Gebser, M., Janhunen, T., Kaufmann, B., Schaub, T.: Answer set programming modulo acyclicity*. Fundam. Inform. 147(1), 63–91 (2016)

6. Erdem, E., Gelfond, M., Leone, N.: Applications of answer set programming. AI Mag. 37(3), 53–68 (2016)

7. Gebser, M., Kaminski, R., Kaufmann, B., Schaub, T.: Clingo = ASP + control: Preliminary report. In: Leuschel, M., Schrijvers, T. (eds.) Technical Communications of ICLP, vol. 14(4–5) (2014). theory and Practice of Logic Programming, Online Supplement

8. Gebser, M., Ostrowski, M., Schaub, T.: Constraint answer set solving. In: Hill, P.M., Warren, D.S. (eds.) ICLP 2009. LNCS, vol. 5649, pp. 235–249. Springer, Heidelberg (2009). https://doi.org/10.1007/978-3-642-02846-5_22

9. Gelfond, M.: Answer sets. Handbook of knowledge representation, vol. 1, p. 285 (2008)

10. Gelfond, M., Lifschitz, V.: The stable model semantics for logic programming. In: ICLP/SLP, vol. 88, pp. 1070–1080 (1988)

11. Hazarika, S.M.: Qualitative spatial change: space-time histories and continuity. Ph.D. thesis, The University of Leeds (2005)

12. Kanellakis, P.C., Kuper, G.M., Revesz, P.Z.: Constraint query languages (preliminary report). In: Proceedings of the 9th Symposium on Principles of Database Systems, pp. 299–313. ACM (1990)

13. Lee, J., Meng, Y.: Answer set programming modulo theories and reasoning about continuous changes. In: IJCAI 2013, Proceedings of the 23rd International Joint Conference on Artificial Intelligence, Beijing, China, August 3–9, 2013 (2013)

14. Ligozat, G.: Qualitative Spatial and Temporal Reasoning. Wiley-ISTE, London (2011)

15. Muller, P.: A qualitative theory of motion based on spatio-temporal primitives. KR 98, 131–141 (1998)

16. Randell, D.A., Cui, Z., Cohn, A.G.: A spatial logic based on regions and connection. KR 92, 165–176 (1992)

17. Suchan, J., Bhatt, M.: Deep semantic abstractions of everyday human activities. In: Ollero, A., Sanfeliu, A., Montano, L., Lau, N., Cardeira, C. (eds.) ROBOT 2017. AISC, vol. 693, pp. 477–488. Springer, Cham (2018). https://doi.org/10.1007/978-3-319-70833-1_39

18. Suchan, J., Bhatt, M., Wałęga, P.A., Schultz, C.: Visual explanation by high-level abduction: on answer-set programming driven reasoning about moving objects. In: McIlraith, S.A., Weinberger, K.Q. (eds.) Proceedings of the 32nd AAAI Conference on Artificial Intelligence, New Orleans, Louisiana, USA, February 2–7, 2018. AAAI Press (2018)

19. Wałęga, P.A., Bhatt, M., Schultz, C.: ASPMT(QS): non-monotonic spatial reasoning with answer set programming modulo theories. In: Calimeri, F., Ianni, G., Truszczynski, M. (eds.) LPNMR 2015. LNCS (LNAI), vol. 9345, pp. 488–501. Springer, Cham (2015). https://doi.org/10.1007/978-3-319-23264-5_41

20. Wallgrün, J.O.: Topological adjustment of polygonal data. In: Timpf, S., Laube, P. (eds.) Advances in Spatial Data Handling, pp. 193–208. Springer, Heidelberg (2013). https://doi.org/10.1007/978-3-642-32316-4_13

Author Index

Printed in the United States
By Bookmasters

Printed in the United States
By Bookmasters